Contributors

Andy Collins revised the South Carolina chapter. He has edited and contributed to numerous Fodor's guides.

Mitzi Gammon, who lives in Atlanta, contributed the original Georgia chapter.

Kevin and Echo Garrett, who live in Marietta, Georgia, updated the Georgia and Tennessee chapters. Echo is a contributing writer for *Money* and *World Trade* and has also written for *Corporate Travel, Hemispheres,* and *The New York Times.* Kevin has written and photographed for *Bridal Guide* and several business publications.

Mary Ann Hemphill, a travel writer who lives in Williamsburg, revised the Virginia chapter. She has published in *Food & Wine* and *The Los Angeles Times* and has contributed to *Fodor's Alaska* and *Fodor's Cruises and Ports of Call.*

Sylvia Higginbotham, who wrote our chapter on Mississippi, is a freelance writer based in Columbus, in that state. She writes business and travel articles and is the principal in a communications company that prepares sales and PR materials.

Playwright **Anto Howard,** who updated the chapter on Alabama, was born in Ireland, where, he says, there are more B&Bs per capita than just about anywhere else. Now living in Florida, he has contributed to *Fodor's Canada* and *Fodor's Great American Vacations.*

The revisor of the chapter on North Carolina, **Susan Ladd** is a feature writer for the *News & Record* in Greensboro. Her travel articles have also appeared in Rodale's *Scuba Diving and Sports View* magazine.

The chapter of Alabama was contributed by **Henrietta MacGuire,** who works for *Montgomery Magazine* and has authored the book *Married to a Legend,* memoirs of her years in Costa Rica. She was ably assisted by **Mickey Ingalls.**

Real-live Southerner **Honey Naylor,** author of our Louisiana chapter, is a freelance writer whose features have appeared in *Travel & Leisure, New Orleans Magazine, USA Today,* and other national publications. She is a contributor to a dozen Fodor's books.

Susan Spano contributed the chapter on Virginia. She has written about travel for *The New York Times, New Woman,* and *British Heritage.*

Carol Timblin, author of our North and South Carolina chapters, won first place in the Lowell Thomas Travel Journalism Competition and the Discover America Award in 1988. She lives in Charlotte, North Carolina.

Contents

FODOR'S BED & BREAKFASTS AND COUNTRY INNS

The South's Best Bed & Breakfasts

2nd Edition

Delightful Places to Stay and Great Things to Do When You Get There

A portion of this book appears in
*Fodor's Bed & Breakfasts and Country Inns:
Mid-Atlantic Region.*

Fodor's Travel Publications, Inc.
New York • Toronto • London • Sydney • Auckland

Fodor's The South's Best Bed & Breakfasts

Editor: Andrea E. Lehman
Contributors: Robert Blake, Andy Collins, Mitzi Gammon, Echo and Kevin Garrett, Mary Ann Hemphill, Sylvia Higginbotham, Anto Howard, Mickey Ingalls, Laura M. Kidder, Susan Ladd, Henrietta MacGuire, Honey Naylor, Susan Spano, and Carol Timblin
Creative Director: Fabrizio La Rocca
Cartographer: David Lindroth
Illustrator: Alida Beck, Karl Tanner
Cover Design: Guido Caroti
Cover Photograph: H. Mark Weidman

Special Sales

Foreword

While every care has been taken to ensure the accuracy of the information in this guide, the passage of time will always bring change and, consequently, the publisher cannot accept responsibility for errors that may occur.

All prices and listings are based on information supplied to us at press time. Details may change, however, and the prudent traveler will avoid inconvenience by calling ahead.

Fodor's wants to hear about your travel experiences, both pleasant and unpleasant. When a B&B or an inn fails to live up to its billing, let us know and we will investigate the complaint and revise our entries where the facts warrant it.

Send your letters to the editors of Fodor's Travel Publications, 201 E. 50th Street, New York, NY 10022.

Introduction

You'll find bed-and-breakfasts in big houses with turrets and little houses with decks, in mansions by the water and cabins in the forest, not to mention structures of many sizes and shapes in between. B&Bs are run by people who were once lawyers and writers, homemakers and artists, nurses and architects, singers and businesspeople. Some B&Bs are just a room or two in a hospitable local's home; others are more like small inns. So every B&B stay has a quality of serendipity.

But while that's part of the pleasure of the experience, it's also an excellent reason to plan your B&B travels with a good B&B guide. The one you hold in your hands serves the purpose neatly.

To create it, we've handpicked a team of professional writers who are also confirmed B&B lovers: people who adore the many manifestations of the Victorian era; who go wild over wicker and brass beds, four-posters and fireplaces; and who know a well-run operation when they see it and are only too eager to communicate their knowledge to you. We've instructed them to inspect the premises and check out every corner of the premier bed-and-breakfasts and inns in the areas they cover, and to report critically on only the best.

They've returned from their trips with glowing reports on the pleasure of B&B travel, which may well become your pleasure as you read their reports in the pages that follow. These are establishments that promise a unique experience, a distinctive sense of time and place. All are destinations in themselves, not just spots to put your head at night, but an integral part of a weekend escape. In our writers' evaluations of each, you'll learn what's good, what's bad, and what could be better; what they liked, and what you may not like.

Fodor's reviewers, at the same time, tell you what's up in the area and what you should and shouldn't miss—everything from historic sites and parks to antiques shops, boutiques, and the area's niftiest restaurants and nightspots. We also include names and addresses of B&B reservation services, just in case you're inspired to seek out additional properties on your own. Reviews are organized by state, and, within each state, by region.

In the italicized service information that ends every review, a second address in parentheses is a mailing address. A double room is for two people, regardless of the size or type of beds it contains. Unless otherwise noted, rooms don't have phones or TVs. Note that even the most stunning homes, farmhouses and mansions alike, may not provide a private bathroom for each individual.

What we call a restaurant serves meals other than breakfast and is usually open to the general public. At inns listed as operating on the Modified American Plan (MAP), rates include two meals, generally breakfast and dinner.

Where applicable, we note seasonal and other restrictions. Although we abhor discrimination, we have conveyed information about innkeepers' restrictive practices so that you will be aware of the prevailing attitudes. Such discriminatory practices are most often applied to parents who are traveling with small children and who may not—in any case—feel comfortable having their offspring toddle amid breakable bric-a-brac and near precipitous stairways.

When traveling the B&B way, always call ahead; and if you have mobility problems or are traveling with children, if you prefer a private bath or a certain type of bed, or if you have specific dietary needs or any other concerns, discuss them with the innkeeper. At the same time, if you're traveling to an inn because of a specific feature, make sure that it will be available when you get there and not closed for renovation. The same goes if you're making a detour to take advantage of specific sights or attractions.

It's a sad commentary on other B&B guides today that we feel obliged to tell you that our writers did, in fact, visit every property in person, and that it is they, not the innkeepers, who wrote the reviews. No one paid a fee or promised to sell or promote the book to be included in it. (In fact, one of the most challenging parts of the work of a Fodor's writer is to persuade innkeepers and B&B owners that he or she wants nothing more than a tour of the premises and the answers to a few questions!) Fodor's has no stake in anything but the truth. If a room is dark, with peeling wallpaper, we don't call it quaint or atmospheric—we call it run-down, and then steer you to another section of the same property that's more appealing.

So trust us, the way you'd trust a knowledgeable, well-traveled friend. Let us hear from you about your travels, whether you found that the B&Bs you visited surpassed their descriptions or the other way around. And have a wonderful trip!

Karen Cure

Editorial Director

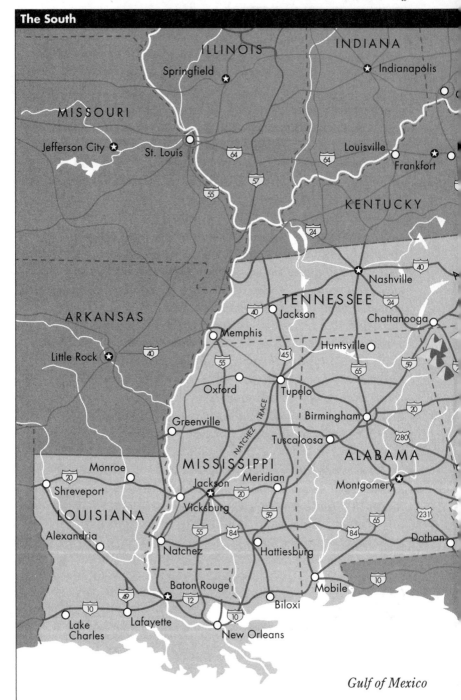

The South

Gulf of Mexico

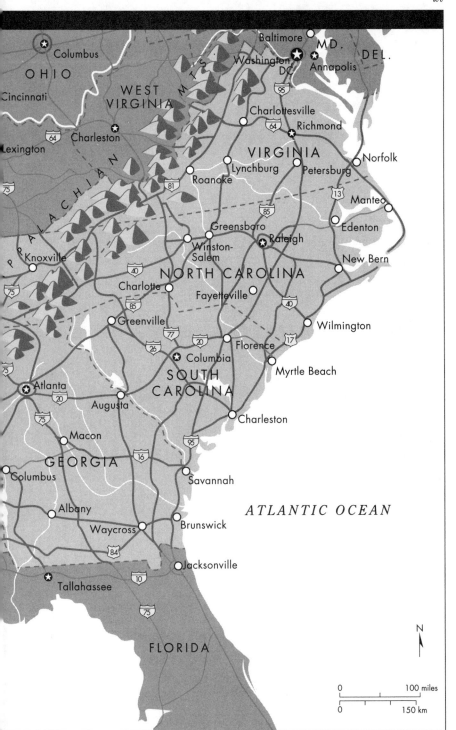

Special Features at a Glance

Name of Property	Accessible for Disabled	Antiques	On the Water	Good Value	Car Not Necessary	Full Meal Service	Historic Building	
ALABAMA								
Bay Breeze	✓	✓	✓	✓				
Blue Shadows		✓		✓				
Church Street Inn		✓			✓		✓	
The Colonel's Rest				✓				
Grace Hall		✓		✓	✓		✓	
The Guest House	✓				✓		✓	
The Lattice Inn		✓		✓			✓	
Mentone Inn				✓				
Oakwood		✓		✓	✓		✓	
Orangevale Plantation		✓		✓			✓	
The Plantation House		✓		✓			✓	
Red Bluff Cottage		✓		✓				
Roses and Lace		✓		✓			✓	
Wood Avenue Inn		✓		✓			✓	
GEORGIA								
Ansley Inn	✓	✓					✓	
Ballastone Inn	✓	✓			✓		✓	
Brunswick Manor	✓	✓			✓		✓	
Captain's Quarters Bed & Breakfast Inn		✓		✓			✓	
The 1842 Inn	✓	✓		✓	✓		✓	
Evans House Bed & Breakfast	✓	✓		✓	✓		✓	
The Gastonian	✓	✓		✓	✓		✓	
Glen-Ella Springs Inn & Conference Center	✓	✓		✓		✓	✓	
The Gordon-Lee Mansion		✓					✓	

Romantic Hideaway	Luxurious	Pets Allowed	No Smoking Indoors	Good Place for Families	Near Arts Festivals	Beach Nearby	Cross-Country Ski Trail	Golf Within 5 Miles	Fitness Facilities	Good Biking Terrain	Skiing	Horseback Riding	Tennis	Swimming on Premises	Conference Facilities
			✓		✓	✓		✓						✓	
✓			✓	✓			✓			✓				✓	
	✓		✓		✓	✓		✓							
✓		✓			✓	✓	✓	✓		✓				✓	✓
✓	✓		✓		✓			✓		✓					
				✓		✓		✓		✓					✓
	✓		✓		✓			✓		✓				✓	
✓			✓	✓	✓		✓	✓		✓	✓				
			✓	✓				✓		✓					
✓			✓	✓						✓		✓			
✓			✓	✓				✓		✓					
✓	✓		✓	✓	✓			✓		✓					
✓			✓	✓						✓					
✓			✓	✓	✓			✓		✓					
✓	✓	✓			✓			✓	✓	✓			✓	✓	✓
✓	✓				✓	✓		✓		✓			✓		
✓	✓	✓	✓	✓	✓	✓		✓		✓		✓	✓		
✓	✓		✓		✓					✓		✓			
	✓			✓	✓			✓		✓			✓		
	✓		✓		✓			✓		✓		✓			
✓	✓		✓		✓	✓		✓		✓			✓		
✓	✓			✓	✓			✓				✓		✓	✓
✓	✓		✓		✓								✓		

Name of Property	Accessible for Disabled	Antiques	On the Water	Good Value	Car Not Necessary	Full Meal Service	Historic Building
Greyfield Inn		✓	✓	✓	✓	✓	✓
Inn Scarlett's Footsteps		✓					✓
Magnolia Place Inn	✓	✓		✓		✓	✓
Morgan Towne House Rest. Bed & Breakfast				✓		✓	✓
Olde Harbour Inn	✓		✓	✓	✓		✓
Open Gates	✓	✓		✓		✓	✓
The Pittman House		✓		✓			
Pulaski Square Inn	✓	✓			✓		✓
Rose Manor Guest House	✓	✓		✓			✓
Statesboro Inn	✓	✓		✓		✓	✓
Susina Plantation Inn		✓				✓	✓
The Tate House	✓	✓		✓			✓
The Veranda		✓		✓		✓	✓
The York House							✓
LOUISIANA							
A la Bonne Veillée		✓					✓
Bois des Chênes	✓	✓					✓
Butler Greenwood		✓		✓			✓
Camellia Cove		✓		✓			✓
The Chimes				✓	✓		✓
Chrétien Point Plantation		✓		✓			✓
Cloutier Townhouse		✓			✓		✓
Cottage Plantation		✓		✓			✓
Fleur-de-Lis	✓			✓			
Girod House		✓		✓	✓		✓

Romantic Hideaway	Luxurious	Pets Allowed	No Smoking Indoors	Good Place for Families	Near Arts Festivals	Beach Nearby	Cross-Country Ski Trail	Golf Within 5 Miles	Fitness Facilities	Good Biking Terrain	Skiing	Horseback Riding	Tennis	Swimming on Premises	Conference Facilities
✓			✓	✓		✓				✓					
✓			✓		✓					✓					
✓					✓					✓					
				✓	✓										
				✓	✓	✓		✓		✓			✓		
✓			✓			✓				✓			✓	✓	
				✓	✓	✓		✓		✓		✓	✓		
✓	✓				✓	✓		✓		✓			✓		
✓			✓		✓	✓		✓		✓		✓	✓		
	✓			✓				✓		✓					✓
✓	✓		✓		✓			✓		✓		✓	✓	✓	
✓	✓			✓	✓			✓				✓	✓	✓	✓
✓			✓		✓			✓		✓			✓		
				✓	✓			✓			✓	✓			
✓			✓		✓			✓		✓					
✓	✓	✓	✓		✓			✓							
✓	✓	✓		✓				✓		✓				✓	
				✓	✓	✓			✓						
✓		✓	✓		✓			✓		✓					
✓	✓		✓					✓		✓			✓	✓	✓
	✓		✓		✓			✓		✓					
✓			✓		✓			✓		✓				✓	✓
					✓			✓		✓					
✓	✓			✓	✓			✓		✓					

Name of Property	Accessible for Disabled	Antiques	On the Water	Good Value	Car Not Necessary	Full Meal Service	Historic Building	
Green Springs Plantation				✓				
Hotel Maison de Ville and Audubon Cottages		✓			✓	✓	✓	
Jefferson House		✓	✓	✓				
Josephine Guest House		✓			✓		✓	
Lafitte Guest House		✓		✓	✓		✓	
Loyd Hall	✓	✓		✓				
Madewood Plantation		✓					✓	
Melrose Mansion		✓			✓		✓	
Nottoway		✓				✓	✓	
Old Castillo Hotel/Place d'Evangeline		✓	✓	✓		✓	✓	
Ormond Plantation		✓					✓	
Pointe Coupee Bed & Breakfast		✓		✓			✓	
Riverside Hills Farm			✓	✓				
St. Charles Guest House				✓	✓			
Salmen-Fritchie House		✓		✓			✓	
Soniat House	✓	✓			✓		✓	
Starlight Plantation			✓					
Sully Mansion		✓			✓		✓	
Terrell House		✓		✓	✓		✓	
T 'Frère's House		✓					✓	
Woods Hole Inn				✓				
MISSISSIPPI								
The Amzi Love House		✓		✓		✓	✓	
Anchuca		✓		✓		✓	✓	
Annabelle		✓					✓	

Romantic Hideaway	Luxurious	Pets Allowed	No Smoking Indoors	Good Place for Families	Near Arts Festivals	Beach Nearby	Cross-Country Ski Trail	Golf Within 5 Miles	Fitness Facilities	Good Biking Terrain	Skiing	Horseback Riding	Tennis	Swimming on Premises	Conference Facilities
			✓	✓	✓			✓		✓					
✓	✓				✓			✓		✓				✓	✓
	✓			✓	✓			✓		✓					
	✓	✓		✓	✓			✓		✓					
✓					✓			✓		✓					✓
✓	✓		✓	✓	✓					✓		✓		✓	
✓	✓		✓							✓					
✓	✓				✓			✓	✓	✓				✓	✓
	✓		✓							✓				✓	
				✓	✓			✓		✓					
			✓		✓					✓					✓
✓				✓	✓			✓		✓					
				✓	✓			✓		✓				✓	
	✓		✓		✓			✓		✓					
✓	✓				✓			✓		✓					✓
✓				✓	✓			✓		✓					
					✓			✓		✓					
	✓				✓			✓		✓					
✓	✓	✓	✓		✓			✓		✓					
✓			✓					✓		✓					
✓								✓		✓					
✓		✓	✓					✓		✓				✓	
			✓					✓							

Name of Property	Accessible for Disabled	Antiques	On the Water	Good Value	Car Not Necessary	Full Meal Service	Historic Building	
The Briars	✓	✓		✓		✓	✓	
The Burn		✓		✓		✓		
Canemount Plantation		✓		✓		✓	✓	
Carpenter Place		✓		✓			✓	
The Cartney-Hunt House		✓		✓			✓	
Cedar Grove	✓	✓	✓	✓		✓	✓	
The Corners		✓	✓	✓		✓	✓	
The Duff Green Mansion	✓	✓		✓		✓	✓	
Dunleith		✓		✓			✓	
French Camp Bed and Breakfast Inn		✓		✓			✓	
Governor Holmes House		✓		✓		✓	✓	
The Guest House Historic Hotel	✓	✓		✓			✓	
Hamilton Place		✓		✓			✓	
Harbour Oaks Inn				✓			✓	
Hope Farm		✓		✓			✓	
Lansdowne		✓		✓			✓	
Liberty Hall		✓		✓		✓	✓	
Lincoln, Ltd.		✓		✓				
Linden	✓	✓		✓			✓	
Millsaps Buie House		✓		✓			✓	
The Mockingbird Inn	✓	✓		✓			✓	
Monmouth	✓	✓		✓		✓	✓	
Mount Repose		✓		✓			✓	
No Mistake Plantation		✓		✓		✓	✓	
Oak Square	✓	✓		✓			✓	
Pleasant Hill		✓		✓			✓	

Romantic Hideaway	Luxurious	Pets Allowed	No Smoking Indoors	Good Place for Families	Near Arts Festivals	Beach Nearby	Cross-Country Ski Trail	Golf Within 5 Miles	Fitness Facilities	Good Biking Terrain	Skiing	Horseback Riding	Tennis	Swimming on Premises	Conference Facilities
✓	✓		✓							✓				✓	
✓	✓		✓							✓				✓	
✓	✓		✓							✓				✓	
✓	✓		✓		✓					✓					
	✓							✓		✓					
✓	✓		✓							✓				✓	
✓			✓							✓					
✓		✓								✓				✓	
✓	✓							✓		✓					
		✓	✓	✓						✓					
✓										✓					
✓	✓	✓		✓						✓					✓
✓	✓									✓				✓	
					✓	✓		✓		✓					
✓	✓									✓					
✓			✓							✓					
✓			✓							✓				✓	
✓										✓					
✓								✓		✓					
	✓		✓		✓			✓	✓	✓					✓
✓	✓		✓					✓		✓					
✓	✓		✓					✓		✓					
✓	✓		✓							✓					
✓	✓		✓							✓					
✓	✓		✓							✓					
✓	✓		✓					✓		✓					

Name of Property	Accessible for Disabled	Antiques	On the Water	Good Value	Car Not Necessary	Full Meal Service	Historic Building	
Puddin Place		✓		✓			✓	
Ravenna		✓		✓		✓	✓	
Redbud Inn		✓		✓			✓	
Red Creek Colonial Inn		✓		✓			✓	
Tally House		✓		✓			✓	
Temple Heights		✓					✓	
Weymouth Hall		✓					✓	
White Arches		✓		✓			✓	
NORTH CAROLINA								
The Arrowhead Inn		✓		✓			✓	
The Blooming Garden Inn		✓					✓	
Catherine's Inn		✓	✓	✓	✓		✓	
Cedar Crest Inn		✓					✓	
The Fearrington House	✓				✓	✓		
First Colony Inn	✓	✓					✓	
Granville Queen Inn		✓		✓	✓		✓	
The Greystone Inn	✓	✓	✓		✓	✓	✓	
Harmony House Inn		✓		✓	✓		✓	
Henry F. Shaffner House		✓		✓			✓	
The Homeplace		✓						
The Inn at Taylor House	✓	✓					✓	
The Island Inn		✓		✓	✓	✓	✓	
The King's Arms Inn		✓			✓		✓	
Langdon House		✓			✓		✓	
The Lodge on Lake Lure		✓	✓				✓	

Romantic Hideaway	Luxurious	Pets Allowed	No Smoking Indoors	Good Place for Families	Near Arts Festivals	Beach Nearby	Cross-Country Ski Trail	Golf Within 5 Miles	Fitness Facilities	Good Biking Terrain	Skiing	Horseback Riding	Tennis	Swimming on Premises	Conference Facilities
			✓		✓					✓					
					✓			✓		✓				✓	
✓			✓					✓		✓					
✓			✓	✓	✓	✓		✓		✓					
			✓							✓					
	✓		✓							✓					
			✓							✓					
✓	✓		✓							✓					
				✓	✓			✓		✓					✓
				✓	✓			✓					✓		
			✓	✓	✓	✓		✓	✓	✓			✓		
✓	✓		✓		✓			✓							
✓	✓				✓			✓		✓			✓	✓	✓
✓	✓		✓			✓		✓		✓				✓	✓
✓	✓		✓					✓		✓					
✓	✓						✓	✓	✓	✓		✓	✓	✓	✓
			✓		✓			✓		✓					
✓	✓		✓		✓			✓	✓	✓					✓
			✓		✓			✓		✓					
✓			✓		✓			✓		✓	✓	✓			
✓				✓		✓				✓				✓	
			✓	✓	✓			✓		✓					
			✓		✓	✓		✓		✓					
✓			✓					✓					✓		✓

Name of Property	Accessible for Disabled	Antiques	On the Water	Good Value	Car Not Necessary	Full Meal Service	Historic Building	
The Magnolia Inn		✓				✓	✓	
New Berne House		✓			✓		✓	
Pecan Tree Inn		✓		✓	✓		✓	
Pilot Knob Inn		✓					✓	
The Pine Crest Inn		✓				✓	✓	
The Randolph House		✓		✓		✓	✓	
Richmond Hill Inn	✓	✓				✓	✓	
The Tranquil House Inn	✓		✓			✓	✓	
The Waverly Inn		✓		✓			✓	
SOUTH CAROLINA								
Annie's Inn		✓		✓			✓	
Belmont Inn	✓					✓	✓	
Brustman House				✓				
Chesterfield Inn			✓	✓	✓	✓		
Constantine House		✓		✓				
DuPre House							✓	
Greenleaf Inn		✓		✓		✓	✓	
Inn on the Square	✓			✓		✓		
John Rutledge House Inn		✓				✓	✓	
Kings Courtyard Inn						✓	✓	
King's Inn at Georgetown		✓					✓	
Litchfield Plantation		✓					✓	
Maison DuPré		✓				✓	✓	
Mansfield Plantation		✓				✓	✓	
New Berry Inn	✓			✓	✓			

Romantic Hideaway	Luxurious	Pets Allowed	No Smoking Indoors	Good Place for Families	Near Arts Festivals	Beach Nearby	Cross-Country Ski Trail	Golf Within 5 Miles	Fitness Facilities	Good Biking Terrain	Skiing	Horseback Riding	Tennis	Swimming on Premises	Conference Facilities
					✓			✓		✓				✓	
			✓					✓		✓					
✓	✓		✓			✓		✓		✓					
✓								✓				✓		✓	✓
✓	✓						✓	✓		✓		✓	✓		✓
			✓					✓							
✓	✓		✓		✓			✓		✓		✓	✓		✓
✓	✓			✓		✓		✓		✓					✓
					✓			✓							
			✓					✓		✓				✓	
				✓				✓							✓
			✓			✓		✓							
				✓		✓		✓						✓	
								✓							
				✓				✓						✓	
				✓				✓	✓	✓					
				✓				✓						✓	✓
✓	✓				✓					✓					
	✓			✓	✓					✓					✓
✓			✓					✓						✓	
✓	✓		✓			✓		✓					✓	✓	
			✓		✓					✓					
✓		✓	✓					✓							
			✓					✓	✓	✓					

Name of Property	Accessible for Disabled	Antiques	On the Water	Good Value	Car Not Necessary	Full Meal Service	Historic Building	
Rhett House Inn		✓				✓	✓	
Sea View Inn		✓	✓			✓		
Serendipity, An Inn				✓				
1790 House		✓					✓	
Two Meeting Street		✓			✓		✓	
TwoSuns Inn			✓	✓				
Victoria House Inn					✓		✓	
Willcox Inn	✓					✓	✓	✓
TENNESSEE								
Adams Edgeworth Inn	✓	✓					✓	
Big Spring Inn		✓				✓	✓	
Bird Song Country Inn	✓	✓	✓	✓			✓	
Blue Mountain Mist Country Inn	✓	✓						
Bluff View Inn	✓	✓	✓			✓	✓	
Buckhorn Inn	✓	✓					✓	
Hachland Hill Dining Inn	✓	✓				✓	✓	
Hale Springs Inn						✓	✓	
Hippensteal's Mountain View Inn	✓	✓						
Lynchburg Bed & Breakfast		✓					✓	
Lyric Springs Country Inn	✓	✓	✓	✓		✓	✓	
Magnolia Manor		✓				✓	✓	
McEwen Farm Log Cabin Bed & Breakfast		✓					✓	
Monthaven Bed & Breakfast	✓	✓					✓	
Moss Rose Inn & Café		✓		✓		✓	✓	
Old Cowan Plantation	✓	✓					✓	

Romantic Hideaway	Luxurious	Pets Allowed	No Smoking Indoors	Good Place for Families	Near Arts Festivals	Beach Nearby	Cross-Country Ski Trail	Golf Within 5 Miles	Fitness Facilities	Good Biking Terrain	Skiing	Horseback Riding	Tennis	Swimming on Premises	Conference Facilities
✓	✓		✓							✓					
						✓		✓		✓					
				✓		✓		✓						✓	
✓			✓					✓							
✓	✓		✓		✓					✓					
			✓							✓					
✓	✓			✓	✓					✓					
	✓			✓				✓	✓	✓					
✓	✓		✓		✓		✓	✓		✓			✓	✓	✓
✓	✓		✓		✓	✓	✓	✓		✓	✓		✓	✓	✓
		✓	✓	✓						✓		✓	✓	✓	
✓	✓		✓		✓		✓	✓		✓	✓				✓
✓	✓		✓	✓	✓					✓					
✓					✓		✓	✓		✓	✓	✓			✓
✓		✓		✓	✓			✓		✓					✓
	✓			✓				✓							
	✓		✓	✓				✓							✓
✓				✓						✓					
✓	✓		✓		✓					✓			✓		✓
✓	✓		✓												
✓			✓	✓	✓	✓				✓		✓			
✓			✓	✓	✓	✓		✓		✓				✓	
✓	✓		✓	✓						✓					
✓		✓	✓	✓	✓			✓		✓					

Name of Property	Accessible for Disabled	Antiques	On the Water	Good Value	Car Not Necessary	Full Meal Service	Historic Building	
The Peach Tree Inn		✓	✓			✓		
Richmont Inn	✓	✓						
Tennessee Ridge Inn		✓						
Von-Bryan Inn		✓				✓		
Wayside Manor	✓	✓				✓	✓	
VIRGINIA								
Applewood		✓		✓	✓			
The Ashby Inn & Restaurant		✓					✓	
Ashton Country House		✓		✓				
The Bailiwick Inn	✓	✓			✓		✓	
Belle Grae Inn	✓	✓				✓	✓	
Bleu Rock Inn						✓		
Brookside		✓		✓			✓	
The Burton House and Hart's Harbor House		✓		✓				
The Channel Bass Inn		✓						
Chester		✓		✓			✓	
Chester House		✓		✓			✓	
Clifton	✓	✓	✓			✓	✓	
Colonial Capital		✓			✓			
The Conyers House		✓					✓	
Edgewood		✓					✓	
1817 Antique Inn		✓					✓	
Fassifern		✓					✓	
Fort Lewis Lodge			✓			✓		
The Garden and the Sea Inn		✓					✓	

Romantic Hideaway	Luxurious	Pets Allowed	No Smoking Indoors	Good Place for Families	Near Arts Festivals	Beach Nearby	Cross-Country Ski Trail	Golf Within 5 Miles	Fitness Facilities	Good Biking Terrain	Skiing	Horseback Riding	Tennis	Swimming on Premises	Conference Facilities
✓			✓	✓	✓					✓					
✓			✓		✓		✓	✓		✓	✓	✓			
✓	✓		✓		✓		✓			✓	✓			✓	
✓	✓		✓		✓		✓			✓				✓	✓
✓	✓		✓	✓	✓			✓		✓			✓	✓	✓
			✓	✓	✓			✓		✓					
✓	✓				✓					✓		✓			✓
			✓		✓			✓		✓					
✓	✓		✓		✓			✓		✓					✓
					✓			✓							✓
✓										✓					✓
✓			✓		✓			✓		✓					
			✓					✓		✓					
✓			✓			✓				✓					✓
		✓			✓					✓					✓
								✓		✓					✓
✓	✓		✓		✓			✓		✓			✓	✓	✓
				✓	✓			✓		✓					✓
✓		✓	✓	✓	✓					✓		✓			✓
✓										✓				✓	✓
					✓			✓		✓					
			✓		✓			✓		✓					
				✓						✓				✓	✓
✓	✓				✓	✓				✓					

Name of Property	Accessible for Disabled	Antiques	On the Water	Good Value	Car Not Necessary	Full Meal Service	Historic Building	
High Meadows and Mountain Sunset	✓	✓					✓	
The Holladay House		✓		✓			✓	
The Inn at Gristmill Square		✓					✓	
The Inn at Little Washington		✓						
The Inn at Monticello		✓						
The Inn at Narrow Passage		✓	✓	✓			✓	
Island Manor House		✓					✓	
Jordan Hollow Farm Inn		✓				✓	✓	
Joshua Wilton House		✓					✓	
Keswick Hall	✓	✓				✓		
L'Auberge Provençale		✓					✓	
Lavender Hill Farm			✓	✓				
Liberty Rose		✓						
Miss Molly's Inn		✓					✓	
The Morrison House	✓	✓			✓	✓		
Newport House		✓						
The Norris House Inn		✓					✓	
North Bend Plantation		✓	✓	✓			✓	
Nottingham Ridge		✓	✓	✓				
Pickett's Harbor		✓	✓					
The Pink House		✓		✓			✓	
Prospect Hill		✓				✓	✓	
The Richard Johnston Inn		✓		✓	✓		✓	
Sampson Eagon Inn		✓		✓	✓		✓	
Sea Gate		✓		✓				
Seven Hills Inn								

Romantic Hideaway	Luxurious	Pets Allowed	No Smoking Indoors	Good Place for Families	Near Arts Festivals	Beach Nearby	Cross-Country Ski Trail	Golf Within 5 Miles	Fitness Facilities	Good Biking Terrain	Skiing	Horseback Riding	Tennis	Swimming on Premises	Conference Facilities
✓	✓	✓	✓		✓					✓					✓
					✓					✓					
			✓		✓			✓		✓	✓		✓	✓	✓
✓	✓									✓					✓
			✓		✓			✓		✓				✓	
				✓			✓			✓	✓	✓			✓
			✓		✓	✓				✓					✓
✓				✓			✓	✓		✓	✓	✓			
					✓			✓		✓	✓				✓
✓	✓				✓			✓	✓	✓			✓	✓	✓
✓	✓									✓					
			✓	✓	✓			✓		✓		✓			
✓					✓			✓		✓					
			✓	✓	✓	✓				✓					✓
✓	✓				✓			✓		✓					✓
			✓	✓	✓			✓		✓					
			✓		✓			✓		✓					✓
			✓	✓	✓					✓				✓	
			✓	✓	✓		✓			✓				✓	
			✓	✓			✓			✓				✓	
✓					✓			✓		✓					
✓	✓								✓	✓				✓	✓
			✓		✓			✓							
			✓		✓			✓		✓					
					✓	✓		✓		✓					
				✓						✓					✓

Name of Property	Accessible for Disabled	Antiques	On the Water	Good Value	Car Not Necessary	Full Meal Service	Historic Building	
The Shadows		✓		✓			✓	
The Silver Thatch Inn		✓					✓	
Sleepy Hollow Farm		✓		✓				
The Spinning Wheel Bed and Breakfast		✓		✓				
Sycamore Hill	✓							
Thornrose House		✓		✓				
Tivoli		✓					✓	
Trillium House	✓			✓				
200 South Street	✓	✓						
War Hill Inn		✓		✓				
The Watson House				✓				
Welbourne		✓		✓			✓	
Willow Grove Inn		✓					✓	

Romantic Hideaway	Luxurious	Pets Allowed	No Smoking Indoors	Good Place for Families	Near Arts Festivals	Beach Nearby	Cross-Country Ski Trail	Golf Within 5 Miles	Fitness Facilities	Good Biking Terrain	Skiing	Horseback Riding	Tennis	Swimming on Premises	Conference Facilities
✓			✓		✓					✓					✓
✓			✓		✓			✓					✓		
		✓		✓	✓					✓		✓		✓	✓
			✓		✓	✓		✓		✓					
			✓		✓										
			✓		✓			✓		✓			✓		
					✓					✓					✓
				✓			✓	✓	✓		✓	✓	✓		✓
					✓			✓		✓					✓
		✓	✓	✓				✓		✓					
✓			✓		✓	✓				✓					
		✓			✓					✓		✓			
					✓					✓					

Virginia

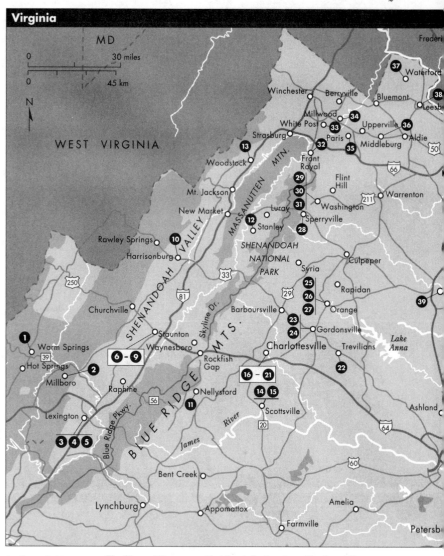

Virginia

0 ⊢ 30 miles
0 ⊢ 45 km
N

WEST VIRGINIA

MD

Frederi

Winchester
Berryville
Bluemont
Waterfor
37

Millwood
White Post **33** **34** Upperville **36**
Strasburg
Paris **35** Aldie
32 Middleburg
13
Woodstock
Front Royal
29
Flint Hill
30
Mt. Jackson
31 Washington
New Market
Luray **211** Warrenton
12 Sperryville
Stanley
28
Rawley Springs **10**
Harrisonburg
SHENANDOAH NATIONAL PARK
Syria
Culpeper
250
33
25
Churchville
29 **26** Rapidan
Barboursville **27** Orange
81
23
Staunton
24 Gordonsville
Warm Springs
Waynesboro
Charlottesville
Trevilians
Lake Anna
6 - 9
Hot Springs
2 Rockfish Gap
16 - 21
22
Millboro
Raphine
14 15
Nellysford
Ashland
56
11
Lexington
Scottsville
3 4 5
20
64
James
River
60
Bent Creek

Lynchburg
Appomattox
Amelia
Farmville
Petersb

Applewood, **44**

The Ashby Inn & Restaurant, **35**

Ashton Country House, **6**

The Bailiwick Inn, **40**

Belle Grae Inn, **7**

Bleu Rock Inn, **29**

Brookside, **34**

The Burton House and Hart's Harbor House, **52**

The Channel Bass Inn, **55**

Chester, **14**

Chester House, **32**

Clifton, **16**

Colonial Capital, **45**

The Conyers House, **28**

Edgewood, **42**

1817 Antique Inn, **17**

Fassifern, **3**

Fort Lewis Lodge, **2**

The Garden and the Sea Inn, **54**

High Meadows and Mountain Sunset, **15**

The Holladay House, **25**

The Inn at Gristmill Square, **1**

The Inn at Little Washington, **30**

The Inn at Monticello, **18**

The Inn at Narrow Passage, **13**

Island Manor House, **56**

Jordan Hollow Farm Inn, **12**

Joshua Wilton House, **10**

Keswick Hall, **19**

L'Auberge Provençale, **33**

Lavender Hill Farm, **4**

Northern Virginia

With verdant scenery, intriguing hamlets, tempting antiquing, top-notch inns, and some of the Old Dominion's most fascinating history, northern Virginia is an ideal getaway. Its rolling hills have nurtured great numbers of American revolutionaries, and almost half the battles of the Civil War were waged in this countryside. Nowadays, though, it's refugees from Washington's bureaucratic wars who are claiming their rewards in northern Virginia. The District's shiny office parks and shopping malls are encroaching. Development, the area's only enemy, is being tenuously held at bay.

The fast track to this Eden west of DC is I–66 (except on Friday and Sunday afternoon), but cognoscenti opt for U.S. 50, which in an easy hour of driving puts you in Middleburg, the capital of hunt country. This discreet town breathes—and caters to—old money, with a collection of upscale galleries, antiques stores, and gun shops. Hunt season in Loudoun, Fauquier, Clarke, and Rappahannock counties begins in late October with an opening meet, peaks around Thanksgiving, and continues into March, provided the ground doesn't freeze.

Frankly, most hunt-country visitors prefer to spend their time window-shopping at Middleburg real-estate offices and driving Loudoun County's back roads. (Routes 622, 626, 710, 713, and 734 are highly recommended, provided you're on the alert for careering Maseratis and BMWs.) These back roads lead to many country pleasures. Hamlets such as Hillsboro, Hamilton, Delaplane, Aldie, Purcellville, and Millwood offer plenty of opportunities for antiquing. All across the countryside, wineries—Naked Mountain, Meredyth, Linden, Piedmont, Oasis—are flourishing. (For a map of them, contact the Virginia Wine Marketing Program, VDACS, Division of Marketing, Box 1163, Richmond, VA 23209, tel. 804/786–0481). Many farms have seasonal tours, pick-your-

own days, and choose-and-cut Christmas trees. (For the "Farms of Loudoun Getaway Guide," contact the Loudoun County Department of Economic Development, Agricultural Development Office, 102 Heritage Way NE, Suite 303, Leesburg, VA 22075, tel. 703/777-0426.)

Northeast of Middleburg lies Leesburg, founded about 1760, which remained in Federal hands during the Civil War and thus retains much of its Colonial architecture. Leesburg's spruced-up storefronts and row houses now function as restaurants and shops.

South and west of Leesburg, a 30-mile corridor between Flint Hill and Syria makes for peak auto idling, too. Here the Blue Ridge asserts itself on the horizon as the roads wind up into the foothills. Fauquier County offers horseback riding in Shenandoah National Park; mounts can be claimed at the Marriott Ranch.

At the southern border of the area sits Fredericksburg, boyhood stomping ground of George Washington, and hotly contested site during the Civil War. Between 1862 and 1864, four major battles were fought—at Chancellorsville, Wilderness, Spotsylvania Court House, and in Fredericksburg itself—resulting in more than 17,000 casualties. Fredericksburg's 40-block national historic district has more than 350 18th- and early 19th-century buildings. Antiquing is big here; there are over 80 dealers in a six-block area.

Established in 1749 by a group of Scottish merchants, Alexandria—a mere 10-minute drive from Washington, DC—has impeccable historical credentials. It was an important Colonial port and a social and political center. Tobacco was shipped from here to the smoky coffeehouses of London, and dissident Scots rankling over the Act of Union with England flocked here (which explains Alexandria's continuing fascination with things Scottish). Alexandria is considered George Washington's hometown; Light Horse

*Harry Lee and Robert E. Lee both lived here. Old Town has
more 18th- and 19th-century architectural gems than any
other city in the country.*

*A walk along Alexandria's shady lanes takes you by
handsome brick homes and offers peeks into mazelike
courtyards. Shoppers will find present-day Alexandria as
mercantile as ever. Ethnic variety makes dining both
outstanding and interesting; there are 80 restaurants within
walking distance of the visitor center.*

Places to Go, Sights to See

Alexandria Archaeology (tel. 703/838–4399). This research facility preserves
the Colonial treasures hidden beneath the paving stones of Old Town.

Carlyle House (Alexandria, tel. 703/549–2997). Built in 1752 by Scottish
merchant John Carlyle (and still the grandest house in town), it
headquartered General Edward Braddock in 1755, when he summoned five
Colonial governors to plot the strategy for the French and Indian War.

Christ Church (Alexandria, tel. 703/549–1450). Its parishioners included
George Washington and Robert E. Lee.

Gadsby's Tavern Museum (Alexandria, tel. 703/838–4242). The rooms have
been restored to their 18th-century appearance; of particular note is the
hanging musicians gallery in the ballroom. George Washington socialized
here. Nearby *Gadsby's Tavern* (tel. 703/548–1288) has been dispensing spirits
and victuals off and on since 1793.

Gunston Hall (15 mi south of Alexandria, tel. 703/550–9220) was the
Georgian mansion of George Mason, author of the first Virginia constitution
and the Virginia Declaration of Rights. Built around 1755, it has a Palladian
parlor and a Chinese-inspired dining room.

Historic Fredericksburg. Sights include the *Mary Washington House*,
bought by a dutiful son for his retired mother, the *James Monroe Museum
and Memorial Library*, the *Hugh Mercer Apothecary* shop, and *Rising Sun
Tavern*. The *Visitors Center* (*see* Tourist Information, *below*) has maps for
several walking tours.

Kenmore (Fredericksburg, tel. 703/373–3381). This Colonial mansion, famous for its decorative plaster moldings, was the home of George Washington's sister, Betty. Its dining room has been called one of the 100 most beautiful rooms in America.

Manassas National Battlefield Park (tel. 703/754–1861) was the scene of the First and Second Battles of Manassas (Bull Run), during which the Confederacy lost 11,456 men and the Union 17,170. General Thomas J. Jackson's famous nickname was coined here when a soldier cried, "There stands Jackson like a stone wall! Rally behind the Virginians!"

Morven Park (near Leesburg, tel. 703/777–2414) is a handsome Greek Revival mansion built by a governor of Virginia. It houses a carriage museum and puts on frequent special events, including steeplechase races.

Mount Vernon (10 mi south of Alexandria, tel. 703/780–2000) is George Washington's home and burial place. The museum holds Jean-Antoine Houdon's bust of Washington, as well as the first president's sunglasses and sword.

Oatlands (near Leesburg, tel. 703/777–3174), a Classical Revival mansion, was built in 1803 by George Carter, grandson of the Williamsburg planter "King" Carter. Its terraced formal gardens are considered some of the most distinguished in the state.

The Saturday Morning Market at Market Square (Alexandria), by City Hall, is the country's oldest operating farmers market. Vendors offer baked goods, fresh produce, plants, flowers, and high-quality crafts. Come early; the market opens at 5 AM, and by 9:30 AM it's all packed up.

Torpedo Factory (Alexandria, tel. 703/838–4565). It's just that: Naval torpedoes were produced here during World Wars I and II. The waterfront building is now a complex of studios where artists produce and sell their works.

Trinity Church (Upperville) is one of the most beautiful Episcopal churches in America. The style was adapted from French country stone churches of the 12th and 13th centuries.

Waterford, a village north of Leesburg so reminiscent of rural England that it could tug at the heart of any Anglophile, is, from one end to the other, a National Historic Site.

White's Ferry (Dickerson, MD, to the edge of Leesburg, tel. 301/349–5200). The historic ferry across the Potomac is now a six-car tugboat, the *General Jubal Early*. It runs daily 5 AM–11 PM.

Restaurants

Many of northern Virginia's top inns offer outstanding meals. Not to be missed are the extraordinary dinners at the **Inn at Little Washington** (*see below*). In Flint Hill, **Four and Twenty Blackbirds** (tel. 703/675–1111) features local ingredients. Leesburg's favorites are **Lightfoot Cafe** (tel. 703/771–2285), which has a bistro-like atmosphere, and **Tuscarola Mills** (tel. 703/771–9300), known for its varied menu and fine wine list. For local color, reasonably priced sandwiches, and a fantastic selection of baked goodies, try **The Upper Crust** (tel. 703/687–5666), across the street from Safeway in Middleburg. **Fiddler's Green** (tel. 703/253–7022) is popular in The Plains. In Fredericksburg, recommended spots are **Sammy T's** (tel. 703/371–2008) and **Merriman's** (tel. 703/371–7723) for casual dining, **Le Lafayette** (tel. 703/373–6895) for French fare, and **Ristorante Renato** (tel. 703/371–8228) for Italian cuisine. In Alexandria, **Le Refuge** (tel. 703/548–4661) and **Le Gaulois** (tel. 703/739–9494) are comfortable French bistros, **Landini Brothers** (tel. 703/836–8404) and **Geranio Ristorante** (tel. 703/548–0088) are the spots for fine Italian dining, and **Bilbao Baggins** (tel. 703/683–0300) is a cozy café with imaginative fare.

Tourist Information

Alexandria Convention and Visitors Bureau (221 King St., Alexandria, VA 22314, tel. 703/838–4200). **Fairfax County Visitors Center** (7764 Armistead Rd., Suite 160, Lorton, VA 22079, tel. 800/724–7329). **Fredericksburg Visitors Center** (706 Caroline St., Fredericksburg, VA 22401, tel. 703/373–1776 or 800/678–4748). **Loudoun County Tourist Information Center** (108-D S St. SE, Market Station, Leesburg, VA 22075, tel. 800/752–6118). **Virginia Division of Tourism** (1021 E. Cary St., Richmond, VA 23219, tel. 804/786–4484).

Reservation Services

Blue Ridge Bed & Breakfast Reservation Service (Rocks & Rills Farm, Rte. 2, Box 3895, Berryville, VA 22611, tel. 703/955–1246). **Princely Bed & Breakfast Reservation Service** (819 Prince St., Alexandria, VA 22314, tel. 703/683–2159). For a copy of **The Bed and Breakfast Association of Virginia's directory,** describing more than 100 establishments, call the Virginia Division of Tourism's B&B line (tel. 800/262–1293). The Division of Tourism's Washington, DC, office also operates a **B&B and small-inn booking service** (tel. 202/659–5523 or 800/934–9184 outside DC).

The Ashby Inn & Restaurant

West of Middleburg and Upperville along U.S. 50, the turnoff for minuscule Paris comes upon you suddenly; half the travelers looking for this hamlet in a hollow below the road probably miss it completely and end up crossing Ashby Gap or the Shenandoah River. At the Ashby's restaurant, you're treated to some of rural Virginia's most sophisticated food, prepared by chef Michelle Beall and masterminded by innkeepers Roma and John Sherman. The menu is changed nightly; crab cakes and New England mussel chowder with pumpkin-smoked bacon and spicy chipolte oil reign as favorites. Dinner runs about $70 for two.

Perhaps the only danger in staying at the inn is that dinner will leave you too blissfully comatose to appreciate your room. The six rooms in the main building are furnished with a spareness that is a calming contrast to the rich food. Quilts, blanket chests, rag rugs, and the occasional cannonball bed set the country tone, though in every case, the views are the chief enhancement. As morning light shines through the windows, you'll spy the garden, the Blue Ridge foothills, lowing cows and other pastoral delights. The coveted Fan Room has two skylights and a glorious fan window opening onto a balcony.

The four expansive rooms in Paris's former one-room schoolhouse are top-of-the-line and excellent values. Each has a private porch that opens onto those splendid countryside views. The Glascock Room has deep red walls, a canopied four-poster bed, and an antique trunk with extra towels. Oriental rugs cover the hardwood floors, and there are two sinks in the large bathroom. Two wing chairs facing the fireplace and a window seat are inviting places for curling up with a book.

Roma, an avid horsewoman, and John are generally too busy during dinner to chat, but at breakfast—featuring fresh eggs cooked to order and succulent muffins—you might get to know your hosts. Roma left advertising for innkeeping, and John, once a House Ways and Means Committee staffer, still writes speeches for politicians and CEOs between stints as the Ashby Inn's maître d'.

Address: *Rte. 1 (Box 2A), Paris, VA 22130, tel. 703/592–3900, fax 703/592–3781.*
Accommodations: *8 double rooms with baths, 2 doubles with sinks share a bath.*
Amenities: *Air-conditioning; TVs, phones, and fireplaces in schoolhouse rooms.*
Rates: *$90–$200; full breakfast. MC, V.*
Restrictions: *No smoking in bedrooms, no pets, closed Jan. 1, July 4, Dec. 25.*

The Bailiwick Inn

The Bailiwick's impeccable restoration befits its location in historic Fairfax. The early 19th-century house sits on the old Ox Road, one of the nation's first toll roads. George Washington's will is filed at the Court House across the street; the first casualty of the Civil War occurred on the Court House lawn.

Thus it was only appropriate that original owners Anne and Ray Smith should hire seven of Washington's top decorators to fashion each room after a famous Virginian. The theme carries through from favorite colors to portraits, accessories, and even biographies. The staff likes to book guests in appropriate rooms; thus, attorneys may find themselves in the John Marshall.

All rooms have plump feather beds and goose-down pillows, and no detail has been slighted. The window treatment and red-and-gold scheme in the Thomas Jefferson repeats the decor of his bedroom in Monticello. The James Monroe has fabric duplicating material used for one of his White House chairs (the 1816 order was still on file). Lord Fairfax's coat of arms determined the colors in his room; its bath has a brocade shower curtain. The sumptuous third-floor bridal suite, the Antonia Ford (she was a Confederate spy), has a pitched ceiling and dormer windows with pillowed seats. Done up in tones of ivory, the suite includes a Chippendale sitting room, a king-size bed, and a bath with whirlpool tub.

There are two elegant parlors for lounging before the fire or taking afternoon tea. One of them has full-length portraits of Anne and Ray in Colonial garb; Anne is holding the keys to the Bailiwick.

Colonial authenticity is carried through to dinners. Such original recipes as Martha Washington's onion cream soup have been adapted to modern tastes. The five-course dinners cost $45 ($55 on Friday and Saturday); menus change every two weeks. From this gem, guests can head west to the countryside or hop the Metro into the capital.

Address: *4023 Chain Bridge Rd., Fairfax, VA 22030, tel. 703/691–2266 or 800/366–7666, fax 703/934–2112.*
Accommodations: *13 double rooms with baths, 1 suite.*
Amenities: *Restaurant, air-conditioning, TV in parlor, phone jacks in rooms, fireplaces in parlors and 4 rooms, turndown service, whirlpool baths in 2 rooms, 2 rooms wheelchair accessible.*
Rates: *$130–$275; full breakfast, afternoon tea. AE, MC, V.*
Restrictions: *No smoking indoors, no pets.*

The Conyers House

I f you want to climb Old Rag, make the scene at the meeting of the Rappahannock Hunt, have a group of companionable dogs lead you to a swimming hole, or go hill-topping on horseback, the Conyers House will suit you like a pair of jodhpurs. This 1790 Hessian soldier–built inn lies on a narrow country road southwest of Sperryville.

Innkeepers Norman and Sandra Cartwright-Brown have made the Conyers House into a very comforting, personal place, stuffed with family mementos and curios the two have collected in their wanderings. In Uncle Sim's Suite there's a stuffed zebra head and a Texas bed with—since everything's big in Texas—seven-foot posts. Sandra has parlayed her penchant for collecting into Conyers Fox and Grape, an antiques shop and tea room in minuscule Sperryville.

She and Norman bought the house, which was a general store in 1810 and a hippie commune in the 1970s, as a summer retreat from their Chevy Chase, Maryland, home. The beige frame structure sits on the side of Walden Mountain. There are four porches and ten fireplaces, seven of which are in the bedrooms. The New Attic is the largest room, but many guests prefer the small Old Attic, which has a claw-foot tub in front of the windows as well as a private deck. In addition to six rooms in the main

building, there's Old Spring House and Hill House out back, where pets are allowed, not to mention a stall for your horse.

With prior arrangement, Sandra and Norman serve a seven-course dinner in the gigantic dining room with such entreés as local trout, tenderloin of pork braised in local cider, and breast of duck in orange sauce. The price of $67.50 per person includes four wines, tax, and service.

The Conyers House has an air of unstuffy, slightly gone-to-seed elegance. It's the kind of place where you can appear for breakfast in jeans, disappear for the day canoeing on the Shenandoah, and return confident of being invited to sip a preprandial sherry.

Address: *Slate Mills Rd. (Rte. 1, Box 157), Sperryville, VA 22740, tel. 703/987–8025, fax 703/987–8709.*
Accommodations: *7 double rooms with baths, 1 suite.*
Amenities: *Air-conditioning, TV with VCR in Old Spring House and Hill House, double whirlpool bath in Hill House; riding arranged.*
Rates: *$100–$195; full breakfast, afternoon refreshments. No credit cards.*
Restrictions: *No smoking indoors, 2-night minimum fall and holiday weekends.*

The Inn at Little Washington

In 1978, in a village of 160 an hour and a half west of (Big) Washington, DC, in the eastern foothills of the Blue Ridge, master chef Patrick O'Connell and his partner, Reinhardt Lynch, opened a restaurant that grew into a legend. From the outside the three-story white frame building looks like any quiet Southern hotel; only the Chinese Chippendale balustrade on the second-floor porch suggests the decorative fantasy within. The rich interior is the work of British designer Joyce Conwy-Evans, who has designed theatrical sets and rooms in English royal houses. The settees in the inn bear as many as 13 elegantly mismatched pillows each; the garden, with crab apple trees, fountain, and fish pond, cries out to be used as a backdrop in *The Importance of Being Earnest.* One bedroom has a bed with a bold plaid spread, shaded by a floral-print half-canopy—and, amazingly, the mélange works. And in the slate-floored dining room with Robert Morris wallpaper, a fabric-swathed ceiling makes guests feel like pashas romantically sequestered in a tent. (A room and a suite in the Guest House, across the street, are good for two couples traveling together, but they lack the sumptuousness of the main building.)

Much has been written about Chef O'Connell's food, all of it giddily rhapsodic. The menu, which changes nightly, makes compelling reading itself, and the six-course dinner costs $98 per person on Saturday, $78 Sunday and weekdays, not including wine and drinks. Some rare vintages rest in the 10,000-bottle cellar.

Breakfast, served overlooking the courtyard garden, is far above the usual Continental fare. Miniature pastries and muffins are tucked in a basket alongside tasty croissants; raspberries glisten in large goblets. Those not still sated from dinner can order, at extra cost, a full breakfast— a lobster omelet with rainbow salsa, a bourbon-pecan waffle.

Clearly the inn, with its staff of 50, is a place for indulgence, and anyone unwilling to succumb to it—both psychologically and financially—should opt for humbler digs. But judging from the waiting list, there are plenty of hedonists out there.

Address: *Middle and Main Sts., Washington, VA 22747, tel. 703/675–3800, fax 703/675–3100.*
Accommodations: *9 double rooms with baths, 3 suites.*
Amenities: *Room service, air-conditioning and phones in rooms, robes, turndown service, whirlpool baths and separate double showers in suites; bicycles.*
Rates: *$240–$580; Continental breakfast, afternoon tea. MC, V.*
Restrictions: *No smoking in dining room, no pets, closed Tues. except in May, Oct., and late Dec.*

L'Auberge Provençale

ourth-generation chef Alain Borel and his wife, Celeste, have brought the romance, personal touches, and fine dining of a French country inn to tiny White Post, an hour and a half west of the Beltway. The 1753 stone house is set on 8½ acres and is surrounded by rolling pastureland. Inside are the Borels' special accents: Alain's great-grandmother's copper pots in the dining room, provincial prints in the guest rooms, whimsical carved carousel animals, painted tiles, and art by Picasso, Buffet, and Dufy.

Don't fill up on the plate of fresh fruit, chocolate, and homemade cookies that welcomes you to your room; you'll want to save your appetite for the five-course dinner ($52). You might start with tempura-style shrimp with saffron sauce and fried plantains, go on to Bahamanian conch chowder, then rack of lamb with black beans, roasted garlic, and rosemary or pompano in parchment and citrus with papaya and tarragon. Celeste, who handles the wine, has assembled a 250-selection list, plus the Captain's List, with rare vintages for the connoisseur. Breakfast in the sunny, bay-windowed, peach-colored dining room starts with a mix of tangerine and orange juice and is followed by such delicacies as fresh fruit, rich croissants, poached egg in phyllo cups, applewood smoked bacon, and house-cured smoked salmon. If you'd like to take a bit of Borel magic

on a picnic along Skyline Drive or at one of the local wineries, they will load a basket with a tablecloth, fruit, cheese, sandwiches, salads, chocolates, and wine. Alain also tends his gardens, fussing over herbs and vegetables grown from seeds imported from France or one of the 54 fruit trees, including such exotics as Asian pears, persimmons, and kiwis.

Celeste is as deft a decorator as she is a wine selector. The three rooms in the new wing are furnished with the fabrics and colors of Provence, accented by hand-painted Spanish tiles; they have fireplaces and private entrances opening onto the gardens. Room 9, the Chambre des Amis, features a canopy bed, cheery yellow and blue prints, and windows facing two directions. For lazy hours with a book or for just viewing the country-side, the large private deck off Room 7 in the main house is perfect.

Address: *Rte. 340 (Box 119), White Post, VA 22663, tel. 703/837–1375 or 800/638–1702, fax 703/837–2004.*
Accommodations: *9 double rooms with baths, 1 suite.*
Amenities: *Restaurant, air-condition-ing, TV in suite, phone jacks in 3 rooms, fireplaces in 5 rooms, living room, and dining room.*
Rates: *$155–$210; full breakfast. AE, DC, MC, V.*
Restrictions: *Smoking in sitting room only, no pets, restaurant closed Tues., inn closed Dec. 25, Jan. 1.*

Bleu Rock Inn

Set on 80 acres of the Bleu Rock Farm, the Bleu Rock Inn enjoys a bucolic setting (if you disregard the front view to the highway). The Blue Ridge Mountains form the backdrop; a pond with ducks and geese, rolling pastures, and 7½ acres of vineyards lie in the foreground. Guests can fish for bass and blue gill in the pond and pluck peaches and apples in the farm's orchards.

The guest rooms are pretty: simply, if unimaginatively, furnished in pastels, light woods, and lace curtains. The four upstairs rooms have private balconies. Number 2's has a mountain view, and the room's window overlooks the serene pond.

The food is the star here. Owners Bernard and Jean Campagne operate the successful La Bergerie Restaurant in Alexandria. Chef Dan Cornish's "modern cuisine" utilizes fresh local ingredients and emphasizes good health and nutrition.

Address: *U.S. 211 (Rte. 1, Box 555), Washington, VA 22747, tel. 703/987-3190 or 800/537-3652, fax 703/987-3193.*
Accommodations: *5 double rooms with baths.*
Amenities: *Restaurant, air-conditioning, fireplaces in dining rooms and lounge, turndown service, wheelchair accessible.*
Rates: *$125–$150; Continental or full breakfast. AE, MC, V.*
Restrictions: *No smoking in dining rooms, no pets, closed Mon. and Dec. 24–25.*

Brookside

Even if Carol and Gary Konkel weren't such nice people, you would still like Brookside. This intimate bed-and-breakfast, right beside Spout Run and the historic Burwell-Morgan Mill, was built in two stages in the 1780s by the grandson of Williamsburg's "King" Carter. It's a frame house with a bay added in the late 1800s, tucked into a picturesque hollow.

Millwood's major industry is antiques, and the Konkels also own an antiques shop. In fact, they opened the B&B as a showplace for such treasures as a mid-1800s schoolmaster's desk, Staffordshire foxes, and everywhere horses—Carol's personal passion.

The guest rooms have high canopied feather beds, bed hangings, working fireplaces, freshly pressed cotton bedding, sherry and a fruit plate, and, for the ladies, antique nighties. The Burwell Room features a cupboard bed. The suite in the toll house, which once taxed traffic over Spout Run, has a full kitchen and a screened porch. A bike trail begins at the mill.

Address: *Millwood, VA 22646, tel. 703/837-1780.*
Accommodations: *3 double rooms with baths, 1 housekeeping suite.*
Amenities: *Air-conditioning, turndown service.*
Rates: *$95–$140; full breakfast. MC, V.*
Restrictions: *No smoking indoors, no pets, closed Mon.–Tues.*

The Morrison House

A Scottish flag snaps in the breeze above the white-pillared portico of the Morrison House, bespeaking the Scottish heritage of the owner, a Washington real-estate developer and world traveler. Robert E. Morrison built the five-story Federal-style building in 1985, under the eye of a curator from the Smithsonian. It's constructed of red brick laid in Flemish bond and has arched windows and a small garden at the foot of the entryway. Luxuries abound, including state-of-the-art marble bathrooms with scales and makeup mirrors, triple-sheeting on the high mahogany beds, afternoon tea (extra charge), and Mrs. Morrison's chocolate-chocolate-chip cookies in every room. All 45 guest rooms are different, with camelback sofas, Chippendale-style chairs, swagged draperies, and a few fireplaces (which, alas, don't work, though two in the parlor do). The house is an eight-block walk from a metro station. Patrons can park beneath the hotel and explore the District and Old Town Alexandria.

Address: *116 S. Alfred St., Alexandria, VA 22314, tel. 703/838–8000 or 800/367–0800, fax 703/684–6283.*
Accommodations: *42 double rooms with baths, 3 suites.*
Amenities: *Restaurant, 24-hr room service, air-conditioning, cable TV and phones in rooms, robes, turn-down service, nonsmoking floor, wheelchair accessible.*
Rates: *$175–$295; breakfast extra. AE, DC, MC, V.*
Restrictions: *No pets.*

The Norris House Inn

B efore leaving their marketing careers in California to become Virginia innkeepers, Pamela and Don McMurray spent four years looking at almost 200 B&Bs. In 1991 they finally settled on the Norris House, a handsome brick Federal-style home in the center of historic Leesburg, and spent two years restoring the 1806 home and landscaping the gardens. Two celebrated early 19th-century builders, the Norris brothers, are responsible for the portico with turned spindles, the Adam-style mantel in the biscuit-toned parlor, and the shiny wild-cherry bookcases in the library. The Garden Room has a stenciled border along the walls and a four-poster bed with lace canopy. Across the gardens is the Stone House Tea Room, another McMurray business. Guests also have access to a full-service business center. The McMurrays are amateur genealogists, and they offer special packages to guests sharing their interest. But since 1991 there hasn't been much time for tracing ancestors.

Address: *108 Loudoun St. SW, Leesburg, VA 22075, tel. 703/777–1806 or 800/644–1806, fax 703/771–8051.*
Accommodations: *6 double rooms share 3 baths.*
Amenities: *Air-conditioning, phone jacks in rooms, fireplaces in 3 rooms, robes, turndown service.*
Rates: *$75–$140; full breakfast, evening refreshments. AE, DC, MC, V.*
Restrictions: *No smoking indoors, no pets, 2-night minimum Apr.–May and Sept.–Oct. weekends.*

The Pink House

The Pink House lies at a crossroads in the wee village of Waterford, founded in 1733 by Quakers. The town resisted embroilment in the Revolution but joined the Union during the Civil War, when Confederate troops laid to waste its rolling Loudoun County farms. Today the whole 1,400-acre town is a National Historic Landmark, special among such places because modern development hasn't touched its periphery. This Brigadoon is accessible by bike path from Alexandria or by car via Routes 7, 9, and 662. The Pink House is owned by Chuck and Marie Anderson, who love opera, books, theater, and long, cozy chats. The Opera Suite features 18th-century antiques, a whirlpool bath, TV with VCR, a baby grand piano, and a folk-arty mural depicting Waterford notables attending a gala at the Met. It also has a fireplace and a private entrance opening onto the Waterford fields, where walking is encouraged. Marie's breakfasts include Irish soda bread, but for lunch or dinner you'll have to drive to Leesburg (20 minutes away), as the village puts itself out for tourists only during the October Waterford Crafts Fair.

Address: *Waterford, VA 22190, tel. 703/882–3453, fax 703/882–3559.*
Accommodations: *1 suite.*
Amenities: *Air-conditioning, phone, turndown service; private outdoor sitting areas.*
Rates: *$95; full English breakfast. No credit cards.*
Restrictions: *No pets, closed Dec. 25.*

The Richard Johnston Inn

In a prime Caroline Street location, just across from the visitor center, is this diminutive-looking 18th-century brick row house with a dormer on the third floor and a pleasant patio adjoining the parking lot in the rear, shaded by magnolia trees. Inside, restoration work has been top-drawer, and owner Susan Thrush has lavished loving care on the immaculate inn.

In the common rooms downstairs, board floors are polished to a rich luster and covered with Oriental rugs. The furnishings are Chippendale- and Empire-style antiques. Of the guest rooms, Room 5 has an imposing, queen-size, 19th-century mahogany plantation bed, and Room 2 has a dormer, a king-size brass bed, and Victorian furnishings. Two commodious suites, with living rooms, wet bars, and wall-to-wall carpeting, have private entrances opening onto the patio.

Susan serves her freshly baked breads and muffins in the vast dining room, set with fine china, crystal, and silver.

Address: *711 Caroline St., Fredericksburg, VA 22401, tel. 703/899–7606.*
Accommodations: *7 double rooms with baths, 2 suites.*
Amenities: *Air-conditioning, cable TV in living room and 3 rooms.*
Rates: *$90–$130; Continental-plus breakfast. AE, DC, MC, V.*
Restrictions: *No smoking, no pets, closed Dec. 24–25.*

Sycamore Hill

Get out your cameras, please, for the serious photo opportunities at Sycamore Hill, a ranch-style house seemingly dropped from the sky onto the crest of Menefee Mountain. As you wind up the mile approach from town, you begin to doubt there could possibly be a lodging at the end of the road. Fear not. Eventually the forest gives way to Kerri Wagner's extensive gardens, and finally you arrive at the Virginia fieldstone house wrapped by a 65-foot veranda. The view from this spot is the raison d'être of Sycamore Hill—there's Old Rag to the right, Tiger Valley, and Red Oak Mountain. And the 52-acre lot is a certified wildlife sanctuary. With its views and gardens, this is a spot for the nature lover. The best view is from the 6-foot picture window in the Master Bedroom, which has a queen-size four-poster bed. Kerri Wagner is an energetic hostess who treats her guests like friends, aided by a shaggy white mop of a dog named Molly Bean and her husband, Steve, an artist whose fascinating magazine covers line the walls.

Address: *Rte. 1 (Box 978), Washington, VA 22747, tel. 703/675–3046.*
Accommodations: *3 double rooms with baths.*
Amenities: *Air-conditioning, TV in living room and 1 room, fireplace in living room, turndown service, wheelchair accessible.*
Rates: *$100–$140; full breakfast, afternoon refreshments. MC, V.*
Restrictions: *No smoking indoors, no pets, 2-night minimum holiday and May weekends and Oct.*

Welbourne

There are so many stories attached to this 1775 mansion that it makes your head spin. Thomas Wolfe visited. F. Scott Fitzgerald came often and set his short story "The Last Case" here. During the Civil War a Dulany of Welbourne served J.E.B. Stuart breakfast on horseback outside the front door. Beyond the stories, Welbourne is the genuine, blue-blooded hunt-country article, a sweeping, stately yellow home fronted by six columns and surrounded by 550 acres. It's been in the same family for seven generations, though as owner Sherry Morison says, "We have the acreage, but not the bank account." Recognizing that the old homestead isn't in peak condition, Mrs. Morison describes it as "definitely faded elegance. The chairs are wobbly because they've been sat in for 150 years." There are no pretensions here, only peeling paint and faded upholstery, countless family antiques and art, and an unequaled wealth of history. There's no place else like it in Virginia.

Address: *Welbourne Rd. (Rte. 1, Box 300), Middleburg, VA 22117, tel. 703/687–3201.*
Accommodations: *5 double rooms with baths, 3 cottages.*
Amenities: *Air-conditioning in rooms, TV in living room, fireplaces in 4 rooms and 2 cottages.*
Rates: *$85–$96 (plus $10 a day for firewood); full Southern breakfast, evening cocktails. No credit cards.*
Restrictions: *No cigars, no cats, 2-night minimum spring, fall, and holiday weekends.*

The Eastern Shore

Most people think of the long peninsula east of the Chesapeake Bay as territory claimed by the states of Maryland and Delaware. Indeed, the most developed and touristy parts of Delmarva are, but if you look closely at a map you'll see a boundary line with the word Virginia printed beneath. The border lies about 75 miles north of the peninsula's tip, and in between is Virginia's very own toehold on the Eastern Shore, encompassing two counties— Northampton and Accomack—with a combined population close to that of Charlottesville. The area was settled in the 1600s, by English colonists; visited by vacationers (who made the trip by ferryboat) in the 19th century; and surveyed by the railroad, which reached the peninsular terminus, at Cape Charles, in about 1885. Several decades ago the peninsula was bisected by a highway, U.S. 13, which brought some—but not many—1950s-style motels and drive-in restaurants. Off U.S. 13, however, the Eastern Shore lives and looks the way it did around the turn of the century—no quaint restored villages or tony resorts. True back-roaders will like it immensely—providing they understand a few basic facts in advance.

Above all, Virginia's Eastern Shore is not a beach haven, except for the stellar sandy stretches at its northeast corner lying within the Chincoteague National Wildlife Refuge. On the bay side, tidal creeks and marshes predominate. Seaside, a string of barrier islands has kept beaches from forming at the shoreline. The islands themselves are either privately owned or, like the islands of Cobb, Smith, and Hog, are provinces of the Nature Conservancy's Virginia Coast Reserve. To reach them you'll need to charter a boat or sign up for one of the VCR's infrequent island trips. There are spring and fall boat tours and three-day photography weekends (tel. 804/442-3049) led by trained naturalists.

Nor are there any cities of note on Virginia's Eastern Shore, with the possible exceptions of Chincoteague, whose meager population swells in peak summer months but otherwise figures at about 3,500, and Cape Charles, which thrived during ferry and railroad days but now has only a cranking cement factory to keep it from becoming comatose. County maps show many other towns (with colorful names such as Temperanceville, Birds Nest, and Oyster), but these are really only crossroads with, if you're lucky, a general store. East of U.S. 13, skinny local arteries such as Routes 679 and 600 reach such villages and the architectural contradictions that surround them. The Virginia peninsula has its own unique building style, followed for hundreds of years: "chain" houses made of frame, consisting, when the pattern holds, of big house, little house, colonnade, and kitchen linked in a row. You can glimpse a good example, the privately owned Holly Brook Plantation, on the west side of U.S. 13, some 8 miles south of Nassawadox.

The town of Chincoteague lies on 8-mile-long Chincoteague Island (not to be confused with the island holding the wildlife refuge, Assateague Island, to which it provides access via a bridge) and exists almost wholly to cater to tourists, with motels, restaurants, and shops. It is atmospherically similar to other Atlantic beach resorts in Maryland and Delaware, but its low-lying, marshy location brings septic and mosquito problems. Nonetheless, it has one attraction that will probably never cease drawing crowds: the legendary Pony Penning event, held in late July. The ponies swim the channel between Assateague and Chincoteague and are then corraled and auctioned off, usually for about $600 each. This roundup began in 1924, though it was made nationally famous by Marguerite Henry's Misty of Chincoteague *in 1947. Misty herself was a real pony; her descendants can be seen roaming free on Assateague throughout the year.*

Places to Go, Sights to See

Accomac. This particularly pretty town has enough restored Colonial architecture to rival Williamsburg, and it is one of two villages on the Eastern Shore (the other is Eastville) with an 18th-century debtors' prison. The Victorian clerk's office on the west side of the courthouse green holds records dating to 1663.

Cape Charles, a place decidedly in the slow lane, was by 1953 abandoned by the passenger railroad and ferry service that made the town boom briefly around the turn of the century. Today most of its 136 acres are a historic district, though an unusual one because the houses date from the first quarter of the century. A walking tour takes you past two Sears-catalog homes built in the mid-1920s, the pleasant bayside boardwalk, and a wonderful art-deco movie house. Some will feel that industrial works to the south mar the townscape, though at these you can watch freight trains being loaded onto barges that take them to Norfolk. In all, it's a funky, beyond-the-pale sort of place that attracts more and more refugees from northern metropolises, who can still buy reasonably priced property here.

Chesapeake Bay Bridge-Tunnel (tel. 804/624–3511). This 17.6-mile, $200 million engineering marvel links the peninsula with Norfolk and Virginia Beach. Completed in 1964, it has brought the Eastern Shore into the Virginia fold only to a degree, largely due to the hefty $10 toll each way—which, as some peninsula dwellers see it, keeps the Navy riffraff out. To support its mammoth span, four islands were built; one has a scenic stopping place, a fishing area, a snack bar, and a gift shop. To accommodate Chesapeake Bay ship traffic, the two-lane bridge gives way to two 1-mile-long tunnels. The trip is either awesome, unsettling, or soporific, depending on the soundness of your stomach and nerves.

Chincoteague National Wildlife Refuge (tel. 804/336–6577). Despite the surfboarders and sun worshipers headed toward its long stretch of Atlantic beach, the refuge exists first and foremost for the benefit of birds, snakes, ponies, rare Delmarva gray squirrels, and Sika deer. Many of the species preserved in this veritable Noah's Ark are visible from a 6-mile loop drive that winds through forests and marshes. There are, as well, a visitor center, lighthouse (built in 1866), crabbing ridge, and fishing area—but no restaurants, camping, or bonfires. In season the refuge sponsors fishing expeditions, evening cruises, and a wildlife safari (tel. 804/336–5593), which takes nature lovers along back roads to observe the intimate habits of the famed Chincoteague feral ponies.

Eastern Shore of Virginia National Wildlife Refuge (Cape Charles, tel. 804/331–2760). This 651-acre refuge provides good birding year-round. Each fall, migrating birds gather in large groups until favorable conditions permit an easy crossing of Chesapeake Bay.

Eyre Hall. The peninsula's handsomest and most historic plantation was built in 1733, on land granted to the owners in 1662. The brick and frame house near the bay is open only during Historic Garden Week in April, but its grounds, with ancient plantings, flowering shrubs, and venerable trees, can be visited year-round. Turn left 3 miles above the Cheriton stoplight, onto the private lane opposite Route 636.

Hopkins & Bro. General Store (Onancock, tel. 804/787–4478). This 1842 country store-cum-restaurant at the town dock is a Virginia Historic Landmark, with a companionable bar and a menu featuring shore inevitables such as crab cakes and seafood salad.

Kerr Place (near Onancock, tel. 804/787–8012). The distinguished brick mansion on the outskirts of town was built in 1799. Housed within are the collections of the Eastern Shore of Virginia Historical Society, including costumes, portraits, and furnishings.

Kiptopeke State Park (tel. 804/331–2267). Located 3 miles north of the Bay Bridge-Tunnel on Route 704, the park has a wide swimming beach, biking and hiking trails, and a lighted fishing pier. Its Atlantic Flyway location has made it a bird-banding site for 30 years.

NASA Goddard Flight Center and Wallops Flight Facility Visitor Center (Wallops Island and areas surrounding Chincoteague, tel. 804/824–2298). The first rocket at this 6,000-acre NASA enclave was launched in 1945. The visitor center (the only part of the complex open to visitors) displays space suits, moon rocks, and scale models of satellites and space probes. On the first Saturday of every month NASA launches model-rockets on the grounds.

Pear Valley (near Johnsontown). Constructed in 1672, this is the peninsula's oldest house. The one-room cottage with a chimney and loft is owned by the Association for the Preservation of Virginia Antiquities and is currently unrestored. It can be seen from Route 689.

Refuge Waterfowl and Oyster Museums (Piney Island, tel. 804/336–5800 and 804/336–6117, respectively). These two tiny museums are neighbors on Piney Island (barely an island, really, as it's only tenuously separated from Chincoteague by skinny Eel Creek). The Waterfowl Museum has a collection of handcrafted decoys, and the Oyster Museum tells the life story of the bivalve and how generations of watermen have pursued it.

Tangier Island. To reach this tiny island, stuck like a buoy in the middle of Chesapeake Bay, catch the *Captain Eulice* at Onancock Harbor (tel. 804/787–8220). The boat sails June–September at 10 and returns at 3. A livestock-grazing range before the Revolution, Tangier is now home to approximately 900 souls—most of them named Crockett, Parks, Thomas, and Pruitt—whose speech is Elizabethan cockney, barely changed since the first settlers moved in. It's an insular place, devoted to seafood harvesting and Methodism, with one main street that's too narrow for cars and the *Chesapeake House* (tel. 804/891–2331), whose reputation for family-style shellfish feasts has spread far and wide. Slightly less renowned is *Double-Six* (tel. 804/891–2410), a local haunt once featured in *National Geographic* because it serves hot oyster sandwiches.

Wachapreague. This sleepy village on the Atlantic side of the peninsula once held a 30-room hotel and attracted vacationers from as far away as New York City. But the hotel burned down, leaving only the 340-odd permanent residents, along with a carnival ground that still lights up in late July. It remains a fishing mecca, especially for flounder.

Restaurants

There are two culinary stars on Virginia's Eastern Shore. At the **Channel Bass Inn** (Chincoteague, tel. 804/336–6148), Jim Hanretta serves Spanish, Basque, and Continental cuisine to 18 guests each night. At **The Garden and the Sea** (New Church, tel. 804/824–0672), Victoria Olian creates a French-flavored menu that changes every two weeks. Both are inns.

For casual dining, try **Ray's Shanty** (Wattsville, tel. 804/824–3429) or **AJ's on the Creek** (Chincoteague, tel. 804/336–9770). Trendy **Armando's** (Onancock, tel. 804/787–8044) has a bistro atmosphere, and intimate **Minda's** (Tasley, tel. 804/787–5656) has exceptional seafood. **Hopkins & Bro.** (Onancock, tel. 804/787–4478) is a pleasant setting for lunch. The casual **Formy's Pit Barbecue** (Painter, tel. 804/442–2426) is the Eastern Shore's only barbecue restaurant. Don't be misled by the truck stop appearance of the **Cape Center Restaurant** (Cape Charles, tel. 804/331–2505). Locals call it "Chez Exxon" and praise the sophisticated dinner entrées and reasonable prices.

Tourist Information

Chincoteague Chamber of Commerce (Box 258, Chincoteague, VA 23336, tel. 804/336–6161). **Virginia Division of Tourism** (1021 E. Cary St., Richmond, VA 23219, tel. 804/786–4484). **Virginia's Eastern Shore Chamber of Commerce/Tourism Commission** (Drawer R, Melfa, VA 23410, tel. 804/787–2460).

Reservation Services

Amanda's Bed & Breakfast Reservation Service (1428 Park Ave., Baltimore, MD 21217, tel. 410/225–0001). **Bed & Breakfast of Tidewater Virginia Reservation Service** (Box 6226, Norfolk, VA 23508, tel. 804/627–1983). **Inns of the Eastern Shore** (1500 Hambrooks Blvd., Cambridge, MD 21613, tel. 800/373–7890). For a copy of **The Bed and Breakfast Association of Virginia's directory,** describing more than 100 establishments, call the Virginia Division of Tourism's B&B line (tel. 800/262–1293). The Division of Tourism's Washington, DC, office also operates a **B&B and small-inn booking service** (tel. 202/659–5523 or 800/934–9184 outside DC).

The Channel Bass Inn

The Channel Bass occupies a pale-lemon building constructed in the 1880s—making it one of Chincoteague's oldest—and added onto in the 1920s, resulting in an untroubled asymmetry and a kind of appealing architectural buxomness, albeit slightly weather-beaten. But the inn's design style, history, even its proximity to Chincoteague National Wildlife Refuge, are all eclipsed by another feature—its restaurant.

Jim Hanretta, who is both innkeeper and chef, opened the Channel Bass in 1972, and since then its culinary reputation has spread. The restaurant is known for its unusual recipes, invented on the premises by Jim, who learned his craft in Barcelona. Here you'll find local seafood brightened with Spanish and Basque sauces, as well as French cuisine. Jim cooks every dish all alone in his compact kitchen, which is why only 18 people can be served each night; dining here is a little like hiring yourself a private chef. The dining room is intimate, with windows providing views of the romantically lit garden in back. Wedgwood china, silver, and linen table napkins are de rigueur. Of course, you pay dearly for the Channel Bass dining experience. With entrées ranging from $36 to $39, a five-course dinner for two runs $150–$200, before wine. (The private reserve list is topped off with an $800 bottle of 1966 Château Lafite Rothschild.) Breakfasts are on the pricey side, too—$12 for Continental, $12–$14 for one of Jim's soufflés.

The 10 guest rooms, on the second and third floors, are extremely large and luxurious, with original art on the walls, plump picture books on the coffee tables, and seating areas. Jim's a perfectionist here—down pillows on the triple-sheeted beds, thick Egyptian-cotton towels in the ceramic-tile baths. Guest rooms share no common walls, and soundproofing ensures quiet. Room 10 is as big as a suite and has a minifridge. Though the rooms lack the restaurant's unique personality, they are immensely comfortable, very private neutral zones. (A romantic dinner can be arranged in the two suites.)

Off season, Jim holds special three-day cooking vacations, which include dinners, rooms, and hands-on lessons during which some of the inn's secrets are revealed.

Address: *100 Church St., Chincoteague, VA 23336, tel. 804/336–6148, fax 804/336–6599.*
Accommodations: *8 double rooms with baths, 2 suites.*
Amenities: *Air-conditioning, TV in suites.*
Rates: *$125–$175; breakfast extra. AE, D, DC, MC, V.*
Restrictions: *No smoking, no pets, 2-night minimum weekends, 3-night minimum during Pony Penning, closed Dec. 15–Jan. 15.*

The Garden and the Sea Inn

When Victoria Olian and her husband, Jack Betz, traveled to southern France in 1986, they hardly imagined that their enchantment with the area would lead to new careers as innkeepers in tiny New Church, just 1½ miles south of the Maryland border.

For 25 years they had lived in Washington, DC, where Jack was an attorney and Victoria an interior designer (her talent is evident at the inn). After the year in France on sabbatical from city life, they bought a country Victorian—the 1802 Bloxom's Tavern and its 1901 addition—which they remodeled and opened as the Garden and the Sea in 1989.

The quietly sophisticated, light and airy Garden and the Sea brings the feel of a small French inn to the Eastern Shore. The decor mixes antique furnishings, French wicker, Oriental rugs, ballooning fabrics, Victorian moldings and detail, and bay windows. From the multicolored gingerbread trim on the wide front porch to the sunny, rose-hued dining room, the inn is exceptionally inviting. Guest rooms are spacious. In the main house, the Chantilly Room, with a wicker sleigh bed and painted dresser, and the Giverny Room, with floral prints and dark green lacquered wrought-iron furniture, both have large baths with double sinks and bidets.

Awhile back, Jack and Victoria moved New Church's oldest house onto the property. It's now the newly remodeled Garden House, with a music room, library, and three guest rooms. The large, private Champagne Room has a two-person whirlpool tub and shower and a wrought-iron canopy bed.

Victoria, who had worked with a chef in Provence, enrolled in culinary school and now creates the marvelous French meals of fresh ingredients from local farms and waters in menus that change every other week. Jack serves as the amiable maître d'. There are two fixed-price menus, as well as à la carte choices (entrées run about $14–$21). Specialties include bouillabaisse, grilled duck breast with cassis berries, and scallops with sautéed cabbage and parsley. There are occasional chamber-music dinner concerts and art shows.

Address: *Rte. 710 (Box 275), New Church, VA 23415, tel. 804/824–0672.*
Accommodations: *5 double rooms with baths.*
Amenities: *Air-conditioning, ceiling fans, robes, whirlpool baths in 3 rooms.*
Rates: *$85–$150; hearty Continental breakfast, afternoon tea. AE, D, DC, MC, V.*
Restrictions: *Smoking in parlor and on open porches only, no pets, 2-night minimum weekends, closed Nov.–Mar.*

The Burton House and Hart's Harbor House

The business of little Wacha-preague, on the Atlantic side of the peninsula, is fishing. The pretty village sits alone, though in late July its amusement park lights up for the Fireman's Carnival. The Burton House, just across the street from the carnival grounds, is a pale green, surprisingly ungingerbready Victorian built in 1883. In back there's a gazebo and deck, and to the side a rack of bikes, which guests may borrow.

Next door is the tan 1870 Hart's Harbor House. Friendly, down-to-earth Pat and Tom Hart have remodeled it into a three-bedroom B&B. It has a fireplace in the living room and a wood-burning stove in the dining room. Both establishments are simply adorned and comfy. Antique furnishings, quilt-covered beds, and the Harts themselves create an inviting, at-home atmosphere. The Harts can arrange guided pontoon boat trips to the barrier islands.

Address: *9 and 11 Brooklyn St. (Box 182), Wachapreague, VA 23480, tel. 804/787-4560.*
Accommodations: *3 double rooms with baths, 6 doubles with ½ baths share 2 showers.*
Amenities: *Air-conditioning, cable TV in parlors.*
Rates: *$75–$85; full breakfast, afternoon tea. MC, V.*
Restrictions: *Smoking on porches only, no pets.*

Island Manor House

In this 1848 three-story T-shaped Maryland house on Main Street, Charles Kalmykow and Carol Rogers have created what Charles terms "a very classy B&B." The house is furnished in Federal style with an impressive collection of antiques. Classical music plays quietly in the impeccable, rose-colored Garden Room, a serene retreat with fireplace, big windows, and French doors opening onto a brick courtyard with roses and a fountain. The large Nathaniel Smith Room has a sloped ceiling, a sitting area, and four dormer windows, each with a window seat. The premier room is the Mark Twain, which has a king-size bed.

While Carol tends the inn, preparing lavish breakfasts with homemade bread each morning, Charles works in western New York, making the 1,200-mile commute to Chincoteague every weekend.

Since Miss Molly's is just across the street, travelers can choose from two distinct personalities—the casual, spontaneous Miss Molly's or the more formal, light-filled Island Manor House.

Address: *4160 Main St., Chincoteague, VA 23336, tel. 804/336-5436.*
Accommodations: *4 double rooms with baths, 4 doubles share 2 baths.*
Amenities: *Air-conditioning; bicycles.*
Rates: *$80–$120; full breakfast, afternoon tea. MC, V.*
Restrictions: *Smoking on sheltered porches only, no pets, 2-night minimum weekends, 3-night minimum holidays.*

Miss Molly's Inn

Effusive hostess Barbara Wiedenheft immediately makes her guests at home in this 1886 Victorian on Chincoteague's Main Street. Miss Molly, daughter of the builder J.T. Rowley, lived in the house until she was 84. The sunny corner room named after her has roses on the walls, bedspread, and linens. The large room next door is where Marguerite Henry stayed while she was writing *Misty of Chincoteague*. The upstairs dormer rooms are light and share a homey sitting area.

Barbara and her husband, David, are expatriates from the Washington, DC, area. (Barbara used to work for the British Embassy and is fluent in three languages.) In good weather she serves what she laughingly calls her "world-famous" breakfasts and her "world-famous" tea (with homemade scones) on the screened-in gazebo, facing the channel and its fishing activity. There are some commercial areas nearby, but not enough to detract from the charms of this cozy, laughter-filled spot.

Address: *4141 Main St., Chincoteague, VA 23336, tel. 804/336–6686.*
Accommodations: *5 double rooms with baths, 2 doubles share 1 bath.*
Amenities: *Air-conditioning, fireplace in dining room, beach towels.*
Rates: *$69–$135; full breakfast, afternoon tea. No credit cards.*
Restrictions: *No smoking, no pets, 2-night minimum weekends, closed Jan.–mid-Feb.*

Nottingham Ridge

Bonnie Nottingham's sister-in-law, Sara Goffigan (of Pickett's Harbor just up the lane), convinced her that she should open her brick Williamsburg-style house, built in 1975, to guests. And so she did. Two miles off the main road, it shares a long stretch of private beach with Pickett's Harbor, as well as the smashing Chesapeake Bay sunsets and visitations by herons and egrets. Situated on the Atlantic Flyway, this is a bird-watcher's paradise. Inside, it's a cheerful, less composed place than Pickett's Harbor, with two fireplaces in common rooms, a back porch, and four bedrooms. Romantics favor a downstairs room with canopy bed and pastel quilt. An upstairs room, with a private entrance, bedroom, and separate sitting and sleeping room, is great for families.

Bonnie is a warm, lovable host. Be sure to sample her sweet-potato biscuits, scrapple, and homemade jam at breakfast. Exact directions to both Nottingham's Ridge and Pickett's Harbor (neither has signs) are given with reservation confirmation.

Address: *28184 Nottingham Ridge La. (Box 97–B), Cape Charles, VA 23310, tel. 804/331–1010 (at night).*
Accommodations: *3 double rooms with baths, 1 suite.*
Amenities: *Air-conditioning, TV in den; beach.*
Rates: *$85; full breakfast, afternoon refreshments. No credit cards.*
Restrictions: *No smoking, no pets, 2-night minimum weekends.*

Pickett's Harbor

Sara and Cooke Goffigan's beige frame-and-brick house sits off an isolated country lane 4 miles north of the Chesapeake Bay-Bridge Tunnel and 2 miles west of U.S. 13. The front yard is a vast stretch of private beach frequented by deer and horseshoe crabs.

Sara's warmth and the high-ceilinged rooms furnished with antiques and family items immediately make you feel like you're sharing an immensely inviting, cozy home with friends. The one downstairs bedroom has a four-poster bed, easy chairs, and an exceptional water view. The upstairs rooms, with quilt-covered beds and water views, are pretty, too.

Sara serves a country breakfast that routinely features sweet-potato biscuits, Virginia ham, and popovers. Before she heads off to teach school, you may want to ask her about her family, a clan that came to the Eastern Shore in the 1600s, not long after Captain John Smith explored the peninsula.

Address: *Box 97–AA, Cape Charles, VA 23310, tel. 804/331–2212.*
Accommodations: *2 double rooms with baths, 4 doubles share 2 baths.*
Amenities: *Air-conditioning, TV with VCR in family room, fireplaces in family and dining rooms; bicycles.*
Rates: *$75–$125; full breakfast. No credit cards.*
Restrictions: *Smoking on porch only, no pets, 2-night minimum holiday weekends.*

Sea Gate

Jim Wells and Chris Bannon, both formerly of New York City (as are so many recent arrivals to the town), have laughingly taken to calling Cape Charles "the Cape." The Sea Gate was built in 1912; it's a rotund pink frame, transitional Victorian house a block from the water, on one of the town's prettiest residential streets. There's a wide porch out front, a grand piano in the entryway, antiques scattered about, and fireplaces in the living room and dining room. The relaxed tone of the place and the congenial hosts are winning. Guest rooms are bright. The corner Blue Room has access to an enclosed upstairs porch. Generally guests sit up late talking in the living room. The next morning at breakfast (perhaps French toast made with homemade cinnamon bread) the conversation picks up as if it had never ended. Then it's off to explore Cape Charles, followed by a visit to the beach, afternoon tea, and phenomenal sunset-watching. For dinner in town, there's Joe's Bayside Cafe or the Cape Charles Pizzeria.

Address: *9 Tazewell Ave., Cape Charles, VA 23310, tel. 804/331–2206.*
Accommodations: *2 double rooms with baths, 2 doubles with ½ baths share 1 hall bath.*
Amenities: *Air-conditioning, TV and clock radio in rooms, cable TV with VCR in living room; bicycles.*
Rates: *$65–$80; full breakfast, afternoon tea. No credit cards.*
Restrictions: *Smoking downstairs only, no pets, 2-night minimum holiday weekends.*

The Spinning Wheel Bed and Breakfast

For five years, this 1890s Victorian home in the heart of Onancock was Karen and David Tweedie's summer home. Then in 1993, they jump-started their plans to open a B&B by converting the house, a job Karen declares was "more fun than we ever expected." Karen, a spinner, displays her collection of antique spinning wheels throughout the house. David serves elaborate breakfasts in the dining room, or you can enjoy a Continental breakfast in bed. Their huge sheepdog, Nellie, is a third host. When not at The Spinning Wheel, which is open late spring to fall, the Tweedies work with the hearing impaired in Washington, DC.

Of the guest rooms, a favorite is Room 2, decorated with oil lamps, an oak dresser, crocheted pillow covers, and a wedding-ring-pattern quilt on the brass bed. Closet space was sacrificed throughout to make room for the private baths. There are just rods or racks with hangers and little drawer space, but who needs a lot of clothes for casual Onancock?

Address: *31 North St., Onancock, VA 23417, tel. 804/787–7311.*
Accommodations: *5 double rooms with baths.*
Amenities: *Air-conditioning, wood-burning stove in living room, turndown service; bicycles.*
Rates: *$75–$85; full or Continental breakfast, afternoon refreshments. MC, V.*
Restrictions: *No smoking indoors, no pets, 2-night minimum weekends, closed Nov.–Apr.*

The Watson House

With freshly painted gingerbread trim, hanging planters, pots of flowers, and wicker rockers, the Watson House porch is a charmer. David and JoAnne Snead, their daughter Jacque Derrickson, and Jacque's husband, Tom, had no experience in inn keeping, but, inspired by a workshop in Cape May, they restored an 1873 Victorian "disaster" to perfection in less than a year.

Chincoteague's newest bed-and-breakfast opened for business in the spring of 1992. The deluxe rooms have sitting porches. The inn blends the new shine of a fine restoration with the traditional B&B touches: It's an immaculate mix of oak, wicker, lace curtains, floral wallpaper, and needlework. Two blemishes mar this pristine house: Hanging on a mirror in the entry are sweatshirts and T-shirts for sale, and in the bedrooms you'll find well-used tip envelopes with various guests' thank-you comments scratched out.

Address: *4240 Main St. (Box 905), Chincoteague, VA 23336, tel. 804/336–1564.*
Accommodations: *6 double rooms with baths.*
Amenities: *Air-conditioning, clock radios and ceiling fans in rooms, TV on request in parlor; bicycles, beach chairs, outdoor shower.*
Rates: *$65–$105; full breakfast, afternoon tea. MC, V.*
Restrictions: *Smoking on porches only, no pets, 2-night minimum weekends, 3-night minimum holidays, closed Thanksgiving–Apr. 1.*

Williamsburg and the Peninsula

"Down in Virginia there is a little old-fashioned city called Williamsburg. It stands on the ridge of the peninsula that separates the James and York Rivers." This is how The City of Once Upon a Time, *a children's book written by Gilchrist Waring in 1946, opens. That book and* The Official Guide to Colonial Williamsburg *are two of the best introductions to the legendary city, which is visited by a million people annually.*

Williamsburg was the capital of Virginia between 1699 and 1780, when the colony was immense, extending west to the Mississippi River. A planned city like Annapolis, Maryland, and a thriving business center serving the farms and tobacco plantations between the rivers, it was a beautiful place and still is. In 1926 the rector at Williamsburg's Bruton Parish Church persuaded John D. Rockefeller, Jr., to restore the town, and the continuing project has resulted in a living-history museum of 173 acres, a mile long and half a mile wide, holding 88 restored and 50 major reconstructed buildings and surrounded by a 3,000-acre "greenbelt." The restoration has become a pattern for similar endeavors nationwide. Outlying discount malls and commercial strips woo travelers with shopping opportunities at bargain emporiums like the Williamsburg Pottery Factory and Berkeley Commons. The charming Merchants Square, adjoining the historic district, houses a movie theater, restaurants, and some 40 shops.

Once you've located Colonial Williamsburg proper, you can simply wander in and soak up the atmosphere, perhaps slaking your thirst on a cup of cider, peddled streetside; or you can stop at the visitor center (tel. 804/220–7645 daily 8:30–5), which lies off the Colonial Parkway (the National Park artery that connects Jamestown, Williamsburg, and Yorktown), to view a 35-minute film and buy passes that entitle you to enter the buildings and ride the fleet of shuttle buses that link the top sights.

*Williamsburg is not the oldest English settlement in the
United States. That title is held by nearby Jamestown, where
a sea-weary party of 104 men and boys aboard the* Sarah
Constant, Godspeed, *and* Discovery *landed in 1607 and hung
on, despite hostile Native Americans, disease bred in nearby
swamps, and chaos engendered by the fear that they'd been
forgotten by suppliers across the Atlantic. Today Jamestown
Island, the site of a national park, is a much more rustic
place than civil Williamsburg.*

*It is entirely understandable that visitors to the area should
feel overwhelmed. Besides Jamestown and Williamsburg
there's nearby Yorktown to explore (the scene of the last
Revolutionary War battle and the surrender of General
Cornwallis) and scores of plantations along the James River
that should not be missed. Charles City County, which hugs
the river between Richmond and Williamsburg, is truly a
place apart. The same handful of families have owned and
farmed its plantations since the 17th century and have
stoically kept development out. So a drive along Route 5,
which offers access to all the historic homes, makes a scenic
trip indeed.*

*Finally, the thing to keep in mind about Williamsburg's bed-
and-breakfasts is that none of them lies within the historic
district; indeed, none of them occupies a historic home,
though a number of them are exceedingly fine places to stay.
Those intent on booking accommodations in a bona fide
Colonial structure with a historic pedigree should contact the
Williamsburg Inn (tel. 804/229–1000 or 800/447–8679). It
manages 85 rooms in taverns and houses in the restored
district.*

Places to Go, Sights to See

Abby Aldrich Rockefeller Folk Art Center (Williamsburg, tel.
804/220–7670). Some 3,000 pieces—furniture, paintings, carvings, textiles, and
decorative useful wares—make this the nation's leading American folk-art
center. Mrs. Rockefeller's 424-work collection forms the core.

Busch Gardens/The Old Country (off U.S. 60, Williamsburg, tel. 804/253–3350). This theme park re-creates things German, French, Italian, and English and offers rides on such curiosities as the Loch Ness Monster, Roman Rapids, Drachen Fire Roller Coaster, and Big Bad Wolf.

Carter's Grove (Williamsburg, tel. 804/220–7452). An 18th-century plantation 8 miles east of the historic district, Carter's Grove was built in 1750 by a grandson of the Colonial tobacco tycoon Robert "King" Carter and renovated and enlarged in 1928. It's now part of the Colonial Williamsburg Foundation, and a lovely one-way country road wends its way back to the historic district. The Winthrop Rockefeller Archaeology Museum explores the discovery of the Wolstenholme Towne site here. This village had fewer than 50 inhabitants; all were massacred by Native Americans in 1622.

The College of William and Mary (Williamsburg, tel. 804/221–2630). The second-oldest college in the United States was founded in 1693 by charter from King William and Queen Mary of England. Its centerpiece, the Wren Building, begun in 1695, is the oldest academic building still in use in the country.

Colonial Williamsburg (tel. 800/447–8679). In the restored district, some of the most interesting historic buildings are the *Capitol*, where Patrick Henry delivered his famous speech; *Bruton Parish Church;* and the handsome *Governor's Palace*, with its stable, kitchen, exquisite gardens, and working wheelwright's shop. The *Courthouse* in *Market Square*, fronted by pillories and stocks, offers reenactments of 18th-century court trials. Along Duke of Gloucester Street are the *Printing Office, Shoemaker's Shop,* the *James Anderson Blacksmith Shop,* and *Golden Ball Silversmith.* Crafts shops in the historic district include *Prentis Store,* for pottery, baskets, soaps, and pipes; the *Post Office,* for books, prints, maps, stationery, and sealing wax; and *Raleigh Tavern Bake Shop,* for ginger cakes and cider.

DeWitt Wallace Decorative Arts Gallery (Williamsburg, tel. 804/220–7724). This modern museum behind the Public Hospital contains 10,000 examples of English and American furniture, ceramics, textiles, prints, metals, and costumes primarily from the 17th and 18th centuries.

Historic Air Tours (Williamsburg Airport, tel. 804/253–8185 or 800/822–9247). Narrated flights over Colonial Williamsburg, Yorktown, Jamestown, the James River Plantations, and Hampton Roads give an intriguing perspective on the area's history and growth.

James River Plantations. On Route 5, where descendants of Virginia's earliest families still live, work, and preserve a way of life spanning three centuries, these estates are open for tours. *Berkeley* (tel. 804/829–6018) is a perfect Georgian. Built in 1726 and later inhabited by a signer of the Declaration of Independence and two U.S. presidents, William Henry Harrison and Benjamin Harrison, it is surrounded by 10 acres of formal boxwood gardens. You can dine in its Coach House Taverns. *Evelynton* (tel. 804/829–5075 or 800/473–5075) was the site of several fierce Civil War skirmishes. Today the 2,500-acre farm is still family-owned and -occupied, the house filled with photographs and portraits. *Sherwood Forest* (tel. 804/829–5377) was purchased in 1842 by John Tyler, the 10th president of the United States, who moved here when he left the White House. The current occupants are the third generation of Tylers to live here. At 321 feet, this is the longest frame house in the country. *Shirley Plantation* (tel. 804/829–5121 or 800/232–1613), a Georgian house surmounted by a hand-carved pineapple finial, has been owned by 10 generations of Hills and Carters (Anne Carter was the mother of Robert E. Lee). Shirley was founded six years after the settlers arrived in Jamestown; the house went up in 1723. Its three-story "flying" staircase, which looks unsupported, and the Queen Anne forecourt are noteworthy. *Westover* (tel. 804/829–2882), seat of the Byrd family, is one of the finest Georgian plantations in the United States. Its grounds are open daily, though the house can be seen only in late April, during Virginia's Historic Garden Week.

Jamestown Colonial National Historical Park (tel. 804/229–1733). The site is an island, which is why the colonists chose it for a settlement in 1607. It was a bad choice; in one year nine-tenths of the settlers died of starvation, violence, or disease, and the capitol burned four times before it was moved to Williamsburg. You'll find a visitor center, museum, paths leading through the ruins of "James Cittie," a scenic loop drive, and Glasshouse, where craftspeople demonstrate one of Virginia's first industries—glassblowing.

Jamestown Settlement (adjacent to the National Historical Park, tel. 804/ 229–1607). Run by the state, this outdoor re-creation of Jamestown village offers reproductions of James Fort, a Powhatan Indian village, and full-scale replicas of the three ships that brought the original settlers.

The Mariner's Museum (Newport News, tel. 804/595–0368). Here maritime history is documented, from the Native American dugout canoe and Chesapeake workboats to modern shipbuilding at Newport News.

Virginia Air & Space Center (Hampton, tel. 804/727–0800). The center depicts Hampton Roads' importance to aviation and serves as the official visitor center for the NASA Langley Research Center, where the first Mercury astronauts trained in the 1960s. It includes an IMAX theater, a full-size aircraft and spacecraft, and a seven-story-high observation deck.

Williamsburg Winery (tel. 804/229–0999). Tours and tastings are given. Especially noteworthy are the chardonnay and the Governor's White.

Yorktown and **Yorktown Battlefield Colonial National Historic Park** (tel. 804/898–3400). Here Washington laid siege to Cornwallis's army, and in 1781 the British surrendered in the (restored) Moore House. English, French, and American breastworks still line the battlefield. It's a good idea to stop at the visitor center first to view the dioramas and rent a taped tour.

Yorktown Victory Center (tel. 804/887–1776), a multimedia museum, offers a film about the Siege of Yorktown, a time-line walkway, and a re-created Continental Army camp with costumed interpreters.

Restaurants

When hunger overtakes you, you'll find Colonial taverns are scattered around Williamsburg's historic district, among them the **King's Arms, Shields,** and **Chownings** (tel. 804/229–2141). These serve such traditional fare as prime rib, game pie, Sally Lunn (slightly sweet raised bread), and peanut soup. For expensive formal dining there's the award-winning **Regency Room,** at the Williamsburg Inn (tel. 804/229–2141). The **Trellis** (tel. 804/229–8610), in Merchants Square, features a changing menu of regional food and decadent desserts. The **Old Chickahominy House** (1211 Jamestown Rd., tel. 804/229–4689) is noted for its Brunswick stew; **Pierce's** (just off I–64, tel. 804/565–2955) has good barbecue. At **Indian Fields** (Rte. 5, Charles City, tel. 804/829–5004) the menu has such Tidewater delicacies as Virginia ham in pineapple-raisin sauce and scallops in puff pastry.

Tourist Information

Colonial National Historical Park (Jamestown–Yorktown) (Superintendent, Yorktown, VA 23690, tel. 804/898–3400). **Colonial Williamsburg Foundation** (Williamsburg, VA 23187, tel. 804/229–1000 or 800/447–8679). **Hampton Visitor Center** (710 Settlers Landing Rd., Hampton, VA 23669, tel. 804/727–1102 or 800/800–2202). **Jamestown-Yorktown Foundation** (Box JF, Williamsburg, VA 23187, tel. 804/253–4838). **Virginia Division of Tourism** (1021 E. Cary St., Richmond, VA 23219, tel. 804/786–4484). **Virginia Plantation Country** (Box 1382, Hopewell, VA 23860, tel. 804/541–2206). **Williamsburg Area Convention & Visitors Bureau** (Box 3585, Williamsburg, VA 23187–3585, tel. 804/253–0192 or 800/368–6511).

Reservation Services

Bensonhouse (2036 Monument Ave., Richmond, VA 23220, tel. 804/648–7560). For a copy of **The Bed and Breakfast Association of Virginia's directory,** describing more than 100 establishments, call the Virginia Division of Tourism's B&B line (tel. 800/262–1293). The Division of Tourism's Washington, DC, office also operates a **B&B and small-inn booking service** (tel. 202/659–5523 or 800/934–9184 outside DC).

Edgewood

Says frothy innkeeper Dot Boulware in her liquid southern accent, "I have to tell you, I am a romantic." And so is Edgewood—three marriage proposals were made in one week here. But before she and her husband, Julian, bought Edgewood Plantation, on scenic Route 5 approximately half an hour from Colonial Williamsburg, in 1978, she didn't care a bit for Victoriana. Fortunately tastes change, and when she became the mistress of an 1850s Carpenter Gothic house she began collecting Victorian antiques like a woman possessed.

Dot's eight-bedroom house, visible from Route 5, looks on the inside like Miss Havisham's dining room, minus the cobwebs. It is full to bursting with old dolls, antique corsets and lingerie, lace curtains and pillows, love seats, baby carriages, stuffed steamer trunks, mighty canopied beds, highboys, Confederate caps . . . the list goes on and on. At Christmastime she personally decorates 18 trees and festoons the banister of the graceful three-story staircase with bows. Clearly, more is better at Dot Boulware's Edgewood.

In her hands, Victoriana is thoroughly feminine, even though in one chamber, the Civil War Room, she's tried to cater to the opposite sex, decorating with intimate details of men's 19th-century apparel. Large people of either sex will have a hard time

moving freely in this wildly crowded bed-and-breakfast. Lizzie's Room, the favorite, has a king-size pencil-post canopy bed and a private bath. The room enshrines the memory of a teenager who, Dot says, died of a broken heart when her beau failed to return from the Civil War. Prissy's Quarters, upstairs in the carriage house, has a kitchen area.

Breakfast is served in the dining room by candlelight. The brick-walled, beam-ceilinged basement is a cozy sitting area with a fireplace, backgammon board, TV, and popcorn machine. There are also fireplaces in the dining room, tea room, and two bedrooms. Outside there's an unrestored mill house dating from 1725, an antiques shop, gazebo, swimming pool, and formal 18th-century garden (which makes a delightful wedding setting). Edgewood is centrally located for touring the James River plantations.

Address: *4800 John Tyler Memorial Hwy., Charles City, VA 23030, tel. 804/829–2962 or 800/296–3343.*
Accommodations: *6 double rooms with baths, 2 suites.*
Amenities: *Tea room, air-conditioning, TV in rooms on request, portable phones, turndown service; pool, bicycles.*
Rates: *$95–$168; full breakfast, afternoon refreshments. MC, V.*
Restrictions: *No smoking in bedrooms, no pets, 3-night minimum holiday weekends.*

Liberty Rose

Bed-and-breakfast keepers in Williamsburg are in something of a bind. Because all the historic buildings in town are owned by either the Williamsburg Foundation or the College of William and Mary, they can't offer travelers authentic Colonial accommodations. Some have Colonial-style decoration anyway, but others, like Sandy and Brad Hirz, owners of the Liberty Rose, have come up with different, imaginative solutions to the dilemma.

Understand first that Sandy and Brad have a tremendously romantic story. They were just friends when Sandy decided to leave the West Coast to open a B&B in Williamsburg. Brad was helping Sandy house hunt when they looked at a 1920s white clapboard and brick home a mile west of the restored district (on the road to Jamestown), and Sandy bought it in five minutes. Then Brad started seriously courting her, but it was Sandy, and not the B&B, who inspired him. Now they're a devoted married couple who run Williamsburg's most romantic B&B, decorated à la nouvelle Victorian with turn-of-the-century touches.

Sandy, a former interior designer, has a special talent for fabrics and is responsible for the handsome tie-back curtains, many-layered bed coverings, and plush canopies. The patterns are 19th-century reproductions. Brad has held up his end of the business by managing remodeling details. The bathrooms are particularly attractive: One has a floor taken from a plantation in Gloucester, a comfortable claw-foot tub, and an amazing freestanding, glass-sided shower. The sumptuous Suite Williamsburg has an elaborate carved-ball-and-claw fourposter bed and a fireplace. (The parlor, too, has a fireplace.) All rooms have a TV with VCR and a collection of films, and an amenities basket bulging with everything the traveler might need, from bandages to needle and thread. The furnishings are a copacetic mix of 18th- and 19thcentury reproductions and antiques. Antique handmade Santas, folk art, dolls, toys, and Noah's Ark carvings are tucked away in corners and sold in the tiny gift shop.

Liberty Rose sits on a densely wooded hilltop, and the lake on the William and Mary campus is a pretty walk away. Romance, above all, is the tone pursued and achieved here.

Address: *1022 Jamestown Rd., Williamsburg, VA 23185, tel. 804/253-1260.*
Accommodations: *1 double room with bath, 3 suites.*
Amenities: *Air-conditioning, TV with VCR in rooms, phone in breakfast room, turndown service.*
Rates: *$105–$165; full breakfast. MC, V.*
Restrictions: *No smoking indoors, no pets.*

North Bend Plantation

Routinely, a stay at this Charles City County plantation begins with a tour of the house and grounds conducted by Ridgely Copland, a farmer's wife and a nurse (several years ago named Virginia nurse of the year). Along the way Ridgely points out Union breastworks from 1864, wild asparagus, herds of deer, a swamp, and the wide James River. Only one other Virginia bed-and-breakfast—Welbourne, near Middleburg—is so strikingly authentic, but North Bend differs from that slightly gone-to-seed mansion in that it's a well-maintained working farm. The Coplands are salt-of-the-earth people striving to keep their 850 acres intact in the face of modern agricultural dilemmas.

North Bend, on the National Register and also a Virginia Historic Landmark, was built for the sister of William Henry Harrison, the ninth president. It's a fine example of the Academic Greek Revival style, a wide white frame structure with a red roof and a slender chimney at each corner. Built in 1819 with a classic two-over-two layout, large center hall, and Federal mantels and stair carvings, it was remodeled in 1853 according to Asher Benjamin designs. But beyond its architectural distinctions, North Bend is drenched in history. The Sheridan Room, the premier guest bedroom, represents both sides of the Civil War. It contains a walnut desk used by the Union general Philip

Sheridan, complete with his labels on the pigeonholes. His map was found in one of its drawers, and a copy is framed on the wall of the billiard room. The room's bed belonged to Edmund Ruffin, the ardent Confederate who fired the first shot of the war at Fort Sumter. The headboard is a reproduction; the Yankees shot out the original one in 1864.

Above all, though, at North Bend history means family. George Copland is the great-great-nephew of William Henry Harrison and the great-great-grandson of Edmund Ruffin. Family heirlooms are everywhere, as is the amazing collection of Civil War first editions, which make fascinating bedtime reading. There's an inviting upstairs wicker-furnished sun porch, and the cozy children's area has vintage toys.

Address: *12200 Weyanoke Rd., Charles City, VA 23030, tel. 804/829–5176 or 800/841–1479 (after 5:30).*
Accommodations: *4 double rooms with baths, 1 suite.*
Amenities: *Air-conditioning, TV in rooms, robes, turndown service; pool, tandem bicycles, croquet, horseshoes, badminton, volleyball.*
Rates: *$95–$120; full breakfast, welcoming refreshments. No credit cards.*
Restrictions: *Smoking on porches only, no pets, closed Jan. 1, Thanksgiving, Dec. 25.*

Applewood

Applewood, so named because its owner collects things with an apple theme, is a spotlessly tidy bed-and-breakfast about four blocks from the historic district. It contains ceramic apples, apple prints, and even a copy of John Cheever's *The World of Apples*. Like other houses in the area, it was built in the late 1920s by a Colonial Williamsburg restorer, who added many of the kinds of details he'd been working on in the historic area: a Flemish-bond brick exterior, a handsome 18th century–style portal, and detail crown moldings in the interior. The trim is painted those milky blues and greens that are so common in Williamsburg. Applewood has four bedrooms for travelers; one suite has a canopy bed, fireplace, private breakfast area and entrance, and a convertible sofa bed— a fine choice for families with children. And the Golden Pippin Room sleeps four, one in a trundle bed. Innkeeper Fred Strout serves afternoon tea and a deluxe Continental breakfast, including, of course, apple muffins.

Address: *605 Richmond Rd., Williamsburg, VA 23185, tel. 804/229–0205 or 800/899–2753.*
Accommodations: *3 double rooms with baths, 1 suite.*
Amenities: *Air-conditioning, cable TV and fireplace in parlor, portable phones, turndown service; bicycles.*
Rates: *$75–$125; Continental-plus breakfast, afternoon tea. MC, V.*
Restrictions: *No smoking indoors, no pets, 2-night minimum holiday and special-events weekends.*

Colonial Capital

The Colonial Capital, a three-story frame house painted spring-mist green, is within walking distance of the historic district, Merchants Square, and the College of William and Mary. The exceedingly nice innkeepers, Phil and Barbara Craig, are a retired stockbroker and a university administrator who moved to Williamsburg after 25 years in North Carolina. The Colonial's five rooms are named after Tidewater-area rivers. The York has an enclosed, canopied high rope bed. Prettiest, though, is sunny Pamlico, with window seats and a white-canopied bed. The third floor can be made into a two-bedroom suite, a plus for families. Downstairs, there's a large parlor with a wood-burning fireplace and access to a sun porch, where the Craigs keep games, books, and puzzles. In the rear, near the Colonial garden, is guest parking, which solves a serious problem in teeming Williamsburg.

Address: *501 Richmond Rd., Williamsburg, VA 23185, tel. 804/229–0233 or 800/776–0570.*
Accommodations: *4 double rooms with baths, 1 suite.*
Amenities: *Air-conditioning, cable TV with VCR in parlor and suite, phone jacks in halls, turndown service; bicycles.*
Rates: *$95–$135; full breakfast, welcoming drink. AE, MC, V.*
Restrictions: *Smoking in parlor only, no pets, 2-night minimum weekends and holidays.*

Newport House

The Newport House takes the prize for the most unusual bed-and-breakfast in Williamsburg, if not all of Tidewater Virginia. The house is a meticulous reproduction of one that once stood in Newport, Rhode Island, designed by the Colonial architect Peter Harrison. The house is totally furnished in period style, with English and American antiques and reproductions. Both guest rooms have canopy beds. The three-story, dormered house, painted creamy yellow, stands just across the street from the William and Mary Law School on a small lot that contains an herb garden. The owners, Cathy and John Millar, are practicing Colonial country dancers; they hold country-dancing evenings in the ballroom on Tuesday and, occasionally, Scottish country dances on Thursday. (They also rent costumes.) Breakfast, from Colonial recipes, is accompanied by a historical lecture from the fascinating host and a visit from this offbeat B&B's pet—a house-trained rabbit named Sassafras, who is let out of its kitchen hutch for morning floor shows.

Address: *710 S. Henry St., Williamsburg, VA 23185, tel. 804/229–1775.*
Accommodations: *2 double rooms with baths.*
Amenities: *Air-conditioning, TV with VCR and phones in rooms, fireplace in living room.*
Rates: *$110, $100 subsequent nights; full breakfast. No credit cards.*
Restrictions: *No smoking indoors, no pets, 2-night minimum weekends and holidays.*

War Hill Inn

The War Hill Inn is 3 miles north of town; this is a drawback or an attraction, depending on whether you prefer to stay overnight in the thick of Colonial things or put some space between your lodging and the crowds. Adding to the inn's feeling of remoteness are the surrounding pastures, where owner Bill Lee's prize-winning Black Angus cows munch on the grass—though a condo development has risen up on one of the property's flanks. Bill is a retired veterinarian who built the house in 1968 to raise a family. It's a copy of the Anderson House in Colonial Williamsburg, and a fine one at that. Inside are architectural features that came from other places—the heart-of-pine floors from a schoolhouse and a staircase from a Lutheran church. The decor in the guest rooms is a mélange of Colonial reproductions and family things; the downstairs chamber is notable for its size and privacy. War Hill is a good choice for families—thanks to its fenced-in grounds, a small orchard of peaches and plums, and a cottage. Two of its rooms sleep four.

Address: *4560 Longhill Rd., Williamsburg, VA 23185, tel. 804/565–0248.*
Accommodations: *5 double rooms with baths.*
Amenities: *Air-conditioning, cable TV in rooms, fireplace in parlor, whirlpool bath in cottage.*
Rates: *$70–$120; full breakfast. AE, MC, V.*
Restrictions: *No smoking, no pets, 2-night minimum weekends.*

Around Charlottesville

Few cities in this country are so deeply devoted to—one might say, so in love with—a single man as is Virginia's Piedmont capital, Charlottesville. On a farm east of town (in the present-day hamlet of Shadwell), Thomas Jefferson, the third president of the United States, was born; and on a mountaintop overlooking a countryside Jefferson himself considered Edenic, he built his home. We have all seen Monticello, for it appears on one side of the nickel, though its minted image hardly does it justice. The breathtakingly beautiful edifice, constructed on architectural principles that would change the face of America, is a house that reveals volumes about the man who built it and lived there.

For instance, in the terraced vegetable gardens (restored according to Jefferson's Garden Book*) he introduced the tomato to North America and raised 19 types of English peas, his favorite food. (Mr. Jefferson, as he is called around here, attributed his long life—he lived to be 83—to his vegetarian eating habits.) Here he built a glass-enclosed pavilion, where he went to read, write, and watch his garden grow. Most of the 20,000 letters he wrote were penned in his study in a reclining chair with revolving desk (he had rheumatism and worked from a semirecumbent position). Jefferson was also a collector; the walls of the formal parlor are lined with portraits of friends, like Washington and Monroe, and the east entrance hall displays mastodon bones and a buffalo head brought back from the West by Lewis and Clark.*

"Architecture," wrote Jefferson, "is my delight and putting up and pulling down one of my favorite pastimes." Originally he built Monticello in 1779 as an American Palladian villa, but after seeing the work of Boullée and Ledoux in France, he returned to Monticello with a head full of new ideas, above all, about its dome, and an aversion to grand staircases, which he believed took up too much room.

*Today the full effect is best seen from the flower gardens on
the west side.*

*There's another reason for Charlottesville's love affair with
Jefferson—the University of Virginia. If Monticello is a taste
of Jeffersonian style, the school's rotunda and colonnade
provide the banquet. Jefferson began designing the
university buildings at the age of 74; in 1976 the American
Institute of Architects voted them the most outstanding
achievement in American architecture. The rotunda was
inspired by the Pantheon, in Rome, but the dual colonnade
that extends from it, intended as both dwelling place and
study center for students and faculty, is all Jefferson's own.
Students still inhabit the colonnade rooms, amid fireplaces,
porches, and rocking chairs.*

*Downtown Charlottesville has been converted into a
pedestrian mall where shoppers find intriguing stores, such
as Spirit Vision, for Native American and Southwestern art;
the Signet Gallery, for extraordinary crafts; and, for great
arrays of vintages, Market Street Wineshop & Grocery and
Tastings, which doubles as a café.*

*Charlottesville lies in the Piedmont, the Blue Ridge foothills,
and the driving here is fun and scenic. Route 20, called the
Constitution Route, takes travelers past Montpelier (James
Madison's home) in Orange, 25 miles north of
Charlottesville, and south to Scottsville. This village on the
James River, once the seat of Albemarle County, is rich in
Revolutionary and Civil War history. It's a favorite spot for
canoe and inner-tube trips. Twenty miles to the west the Blue
Ridge rises, with access to the Skyline Drive or Parkway at
Rockfish Gap.*

Places to Go, Sights to See

Ash Lawn—Highland (Charlottesville, tel. 804/293–9539). Just down the
road from Monticello, this is the restored home of James Monroe; its
mountaintop site (selected by Jefferson) offers views of Monticello's dome. A

tour covers the original rooms and the warming kitchen. Today it's still a working 550-acre farm where sheep and peacocks roam. Summertime brings a Festival of the Arts and Plantation Day.

Barboursville Vineyards (north of Charlottesville, tel. 703/832–3824). In addition to tasting the several varieties produced here, you can explore the ruins of Governor James Barbour's plantation home. Other area vineyards include *Oakencroft* and *Montdomaine*. (For a map of Virginia wineries, contact the Virginia Wine Marketing Program, VDACS, Division of Marketing, Box 1163, Richmond, VA 23209, tel. 804/786–0481).

Court Square (downtown Charlottesville) is the focus of Albermarle County government. In addition to a courthouse, built between 1803 and 1867, the square holds an impressive equestrian statue of Stonewall Jackson.

The Exchange Hotel & Civil War Museum (Gordonsville, tel. 703/832–2944). Built in 1860 as a railroad hotel, this Greek Revival structure served as a military hospital during the Civil War and is now a museum devoted to the military and medical history of that conflict.

Michie Tavern (Charlottesville, tel. 804/977–1234). This tavern, dating from 1765, was moved to its present location on the road to Monticello in 1920. With its ceaseless crowds, recorded tours, and cafeteria-style restaurant, serving such historic dishes as fried chicken, black-eyed peas, and stewed tomatoes, it's very commercial. The Virginia Wine Museum is adjacent.

Monticello (Charlottesville, tel. 804/984–9800). Jefferson's home lies about 2 miles southeast of the intersection of I–64 and Route 20. The tour, which ascends Mr. Jefferson's "little mountain" by shuttle bus, lasts about half an hour and is extremely rewarding. Afterward visitors are free to roam the gardens, view the hidden dependencies, and make a pilgrimage to the great man's grave. The earlier you arrive, the shorter the wait.

Montpelier (south of Orange, tel. 703/672–2728). James Madison, Jr., served as president after Jefferson and before Monroe. Known as the Father of the Constitution, Madison saw America through the War of 1812. He and his wife, Dolley, lived here from 1817 to 1836, followed by William du Pont, Sr., who bought it in 1901. The guided tour of the estate leads visitors over the 2,700-acre grounds, through the 55-room house, and past Madison's grave. The Montpelier Hunt Race takes place here on the first weekend in November.

Rapidan. This village about 5 miles northeast of Orange is bisected by the Rapidan River and holds the *Waddell Memorial Presbyterian Church*, an architectural hymn in Carpenter Gothic. Nearby you'll also find *Marmont Orchards* (tel. 703/672–2730 or 800/572–2262), where, in season, you can pick your own apples, peaches, plums, and nectarines.

Scottsville sits on the James River and is where Lafayette made a successful stand against General Cornwallis in 1781. The village holds 32

Federal-style buildings and the locks of the James River Kanawha Canal, which were a target for 10,000 bluecoats under General Sheridan during the Civil War. The nearby *James River Runners* (tel. 804/286–2338) rents tubes, rafts, and canoes.

University of Virginia (Charlottesville, tel. 804/924–7969). Wander the grounds or take one of the tours that leave the rotunda several times daily (except holidays and exams). Inside the rotunda is Alexander Galt's statue of Jefferson, which students saved from the fire of 1895.

Walton's Mountain Museum (Schuyler, tel. 804/831–2000). Earl Hamner, Jr., creator of the long-running TV series "The Waltons," based the family's tales on his own experiences growing up in this small village. The simple museum re-creates the TV sets and has lots of memorabilia, videotapes, and photos of the show and cast.

Restaurants

In addition to top dining at the area's inns, there's a cosmopolitan assortment of restaurants in Charlottesville. **Metropolitan** (tel. 804/977–1043) serves popular nouvelle American cuisine. **Memory & Company** (tel. 804/296–3539) offers $25 prix-fixe dinners and a terrific wine list. **C & O** (tel. 804/971–7044) has a bistro downstairs and formal French dining upstairs. In Orange, the **Orange Gourmet** (tel. 703/672–3514) gets top ratings. For casual dining in Charlottesville, there's **Kafkafe** (tel. 804/296–1175), on University Corner; **Court Square Tavern** (tel. 804/296–6111), with a pub atmosphere and more than 120 imported beers; and **Southern Culture** (tel. 804/979–1990), a reasonably priced mix of Caribbean and Cajun. **Pig 'N Steak** (tel. 804/286–4114) is a country café in Scottsville.

Tourist Information

Charlottesville/Albemarle Convention & Visitors Bureau (Box 161, Charlottesville, VA 22902, tel. 804/977–1783). **Orange County Visitors Bureau** (Box 133, Orange, VA 22960, tel. 703/672–1653). **Virginia Division of Tourism** (1021 E. Cary St., Richmond, VA 23219, tel. 804/786–4484).

Reservation Services

Guesthouses Bed & Breakfast, Inc. (Box 5737, Charlottesville, VA 22905, tel. 804/979–7264) can arrange entrée to private houses that are otherwise closed to the public. For a copy of **The Bed and Breakfast Association of Virginia's directory,** describing more than 100 establishments, call the Virginia Division of Tourism's B&B line (tel. 800/262–1293). The Division of Tourism's Washington, DC, office also operates a **B&B and small-inn booking service** (tel. 202/659–5523 or 800/934–9184 outside DC).

Clifton

From the cozy paneled library and the comforter-covered beds to the sunny terrace and the languid lake, there are reasons aplenty to settle in here at one of the state's top inns.

Clifton stands in quiet Shadwell, near Jefferson's birthplace. No wonder it's a National Historic Landmark—the handsome white-frame, six-columned manse was once home to Thomas Mann Randolph, governor of Virginia, member of Congress, and husband of Jefferson's daughter, Martha. It's now owned by a Washington attorney but ably administered by innkeepers Craig and Donna Hartman. As chef, Craig also oversees Clifton's wonderful meals (applewood-smoked loin of veal with Vidalia-onion marmalade, anyone?). Saturdays' five-course, prix-fixe dinners ($48) are served to period music.

There are guest rooms in the manor house, the carriage house, the livery, and Randolph's law office. All have wood-burning fireplaces, antique or canopy beds, and large baths; they may also feature French windows, lake views, and antique bed-coverings. Rooms in the dependencies have a fresh, cottage feel: whitewashed walls, bright floral prints, lots of windows. Suites in the carriage house boast shutters, windows, and other artifacts from the home of the explorer Meriwether Lewis.

The grounds spread through 48 acres of woods. The 20-acre lake offers good fishing (the inn has fishing rods and tackle boxes) and lazy floats on inner tubes. Vines and slate stonework blend the swimming pool and heated spa tub into the bucolic setting. There's also a clay tennis court, as well as croquet, volleyball, horseshoes, and badminton. For pure loafing, there are gardens off the dependencies, wooden chairs scattered across the lawns, and a small gazebo. The extensive gardens are carefully tended: The estate grows its own flowers, lettuce, and herbs.

Clifton offers a magical combination of elegance and hominess. Common areas, too, have fireplaces. A corner of the big butcher-block island in the kitchen is for guests, who often sit and chat with Craig as he cooks. A jar of cookies is always there, and sodas are in the refrigerator.

Address: *Rte. 729, Shadwell (Rte. 13, Box 26, Charlottesville, VA 22901), tel. 804/971–1800, fax 804/971–7098.*
Accommodations: *3 double rooms with baths, 11 suites.*
Amenities: *Restaurant, air-conditioning, wheelchair accessible.*
Rates: *$155–$198; full breakfast, afternoon tea. AE, DC, MC, V.*
Restrictions: *No smoking, no pets, 2-night minimum weekends.*

High Meadows and Mountain Sunset

High Meadows, which stands on 50 acres in Scottsville, is above all a bed-and-breakfast inn done by hand. The hands in question are those of Peter Shushka, a retired submariner, and his wife, Mary Jae Abbitt, a financial analyst. In this unique B&B, Federal and late-Victorian architecture exist side by side, happily joined by a longitudinal hall. It wasn't always so. The Italianate front section was built in 1882 by Peter White, who had intended to level the older house several paces behind it. But bearing in mind her growing family, his wife refused to give up the old place, built in 1830, and for a time a plank between the two was the tenuous connector that kept the marriage intact. Today High Meadows is on the National Register.

Peter and Mary Jae have decorated the place with great originality, keeping intact the stylistic integrity of each section. They've also used fabrics on the bed hangings and windows imaginatively. Fairview, in the 1880s portion, is the quintessential bride's room, with a fireplace, flowing bed drapery, a three-window alcove, and a claw-foot tub. The Scottsville suite, upstairs in the Federal section, has stenciled walls lined with antique stuffed animals, a fireplace, and rafters across the ceiling. A two-person whirlpool sits in the middle of the Music Room. The Carriage House is a contemporary building of cedar, glass, and slate on the site of the original; this two-room suite has a kitchen and a deck. The property also includes the Mountain Sunset (named for its view), a 1910 Queen Anne manor house with two suites, two rooms, fireplaces, decks, and plenty of privacy.

Breakfast consists of Shushka specialties like cranberry-almond muffins and ham-and-egg cups laced with tomatoes and Gruyère cheese. The dining room is open for dinner on the weekends; Saturday, the meal's a six-course affair with wine for $45. And to cap all this off, there are 5 acres of vineyards, which produce pinot noir grapes for the inn's own private-label wine.

Address: *High Meadows La. (Rte. 4, Box 6), Scottsville, VA 24590, tel. 804/286-2218.*
Accommodations: *7 double rooms with baths, 5 suites.*
Amenities: *Air-conditioning, cable TV in 1 suite, fireplaces in 9 rooms and 2 common areas, robes, turndown service, whirlpool baths in 2 rooms, some rooms wheelchair accessible.*
Rates: *$95–$155; full breakfast, evening hors d'oeuvres. MC, V.*
Restrictions: *No smoking, pets permitted in ground-level rooms by arrangement only, 2-night minimum in spring and fall and on holiday weekends, closed Dec. 24–25.*

Keswick Hall

A visit to Keswick Hall is like spending a weekend with friends in the English countryside—that is, if your friends are very wealthy and live in a vast house with scads of antiques, plump chairs and couches in which to lounge and chat, a butler to serve you drinks, and a golf course in the backyard. Keswick sits on 600 acres in the wooded, rolling countryside east of Charlottesville. It's owned by Sir Bernard Ashley, who was married to the late Laura Ashley, so fabrics and furnishings from the company are used throughout. Rooms are not furnished in endless yards of tiny floral prints, however. Fabrics, none of which are repeated, run the gamut from crisp stripes to elegant brocades. Sir Bernard's personal collection of antiques, century-old books, paintings, and silver-framed family photos give the house the lived-in-for-generations look.

Bedrooms are individually decorated in color schemes ranging from soft beige and white to crisp blues to cozy dark green. All have comfy chairs, couches, or cushioned window seats. Baths have extra touches, such as whirlpool tubs in six rooms, extra-long tubs in several others, heated towel racks, hair dryers, an abundance of thick towels, terry robes, and dishes with cotton balls. Some rooms have private terraces with golf-course views, and several have decorative fireplaces.

You'll want to loaf here, perhaps in front of a roaring fire on chilly days, lingering over coffee and the paper in the sunny morning room, having afternoon tea with delicate madeleines and scones in the yellow Crawford Lounge, or penning a letter at Sir Bernard's desk in the library. The all-red snooker room is the spot for predinner drinks and canapés and a late-night brandy, served by the friendly butler.

There's a full country breakfast with a wide range of choices in the garden room. Dinner in the elegant white-and-pastel dining room is a five-course affair ($55), or choose the seven-course degustation menu ($75).

Guests have access to the facilities of Keswick Club, a private club with an 18-hole golf course, fitness facilities, indoor/outdoor pool, tennis courts, and a wood-paneled casual dining room.

Address: *701 Country Club Dr. (Box 68), Keswick, VA 22947, tel. 804/979–3440 or 800/274–5791, fax 804/979–3457.*
Accommodations: *43 double rooms with baths, 3 suites.*
Amenities: *Air-conditioning, cable TV and phones in rooms, turndown service, conference facilities, wheelchair accessible; bicycles.*
Rates: *$195–$645; full breakfast, afternoon tea. AE, DC, MC, V.*
Restrictions: *No smoking in dining rooms, no pets.*

For elegance and luxury, Prospect Hill is one of Virginia's finest inns. Added to its architecturally noteworthy setting, that makes staying here something worth filling your piggy bank for. Prospect Hill lies east of Charlottesville, in the 14-square-mile Greensprings National Historic District. It's the oldest continuously occupied frame manor house in Virginia. But except for the obligatory dependencies and impressive boxwood hedges, Prospect Hill doesn't look like a plantation, because it was rebuilt in the Victorian era, when a columned facade and decorative cornices were added. The innkeepers have painted it lemony yellow.

Fresh flowers, a basket of fruit, and just-baked cookies welcome guests to their rooms. There are four nicely furnished rooms in the main house, but the big treat is the six refurbished dependencies. Sanco Pansy's cottage, 100 feet from the manor, has a sitting room and whirlpool tub for two. The Carriage House, lit by four Palladian windows, offers views of ponies in the meadow nibbling the green Virginia turf. Surrounded by such *luxe, calme, et volupté*, it's strange to consider that in the last century the dependencies were filled with hams, ice blocks, and livestock.

Dinner at the inn is a marvelous production, not so much for the cuisine (French-inspired and well above average) as for the ceremony.

You begin with complimentary wine and cider a half-hour before supper— outdoors in good weather. When the dinner bell rings, in you file to hear the menu recited by innkeeper Bill Sheehan or his son, Michael. (Michael looks like a college halfback, but thanks to his delightful mama, Mireille, his French is impeccable.) Then comes an earnest grace and five excellent courses.

A hot breakfast is brought to your dependency on a tray. You can take it in the dining room, but why spoil the fun? In your dependency, you can eat in a whirlpool tub. This really splendid inn is a class act that hasn't become too smoothly professional. You're bound to meet the gregarious innkeepers and appreciate the way they've put their stamp on Prospect Hill.

Address: *Rte. 613 (Rte. 3, Box 430), Trevilians, VA 23093, tel. 703/967–0844 or 800/277–0844, fax 703/967–0102.*
Accommodations: *5 double rooms with baths in main house, 5 doubles with baths and 3 suites in dependencies.*
Amenities: *Air-conditioning, TV with VCR in meeting room, fireplaces in 12 rooms, Jacuzzis in 7 rooms, clock radios; pool.*
Rates: *$195–$300; MAP, afternoon tea. MC, V.*
Restrictions: *No pets, 2-night minimum with Sat. stay, closed Dec. 24–25.*

Chester

A number of years ago, Gordon Anderson, a legal administrator, and Dick Shaffer, an investment banker, retired from the New York rat race and bought an 1847 Greek Revival mansion in Scottsville. They brought their antiques along, their sophisticatedly urban lifestyle, their Russian wolfhounds, videotapes of Leontyne Price's farewell appearance at the Met, and details seen nowhere else in Virginia—like candies laid out in dishes on coffee tables. The two of them are relaxed hosts who run their bed-and-breakfast like a Noel Coward house party. Take dinner, which they serve by arrangement, cook themselves, and eat along with guests: It's a four-course affair for $24 per person, including Virginia wine, with Gordon and Dick chatting until the wee hours of the night about movies, art, and the Chester's brush with the Civil War. They also know interesting facts about the area—for instance, where one of the richest men in America lives. There are five bedrooms, eight fireplaces, and a laundry room, which guests are free to use.

Address: *James River Rd., Rte. 726 (Rte. 4, Box 57), Scottsville, VA 24590, tel. 804/286–3960.*
Accommodations: *1 double room with bath, 4 doubles share 2 baths.*
Amenities: *Air-conditioning, TV in library, fireplaces in 4 rooms, robes; bicycles, kennel.*
Rates: *$65–$100; full breakfast, complimentary beverages. AE.*
Restrictions: *2-night minimum some weekends.*

1817 Antique Inn

The 1817 Antique Inn is ideal for parents and alums visiting the University of Virginia since the campus is just a block away. The Federal-style town house, built by James Dinsmoor, one of Thomas Jefferson's craftsmen, was just the historic gem that interior designer Candace DeLoach Wilson and her husband, Jon, an industrial engineer, were looking for when Jon was transferred from New York. Raised in Savannah, with parents in the antique business, Candace used her background in southern hospitality and decorating to create an eclectically furnished inn connected to her antiques shop.

Guest rooms include a small hall room (without windows), filled with Candace's grandmother's furniture; a white paneled sleeping porch with two double white-metal beds; and a vast suite with yellow walls and a rose ceiling. The inn's small tea room offers imaginative sandwiches and homemade soups.

Address: *1211 W. Main St., Charlottesville, VA 22903, tel. 804/979–7353 or 800/730–7443.*
Accommodations: *3 double rooms with baths, 1 suite.*
Amenities: *Air-conditioning, cable TV in rooms; bicycles.*
Rates: *$89–$179; Continental-plus breakfast. MC, V.*
Restrictions: *Smoking on porch and in tea room only, no pets, 2-night minimum on UVA-event weekends, 3-night minimum at graduation.*

The Holladay House

The Holladay House, in the center of Orange, makes a good stop for anyone visiting Montpelier or driving the pretty country roads in between. Pete Holladay, a former school administrator, and his wife, Phebe, welcome guests in the 1830 Federal-style home where his grandfather raised Pete's father. Pete says that despite his extensive renovations, much of the house looks just as it did then. His great-grandmother's crazy quilt hangs on one wall; most of the furniture is family pieces.

The simply furnished guest rooms have modern black-and-white tiled baths. Pete's most recent projects are a recreation room and the "decadent" (his word) bathroom in the suite: a vast whirlpool tub, a double-head shower, and heated towel racks. Downstairs, Room 7, with a kitchen, TV, and phone, is ideal for business travelers.

Pete, acclaimed by other innkeepers as "Virginia's best muffin maker," brings breakfast to his guests' rooms.

Address: *155 W. Main St., Orange, VA 22960, tel. 703/672–4893 or 800/358–4422, fax 703/672–3028.*
Accommodations: *5 double rooms with baths, 1 suite.*
Amenities: *Air-conditioning, cable TV in 2 rooms and recreation room.*
Rates: *$75–$185; full breakfast. MC, V.*
Restrictions: *No smoking in rooms, no pets, 2-night minimum weekends in Oct., closed Thanksgiving, Dec. 24–25.*

The Inn at Monticello

Carol and Larry Engel forsook the plains of the upper Midwest because they were enchanted with Virginia. The Inn at Monticello, which they found and renovated, is an 1850s farmhouse with a two-story front gallery and a brook trickling over the long front lawn. The prospect from the back—condos on a hill—is not as bucolic, but curtains block the view from guest rooms.

Downstairs there's a parlor, a twin-bedded room, and a nicely furnished honeymoon room. Of the three upstairs bedrooms, the Yellow Room is nicest because of its white cotton balloon shades and plump rope bed. The Engels take special care with the bed linen, which is downy soft and complemented by European coverlets.

Mornings begin with gourmet breakfasts (for instance, orange yogurt pancakes topped with fresh berries). The rest of the day can be spent visiting nearby Monticello or snoozing in a rocker on the wide front porch.

Address: *Rte. 20 S (RR 19, Box 112), Charlottesville, VA 22901, tel. 804/979–3593, fax 804/296–1344.*
Accommodations: *5 double rooms with baths.*
Amenities: *Air-conditioning, fireplaces in 2 rooms, turndown service; lake for swimming.*
Rates: *$105–$135; full breakfast, afternoon refreshments. MC, V.*
Restrictions: *No smoking, no pets, 2-night minimum some high-season weekends, closed Dec. 22–28.*

The Shadows

Yu won't find a home (or guests) more lovingly tended than at The Shadows. Pat and Barbara Loffredo have filled their 1913 stone farmhouse, serenely set in a grove of old cedars just up the road from Montpelier, with a cheerful collection of country Victorian antiques. Prize pieces include an intricately carved Civil War–era board, an old pump organ, numerous claw-foot tubs, and Maxfield Parrish prints wherever the eye rests. The house is what Barbara calls Gustav Stickley Craftsman style, a modified bungalow built of wood and local fieldstone. It has lustrous oak floors and windowsills around which lace curtains flutter. The four spotless guest rooms upstairs all have standard Victorian trappings. All the tangibles here are pleasant enough,

but Pat and Barbara put The Shadows over the mark. They're refugees from New York, where Pat was a policeman, and their joy in their newfound home is infectious. The two of them delight in coddling guests, overwhelming them at breakfast, laying open their library, and sending them on their way with a hug.

Address: *14291 Constitution Hwy., Orange, VA 22960, tel. 703/672–5057.*
Accommodations: *4 double rooms with baths, 2 cottage suites.*
Amenities: *Air-conditioning, fireplace in 1 cottage, turndown service.*
Rates: *$80–$110; full breakfast, afternoon refreshments. MC, V.*
Restrictions: *No smoking, no pets, 2-night minimum some weekends.*

The Silver Thatch Inn

The Silver Thatch is 7 miles north of downtown Charlottesville off U.S. 29. The oldest part of its semicircle of connected buildings is log, built by Hessian prisoners during the Revolution. New owners Vince and Rita Scoffone became innkeepers because they wanted to spend more time together. (He was a workaholic banker.) The inn is decorated in a comfortable country-Colonial style with richly colored walls and trim. The guest rooms all have quilts, down comforters, and antiques; four have fireplaces. The four cottage rooms surpass those in the main house because of their sparkling new bathrooms.

The restaurant menu, which changes every six to eight weeks, has flair: Rock Cornish hen rubbed with

mustard and Caribbean jerk spices, shrimp and Moroccan sausage with currant and couscous salad. The wine list has received an award of excellence from the *Wine Spectator*. Silver Thatch guests may use a pool and tennis courts nearby.

Address: *3001 Hollymead Dr., Charlottesville, VA 22901, tel. 804/978–4686, fax 804/973–6156.*
Accommodations: *7 double rooms with baths.*
Amenities: *Air-conditioning, cable TV in bar.*
Rates: *$105–$125; Continental-plus breakfast. MC, V.*
Restrictions: *No smoking, no pets, 2-night minimum weekends Apr.–June and Sept.–Nov., closed Dec. 24–25.*

Sleepy Hollow Farm

North of Charlottesville, as you roller-coaster past cattle farms and vineyards on Route 231, you'll also pass the bright red roof of the barn at Sleepy Hollow Farm. This two-story brick house, begun in the 18th century, is surrounded by fields grazed by Black Angus and Tarentais cattle. It's homey, eminently suited to families with children: There's a play set on the grounds, bunnies in the hedgerows, and a spring-fed pond for swimming. The main house has four rooms, and there are two suites, one with kitchen and deck, in the Chestnut Wood Cottage. Sleepy Hollow's owner, Beverley Allison, came to the house as a bride, raised a family, was a news producer, served as an Episcopal missionary in Central America, then returned to open her comfortable bed-and-breakfast. Thus, she has stories to tell, if you can persuade her; ask for the one about a ghost who frequented one of the guest rooms.

Address: *16280 Blue Ridge Turnpike, Gordonsville, VA 22942, tel. 703/832–5555 or 800/215–4804, fax 703/832–2515.*
Accommodations: *3 double rooms with baths, 1 housekeeping suite, 2 suites.*
Amenities: *Air-conditioning, TV in 2 rooms, TV with VCR in sitting room, 3 fireplaces and 2 stoves in common rooms and suites; kennel, riding arranged.*
Rates: *$65–$95; full breakfast, afternoon refreshments. MC, V.*
Restrictions: *No smoking in dining room, 2-night minimum some weekends.*

Tivoli

Sitting high on a hill outside Gordonsville, in the midst of Phil and Susie Audibert's 235-acre working cattle farm, is Tivoli, a three-story, Corinthian-columned, 24-room brick house. Phil grew up in the house, but he and Susie now live in the farmhouse, so Tivoli stood vacant for several years. Transforming it into a stately B&B has been a major, but worthwhile, undertaking.

The Audiberts have concentrated first on what counts most—the guest rooms. The biggest one is the Gold Room, which has an antique Venetian headboard and the original claw-foot tub. The corner Peach Room commands sweeping views of the Piedmont and the Blue Ridge Mountains. All have fireplaces. Impressive family antiques fill the house. Downstairs there's a large dining room, living room, and a ballroom with a Steinway grand piano. These rooms still bear signs of age—watermarks, some peeling paint and paper—but they will be spiffed up when Phil and Susie finish the bedrooms. Complimentary beverages are always available.

Address: *9171 Tivoli Dr., Gordonsville, VA 22942, tel. 703/832–2225 or 703/832–3509.*
Accommodations: *2 double rooms with baths, 2 doubles share 1 bath.*
Amenities: *TV with VCR in reading room, phones in 2 rooms; bicycles.*
Rates: *$75–150; full or Continental breakfast. MC, V.*
Restrictions: *No smoking in bedrooms, no pets, 2-night minimum preferred weekends.*

200 South Street

This popular small hotel in downtown Charlottesville is across the street from and next door to two trendy eateries, Memory and Company and South Street. The complex consists of two Victorian homes built between 1850 and 1900, painted yellow, which cheers up South Street considerably. They're brimming with English and Belgian antiques, including capacious armoires and lace-canopied four-posters. The walls are lined with occasional displays of local art and an interesting collection of historic Holsinger photographs. The 10 rooms and suite in No. 200 are preferable to those in the neighboring cottage, because there's a parlor there, and train tracks in back make a front room desirable. But all the rooms are inviting and immaculately renovated, and some of them contain such luxuries as whirlpool baths and fireplaces. Youthful innkeeper Brendan Clancy fixes breakfast, and in the afternoon, tea and wine are served in the sitting room.

Address: *200 South St., Charlottesville, VA 22901, tel. 804/979–0200 or 800/964–7008, fax 804/979–4403.*
Accommodations: *17 double rooms with baths, 3 suites.*
Amenities: *Air-conditioning, cable TV in 3rd-floor lounge, phones in rooms, fireplaces in 9 rooms, turndown service, whirlpool baths in 7 rooms, wheelchair accessible.*
Rates: *$95–$175; Continental-plus buffet breakfast, afternoon tea and wine. AE, DC, MC, V.*
Restrictions: *No smoking in public rooms, no pets, 2-night minimum weekends Apr.–May and Sept.–Oct.*

Willow Grove Inn

Angela Mulloy, who runs Willow Grove, is friendly but no-nonsense. She adamantly insists that Willow Grove is not one of those country inns where they force camaraderie with social hours and hors d'oeuvres. Instead, she offers good food and plenty of it, rooms that are clean and antiques laden, but a tad ragged around the edges. Convivial surroundings and comfort (triple sheeting, down pillows and comforters) take precedence over pristine conditions. Angela is also extremely proud of Willow Grove's architectural distinctiveness. This grand plantation house with a Greek Revival facade was built in numerous stages beginning in the 1770s and lived in by just a handful of families who didn't remodel during its long history.

Dinners are served in the elegant dining rooms and the casual tavern; guest rooms occupy the second and third floors. Continental breakfasts are delivered to your room, accompanied by the morning newspaper, and a full breakfast is served downstairs.

Address: *14079 Plantation Way, Orange, VA 22960, tel. 703/672–5982 or 800/949–1778.*
Accommodations: *3 double rooms with baths, 2 suites.*
Amenities: *Restaurant, air-conditioning, phone jacks in rooms, fireplaces in 3 rooms.*
Rates: *$95–$155, full breakfast; $195–$255, MAP. No credit cards.*
Restrictions: *No pets, restaurant closed Mon.–Wed.*

The Blue Ridge/ Shenandoah Valley

The standard way to see the Blue Ridge Mountains is to pile into a car on a weekend in October and drive south from Front Royal along the Skyline Drive. If you do this, bumper-to-bumper traffic could keep you from covering the full 105-mile course, and you probably won't get past Rockfish Gap (just east of Waynesboro), where the drive becomes the equally (some would claim more) splendid Blue Ridge Parkway. Above all, you'll have only the foggiest idea of the landscape at Virginia's western border, markedly different from the rest of the state.

In geographical terms the Blue Ridge is the eastern wall of the wide Shenandoah Valley, which is retained at the other side by the Allegheny Mountains. Down the middle of the valley, bisecting it for some 50 miles, rises a mini-mountain range called Massanutten Mountain, even though it holds a pretty valley of its own. The Shenandoah River, which runs through the valley, divides north of Massanutten—to further confuse the issue—into a North and South Fork.

Once you've got the geography down you can plot a more informed assault by crossing the ridge along such strategic and scenic routes as U.S. 211 and 33 and especially Route 56, an untrammeled two-laner that's a favorite even of view-jaded locals. These paths lead into the central and southern sections of the Shenandoah Valley.

Shenandoah National Park holds the heights of the Blue Ridge in a 100-mile strip from Front Royal to Waynesboro and provides nonpareil views of the Virginia Piedmont to the east and the splendid Shenandoah Valley to the west. To the park come anglers to catch the crafty brook trout and hikers who find meanders aplenty. Even a short stroll from a trailhead on the Skyline Drive brings visitors within viewing range of the park's abundant and varied wildlife. Spring and fall are peak seasons for nature lovers. In May the green of new foliage moves up the ridge at a rate of 100 feet a day, with clouds of wild pink azaleas providing contrast. Fall colors are at their most vivid between October 10 and 25, when migrating hawks join the human leaf-gazers to take in the display.

Once over the ridge and in the valley there are better ways to take in the countryside than by zooming along I–81. U.S. 11 parallels the superhighway in a delightfully labyrinthine fashion, providing access to big-name sights, such as the New Market Battlefield and Luray Caverns, and running through small towns, including Woodstock, Edinburg, Mt. Jackson, and Steele's Tavern, where produce stands, flea markets, and local-history museums further delay your progress.

Among Shenandoah's gems, the town of Staunton, as hilly as Rome, was Woodrow Wilson's home; it also boasts pretty Mary Baldwin College and the Museum of American Frontier Culture. Lexington lives and breathes for Stonewall Jackson and Robert E. Lee, who was president of Washington and Lee University after the Civil War. Nearby stands Virginia Military Institute, where Jackson taught before bedeviling Union armies as a Confederate general.

West along winding country roads from Staunton and Lexington lies a countryside often neglected by valley visitors. U.S. 33 and 250 and Route 39 lead to the Appalachian plateau and West Virginia, bordered by the thick foliage of the George Washington National Forest. The roads frequently cross rocky waterways—such as that lovely trio of rivers, the Bullpasture, Cowpasture, and Calfpasture—providing excellent spots for wading and picnicking. Most of the towns in this area are no more than crossroads, with the exception of Hot Springs, site of The Homestead, a 15,000-acre resort that's a Virginia institution. The town has a pleasant collection of arts-and-crafts shops, gourmet delis, and restaurants.

Places to Go, Sights to See

Belle Grove (1 mi south of Middletown, tel. 703/869–2028). The mansion, built of local limestone in 1794, shows the architectural influence of Thomas Jefferson. It suffered greatly in 1864, when Confederate forces launched an attack on a Union Army headquartered at the mansion.

Blue Ridge Parkway (tel. 704/627–3419). One of the country's most breathtaking drives begins at the southern end of the Skyline Drive and follows the mountain crest south to Tennessee.

George C. Marshall Museum and Library (Lexington, tel. 703/463–7103). The general was a 1901 graduate of VMI. He is the only professional soldier awarded the Nobel Peace Prize (on display here), which he received for his plan to rebuild Europe's economy after World War II.

Luray Caverns (tel. 703/743–6551). They're famed for the "stalacpipe organ," which gets played on cave tours. The valley's underground world can also be surveyed at Grand, Shenandoah, Endless, Skyline, and Dixie caverns.

Massanutten (near Harrisonburg, tel. 703/289–9441). A four-season resort has downhill skiing on 11 slopes, golf, tennis, and indoor swimming.

Museum of American Frontier Culture (Staunton, tel. 703/332–7850). In four farmsteads reminiscent of those the early settlers left behind in Europe, costumed workers show how families planted, harvested, and did chores.

Natural Bridge (tel. 703/291–2121 or 800/533–1410). As a young surveyor, George Washington carved his initials in the limestone walls. Thomas Jefferson was so impressed by this 215-foot-high, 90-foot-long rock span that he bought it in 1774. Focus on the spectacular rock formation, and overlook commercial intrusions, such as the wax museum.

New Market Battlefield (tel. 703/740–3101). Of all Civil War memorials, this is one of the most affecting, for in 1864, 247 cadets from the Virginia Military Institute were sent here to a "baptism of fire." Though some in the battalion were just 15, the VMI soldiers became heroes that day.

The Shenandoah National Park (Luray, tel. 703/999–2266). Extending 80 miles along the Blue Ridge, the park was created to restore the scenic terrain to the condition in which the earliest settlers found it. A movie shown at the Byrd Visitors Center at Big Meadows tells the story of the park's regeneration. Information on trails, overlooks, facilities, and activities is available here and at the Dickey Ridge Visitors Center south of Luray.

Shenandoah River Floating. The lazily meandering river offers opportunities for mostly gentle canoe and raft rides, with a little fishing, swimming, and inner-tubing thrown in. Good outfitters include the *Downriver Canoe Company* (Bentonville, tel. 703/635–5526) and *Shenandoah River Outfitters* (Luray, tel. 703/743–4159).

Shenandoah Valley Heritage Museum (Dayton, tel. 703/879–2681). The museum focuses on local history, culture, and tradition. An electronic map traces the movements of troops in Stonewall Jackson's Valley Campaign.

Skyline Drive. The spectacular 105-mile route that meanders through Shenandoah National Park passes scenic overlooks, hiking trails, restaurants, and visitor centers along the way.

Statler Brothers Complex (Staunton, tel. 703/885–7297). Staunton loves the Statlers, because the four country musicians are local boys who defied Nashville by cutting their records in their hometown. A converted elementary school showcases artifacts from their career.

Stonewall Jackson House (Lexington, tel. 703/463–2552). This trim, brick two-story is where Thomas Jonathan Jackson, a natural philosophy professor at VMI, lived with his second wife before he rode away to lead the men in gray. General Jackson died at the Battle of Chancellorsville at the age of 39.

Theater at Lime Kiln (Lexington, tel. 703/463–3074). Set in an abandoned lime quarry, this stage for a professional company of actors has been called the most unusual theater setting in the United States. The Memorial Day–Labor Day schedule includes concerts and plays.

Virginia Horse Center (Lexington, tel. 703/463–7060). The huge equestrian complex has 577 stalls, a 1,000-seat grandstand, regulation dressage areas, horse trails, cross-country courses, and a full calendar of shows and events.

Virginia Military Institute (Lexington, tel. 703/464–7000) was founded in 1839 as the nation's first state-supported military school. Uniformed cadets conduct tours of the campus (an austere and blocky Gothic Revival fortress) and parade most Fridays at 4 PM. *VMI's Museum* (tel. 703/464–7232) highlights the institute's history and most famous graduates. A taxidermic Little Sorrel, Stonewall Jackson's horse, is here, as is the black raincoat that Jackson was wearing when he was shot in 1863.

Washington and Lee University (Lexington, tel. 703/463–8400) was founded in 1749, subsidized by George Washington when the institution was near bankruptcy in 1796, and presided over by Robert E. Lee in the late 1860s. An extraordinary front colonnade and the Lee Chapel and Museum, beneath which the general is buried, are its most noteworthy sights.

Wintergreen (tel. 804/325–2200 or 800/325–2200). This 11,000-acre, four-season resort lies on the eastern flanks of the Blue Ridge. It has golf, skiing, horseback riding, swimming, restaurants, and an acclaimed nature program.

Woodrow Wilson Birthplace and Museum (Staunton, tel. 703/885–0897).
The imposing white Greek Revival home, in the prettiest section of town,
offers lots of Wilson memorabilia, including his Pierce Arrow limousine.

Restaurants

In Staunton, there's a varied menu in the formal dining rooms or casual pub
at **McCormick's** (tel. 703/885–3111); steak and seafood at **The Depot Grill**
(tel. 703/885–7332); traditional Southern cooking at **Rowe's Family Restaurant** (tel. 703/886–1833); casual meals at the small **Beverley Restaurant**
(tel. 703/886–4317); pasta, seafood, and steaks at **The Concourse Cafe** (tel.
703/885–6612); and the town's best ice cream treats at the old-fashioned
Whistle Stop Soda Shoppe (tel. 703/885–6612). **Oliver's** (tel. 703/ 635–3496)
is Front Royal's small, eclectic favorite. **McSylvies** (Middletown, tel. 703/869–
1911) has a well-rounded menu, and **The Springhouse** (Woodstock, tel. 703/
459–4755) serves up reasonably priced food in a comfortable setting. In Lexington, **Il Palazzo** (tel. 703/464–5800) serves traditional Italian food, **The
Willson-Walker House** (tel. 703/463–3020) offers fine American cuisine in a
Colonial setting, and when a burger sounds best, try **The Palms** (tel. 703/
463–7911).

Tourist Information

Augusta–Staunton–Waynesboro Visitors Bureau (Box 58, Staunton, VA
24402, tel. 703/332–3972). **Front Royal Chamber of Commerce** (Box 568,
Front Royal, VA 22630, tel. 703/635–3185). **Harrisonburg–Rockingham
Convention and Visitors Bureau** (800 Country Club Rd., Box 1, Harrisonburg, VA 22801, tel. 703/434–2319). **Lexington Visitors Center** (106 E.
Washington St., Lexington, VA 24450, tel. 703/463–3777). **Shenandoah Valley Travel Association** (Box 1040, New Market, VA 22844, tel. 703/740–
3132). **Virginia Division of Tourism** (1021 E. Cary St., Richmond, VA
23219, tel. 804/786–4484). **Winchester and Frederick County Visitors Center** (1360 S. Pleasant Valley Rd., Winchester, VA 22601, tel. 703/662–4135).

Reservation Services

Bed & Breakfasts of the Historic Shenandoah Valley (402 N. Main St.,
Woodstock, VA 22664, tel. 703/459–4828). **Blue Ridge Bed & Breakfast
Reservation Service** (Rock & Rills Farm, Rte. 2, Box 3895, Berryville, VA
22611, tel. 703/955–1246). **Historic Country Inns of Lexington** (11 N. Main
St., Lexington, VA 24450, tel. 703/463–2044). **Virginia's Inns of the Shenandoah Valley** (Box 1387, Staunton, VA 24401). For a copy of **The Bed and
Breakfast Association of Virginia's directory,** describing more than 100
establishments, call the Virginia Division of Tourism's B&B line (tel. 800/
262–1293). The Division of Tourism's Washington, DC, office also operates a
B&B and small-inn booking service (tel. 202/659–5523 or 800/934–9184
outside DC).

Jordan Hollow Farm Inn

A s anyone who's traveled much in rural America knows, farms aren't always the idyllic-looking places city folk fantasize about. However, Jordan Hollow, a working horse farm set in its own little valley beneath Hawksbill Mountain (on the western side of the Blue Ridge), comes as close to the ideal as possible. It's surrounded by 150 acres of fields and meadows where the horses graze, one can only assume in deep contentment. The passel of cats who have the run of the place also have it good—they sleep on the porch on top of an electric blanket!

Marly and Jetze (pronounced Yetsuh) Beers are the proprietors, and they're a handsome, outdoorsy couple; Marly's blond, and Jetze strikingly tall and dramatically bearded. They met in Liberia, where she was working for AID and he represented a Dutch marine engineering firm. They opened Jordan Hollow as an inn in 1981. Half the guests come for the riding, half to savor the tranquillity. Every day, several equestrian groups (including beginners) leave the farm to wander over the foothills; youngsters go on pony rides. And when Marly gets a break from her cooking duties, she might be prevailed upon to hitch up the carriage. Jetze's forte is keeping things jovial at the Watering Trough, a lounge and game room several paces from the barn. Guests can play volleyball, croquet, and boccie ball; hike along 6 miles of trails; or swim at the public pool across the street. You can even bring your horse; a stall is $10.

The main section of the inn is in a white clapboard farmhouse fronted by a galleried porch. Portions of this structure were built of log around 1790, and in two dining rooms the rough wood and chinking is still visible. Breakfast and dinner are served here and in two other dining rooms. Box lunches are available, too.

Guests can choose from the low-ceilinged Farmhouse Room in the main house, 16 more in the Arbor View Lodge, and four upscale rooms in the Mare Meadow Lodge, which is built of hand-hewn logs. The latter are carpeted and have fireplaces, quilts and matching curtains, cedar furniture, and Jacuzzi tubs.

Address: *Rte. 626 (RR 2, Box 375), Stanley, VA 22851, tel. 703/778-2209 or 703/778-2285, fax 703/778-1759.*
Accommodations: *21 double rooms with baths, 1 suite.*
Amenities: *Restaurant, air-conditioning, cable TV in 5 rooms and lounge, phones in rooms, fireplace in lounge.*
Rates: *$140–$180; MAP. D, DC, MC, V.*
Restrictions: *No pets.*

Trillium House

You've got to hand it to Ed and Betty Dinwiddie. To them, building a bed-and-breakfast on the grounds of Wintergreen resort may have seemed the most natural thing in the world; after all, their family had vacationed there for years. But to skiers, refugees from the Blue Ridge Parkway, wildflower enthusiasts, and all-round mountain devotees, the idea was a stroke of genius. The fact that Trillium House lies across the road from the gargantuan sports complex, with its indoor pool, tennis courts, ski slopes, hiking trails, golf course, and stables, should give you a clue as to the activities available.

From Wintergreen's gate, a roller-coasterish road brings you 3½ miles to the doorstep of Trillium House. The beige frame building fronted by a porch and a Palladian window, surrounded by trees and stylish condominiums owned by Wintergreen residents, was built in 1983. You enter the Great Room, which is two stories high, near a staircase at the side leading to a loft library. The front sitting area has a wood-burning stove, above which hang several organ pipes; by the front door, a canister holds a collection of walking sticks. Breakfast is served in the dining rooms, with views of bird feeders and the backyard gazebo, and on Friday and Saturday dinners (by reservation) are cooked by chef Ellen, who formerly worked in one of Wintergreen's restaurants. The 12 guest rooms at

Trillium House lie in two wings off the Great Room. Their architectural tone is slightly motelish, but decorative touches add some personality— here a quilt or a framed picture that could only have been created by one of the Dinwiddie brood, there a writing desk from The Homestead or a bed with a lace canopy.

The odds are that you'll spend most of your stay here pursuing varieties of R&R on the resort or ensconced in the Great Room, chatting with other guests or Ed and Betty, who manage to seem amazingly relaxed despite their demanding housekeeping duties. The single disappointment is that Trillium House doesn't have mountain views; if that's what you're after, you'll have to grab a stick and walk.

Address: *Wintergreen Dr., Wintergreen (Box 280, Nellysford, VA 22958), tel. 804/325–9126 or 800/325–9126 (reservations only), fax 804/325–1099.*
Accommodations: *10 double rooms with baths, 2 suites.*
Amenities: *Air-conditioning, TV in rooms on request, cable TV with VCR and movie collection in sitting room, turndown service, wheelchair accessible.*
Rates: *$90–$150; full buffet breakfast. MC, V.*
Restrictions: *No smoking in dining room, no pets, 2-night minimum weekends, 3-night minimum some holidays.*

Ashton Country House

Sheila Kennedy, a teacher, says she turned this 1860 Greek Revival home on the outskirts of Staunton into a B&B because she likes meeting people and loves to cook, entertain, and spend money. And she knows the extras that please guests: four plump pillows on each bed, good mattresses, cozy flannel sheets in winter, reading lights, oversize showers, two bath towels per person, bathroom vanities with lots of counter space, big armoires with padded hangers. The large Master Bedroom Suite features a high four-poster Charleston Rice bed. The Cottage Room has a Victorian bedroom suite with faux wood-grain finish and a second-floor porch. Stanley Polanski, Sheila's husband, works with computers by day; by night and during breakfast he's the inn's accomplished jazz pianist. The resident goat often accompanies guests on walks in the surrounding 20 acres of pasture. Lots of books, family quilts, and keepsakes and the owners' hospitality make this a very inviting place.

Address: *1205 Middlebrook Ave., Staunton, VA 24401, tel. 703/885–7819 or 800/296–7819.*
Accommodations: *3 double rooms with baths, 1 suite.*
Amenities: *Ceiling fans in rooms, fireplace in dining and living rooms.*
Rates: *$75–$90; full breakfast, afternoon tea. No credit cards.*
Restrictions: *No smoking indoors, no pets, 2-night minimum on holiday weekends and during fall-foliage season, closed nonholiday weekdays Sept.–May.*

Belle Grae Inn

The Belle Grae is a classic small-town hotel occupying an old Victorian house and several restored buildings close to Staunton's downtown. On your arrival you'll be met by Bellboy, a sanguine boxer, who, according to owner Michael Organ, works for biscuits. The Old Inn, built circa 1870, has a wide porch offering views of Bessie Belle and Mary Grae, two of the town's many hillocks. Its six bedrooms have high ceilings and are decorated with amiable Victorian antiques, and downstairs there are two restaurants—one fancy, in Staunton terms, the other a bistro bar lined with windows. The suites in the 1870 Jefferson House are Belle Grae's top-of-the-line, for their spaciousness and such amenities as fireplaces, balconies, phones, and cable TV. Townhouse rooms are oversize and contain fireplaces and four-poster or canopy beds. The mission oak- and wicker-furnished Cottage has a kitchen, and the Bishop's Suite, with fireplace, kitchen, and garden, is extremely private.

Address: *515 W. Frederick St., Staunton, VA 24401, tel. 703/886–5151, fax 703/886–6641.*
Accommodations: *10 double rooms with baths, 7 suites, 2 cottages.*
Amenities: *Air-conditioning, cable TV and phones in 14 rooms, fireplaces in 14 rooms and 3 common areas, turndown service, wheelchair accessible.*
Rates: *$99–$139; full breakfast. AE, MC, V.*
Restrictions: *No smoking in some rooms, no pets.*

Chester House

Chester House is an architectural gem. Built in 1905 by an international lawyer who participated in drawing up the Treaty of Versailles, the stately Georgian mansion features exquisite dentil molding, an incredible carved Italian-marble fireplace in the dining room, and thick walls. Dogwoods, wisteria, tall boxwoods, a fountain, and statuary grace the 2-acre grounds. The huge Royal Oak Suite has a queen-size poster bed, fireplace, sitting room, and 6-foot bathtub. The Blue Ridge Room is also spacious, with a wrought-iron king-size bed and light floral prints.

Front Royal sits at the foot of the Blue Ridge, and the house is a short walk from Main Street's antiques and crafts shops and from summer concerts at the Village Common's gazebo. Hospitality is Bill Wilson's seventh career; along with his wife, Ann, he's adding it to his list of successful ventures.

Address: *43 Chester St., Front Royal, VA 22630, tel. 703/635–3937 or 800/621–0441 for reservations.*
Accommodations: *5 double rooms with baths.*
Amenities: *Air-conditioning, cable TV in TV lounge, fireplaces in 2 rooms and public rooms, phone in living room, phone jacks in 2 rooms, robes, clock radios.*
Rates: *$85–$110; Continental-plus breakfast, afternoon refreshments. AE, MC, V.*
Restrictions: *Smoking in TV lounge only, no pets, 2-night minimum some weekends.*

Fassifern

Think of it. There are 96,000 horses in Virginia. If you want to buy or show one of them, the place to do it is the Virginia Horse Center, just north of Lexington. And if you make the trip, you'll be glad to know there's one of the Shenandoah Valley's prettiest bed-and-breakfasts just a trot down the road. It's Fassifern, named after the Scottish ancestral home of its builder, who erected this three-story, smoky lavender brick farmhouse circa 1867. It's owned by Francis Whitsel Smith and managed by her animated daughter, Ann Carol Perry, who keeps two Welsh ponies and a horse in the pasture. There's no particular history connected to Fassifern; it's just a lovely country place with a pond, towering maple trees, and an old icehouse that's been converted into two extra guest rooms. The Colonel's Quarters, perhaps the best, has wide plank floors and pasture views. The small Pond Room over-looks the flower-surrounded pond—and the nearby road. In the main house, three more guest rooms are furnished with Victorian armoires, Oriental rugs, and crystal chandeliers.

Address: *Rte. 39 W (RR 5, Box 87), Lexington, VA 24450, tel. 703/463–1013.*
Accommodations: *5 double rooms with baths.*
Amenities: *Air-conditioning, fireplace in living room.*
Rates: *$79–$87; Continental-plus breakfast. MC, V.*
Restrictions: *No smoking, no pets, closed Thanksgiving, Dec. 24–25, Dec. 31.*

Fort Lewis Lodge

On a 3,200-acre farm in the Allegheny foothills, 10 miles off the main road, John and Caryl Cowden raise Angus cattle, soybeans, and corn. The beautiful Cowpasture River deepens into a swimming hole nearby, and Shenandoah Mountain looms above, traversed by paths and logging roads. Below the manor house there's a dining hall in an old mill, and a lodge. Common rooms contain stuffed bears, raccoons, and red fox—all Allegheny Highland species. Lodge rooms are comfortable, with locally handcrafted furniture. The Cowdens have reconstructed two historic log cabins, now cozy accommodations with fireplaces. There's a stone hearth in the gathering room, and a laundry room is available. Rooms in the converted silo are round. In this setting of fields, rivers, mountains, and forests, it's not surprising that Fort Lewis Lodge is blissfully outdoorsy: In addition to swimming, there's tubing down the river, fishing, hiking, biking, and terrific bird-watching. It's great for kids. And at day's end you return to Cowden hospitality—starring Carol's homemade dinners.

Address: *Rte. 625 (HCR3, Box 21A), Millboro, VA 24460, tel. 703/925-2314, fax 703/925-2352.*
Accommodations: *8 double rooms with baths, 3 suites, 2 cabins.*
Amenities: *TV with VCR in game room; bicycles, hot tub.*
Rates: *$130-$180; MAP. MC, V.*
Restrictions: *No smoking in bedrooms, no pets, closed mid-Oct.-mid-Apr.*

The Inn at Gristmill Square

Bath County in western Virginia covers 540 bumpy square miles inhabited by just 5,000 souls, and it hasn't got a single stoplight. Warm Springs, the county seat, boasts a post office, courthouse, and inn—and that's about all. Still, the Inn at Gristmill Square, occupying several 19th-century buildings—a blacksmith's barn, restored mill, miller's house, and hardware store—is reason enough to visit this quintessentially peaceful spot. Its Waterwheel Restaurant is one of the area's best places to sup. Wander down to the cool subterranean wine cellar to select a bottle. The Steel House, across the lane, has a small swimming pool, sauna, and three tennis courts. The Silo has a round living room, and the large, rustic Board Room, a favorite, is paneled with barn siding and features a claw-foot tub. Janice McWilliams and her son, Bruce, are the able proprietors, former owners of an inn in Vermont. They serve a simple breakfast and the *Richmond Times Dispatch* in a picnic basket at your door.

Address: *Rte. 619, Court House Hill (Box 359), Warm Springs, VA 24484, tel. 703/839-2231.*
Accommodations: *14 double rooms with baths, 2 apartments.*
Amenities: *Air-conditioning in 10 rooms, cable TV, phones, and minifridges in rooms, fireplaces in 8 rooms.*
Rates: *$80-$95; Continental breakfast; MAP available. D, MC, V.*
Restrictions: *No pets.*

The Inn at Narrow Passage

Pack your inner tubes, gang, and your swimming togs and fishing rods; they'll all prove useful at the Inn at Narrow Passage, which sits right above the North Fork of the Shenandoah River. Ed Markel, owner of the inn, will kindly put you in about a mile south, and from there it's a 3½ hour float to reach home. The oldest section of the inn was built as a way station on the Great Wagon Road (now U.S. 11) around 1740, and the Markels meticulously restored it. There are three guest rooms on the second floor of this section, each with handmade hinges, tongue-and-groove pine walls, and pegs instead of closets. The rooms in the 1985 addition have canopy beds, fireplaces, and some water views. When the valley is blanketed in snow, the inn is a cozy place—especially the living room with its blue plaid couches and big limestone fireplace (one of 10 here, 7 in guest rooms).

Address: *U.S. 11 S, Woodstock, VA 22664, tel. 703/459–8000, fax 703/459–8001.*
Accommodations: *10 double rooms with baths, 2 doubles share a bath.*
Amenities: *Air-conditioning, TV with VCR in sitting room, clock radios.*
Rates: *$55–$95; full breakfast, afternoon refreshments. MC, V.*
Restrictions: *No smoking in bedrooms, no pets, 2-night minimum fall and holiday weekends, closed Dec. 25.*

Joshua Wilton House

In Harrisonburg's neighborhood of well-kept, handsome old homes, the Joshua Wilton House strikes the highest note. It's a lovingly renovated and luxuriously equipped mauve, lavender, and pink Queen Anne cottage with triple-decker bays and a turret. Throughout, owners Roberta and Craig Moore have provided a sense of polished professionalism, a put-together look of coordinated decor.

You enter by way of a front door surrounded by leaded glass and through a foyer with gleaming parquet floor, a chandelier, and bushy potted plants. Throughout the four downstairs dining rooms you'll find painted mantels and pictures displayed by the Shenandoah Valley Watercolor Association. The guest chambers are really lovely, particularly Room 5, with its four-poster bed and white wing chairs, and Room 4, which has a three-window alcove in the turret. The café is casual, and the restaurant offers fine dining that includes such breakfast specialties as crab-and-cheese omelets.

Address: *412 S. Main St., Harrisonburg, VA 22801, tel. 703/434–4464.*
Accommodations: *5 double rooms with baths.*
Amenities: *Air-conditioning, phones in rooms, fireplace in 1 room; bicycles.*
Rates: *$85–$100; full breakfast. AE, MC, V.*
Restrictions: *Smoking in café bar only, no pets, 2-night minimum some weekends, closed Dec. 24–25.*

Lavender Hill Farm

Four miles west of Lexington, in a hollow across the road from a river, stands Lavender Hill, a working 20-acre farm with pet goats, sheep, dogs, and cats. The central section of the main building is a 200-year-old log cabin. (One guest stayed here because his research revealed that it was his grandfather's birthplace.) Cindy Smith, a former investment banker in Europe, and her jovial husband, Colin, a retired British military officer, designed Lavender Hill to impart the feel of a country English B&B—not antiques-filled, not laden down with quaintness. In keeping with the farm setting, rooms are simply furnished (lace curtains and, say, fresh blue and white stripes). Colin is the chef, providing sophisticated four-course meals (by reservation) for $20; his homegrown herbs are his culinary trademark. Cindy spins wool from the farm's sheep. Guests can fish in the river, bird-watch, or—the usual favorite—lounge on the porch with a cool drink. Special horseback-riding packages are available.

Address: *Rte. 631 (RR 1, Box 515), Lexington, VA 24450, tel. 703/464-5877 or 800/446-4240.*
Accommodations: *2 double rooms with baths, 1 suite.*
Amenities: *Ceiling fans, satellite TV with VCR in living room, portable phones.*
Rates: *$55–$75; full breakfast. MC, V.*
Restrictions: *No smoking indoors, no pets, 2-night minimum some weekends.*

Sampson Eagon Inn

Beltway burnouts Frank and Laura Mattingly—he from hospital administration, she from college administration—have lovingly created an inn that is affordable, elegant, and comfortable. The Mattinglys' two-year restoration of the 1795 Federal mansion with Greek Revival, Italianate, and Victorian additions earned them the Historic Staunton Foundation's Preservation Award for 1992. Furnished with antiques, the yellow mansion perches on Gospel Hill, which, like the inn, is named after the home's first resident, blacksmith and preacher Sampson Eagon. It's across from the Woodrow Wilson Birthplace, a short walk to downtown.

The spacious, high-ceilinged rooms have canopied, queen-size beds, down or nonallergenic pillows and comforters, sitting areas, and cable TV/VCR units. The Holt Room showcases Laura's Delft tile collection, setting the theme for the soothing blue-and-white decor.

Address: *238 E. Beverley St., Staunton, VA 24401, tel. 703/886-8200 or 800/597-9722.*
Accommodations: *3 double rooms with baths, 2 suites.*
Amenities: *Air-conditioning, portable phones, turndown service, fax, photocopying.*
Rates: *$80–$95; full breakfast, afternoon refreshments. No credit cards.*
Restrictions: *No smoking indoors, no pets, 2-night minimum May, Oct., and some holiday weekends.*

Seven Hills Inn

Seven Hills Inn, a classic brick white-columned southern Colonial dwelling in the heart of Lexington's historic Main Street district, was built in 1928 as a fraternity house for nearby Washington and Lee University. Hence the expansive living room (with fireplace), dining room, and casual downstairs chapter room (also with a fireplace as well as TV with VCR and games). It's doubtful, though, that the house had such an impeccably fresh and inviting appearance when the college crowd occupied it. Ben Grigsby, a Washington and Lee alumnus, bought the place and restored it, removing walls between the small fraternity bedrooms to create large guest rooms. When Ben's work sent him out of the country, he asked his mother, Jane Grigsby, and innkeeper Jeanne Tomlinson to operate the bed-and-breakfast.

The pale-yellow third-floor Holly Hill Room, with a sloping ceiling, has a bath that's bigger than the bedroom. Fruit Hill has a Jacuzzi tub and a four-poster bed, and it can be opened into a suite with a parlor.

Address: *408 S. Main St., Lexington, VA 24450, tel. 703/463–4715, fax 703/463–6526.*
Accommodations: *5 double rooms with baths, 2 doubles in suite share 1 bath.*
Amenities: *Air-conditioning.*
Rates: *$75–$140; Continental-plus breakfast. MC, V.*
Restrictions: *No smoking in bedrooms, no pets, 2-night minimum some weekends.*

Thornrose House

In 1984, Susie and Otis Huston spent the night at their first B&B. Someday, they said, *we'll* do this, and they started a portfolio of properties and ideas. After a lengthy search they bought Thornrose and moved down from Buffalo, New York, where Otis had been in management with DuPont and Susie taught school.

Thornrose has a light, fresh appearance. Windsor (all the guest rooms bear English names) has antique twin beds pushed together, with a white down duvet and white lace-trimmed pillows, and an antique armoire and dresser. Although it's the smallest room, sunny Yorkshire is favored for its garden view and claw-foot tub. The blue-and-rose Canterbury Room overlooks bucolic Gypsy Hill Park, where there are a swimming pool, tennis courts, a golf course, and summer concerts. You might prefer to just linger on the wraparound veranda or in the flower-filled gardens, where an 80-year-old climbing, white hydrangea and a wisteria cover two arbors.

Address: *531 Thornrose Ave., Staunton, VA 24401, tel. 703/885–7026.*
Accommodations: *5 double rooms with baths.*
Amenities: *Air-conditioning, cable TV in sitting room, portable phones, fireplaces in dining and living rooms, turndown service; bicycles.*
Rates: *$55–$75; full breakfast, afternoon tea. No credit cards.*
Restrictions: *No smoking, no pets, 2-night minimum Oct. weekends and Mary Baldwin graduation.*

North Carolina

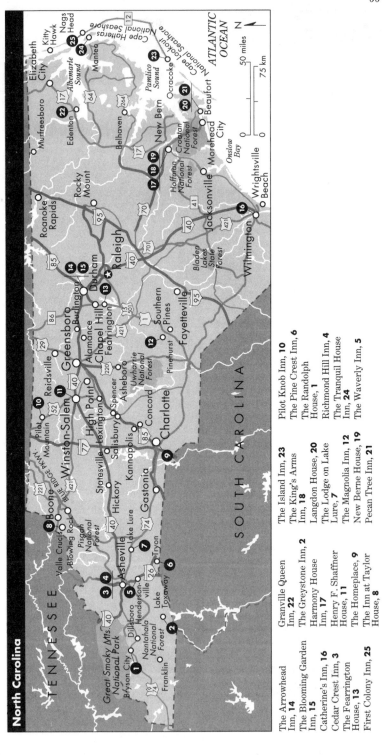

North Carolina

66

ATLANTIC OCEAN

N

50 miles

75 km

The Arrowhead Inn, **14**
The Blooming Garden Inn, **15**
Catherine's Inn, **16**
Cedar Crest Inn, **3**
The Fearrington House, **13**
First Colony Inn, **25**

Granville Queen Inn, **22**
The Greystone Inn, **2**
Harmony House Inn, **17**
Henry F. Shaffner House, **11**
The Homeplace, **9**
The Inn at Taylor House, **8**

The Island Inn, **23**
The King's Arms Inn, **18**
Langdon House, **20**
The Lodge on Lake Lure, **7**
The Magnolia Inn, **12**
New Berne House, **19**
Pecan Tree Inn, **21**

Pilot Knob Inn, **10**
The Pine Crest Inn, **6**
The Randolph House, **1**
Richmond Hill Inn, **4**
The Tranquil House Inn, **24**
The Waverly Inn, **5**

The Outer Banks and Albemarle Region

The northern part of the North Carolina coast, a region of broad bays, meandering rivers, and shallow inlets protected by a chain of barrier islands, was settled very early. Long before Plymouth Rock, earlier than Jamestown, English colonists came in 1584, lived for a time on Roanoke Island, and disappeared mysteriously in 1591. For 100 years or more, Native Americans and the dunes were left mostly undisturbed, and the shifting shoals garnered their annual harvest of shipwrecks. A few towns were founded, a Colonial capital was established, and farming and fishing flourished. In this mild and mannerly land much remains the same.

The old character of the Outer Banks is most evident on Ocracoke Island and in fishing villages like Wanchese and Hatteras. The descendants of early settlers of these isolated places speak their own dialect of Elizabethan English, and the wild ponies that roam the Shackleford Banks are another reminder of a bygone era.

On the 130 miles of barrier islands that stretch from Cape Lookout to the Virginia line, large areas are protected as national seashores, which helps to preserve the marshes, dunes, rare plants, birds, and aquatic life. Although fishing is still the main industry in some of the small villages, tourism has taken hold in others. In summer, the ferries and bridge from the mainland are loaded with cars bound for Ocracoke, Kill Devil Hills, Nags Head, and Manteo. And only when school starts do the towns and villages return to their normal, quiet pace.

Today the image of the coastal region is changing as more people take up residence and its popularity as a travel destination grows. Tourists visit the historic houses in Edenton, flashes of bright nylon on the backs of windsurfers and hang gliders are seen in Nags Head and Kill Devil Hills, and charter boats and head boats leave daily for deep-sea fishing. In the northernmost part of the Outer Banks, where exclusive hunting clubs once flourished, posh residential communities are taking shape. Even with all the changes, though, the area still has that uncrowded, laid-back, old-sneakers feel. The ocean view remains unobstructed, the roads aren't lined with tacky neon signs, and people don't dress to go out to dinner. Though you can swim or fish, sail or dive, the Outer Banks is one of the great places on Earth to do nothing.

Places to Go, Sights to See

Beaches. Most of the Outer Banks' 130 miles of unspoiled beaches are part of the national seashores and are ideal for a variety of water sports. Lifeguards are stationed at Coquina Beach, Salvo, Cape Hatteras, Frisco, and Ocracoke in the *Cape Hatteras National Seashore;* many motels and hotels also have lifeguards.

Cape Hatteras Lighthouse (tel. 919/995–4474), 208 feet high, is the tallest lighthouse in America. Exhibits in the visitor center explain the flora and fauna of the Cape Hatteras National Seashore and show graphically how the ocean is fast encroaching on the lighthouse—you'd better see it soon.

Edenton. Several towns on the mainland side of Albemarle Sound compose the historic Albemarle Region, but this one is the primary attraction. Here, in 1774, a rebellion against the Crown took place that is known as the Edenton Tea Party. The first provincial capital of North Carolina, dating to 1685, Edenton has many historic buildings; four of them can be seen on a walking tour run by *Historic Edenton* (tel. 919/482–2637), which leaves from the 1782 *Barker House* on South Broad Street. You'll see *St. Paul's Episcopal Church* (built between 1736 and 1760); the *Cupola House* (1725), a Jacobean wood building; the Georgian *Chowan County Courthouse,* on the village green; and the waterfront on Albemarle Sound.

Ocracoke Island, ideal for walking and bicycling, is accessible only by ferry and has a quiet village of shops, inns, and restaurants.

Roanoke Island. During the summer, historical interpretations and guided tours are given at the *Elizabeth II State Historic Site* (tel. 919/473–1144), a replica of a 16th-century sailing vessel, harbored in Shallowbag Bay in downtown *Manteo.* The town, which has a New England look to it, is fun to explore. You can buy a walking-tour guide at Manteo Booksellers. Each summer since 1937, *The Lost Colony* (tel. 919/473–3414), an outdoor drama, has reenacted the story of the first colonists, who mysteriously disappeared when some of their party returned to England for supplies. In summer, performances are given nightly, and backstage tours are in the afternoon.

Also on Roanoke Island are the *Ft. Raleigh National Historic Site* (tel. 919/473–5772), a reconstruction of what's thought to be the first colonists' fort; the *Elizabethan Gardens* (tel. 919/473–3234), with walking trails amid period plantings; and the *North Carolina Aquarium* (Airport Rd., tel. 919/473–3493), which offers exhibits, tours, and expeditions to coastal habitats.

Wright Brothers National Memorial (Kill Devil Hills, tel. 919/441–7430). The visitor center has on display a replica of the plane that the two bicycle mechanics from Ohio, Wilbur and Orville Wright, used in their first successful flight on December 17, 1903. National Park Service rangers give interpretive talks on the historic event. The aviators' four takeoffs and landings are marked on the grassy strip outside.

Restaurants

The **Sanderling Inn and Restaurant** (Rte. 12, Duck, tel. 919/261–4111) serves gourmet Continental and Southern regional dishes in an elegantly restored lifesaving station on the oceanfront. Some of the best seafood can be found at **Queen Anne's Revenge** (Old Wharf Rd., Wanchese, tel. 919/473–5466) on Roanoke Island, and at **Café Atlantic** (Rte. 12, tel. 919/928–4861) on Ocracoke Island. Gourmet Italian, including seafood, is found at **Chardo's** (milepost 9, U.S. 158 Bypass) in Kill Devil Hills. The **Weeping Radish Brewery and Restaurant** (U.S. 64, Manteo, tel. 919/473–1157) serves Bavarian-style cuisine and Holpen beer, made on site. The **Elizabethan Dinner Theatre** (U.S. 64, Manteo, tel. 800/346–2466) puts on five-course Renaissance dinner shows on certain days from June through late October. In Edenton, **Caroline's** (Broad St., tel. 919/482–2711) offers gourmet made-from-scratch dishes.

Tourist Information

Dare County Tourist Bureau (Box 399, Manteo, NC 27954, tel. 919/473–2138). **Historic Albemarle Tour, Inc.** (Box 759, Edenton, NC 27932, tel. 919/482–7325). **Outer Banks Chamber of Commerce** (Box 1757, Kill Devil Hills, NC 27948, tel. 919/441–8144).

Reservation Service

North Carolina Bed & Breakfast Assn. (318 W. Queen St., Hillsborough, NC 27278, tel. 800/849–5392).

First Colony Inn

The last of Nags Head's old shingle-style inns was scheduled for demolition when two generations of a Lexington family pooled their resources, mortgaged their homes, and bought the First Colony Inn in 1988. Richard and Camille Lawrence had two things going for them: a piece of land where the inn could be relocated and children with expertise, including a preservation architect, an engineer, an accountant, and a designer. The whole town lined the streets the night the inn (sawed into three pieces) was moved away from the ocean's grasping fingers and down the road to its new home.

Today the inn is listed on the National Register of Historic Places and is far more luxurious than it was in 1932, when it was first constructed. In all, nine of the Lawrences own and operate the inn, and they all helped to restore it with their own hands. The exterior has been returned to its original beauty, complete with two-story, continuous wraparound porches and a brown-shingled roof. The whole interior was reconfigured; now the 26 rooms have private baths and lots of extras, such as heated towel bars, English toiletries, an iron and ironing board, and refrigerators. Luxury rooms also have wet bars or kitchenettes, as well as whirlpool baths and private screened porches. White walls give the inn a fresh feeling, and each room is furnished differently.

Some have cherry beds and dressers, others feature white wicker with floral-print cushions, and still others have canopy beds with crocheted lace.

A Continental breakfast of croissants, pastries, and fruit is served in the first-floor dining room, which contains antique buffets, enormous old mirrors, and vintage photos of Nags Head. The second-floor library is a cozy enclave where guests can read or play games. There's a 50-foot pool with a roomy wooden deck in back, and the ocean is a short walk across the street.

The inn is also convenient to *The Lost Colony* outdoor drama in Manteo, hang gliding at Jockey's Ridge, first-flight history at the Wright Brothers National Memorial, and the many attractions of the Cape Hatteras National Seashore.

Address: *6720 S. Virginia Dare Trail, Milepost 16, Nags Head, NC 27959, tel. 919/441–2343 or 800/368–9390.*
Accommodations: *26 double rooms with baths.*
Amenities: *Air-conditioning, cable TV and phones in rooms.*
Rates: *$125–$200; Continental breakfast, afternoon tea. AE, D, MC, V.*
Restrictions: *No smoking, no pets, 2-night minimum summer weekends, 3-night minimum holidays.*

Granville Queen Inn

Guests get to live out their fantasies at this bed-and-breakfast inn in the heart of Edenton. The ornate sign with its elaborate crown is the first clue to what's inside, and the peach paint on the neoclassic 1907 house hints at the romance to be found within. For Marge and Ken Dunne, it was love at first sight. After staying at the inn themselves, they sold their chain of gourmet cheese shops on Long Island, New York, and bought the inn in 1992. They've retained the unique character that has charmed guests since the inn was first created in 1989.

The first thing you encounter after entering the front door is a sculpture of a pair of cranes, their feet planted in a square white marble fountain and their heads pointed upward to a dark ceiling made of plaster squares hand-molded with cupid faces and then gilded. There's a formal dining room with a crystal chandelier; a side porch sporting white wicker, glass-top tables, and ceiling fans has been enclosed as another dining area.

Each of the guest rooms provides an ambience you might find by taking a trip to a foreign country or stepping into the pages of a storybook. In the Egyptian Room, the most exotic and most requested, guests go to sleep under a leopard coverlet, watched over by two black sphinxes flanking a pair of thronelike chairs draped with the same sheer gold-shot fabric that's at the windows. In the Queen of Italy bathroom, the water spouts from a cherub's mouth. All the oversize tubs have waterfalls. The Queen Victorianna Room is bright and airy and has window seats, a canopy bed, and a claw-foot tub. The Captain's Quarters is furnished in dark mahogany, with a decorated, lacquered dinghy suspended over the bed. The Queen of Queens Room has a massive bed with a bronze plaque of the Blessed Mother set into the headboard. Some rooms have gas-log fireplaces and private patios.

Dining at the Granville Queen is just as lavish. The five-course gourmet breakfast includes grilled chicken breast or filet mignon with eggs and potatoes. Wine and cheese are served on weekend afternoons.

Address: *108 S. Granville St., Edenton, NC 27932, tel. 919/482-5296.*
Accommodations: *9 double rooms with baths.*
Amenities: *Air-conditioning; cable TV, VCRs, and phones in rooms.*
Rates: *$85–$95; full breakfast, weekend-afternoon refreshments. No credit cards.*
Restrictions: *No smoking, no pets.*

The Island Inn

This historic inn, the oldest one on the Outer Banks, has stood for nearly a century. It got its name because it sat on Ocracoke's highest point, with a creek on either side. Built in 1901 of old ship timbers, it served as an Odd Fellows Lodge, public school, and officers' club before becoming an inn in 1945. You may see a water spot on the ceiling or rust on a tub, but the inn also has the character and atmosphere you won't find in a contemporary lodging. It even has a ghost, Mrs. Godfrey, the wife of a former innkeeper; she opens the kitchen door from time to time and leaves things out of place. People have such a good time here, they don't miss luxury; they do find good food and very caring, hospitable hosts. Bob and Cee Touhey, formerly of Winston-Salem, gave up careers in marketing and teaching and are renovating the inn in stages, beginning with air-conditioning, wiring, and other basics.

The best rooms, with panoramic water views, are in the Crow's Nest, up some steep stairs. These rooms feature light-gray natural-wood walls and ceilings and contemporary furnishings with a beach motif. The ocean breeze pours in from sliding glass doors on two sides. In the main inn, rooms have antique furnishings and vintage photographs and feel like Grandma's house. Families prefer the modern annex, where extra-large rooms open on the heated pool. The dining room, the oldest Outer Banks restaurant, is hung with old ships' flags and lanterns. A no-smoking area is on the enclosed sun porch. Many cooks are children of people who cooked here decades ago; they use the same recipes for such trademark dishes as oyster omelets, crab cakes, clam chowder, and scrambled eggs with herring roe. A winter special is popular; one couple decided to marry early to get two nights' lodging, two breakfasts, and a dinner for $120 per couple. The village of Ocracoke is on the island of the same name, accessible only by ferry. The laid-back, casual atmosphere seems a little like Cape Cod. The pirate Blackbeard was killed close to where the Ocracoke Lighthouse is. At the British Cemetery, the Union Jack flies over the graves of British sailors killed offshore, and everyone loves Ocracoke's wild ponies.

Address: *Lighthouse Rd., Rte. 12, Ocracoke, NC 27960, tel. 919/928-4351.*
Accommodations: *35 double rooms with baths.*
Amenities: *Air-conditioning, TV in most rooms.*
Rates: *$30–$95; breakfast extra. D, MC, V.*
Restrictions: *No smoking upstairs in inn, no pets, 3-night minimum holidays.*

The Tranquil House Inn

This inn, on Manteo's waterfront in the heart of the village, looks old but was actually built in 1988. It combines the architecture of the old Roanoke Hotel with the name and reputation for hospitality of another local inn that flourished in the first half of this century. Both have since disappeared from the scene.

The inn is a three-story, gray-shingled building with a green roof, overlooking Shallowbag Bay. Guests sit and watch the goings and comings on the waterfront from long verandas and a spacious second-floor deck furnished with Adirondack chairs. The small, functional lobby with its registration desk is in the center of the building, as is the new restaurant, 1587, which overlooks the waterfront. A Continental buffet breakfast is served here, as is dinner, which features such entrées as sesame-crusted tuna with wasabi vinaigrette and shiitake mushrooms.

Don Just, a retired bank and advertising executive, bought the inn in 1993. His wife, Lauri, is overseeing the redecorating, which includes handmade comforters, dust ruffles and shams in designer fabrics, and room molding and trim painted in coordinating colors. Bathroom mirrors in some rooms were hand-stenciled to match flowers in the wallpaper. The furnishings are all pine reproductions. Beds are kings, queens, and doubles; canopies and four-posters; and sleep sofas. Porta-cribs and cots are available. Two suites have galley kitchens. Each evening, guests gather for a wine-and-cheese reception.

Because the inn is right in the middle of everything, you can leave your car, walk to the local shops and restaurants, and stroll around the quaint seaside village. You can also use the inn's bicycles for getting around town.

Address: *405 Queen Elizabeth St. (Box 2045), Manteo, NC 27954, tel. 919/473–1404 or 800/458–7069, fax 919/473–1526.*
Accommodations: *23 double rooms with baths, 2 housekeeping suites.*
Amenities: *Air-conditioning, cable TV, and phones in rooms; bicycles, gas grill.*
Rates: *$99–$149; Continental breakfast, evening refreshments. AE, D, MC, V.*
Restrictions: *No pets, 2-night minimum summer weekends, 3-night minimum holiday weekends.*

Cape Fear and the Crystal Coast

Unlike the Outer Banks region, where the treacherous coastline and fragile barrier islands have restricted development, the sheltered southern arc of the North Carolina coast gave rise to the first commercial ports and some of its oldest cities. In the northern part of this region, at the confluence of the Trent and Neuse rivers, lies New Bern, a quiet town that served for a time as North Carolina's Colonial capital. The reconstructed Tryon Palace is one of the major tourist attractions in the state, and the town also contains a large historic district.

Beaufort was an early port and today draws sailors and yachters who tie up at the picturesque docks, which are lined with shops and restaurants. This seaside village, founded in 1713, is the state's third-oldest town and has more than 100 historic houses and a complex of restored Colonial buildings. Morehead City, just slightly south, is still a commercial port. The popular beaches of Atlantic Beach, Emerald Isle, and Pine Knoll Shores complete the area known as the Crystal Coast.

Wilmington, in the Cape Fear region, to the south, is located on the peninsula between the Atlantic Ocean and the Cape Fear River. It blossomed into a commercial port when cotton was king and is still the state's largest port, but despite its size, it remains picturesque and charming, with tall church spires and scores of historic homes and buildings. Most recently, it has become the movie-making center of the state, thanks to the soundstages of Carolco Studios.

Places to Go, Sights to See

Beaches. On the Crystal Coast, *Atlantic Beach* is a popular spot with young people, while families gravitate to *Salter Path, Indian Beach,* and *Emerald Isle. Hammocks Beach State Park,* just slightly south of Swansboro, is a completely undeveloped island accessible only by ferry. In the Cape Fear region, *Wrightsville Beach,* about 7 miles from Wilmington, appeals to families. *Carolina* and *Kure,* 20 miles south, are other options. *Bald Head Island,* where people gather to watch the hatching of loggerhead turtles each year, is accessible only by passenger ferry (no cars are permitted).

Beaufort Historic Site (138 Turner St., tel. 919/728–5225) is a complex of 13 restored buildings, including the 1796 *Carteret County Courthouse,* 1859 *Apothecary Shop,* and 1829 *County Jail.* Nearby is the *Old Burying Ground,* listed on the National Register of Historic Places; inhabitants include a privateer with a cannon on his tomb, a sailor buried upright in his casket, and a little girl buried in a cask of rum.

Burgwin-Wright House (224 Market St., Wilmington, tel. 910/762–0570), built in 1770 on the foundation of an early jail, is open for tours.

Chandler's Wharf (Water and Ann Sts., Wilmington), a restored warehouse district on the waterfront, and the **Cotton Exchange** (321 Front St., Wilmington), in a pre–Civil War building, contain some of the city's best restaurants and most interesting shops.

Ft. Fisher State Historic Site (Kure Beach, tel. 910/458–5538), the largest earthwork fortification in the South during the Civil War, has exhibits of war relics and artifacts from sunken blockade-runners. The *North Carolina Aquarium* (tel. 910/458–8257), also at Ft. Fisher, has a 20,000-gallon shark tank, a touch pool, and a whale exhibit, among other attractions.

Ft. Macon State Park (Atlantic Beach, tel. 919/726–3775) contains a Civil War fort. The five-sided fortress, still in good condition, features cannons and restored soldiers' quarters. Audio recordings describe life in the fort. The park also has a museum, bathhouse, and miles of undeveloped beach.

The New Bern Civil War Museum (301 Metcalf St., tel. 919/633–2818), a private collection, has the most complete display of 19th-century firearms, other weapons, and accoutrements on the East Coast.

The **North Carolina Aquarium** (Pine Knoll Shores, tel. 919/247–4003) contains exhibits on the endangered loggerhead turtle, which nests on nearby beaches, as well as "The Living Shipwreck." Another aquarium is located at the Ft. Fisher State Historic Site (*see above*).

The **North Carolina Maritime Museum** (315 Front St., Beaufort, tel. 919/728–7317) explores the state's maritime history, including fishing, whaling, and wartime sinkings that took place just offshore. The *Watercraft Center,* just across the street, demonstrates traditional boat building.

Thalian Hall (102 N. 3rd St., Wilmington, tel. 910/763–3398) was built in 1858 for performances by such greats as Buffalo Bill, John Philip Sousa, General Tom Thumb, Lillian Russell, and Oscar Wilde. It's been restored and is now the site of plays and concerts.

The **Tryon Palace Restoration** complex (610 Pollock St., New Bern, tel. 919/638–1560) includes the reconstructed *palace of Governor William Tryon* (1770s), the *John Wright Stanley House* (ca. 1783), the *Dixon-Stevenson House* (ca. 1826), and *New Bern Academy* (ca. 1764). Throughout the year many special events are staged, and costumed guides give tours of the palace, which is elaborately decorated during the Christmas holidays and is the site of historical interpretations by actors in summer.

The USS *North Carolina* **Battleship Memorial** (Wilmington Harbor, tel. 910/251–5797). The *North Carolina* took part in every major naval offensive in the Pacific during World War II and has been restored as a museum. An orientation film prepares visitors for the two-hour self-guided tour, and a narrated tape is available for rent. On summer evenings "The Immortal Showboat," a 70-minute sound-and-light spectacular staged on board, dazzles audiences seated in grandstands across from the ship's bow.

Wilmington sightseeing tours. Bob Jenkins of *Wilmington Adventure Tours* (tel. 910/763–1785) will give you the inside story on the city during his animated walking tour. Or you can get acquainted with Wilmington through *Sightseeing Tours by Horse Drawn Carriage* (tel. 910/251–8889). Captain Carl Marshburn conducts river tours and dinner excursions aboard the paddle wheeler *Henrietta II* (tel. 910/343–1611).

Restaurants

In Beaufort, the best place for lunch is **Beaufort Grocery** (117 Queen St., tel. 919/729–3866); for dinner, try the seafood supreme at **Spouter's Inn** (218 Front St., tel. 919/728–5190) or any of the nightly specials at the **Bogue's Pocket Cafe** (708 Evans St., Morehead City, tel. 919/247–5351). In New Bern, there's fine dining at the **Harvey Mansion** (221 Tryon Palace Dr., tel. 919/638–3205). Wilmington's **The Pilot House** (Chandler's Wharf, tel. 910/343–0200) serves excellent, fresh seafood.

Tourist Information

Cape Fear Coast Convention and Visitors Bureau (24 N. 3rd St., Wilmington, NC 28401, tel. 910/341–4030 or 800/222–4757). **Carteret County Tourism Bureau** (201 N. 17th St., Morehead City, NC 28557, tel. 919/726–8148 or 800/SUNNY–NC).

Reservation Service

North Carolina Bed & Breakfast Assn. (318 W. Queen St., Hillsborough, NC 27278, tel. 800/849–5392).

Harmony House Inn

The low and melodious chime of an ornate Italian clock marks the hours at this Greek Revival house in New Bern's historic district. The house was built in the early 1850s and enlarged three times. It was even sawed in half as part of one enlargement around the turn of the century and converted to apartments in the '70s. When Buzz and Diane Hansen bought it in 1985, they wanted to make it whole again, as its name reflects. Their renovations have produced an inn that's elegant and homey at the same time.

The double front doors and hallways are the only hint of its strange architectural past. Its history can be seen in framed photos from *Harper's Weekly* depicting the Battle of New Bern. The town fell to Union forces and served as their base of operations in eastern North Carolina for the duration of the war. The Harmony House was occupied by Company K of the 45th Massachusetts Regiment, who posed for a picture in front of the house in 1863.

The Hansens, who moved here from Illinois after Buzz retired from the paper industry, have furnished Harmony House with family photos, handcrafted local furniture, and antiques, including an 1875 pump organ. The soft pastel colors of the walls set off the canopy beds and colorful comforters. Diane's needle-point of North Carolina scenes and "HH"-crocheted coasters, along with her mother's framed wedding handkerchief, give the house a personal touch.

Breakfast is a time for socializing in the formal dining room, where the Hansens lay out a different hot dish on the Empire sideboard each day: pancakes stuffed with cottage cheese, quiche, Scotch eggs, ham Strata, or bacon and eggs, plus fruit and homemade granola. There's also fresh-ground coffee and an assortment of teas.

The Hansens are the kind of hosts who are careful not to intrude on their guests' privacy, but they are always available to answer questions about local attractions and restaurants. There are many within walking distance; convenience is one of the inn's best features. The place could pass a white-glove inspection any day, and it is a favorite overnight stop for bike tours from all over the country.

Address: *215 Pollock St., New Bern, NC 28560, tel. 919/636–3810.*
Accommodations: *9 double rooms with baths.*
Amenities: *Air-conditioning, ceiling fans, cable TV in rooms.*
Rates: *$55–$85; full breakfast, complimentary beverages. AE, MC, V.*
Restrictions: *No smoking, no pets.*

The King's Arms Inn

New Bern was ravaged by fire in the early 1840s, and the home that is now the King's Arms Inn was constructed in the aftermath. The Federal-style frame house with a small balcony over the entrance was built by John Alexander Meadows in 1848. It was enlarged in 1895 to include a "bellcast" (bell-shaped) mansard roof with gabled dormers. The late-Victorian stairway has a polished newel post as thick as a tree trunk, and much of the original woodwork is evident in mantels, doors, and trim. In 1980, the house became an inn, named for an old New Bern tavern frequented by members of the First Continental Congress when they visited Tryon Palace.

Richard and Pat Gulley, originally from Illinois, took over the King's Arms in 1993. Richard had his own construction and upholstery business, and Pat worked in broadcasting. They fell in love with bed-and-breakfasts shortly after they fell in love with each other. Their honeymoon was spent touring New England, staying in B&Bs along the way.

The Gulleys are in the process of freshening up the inn with new paint, wallpaper, and curtains. In one room, a Colonial-style four-poster is draped with tulip-patterned fabric that matches the comforter and draperies. Old paneling was removed in the attic, revealing beadleboard walls, now painted white, and peaked windows. Dried-flower arrangements are hung over the windows. Work is also underway to turn another attic room into a sitting room, something the inn has always lacked. From this vantage point, guests will have a view of the Neuse and Trent rivers.

The rear porch with its white wicker furniture is appealing in good weather. Cribs and cots are provided for children, who are welcome to use the backyard playground equipment. Business travelers seem to love the inn's privacy and convenience.

A morning newspaper and a Continental breakfast are delivered to the rooms. Pat is particularly imaginative with muffins. Kids love her peanut butter and jelly muffins, while adults are treated to creations made with whatever fresh fruits are available. The inn also serves its own coffee blend, a mixture that includes Guatemalan and Indonesian cinnamon coffees, and complimentary beverages are available all day.

Address: *212 Pollock St., New Bern, NC 28560, tel. 919/638-4409 or 800/872-9306.*
Accommodations: *8 double rooms with baths, 2 doubles share 1 bath.*
Amenities: *Air-conditioning, cable TV, and phones in rooms.*
Rates: *$76; Continental breakfast. AE, MC, V.*
Restrictions: *Smoking on porch only, no pets.*

Langdon House

angdon House, a block from the Beaufort waterfront and across the street from the Old Burying Ground, is just about as old as that historic cemetery. It's built of hand-hewn heart-pine timbers, put together with hand-forged nails, and owner Jimm Prest is fairly sure the ballast-stone foundation was laid in 1733. (The cemetery was deeded to the town in 1731.)

A Colonial/Federal-style house with a Bahamian roofline, Langdon House is painted white with dark green shutters and has upstairs and downstairs porches across the front. The floor plan is very simple—a central hall and stairway running down the middle, a parlor on the left side, a bedroom to the right (the largest and sunniest), and three to the rear. All the rooms have queen-size beds (with no headboards but with lots of comfy pillows) and are named for different guests. The dining room, upstairs over the parlor, resembles an 18th-century tavern; an Edwardian oak table takes up most of the room. The kitchen is also upstairs—an arrangement already in place when Prest renovated the house in 1985. Furnishings are an assortment of antiques, some on loan from local residents. The parlor contains an Estes pump organ, an 1840s Empire secretary, and other treasures—all furniture that is friendly and familiar, not museum pieces you wouldn't dare touch.

What really sets Langdon House apart is Prest himself. Having spent 365 days a year on the road for Coca-Cola before he became an innkeeper, he knows what it is to be a traveler, and he's accommodating to a remarkable degree. He'll arrange excursions, make sure guests are fishing with the right lure, and furnish beach baskets with towels and suntan lotion; complimentary beverages are always available. To top it off, he's just plain friendly, the kind of innkeeper who likes to share a glass of wine and good conversation with guests on the rocking-chair-dotted verandas.

Prest encourages his guests to sleep late and will cook a full breakfast for them anytime after 7:30 AM. He describes the food as wholesome but not without sin, such as too-pretty-to-eat orange-pecan waffles or omelets. He describes his business not just as the renting of rooms but rather as the fine art of innkeeping.

Address: *135 Craven St., Beaufort, NC 28516, tel. 919/728-5499.*
Accommodations: *4 double rooms with baths.*
Amenities: *Air-conditioning, cordless phone; bicycles, fishing rods, ice chests.*
Rates: *$88–$120; full breakfast. No credit cards.*
Restrictions: *No smoking indoors, no pets, 2-night minimum summer weekends and holidays.*

Pecan Tree Inn

On Joe and Susan Johnson's first visit to Beaufort, they sat in a waterfront restaurant and watched wild ponies graze on nearby Carrot Island. When dolphins swam up the river to complete the scene, the Johnsons took it as a sign they were now where they belonged. Joe, who ran a chain of hardware stores, and Susan, who sold auto insurance, left New Jersey and bought a Victorian home less than a block from the waterfront. The home was actually built in 1856, and Victorian embellishments, including porches, turrets, and gingerbread trim, were added in the 1890s. Now restored to its original splendor, it's a charmer that lures 20–30 people a week just for a tour.

Rooms are bright and airy, with light floral wallpapers and bed covers. The furnishings are a mix of antiques and reproductions from different periods. The Blue Room, for example, features a white wrought-iron bed with a wicker wardrobe and dresser. The Country Room has a pine pencil-post canopy bed and an antique trunk. The Green Room was renamed the Wow Room for the response it inevitably provokes. Here, deep-green carpeting and fabrics provide a dramatic contrast to the white walls. The Bridal Suite is pure romance. The four-poster canopy bed is accented with a brocade coverlet, and the rose-and-white tile bath includes a two-person Jacuzzi.

A small library is outfitted with books, games, and a guest refrigerator stocked with complimentary beverages. Other favorite places for relaxing are the porches, where breakfast is often served in fair weather. The fare includes homemade muffins, cereals, fresh fruit, and, of course, pecan sticky buns.

Named for two ancient pecan trees that grow on the property, the inn is beautifully landscaped. There's a small yard in front and a huge garden in back, planted with more than 1,000 flowers, shrubs, and trees. (The local chefs also stroll back here to pluck some of Susan's herbs.) The city's best restaurants are all within walking distance, as are the historic district and the waterfront.

Address: *116 Queen St., Beaufort, NC 28516, tel. 919/728–6733.*
Accommodations: *7 double rooms with baths.*
Amenities: *Air-conditioning, cordless phone.*
Rates: *$80–$120; Continental breakfast. MC, V.*
Restrictions: *No smoking, no pets.*

Catherine's Inn

Catherine Ackiss, who formerly operated Catherine's Inn on Orange, has moved her bed-and-breakfast inn to a larger home overlooking the Cape Fear River in Wilmington's historic district. The 1883 Italianate home is painted a crisp white and has a brick and wrought-iron fence. Guests can pass the time rocking on the wraparound porch, which includes a screened area overlooking the river. Another big attraction is a lush sunken garden.

Guests of Catherine's former inn will feel right at home, since she has duplicated much of the decor. The twin room is once again painted a striking dark purple, while other rooms feature four-poster and canopy beds. Catherine's mother's grand piano made the move, along with many other family items that give the inn warmth and charm.

Walter Ackiss, a retired chemist, now works his magic in the kitchen; pancakes with orange or blueberry syrup are served alongside homemade sausage on family silver and china. Conveniences include a stocked refrigerator and library.

Address: *410 S. Front St., Wilmington, NC 28401, tel. 910/251-0863 or 800/476-0723.*
Accommodations: *3 double rooms with baths.*
Amenities: *Air-conditioning, ceiling fans, cable TV in library, phones in rooms, turndown service.*
Rates: *$60–$88; full breakfast. MC, V.*
Restrictions: *Smoking on porches only, no pets.*

New Berne House

Mystery weekends are the big attraction at this Colonial Revival house built in 1923. Owners Marcia Drum and Howard Bronson present their guests with a case at a Friday evening reception, and the guests search out clues in a scavenger hunt that takes them through the shops and homes of the historic district. The solution is revealed after dinner on Saturday.

Howard, a retired sea captain, and Marcia moved from Mystic, Connecticut, to take over the inn two years ago and added a few touches of their own, like family antiques and a privacy fence around the large back yard. A breakfast of praline waffles or spiced apple crepes is served on a dining room table that belonged to Howard's mother.

The most popular guest rooms are No. 5, which has pink pickled floors and a claw-foot tub, and No. 6, with a brass bed rescued from a burning brothel in Prescott, Arizona. The inn is within walking distance of Tryon Palace but is located on a busy thoroughfare.

Address: *709 Broad St., New Bern, NC 28560, tel. 919/636-2250 or 800/842-7688.*
Accommodations: *7 double rooms with baths.*
Amenities: *Air-conditioning, ceiling fans, cable TV in parlor, phones in rooms; bicycle built for two, free airport transportation.*
Rates: *$80, mystery weekends $259 per couple; full breakfast. AE, MC, V.*
Restrictions: *No smoking indoors, no pets.*

The Piedmont

Between the mountains and the coastal plain of North Carolina lies a region of rolling hills, large rivers, and lakes. In his journal (published in 1709), John Lawson called it "the finest part of Carolina." In the 1700s, the Piedmont, populated by Native American tribes and teeming with game and fish, was the western frontier. Today, with its interstate crossroads and the large cities, the area, long devoted to commerce, is beginning to be recognized for its travel appeal. People riding the interstates on their way north, south, or west are likely to spend some time in the Piedmont.

The region is rich in historic attractions and museums of history, art, science, transportation, tobacco, furniture, and textiles. You can spend an entire day exploring the Moravian settlements of Old Salem and Bethabara near Winston-Salem; retrace Revolutionary War battles at Kings Mountain, Guilford Courthouse, and Alamance; or visit the Civil War site at Bentonville. You can see animals from around the world at the North Carolina Zoological Park in Asheboro; enjoy opera, Shakespeare, and concerts; and see government at work in Raleigh, the state capital.

Busloads of travelers shop for clothing, furniture, and household goods at large outlet centers along the interstates in Burlington ("Outlet Capital of the World"), Greensboro, High Point, Winston-Salem, Hickory, Kannapolis, and Charlotte. Antiques are also hot; in fact, entire towns like Waxhaw and Pineville are devoted to buying and selling them. Philip Morris, R.J. Reynolds Tobacco, Fieldcrest-Cannon, and Stroh offer tours of their plants. Long recognized for its handmade pottery, the sandy, pine-treed area called the Sandhills has several dozen shops where you can buy utilitarian and decorative pieces.

North Carolina prides itself on its golf courses, its tennis facilities are increasing, and croquet is making a comeback.

The craze for basketball is contagious in the Tarheel State, thanks to the NBA's Charlotte Hornets and NCAA standouts Duke, UNC, and NC State. The Durham Bulls immortalized in the film Bull Durham, *are also wildly popular, as is NASCAR racing. Carowinds theme park on the South Carolina line has hair-raising rides, and the state's parks and lakes offer other recreation, as well as natural beauty.*

Places to Go, Sights to See

Discovery Place (301 N. Tryon St., Charlotte, tel. 704/372–6261), one of the best science museums in the country, offers hands-on and rotating exhibits; it has aquariums, a rain forest, and an Omnimax theater.

Duke Chapel (Chapel Rd., West Campus, Durham, tel. 919/684–3214), a Gothic structure patterned on a European cathedral, was built in 1924 as the focal point of Duke University. Free organ concerts are given regularly.

Duke Homestead and Tobacco Museum (2828 Homestead Rd., Durham, tel. 919/477–5498). At the mid-19th-century home of Washington Duke, tobacco barns, an original factory, and a museum are open for tours. The complex is a National Historic Landmark.

Furniture Discovery Center (101 W. Green Dr., High Point, tel. 910/887–3876). Opened in 1991 in a renovated warehouse near hundreds of showrooms, this unique museum is devoted entirely to furniture production.

Golf Courses. More than three dozen golf resorts, among them *Pinehurst Resort and Country Club* (tel. 910/295–6811), *Pine Needles* (tel. 910/692–7111), and *Mid-Pines Resort* (tel. 910/692–2114), are in the North Carolina Sandhills. (Some courses are open only to guests at the resort.) *Southern Pines* is home to the PGA/World Golf Hall of Fame (tel. 910/295–6651).

The **Mint Museum of Art** (2730 Randolph Rd., Charlotte, tel. 704/337–2000), built in 1837 as a U.S. mint, has an outstanding collection of pre-Columbian pottery and attracts traveling exhibits.

North Carolina Transportation Museum (411 S. Salisbury Ave., Spencer, tel. 704/636–2889), in the old railroad repair shops, traces the history of transportation from pre-settler days through the heyday of railroading to the present. A restored steam train takes visitors on a short loop tour.

Old Salem (600 S. Main St., Winston-Salem, tel. 910/721–7300), a restored Moravian village dating to the 1700s, comprises 60 buildings where visitors can see Colonial cooking, gardening, and the making of pewter, candles, furniture, and cloth. At Christmas there are candlelight teas and worship services. The *Museum of Early Southern Decorative Arts* (tel. 910/721–7360) has rooms reconstructed from Southern houses.

Reed Gold Mine (off U.S. 601 at Rte. 200, 10 mi east of Charlotte, tel. 704/786–8337) is where America's first gold, a 17-pound nugget, was found in 1799. Explore the mine, pan for gold, and learn about mining in the museum.

State Capitol (Capitol Sq., Raleigh, tel. 919/733–4994). Completed in 1840 and restored in 1976, this building once housed all the functions of state government. The *Capitol Area Visitor Center* (301 N. Blount St., tel. 919/733–3456) conducts free guided tours daily, which include the contemporary State Legislative Building and the executive mansion.

Restaurants

North Carolina's best hickory-smoked pork barbecue is served with red slaw and hush puppies at **Lexington Barbecue** (I–85 Business, tel. 704/249–9814) in Lexington. (World leaders sampled it at the Williamsburg summit meeting several years ago.) **The Lamplighter** (1065 E. Morehead St., tel. 704/372–5343) in Charlotte serves gourmet cuisine in the elegant atmosphere of a house in the old Dilworth neighborhood. Authentic food of the 18th century is offered at the **Salem Tavern** (736 S. Main St., tel. 910/748–8585) in Old Salem. **The Angus Barn, Ltd.** (U.S. 70, tel. 919/781–2444) in Raleigh is famous for its steaks and ribs. At the **Colmant House** (Main St., Pilot Mountain, tel. 910/368–2823), John and Sue Colmant, formerly of New Orleans, serve wonderful Cajun fare at dinner Thursday through Sunday.

Tourist Information

Charlotte Convention & Visitors Bureau (122 E. Stonewall St., Charlotte, NC 28202, tel. 704/371–8700 or 800/231–4636). **Durham Convention & Visitors Bureau** (101 E. Morgan St., Durham, NC 27701, tel. 919/688–2855 or 800/772–2855). **Greensboro Area Convention & Visitors Bureau** (312 Greene St., Greensboro, NC 27401, tel. 910/274–2282 or 800/344–2282). **High Point Convention & Visitors Bureau** (Box 300 S. Main St., High Point, NC 27261, tel. 910/884–5255). **Pinehurst Area Convention & Visitors Bureau** (Box 2270, Southern Pines, NC 28288, tel. 910/692–3330 or 800/346–5362). **Raleigh Convention and Visitors Bureau** (225 Hillsborough St., Suite 400, Raleigh, NC 27602, tel. 919/834–5900 or 800/849–8499). **Winston-Salem Convention & Visitors Bureau** (Box 1408, Winston-Salem, NC 27102–1408, tel. 910/725–2361 or 800/331–7018).

Reservation Service

North Carolina Bed & Breakfast Assn. (318 W. Queen St., Hillsborough, NC 27278, tel. 800/849–5392).

The Arrowhead Inn

The large arrowhead monument from which this inn draws its name designates an old Native American trading route called the Great Path, which once stretched from eastern Virginia to the North Carolina mountains. It's a proper frame of reference for this house, which, like the path, predates the United States. The manor house was built about 1775 on a 2,000-acre land grant purchased from Joseph Brittain, and for more than 100 years, slaves worked the land. The original house had four rooms—two upstairs and two down—but several were added over the years. Situated on 4 acres, it is a two-story Colonial-style house with brick chimneys and tall Doric columns that support the long front porch. The house is painted white with black shutters. The boxwood, magnolias, and flower beds around it are about 150 years old, and more than 40 species of birds live on the property.

After a succession of owners, Jerry and Barbara Ryan bought the house in 1985 and turned it into a bed-and-breakfast, winning an award from the Durham Historic Preservation Society for adaptive reuse. Jerry had worked as a publisher of business magazines, and Barbara, a former editor and ghostwriter, continues to write magazine articles.

Guest rooms are decorated with an assortment of antiques and collectibles from the Colonial through the Victorian period. The front rooms of the house look out on the flower beds, while the back view is dominated by an enormous magnolia. For those wanting more privacy, there are two rooms in an adjacent carriage house. The Land Grant Cabin, which has a downstairs sitting room and a loft bedroom, is a favorite. In addition to families and couples, the inn is quite popular with traveling business-women.

The Ryans greet arriving guests with complimentary refreshments and are always available in the evening when everyone gathers in the keeping room to work puzzles, read, or talk. Barbara promises guests a different breakfast every day. They range from hearty country breakfasts with bacon, eggs, fruit, and muffins to more exotic fare. Lower-fat alternatives are prepared on request.

Address: *106 Mason Rd., Durham, NC 27712, tel. and fax 919/477–8430 or 800/528–2207.*
Accommodations: *4 double rooms with baths, 2 doubles share 1 bath, 1 suite, 1 cabin.*
Amenities: *Air-conditioning; ceiling fans in public rooms; TV in keeping room, cabin, and suite; phone in rooms on request; guest refrigerator.*
Rates: *$70–$150; full breakfast, afternoon tea. AE, D, DC, MC, V.*
Restrictions: *No smoking in bedrooms, no pets.*

The Fearrington House

If you didn't know better, you'd think a click of the heels had transported you to the Cotswolds of England. Actually, this bucolic setting is Fearrington Village, a 200-year-old farm remade into a residential community just off U.S. 15–501 between Chapel Hill and Pittsboro. The village consists of the inn and private homes, a restaurant (in the former farmhouse), a bank, pharmacy, pottery, jewelry store, bookstore, fine art gallery, and garden shop.

Fearrington Village is the creation of R.B. and Jenny Fitch, who studied inns and restaurants all over Europe before they began the 1,100-acre project in 1974. The guest rooms are clustered around a charming courtyard with a central fountain and look out over the gardens and the pasture, where Galloway cows and Tunis sheep graze. The rooms are furnished in English pine that matches the flooring from a London workhouse; they are complemented by polished floral print fabrics and dried arrangements. The luxurious bathrooms have towel warmers. Jenny has had a hand in decorating just about every building in the village, and she helps the chef plan meals for the restaurant. She's quite an accomplished chef herself and has produced a cookbook.

Breakfast is served in the restaurant, comprising different rooms done up in the elegant country style that is Fearrington's hallmark. One room is peach, with matching tablecloths and draperies; another has a white and green ivy design. Dinner draws not only inn guests but diners from Chapel Hill. Often requested entrées include sautéed scallops with lemon-garlic butter and toasted almonds, Carolina crab cakes with mustard mayonnaise, and beef tenderloin with a merlot and peppercorn sauce. Most guests eat lunch in the Market Café or go for a picnic, which can be ordered from the deli. Then they gather for afternoon tea in the Garden Room.

One of the most pleasant things about the Fearrington is its low-key country atmosphere. You won't be subjected to a schedule here, but you might try a round of croquet or ride one of the bikes to the swimming pool and tennis courts. Of course, there are plenty of diversions nearby—the Morehead Planetarium at Chapel Hill, Duke Chapel, and the Duke Homestead. The inn is affiliated with Relais & Chateaux.

Address: *Fearrington Village Center, U.S. 15/501, Pittsboro, NC 27312, tel. 919/542–2121, fax 919/542–4202.*
Accommodations: *15 double rooms with baths, 9 suites.*
Amenities: *Air-conditioning, TVs and phones in rooms.*
Rates: *$150–$250; full breakfast, afternoon tea. MC, V.*
Restrictions: *No smoking in bedrooms, no pets.*

Henry F. Shaffner House

The Henry F. Shaffner House was built between 1907 and 1909 by Henry Fries Shaffner, one of the founders of Wachovia Bank. The first time the house was saved, it was by Shaffner himself, who went onto the rooftop with buckets of water to keep a fire from taking his home. He later replaced the cedar shingles with copper, which helped to preserve the mansion through the next 70 years, even after it was abandoned and neglected. The house was saved again in 1990 by Henry and Betty Falls, who spent two years renovating it. Henry, who owns the insurance agency across the street, initially had designs on the overgrown back lot, which he needed for parking. But once he stepped inside the home, he saw past the layers of paint and dirt to the treasure underneath.

The house was built using the finest materials and workmanship. Tiger oak paneling covers the walls of the entry hall and adorns the doors, windows, and exposed ceiling beams. Many of the brass fixtures remain, as do the tile fireplaces and a huge ornate radiator in the library. The Queen Anne detailing on the exterior, with large wraparound porches and a wrought-iron fence, is stunning enough to stop traffic, even on the busy main thoroughfare that now runs past it. It was the coming of the interstate, which cuts alongside the house, that moved Shaffner's widow to sell it in 1949. For today's travel-ers, the location provides easy access from downtown to any Winston-Salem attraction.

Once inside, however, you may not want to go anywhere. Rooms are beautifully appointed with rich fabrics, comfortable sofas and chairs, and gleaming reproduction furniture. Each room is different. The Winston Room is decorated in English regency—deep sapphire-blue carpet, stucco walls, and a queen-size sleigh bed. The Reynolda is bright and feminine; the Bethabara is darkly masculine. The Piedmont Room is a remarkable penthouse suite in the 18th-century Biedermeier style. The king-size canopy bed is covered with a leopard-print comforter, and leopard-print accents are echoed tastefully in the wallpaper and bolster pillows. There is a waiting list for a huge suite that contains a whirlpool bath and wet bar. Throughout, the inn combines the charm of the past with modern amenities.

Address: *150 S. Marshall St., Winston-Salem, NC 27101, tel. 910/777–0052.*
Accommodations: *5 double rooms with baths, 3 suites.*
Amenities: *Air-conditioning, cable TV and phones in rooms; passes to nearby fitness center.*
Rates: *$89–$189; Continental breakfast, afternoon refreshments. AE, MC, V.*
Restrictions: *No smoking, no pets.*

The Homeplace

The Homeplace, a well-preserved remnant of the past, has somehow survived modern development in the bustling Sunbelt city of Charlotte. The almond-colored house, on 2½ wooded acres with profuse plantings of flowers, is located at the corner of a busy residential intersection but is so quiet inside, you might just as well be at the top of Walton's Mountain.

Frank and Peggy Dearien had admired the 1902 country Victorian farmhouse for several years before the chance arose in 1984 for them to buy it and turn it into a bed-and-breakfast. Frank took early retirement from his accounting job, and the inn is now their full-time occupation. They furnished the house in Victorian period pieces, quilts, cross-stitch pictures, and family memorabilia. Peggy made all the curtains. The most cherished artwork in the house is a collection of primitive paintings reminiscent of Grandma Moses that Peggy's father did during the last years of his life.

The Victorian Lady Room, done in mauve and green, was planned around a cross-stitch picture made by their daughter Debra Moye. The largest room in the inn, it has a four-poster rice bed and a twin bed. The blue and white English Country Room overlooks the garden and the gazebo. The two Cottage Rooms upstairs, which have an adjoining bath, are great for families or honeymooners. One bedroom is particularly romantic; it has a queen-size feather bed draped with a rose-print fabric. When honeymooners stay here, the other bedroom is used as a sitting room where Peggy will serve a private breakfast. All the rooms have little personal touches, such as a purse or hand mirror that belonged to Frank's mother.

The Deariens, who live on the property, are great believers in practicing Southern hospitality. There's always hot water for tea or coffee on the old-fashioned cupboard, as well as ice and soft drinks. Breakfast, served in the dining room or the new addition overlooking the garden, might be poached pears with raspberry sauce, scrambled dill eggs with cheese sauce, or waffles and cinnamon cream.

Address: *5901 Sardis Rd., Charlotte, NC 28270, tel. 704/365–1936.*
Accommodations: *2 double rooms with baths, 1 suite.*
Amenities: *Air-conditioning, ceiling fans, cable TV in common areas, phone in parlor, irons and ironing boards in rooms.*
Rates: *$68–$88; full breakfast. AE, MC, V.*
Restrictions: *No smoking indoors, no pets, 2-night minimum holiday weekends.*

Pilot Knob Inn

The two-story log tobacco barns that dot this rural landscape aren't usually the kind of places you'd consider spending the night. Here, however, they have become a one-of-a-kind B&B. The property adjoins Pilot Mountain State Park, and the knob that crowns the 1,500-foot mountain is within view. (If the names ring a bell, it's because they inspired the place names in Andy Griffith's mythical Mayberry.)

Five small barns and a slave cabin, all at least 100 years old, were moved to the 50-acre wooded site by innkeeper Jim Rouse, who added decks and porches to the barns, while keeping their rustic look, and enlarged the slave cabin for himself. Jim's father, Don, who is also involved in the operation, can always find something that needs fixing or changing. Norman Ross, his silent business partner from Chicago, owns the collection of 6,000 records in the library. The barns are furnished in a mix of 18th-century reproductions, Southern primitive, and country English antiques, in addition to Oriental and dhurrie rugs. Each has a whirlpool tub for two and a fireplace and is equipped with such amenities as bathrobes, hair dryers, fresh fruit, and flowers. Some of the barns have massive "Paul Bunyan" beds, handmade of juniper logs by a local craftsman. The common room, downstairs in the bilevel central barn—where guests gather to read,

listen to music, and watch videos—features a 300-year-old Italian-marble fireplace, a William and Mary love seat, and a coffee table made of parquet flooring from Versailles (really!). There's a dry sauna and a pool, and a 6-acre lake and gazebo are ideal for fishing. The most recent addition is a contemporary building overlooking the pool and the mountain beyond; it will house the office, kitchen, a conference room, and a gift shop that sells community crafts.

Privacy and isolation are the main attractions at Pilot Knob. It's tucked away with no signs or billboards to point the way. It's the perfect place to commune with nature, slow down, and rekindle romance. Guests usually get together at breakfast, which is served in the central barn and prepared by Jim's mother, Pat. Her specialties are chocolate-chip sour-cream coffee cake, waffles and sausage, poached pears, and a peach and cream-cheese concoction called Peach Pilot—all served with fresh berries in season.

Address: *Box 1280, Pilot Mountain, NC 27041, tel. 910/325–2502.*
Accommodations: *5 cabins.*
Amenities: *Air-conditioning, TV and phones in rooms.*
Rates: *$90–$105; deluxe Continental breakfast. MC, V.*
Restrictions: *Smoking in cabins only, no pets, 2-night minimum Oct. and holidays.*

The Blooming Garden Inn

Aptly named, this inn is an oasis in Durham's Holloway Historic District, where many stately old homes still await renovation. The sunny yellow Victorian is surrounded with flower beds and bordered with a neat white fence. It's like a riotous garden inside, too, overflowing with floral-print fabrics, stained-glass pieces, marbles, kaleidoscopes, and other whimsical accents. Dolly Pokrass, a nurse by profession, ran an antiques and handicrafts shop in Hillsborough for several years before she and husband, Frank, a retired medical sociologist, bought the inn. It's largely decorated with the items she could never bear to sell. Each guest room is named according to its colors—Ivy (dark green with cheery accents), Tiffany (stained glass), Moroccan (dark green, gold, and red),

and so on. Fresh flowers from the garden adorn each one.

Breakfast begins with original juice blends and home-ground coffee and can include walnut crepes with ricotta cheese and warm raspberry sauce.

Address: *513 Holloway St., Durham, NC 27701, tel. 919/687–0801.*
Accommodations: *3 double rooms with baths, 2 suites.*
Amenities: *Air-conditioning, ceiling fans, cable TV in library and 1 suite, whirlpool baths in suites, refrigerator.*
Rates: *$75–$150; full breakfast. AE, MC, V.*
Restrictions: *No smoking indoors, no pets.*

The Magnolia Inn

Pinehurst has been a favorite vacation spot for more than a century, as this historic inn attests. Built in 1896, it is now on the National Register of Historic Places. Owners Jan and Ned Darby cater to golfers, who come in droves to enjoy the many courses of the Sandhills. The inn has package arrangements with several clubs, including the prestigious Pinehurst. The outdoor pool and wraparound porches are a welcome sight after several rounds.

Guest rooms are furnished in a turn-of-the-century Victorian style, with brass beds and wicker. The original bathroom fixtures and claw-foot tubs have been returned to their former luster, and accent pieces, like an old Victrola, add to the ambience.

Chefs John Salmon and Lucille Falk serve unforgettable gourmet food. The dark bar has the feel of an old English pub and offers unusual brews, such as Watney's Red Barrel and Belhaven Scottish Ale.

Address: *Magnolia St. and Chinquapin Rd. (Box 818), Pinehurst, NC 28374, tel. 910/295–6900 or 800/526–5562.*
Accommodations: *12 double rooms with baths.*
Amenities: *Restaurant, air-conditioning, cable TV in rooms and pub, pay phone at front desk.*
Rates: *$130; MAP. AE, MC, V.*
Restrictions: *No smoking in bedrooms, no pets, 2-night minimum spring and fall weekends.*

The Mountains

Western North Carolina is blessed with two major ranges in the Southern Appalachian chain: the Blue Ridge Mountains, extending from Virginia, and the Great Smokies, called Shaconage ("place of blue smoke") by Native Americans. The gentle foothills of both ranges crest into peaks of blue and purple grandeur, many over 5,000 feet high. Grandfather Mountain, near Linville, is said to be a billion years old. Mt. Mitchell, at 6,684 feet, is the highest point east of the Mississippi.

The Cherokees lived in these mountains for thousands of years before the arrival of Scotch-Irish farmers and enterprising lumberjacks in the mid-1800s. Later, Georgia and Carolina lowlanders, seeking to escape the scorching summer heat, established retreats at Flat Rock, Hendersonville, Highlands, Linville, and Blowing Rock. Around the turn of the century, George Vanderbilt and Edwin Wiley Grove fashioned their dreams into fabulous estates at Asheville and invited their friends to breathe the pure mountain air amid incredible beauty. In the past 25 years, the region has become a magnet for skiers and golfers, and resort communities like Linville Ridge, Elk River, Fairfield, Chetola, and Etowah Valley have sprung up.

Today there's year-round recreation, not only for the silk-stocking set but also for anyone who loves the outdoors. You can camp, hunt, and fish in the Great Smoky Mountains National Park; dig for rubies in Franklin; ride a steam train through the Nantahala Gorge; join thousands of other rubberneckers during leaf season on the Blue Ridge Parkway; and shoot the rapids on the French Broad. Many come to play golf and tennis at posh resorts like the Hound Ears Club or schuss through white powder at Ski Beech and Sugar Mountain. You can attend plays at the Flat Rock Playhouse, listen to classical music at the Brevard Music Festival, watch European folk dancers at Folkmoot, or learn to clog (the native dance) at the Stompin' Ground. If it's not a B&B you're after, you can stay in century-old log cabins at Cataloochee Ranch or live it up at the luxurious Grove Park Inn and Country Club. To complete the experience, dine on rainbow trout and vinegar pie at Jarrett House in Dillsboro or have a seven-course gourmet dinner at Eseeola Lodge.

Most people like the high drama of the mountains' four seasons. Many fall in love and decide to sink in deeper roots: Look at the preserved cabins, A-frames, and million-dollar second homes that dot the hillsides. When Rand McNally rated Brevard and Asheville among the most desirable places to live in America, residents were not surprised.

Places to Go, Sights to See

Biltmore (Biltmore Ave., Asheville, tel. 704/255–1770 or 800/543–2961). The best times to see the fabulous 12,000-acre George C. Vanderbilt estate are April and May, when the gardens are in bloom, and December, when the 250-room mansion is decorated for Christmas as it would have been in 1895. A modern winery is housed in the former dairy, where you can see the entire process and sample some of the products.

The Blue Ridge Mountain Frescoes (Glendale Springs and Beaver Creek, near West Jefferson, tel. 910/982–3076). In the 1970s, North Carolina artist Ben Long painted these frescoes of New Testament scenes in two abandoned churches (now restored).

Blue Ridge Parkway. Thousands of Americans travel this famous crestline highway every year from its beginning at Front Royal, Virginia, to its terminus near Great Smoky Mountains National Park and the Cherokee Indian Reservation. The way is dotted with scenic overlooks, mountain cabins, and markers that explain the history and natural phenomena of the area.

Connemara (1928 Little River Rd., Flat Rock, tel. 704/693–4178). During the final years of his life, Lincoln biographer and poet Carl Sandburg lived at this estate with his wife, Lilian, who raised champion goats. The National Park Service gives daily tours.

Great Smoky Mountains National Park (tel. 615/436–1200 or 615/436–5615). The most visited park in the United States straddles the North Carolina–Tennessee border and offers a wealth of outdoor activities amid its 517,368 acres. There are more than 800 miles of hiking and riding trails and 16 summits higher than 6,000 feet.

Great Smoky Mountains Railway (Sylva, tel. 704/586–8811 or 800/872–4681). Excursion trains traverse the route through rock tunnels and along river gorges between Dillsboro, Bryson City, and Nantahala. Travelers can ride in coach, caboose, or "Kodak" (open) cars.

Mountains. *Grandfather Mountain* (tel. 704/733–4337 or 800/468–7325) is a must. Known for a rocky profile that resembles an old man, it stands 5,964 feet tall and has a mile-high swinging bridge; hiking trails; an "environmental habitat" for bear, deer, and other animals; and a nature center with a restaurant and movie theater. *Mt. Mitchell* (Blue Ridge Pkwy., tel. 704/675–4611)—at 6,684 feet the highest point east of the Mississippi River—is surrounded by a large state park, with camping and hiking, an observation lounge, tower, and museum. In the heart of Great Smoky Mountains National Park is *Clingmans Dome,* whose 6,643-foot peak is actually in Tennessee.

Thomas Wolfe Memorial (48 Spruce St., Asheville, tel. 704/253–8304). The famous writer's mother operated a boardinghouse at this downtown dwelling. Now a state historic site, it is open for tours.

Restaurants

You can make an evening of dining at **Gabrielle's** (87 Richmond Hill Dr., tel. 704/252–7313), in the Richmond Hill Inn in Asheville; at **The Market Place on Wall Street** (20 Wall St., tel. 704/252–4162), also in Asheville; or at the **Eseeola Lodge** (U.S. 221, tel. 704/733–4311) in Linville. Another option is **Heidi's Swiss Inn** (Rte. 184, Banner Elk, tel. 704/898–5020), which serves authentic Swiss cuisine, or the **Green Park Inn** (U.S. 321, Blowing Rock, tel. 704/295–3141), which some critics number among the best in the mountains.

Tourist Information

Asheville Convention and Visitors Bureau (151 Haywood St., Box 1011, Asheville, NC 28802, tel. 704/258–6109 or 800/257–1300). **North Carolina High Country Host** (701 Blowing Rock Rd., Boone, NC 28607, tel. 704/264–1299 or 800/438–7500).

Reservation Service

North Carolina Bed & Breakfast Assn. (318 W. Queen St., Hillsborough, NC 27278, tel. 800/849–5392).

Cedar Crest Inn

The Cedar Crest Inn, its yellow paint and high-pitched roof exuding warmth and cheer, sits on a hill overlooking Biltmore Village. The Victorian inn has close ties to Vanderbilt's 250-room French château. Built in 1891 by the craftsmen who worked on the famous mansion, Cedar Crest has the same hand-carved mantels, beveled glass, and other fine detailing found in Biltmore.

Innkeepers Jack and Barbara McEwan, former residents of Racine, Wisconsin, looked for a year and a half before finding Cedar Crest, which in 1930 had been converted into a guest house. The McEwans restored it in 1984, removing 13 layers of wallpaper and adding several bathrooms. Barbara did the decorating herself, using family heirlooms and antiques and filling in with pieces found at estate sales; Jack drew upon the management skills he had learned as a hotelier; and the McEwans' grown-up children, all talented musicians, found themselves entertaining guests at afternoon tea.

Dark, rich paneling and wide ornate window frames are set off with white lace curtains in the common rooms downstairs. Each of the guest rooms has its own Victorian character, accomplished with lace and silk fabrics, soft colors, and wallpapers. The Queen Anne Room, which has shirred fabric on the ceiling, is a favorite; another is the Garden Room, with a brass bed, mosquito netting, and white linen bedding. Honeymooners and anniversary couples love the guest cottage. The Celebrity Suite has a large bedroom, sitting room, and a whirlpool.

Visitors enjoy gathering around the fire in the parlor; in the formal dining room, where the McEwans serve breakfast; or in the study, which has a coffee table made from a Washington, DC, street grating. Depending on the season, iced tea, lemonade, pressed cider, hot chocolate, or wassail is served in the parlor or library. When the weather is warm, guests often team up for badminton or croquet; otherwise, they like to stay indoors reading or playing cards and board games. In addition to visiting the Biltmore estate, guests can explore the sights and shops in the village, including All Souls Episcopal Church, which George Vanderbilt had built in 1896 for his daughter's wedding.

Address: *674 Biltmore Ave., Asheville, NC 28803, tel. 704/252–1389.*
Accommodations: *8 double rooms with baths, 1 suite, 1 cottage.*
Amenities: *Air-conditioning, cable TV in study, phones in rooms.*
Rates: *$115–$185; Continental breakfast, afternoon tea. AE, D, MC, V.*
Restrictions: *No smoking, no pets, 2-night minimum weekends and holidays.*

The Greystone Inn

In the early 1900s, the rich arrived in their private railcars to vacation at secluded Lake Toxaway. Modern travelers head for The Greystone Inn, a Swiss-style mansion on 3,000 acres that's on the National Register of Historic Places. Built in 1915, the house was converted to an inn in 1985 by Tim Lovelace, a retired financial consultant, who later added Hillmont, a 12-room annex.

Guests can choose between staying in the historic house, which has casement windows, glass doorknobs, and antique beds, and enjoying the modern luxury of the Hillmont Annex, whose rooms contain fireplaces with gas logs, king-size beds, and private balconies overlooking the lake. These contemporary rooms are quite spacious. There are floral-print chairs by the fireplace and leather chairs by the window, and the huge bathrooms have large whirlpool baths and separate, freestanding glass showers. The Presidential Suite, the former library, is the most impressive of the mansion rooms, highlighted by soaring 25-foot ceilings, floor-to-ceiling bookcases, a huge stone fireplace, and a sleeping loft. The Firestone Room, formerly the kitchen, still has a wood-burning stove, a stone fireplace, and exposed beams.

In the dining facility, open only to guests, vast windows frame the mountains and the lake. Chef Chris McDonald serves Southern cuisine with a modern twist, such as trout Ponchartrain and delicate baby corn fritters. The six-course gourmet dinner and lavish breakfast are included.

Greystone guests can play tennis and golf at the adjoining Lake Toxaway Country Club and go swimming, waterskiing, windsurfing, sailing, and canoeing on the lake. Many guests hike or ride horses (from a nearby livery stable) to Mills Creek Falls or Deep Ford Falls for a picnic. Rainy days are devoted to bridge and reading.

After tea, a social highlight of the day, Tim conducts animated lake tours on the *Mountain Lily II.* Everyone gathers in the library lounge for hors d'oeuvres and cocktails before dinner.

Address: *Greystone La., Lake Toxaway, NC 28747, tel. 704/966-4700 or 800/824-5766, fax 704/862-5689.*
Accommodations: *33 double rooms with baths.*
Amenities: *Air-conditioning, ceiling fans, cable TV with VCR and phones in rooms, turndown service, morning newspaper, airport transportation available.*
Rates: *$270–$450; MAP, afternoon tea, hors d'oeuvres, all sports except golf. AE, MC, V.*
Restrictions: *No pets, 2-night minimum weekends, closed Jan.–Mar.*

The Pine Crest Inn

Jennifer and Jeremy Wainwright, owners of this inn nestled under the pines in the hunt country, are originally from England. In 1990 they bought the 10-building complex and refurbished the rooms, retaining the charm and architectural integrity. Although relatively new to innkeeping, they have traveled enough to know what guests expect and appreciate. Good beds, excellent food, peace and quiet, lots of books, and stuffed teddy bears are but a few of the components of their success.

Pine Crest was established in 1917 by Carter Brown, a local horseman who was instrumental in making Tryon a riding and fox-hunting center. The main inn, a two-story green-and-white frame building, is on the National Register of Historic Places. The lobby is decorated in rich, dark fabrics, leather, brass, wood, and pictures of hunting; the lounge is called, appropriately, the Fox and Hounds Bar. Among the small buildings around the main inn are a one-room log cabin, a three-bedroom stone cottage, and a two-bedroom woodcutter's cottage, all dating from the time the inn was built.

Many of the rooms at The Pine Crest sport a Ralph Lauren or English-cottage look. Sporting prints, fluffy comforters, hardwood floors, and wood-burning fireplaces give the guest rooms a welcoming, comfortable feeling. Swayback Cottage and Woodcutter Cottage offer the ultimate in privacy; F. Scott Fitzgerald stayed in Swayback in 1930.

Meals at the inn are something to write home about. Chef Bill Squires is famous for his rack of lamb, grilled mountain trout, roast duck, and Maryland crab cakes, served in the tavernlike dining room. (He'll even prepare a picnic lunch if you request it the evening before.) Because of its proximity to the Foothills Equestrian Nature Center and its affiliation with the Tryon Country Club, Pine Crest offers a full array of recreational and social activities—from golf and tennis to tailgating at the annual Block House Steeplechase.

Blending with the older structures is a new conference center that can accommodate groups of up to 30.

Address: *Pine Crest La., Tryon, NC 28782, tel. 704/859–9135 or 800/633–3001, fax 704/859–9135.*
Accommodations: *30 double rooms with baths, 2 cottages.*
Amenities: *Air-conditioning, cable TV and phones in rooms, fireplaces in most rooms.*
Rates: *$125–$165, 3-bedroom cottage $450; full breakfast. AE, D, DC, MC, V.*
Restrictions: *No smoking in dining room, no pets, 2-night minimum steeplechase weekend, 3-night minimum Thanksgiving, closed first 3 weeks of Jan.*

Richmond Hill Inn

As a young man, Thomas Wolfe used to look up at the Richmond Hill mansion and wonder what kind of people lived in such a glorious place. Years later he would meet members of the Pearson family and write that they were as grand as the house itself. The Queen Anne–style mansion was built in 1889 as the home of Richmond Pearson, a diplomat and statesman, and his wife, Gabrielle. It had long since fallen into disrepair when Jake and Marge Michel of Greensboro bought the home in 1987 and invested $3 million to restore it. The Richmond Hill Inn opened in 1989, and the Michels' daughter, Susan Michel-Robinson, is the innkeeper.

The Michels retained not only the elegant architecture but also the gracious ways of the past, from valet service at the carriage entrance to afternoon games of croquet on the manicured lawn. Afternoon tea is served in the sweeping oak-paneled entry hall, where velvet-covered Victorian chairs are grouped around the fireplace under the benevolent gaze of Gabrielle herself. The restored portrait is one of many Pearson family items that the Michels have recovered. Guests can relax on the porches or in a cozy oak-paneled library.

The 12 guest rooms in the mansion are named for historic figures of the era and North Carolina writers with Asheville ties, and are furnished in antiques, such as canopy beds and claw-foot tubs. The most popular is the romantic Gabrielle Pearson Room, where the canopy bed is draped in peach-colored fabric and lace curtains grace the windows. The Chief Justice Suite has a whirlpool bath, wet bar, and fireplace with gas logs. In a more contemporary style, the Croquet Cottages also have fireplaces with gas logs as well as pencil-post beds and private porches with rocking chairs.

Breakfast is served in the elegant cherry-paneled dining room named for Gabrielle—also one of the best restaurants in Asheville for dinner. Fresh fruit crepes and exotic omelets are common breakfast fare, while dinner entrées include grilled medallions of antelope with smoked wild-boar sausage. And just to make sure you really feel pampered, the turndown service includes fresh flowers, a box of chocolates, and a gift to take home.

Address: *87 Richmond Hill Dr., Asheville, NC 28806, tel. 704/252–7313 or 800/545–9238, fax 704/252–8726.*
Accommodations: *12 double rooms with baths, 9 cottages.*
Amenities: *Air-conditioning, cable TV and phones in rooms.*
Rates: *$125–$295; full breakfast, afternoon tea. AE, MC, V.*
Restrictions: *No smoking, no pets, 2-night minimum weekends, closed 2 weeks in Jan.*

The Inn at Taylor House

In a green mountain valley dotted with grazing Charolais cattle and Christmas trees, this inn, built in 1911 and looking as fresh as the daisies, is still an attention-grabber. Passing motorists stop to ask if there is a vacancy at the white house with wraparound porches. Guests are also captivated by the miniature goats kept in little Swiss barns on the grounds.

Chip Schwab, who used to operate the Truffles Cooking School in Atlanta, runs the inn with her husband, Roland, a fifth-generation innkeeper who graduated from École Hôtelière de Lausanne. The Schwabs opened the inn in 1987; filled it with their eclectic antiques, Oriental rugs, and art; and turned the old smokehouse into a gift shop.

Guests sleep under duvets and then sit down to sour cream pancakes or crab hash with orange hollandaise. Valle Crucis has one of the hottest attractions around—the Mast general store—more than 100 years old and still going strong.

Address: *Rte. 194 (Box 713), Valle Crucis, NC 28691, tel. 704/963–5581, fax 704/963–5818.*
Accommodations: *5 double rooms with baths, 2 suites.*
Amenities: *Air-conditioning on 3rd floor, ceiling fans in rooms.*
Rates: *$110–$145; full breakfast. MC, V.*
Restrictions: *No smoking indoors, no pets, 2-night minimum weekends, closed Jan.–Mar.*

The Lodge on Lake Lure

This lakeside mountain lodge, which provided R&R for North Carolina highway patrolmen in the '30s, now attracts honeymooners and vacationers, who love its rustic elegance. Texans Robin and Jack Stanier jumped at the property when they were scouting for inns in 1989; he had worked in the steel industry, she in oil. Though they had little experience, they love what they do, especially the afternoons spent on the veranda or on the deck at the lake.

Robin's breakfast is served on the sun porch, to the strains of recorded dulcimer music. The Staniers provide books and games, and there is plenty of space outside to be by yourself. The great room has a beamed cathedral ceiling, piano, and an enormous stone fireplace. Antiques

and items from their travels—one is a Malaysian temple gong—add interest in the library, where you can watch TV or read a magazine. Wormy chestnut paneling throughout the inn lends beauty and warmth, as do the quilts and white eyelet comforters in the guest rooms.

Address: *Charlotte Dr. (Rte. 1, Box 529-A), Lake Lure, NC 28746, tel. 704/625–2789 or 800/733–2785.*
Accommodations: *10 double rooms with baths, 1 suite.*
Amenities: *Air-conditioning in suite, ceiling fans, cable TV in library, pay phone in hall; boats, canoes.*
Rates: *$80–$115; full breakfast. AE, D, MC, V.*
Restrictions: *No smoking indoors, no pets, 2-night minimum weekends, 2- or 3-night minimum holidays.*

The Randolph House

When Ruth Randolph Adams and her husband, Bill, retired from their professions in Atlanta in 1970, they wanted to share their Bryson City family home with others. Ruth is a descendant of John Randolph, who married the only daughter of Captain Amos Frye, the attorney and land baron who built this 12-gabled mansion in 1895. Now on the National Register of Historic Places, The Randolph House contains some of the original furnishings and dishes, and guests sleep on beds that have been in the family for years.

Ruth's Southern gourmet cooking is acclaimed far and wide, and guests return year after year for her country breakfasts, fresh vegetables, and homemade cobblers and breads. The inn accepts nonguests for breakfast and dinner if they make reservations. Bill, a natural with people, enjoys his role as host. Guests may rock on the stone-pillared veranda, go white-water rafting, or hike in the Great Smoky Mountains National Park.

Address: *Fryemont Rd. (Box 816), Bryson City, NC 28713, tel. 704/488–3472 or 404/938–2268 (Nov.–mid-Apr.).*
Accommodations: *3 double rooms with baths, 4 doubles share 2 baths.*
Amenities: *Air-conditioning in 6 rooms, window fans.*
Rates: *$65–$85, full breakfast; $110–$130, MAP. AE, D, MC, V.*
Restrictions: *No smoking indoors, no pets, 2-night minimum holiday weekends and Oct., closed Nov.–mid-Apr.*

The Waverly Inn

Hendersonville's oldest inn has been serving guests for more than nine decades and is on the National Register of Historic Places. The present owners, John and Diane Sheiry, have breathed new life into the old place, putting into practice all the skills and knowledge they acquired in the Atlanta hotel industry and staging special murder-mystery weekends, wine tastings, and romance packages.

The three-story inn with a wrap-around porch and upper balcony sits on a small lot overlooking busy North Main Street. Waverly print wallpaper and curtains complement the antiques and family treasures. Named for native plants and flowers, the guest rooms have four-poster canopy and brass beds, and bathrooms have claw-foot tubs and pedestal sinks. The Mountain Magnolia Suite has a king-size canopy bed and a 6-foot claw-foot tub. Complimentary refreshments are available around the clock, and John's cooked-to-order breakfasts get rave reviews.

Address: *783 N. Main St., Hendersonville, NC 28792, tel. 704/693–9193 or 800/537–8195, fax 704/692–1010.*
Accommodations: *13 double rooms with baths.*
Amenities: *Air-conditioning, ceiling fans in most rooms, cable TV in parlor and 4 rooms.*
Rates: *$79–$165; full breakfast. AE, D, MC, V.*
Restrictions: *Smoking in bedrooms only, no pets, 2-night minimum holidays.*

South Carolina

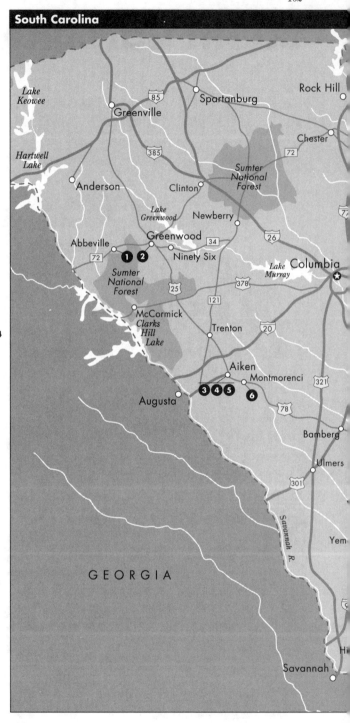

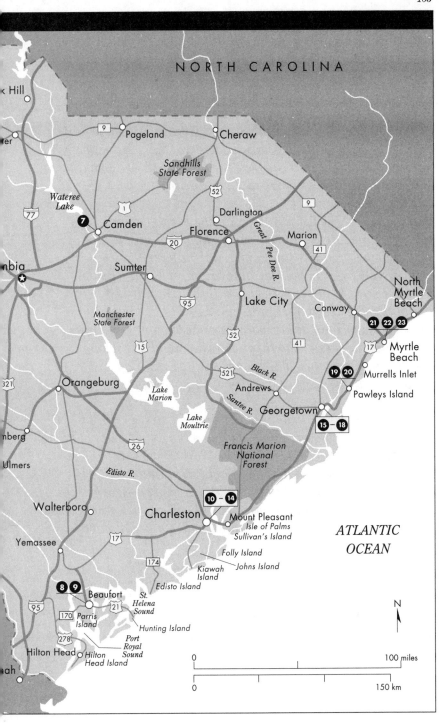

Myrtle Beach and the Grand Strand

The extended necklace that is the Grand Strand begins at Little River on the North Carolina border and reaches about 60 miles south to Georgetown, a Colonial settlement of the 1500s. The jewels dotting the Strand from end to end—glitzy, neon, and natural at the same time—are the oceanside condos and hotels, golf courses, tennis courts, water parks, amusement centers, shops, and restaurants.

Myrtle Beach, the largest town on the Strand, is comparable to Miami Beach in the '50s. It has high-rise hotels, nightclubs, upscale restaurants, and bumper-to-bumper traffic. No longer is the tide of tourism tied to the golden days between Memorial Day and Labor Day; it is a year-round flood. Though the region still draws many visitors from the Carolinas, it has become a mecca for Canadians and midwesterners, who think nothing of a little nippy weather in November. The beach is the area's biggest attraction, with miles and miles of sugary sand.

The Grand Strand, also famous for golf courses (more than 80) and tennis courts (about 200), has the distinction of being the "Miniature Golf Capital of the World," with at least 50 courses, each new one more outrageous than the last. (Be sure to see Hawaiian Rumble in North Myrtle Beach, with its 45-foot mountain that rumbles, lets off vapors, and erupts fire every 20 minutes.) The Strand is also a great place for fishing, particularly in fall, and anglers vie for cash prizes in contests like the Arthur Smith King Mackerel Tournament, one of the world's largest. Shoppers flock to beachwear/souvenir shops, outlet centers like Waccamaw Pottery, and Barefoot Landing, an enormous shopping center built over marshland and water in North Myrtle Beach.

Places to Go, Sights to See

The **Bellefield Nature Center Museum** (U.S. 17, north of Georgetown, tel. 803/546–4623), a field station for botanical and marine research, has aquariums, terrariums, and a saltwater touch tank. It offers weekly tours of its 1,300-acre wildlife refuge and Waccamaw River excursions.

Georgetown has a historic district dating to 1729, where time has stood still; there are more than 50 early buildings and sites. The area was settled by the Spanish in 1526, claimed by the English 200 years later, and by the mid-1800s was the rice-producing capital of America. Today it is famous for ghost-busting tours of old haunts and for *Ghosts of the Coast,* a theatrical production staged at the Strand Theatre on Front Street every other summer. On a self-guided tour (information at the Chamber of Commerce, 102 Broad St., tel. 803/546–8437 or 800/777–7705), you'll see the *Harbor Walk,* a boardwalk lined with shops, galleries, and restaurants; the *Rice Museum* (Front and Screven Sts., tel. 803/546–7423), for the history of rice and indigo production; the 1721 *Prince George Winyah Episcopal Church* (Broad and Highmarket Sts.); and the *Harold Kaminski House* (1003 Front St., tel. 803/546–7706), a restored seafarers' house (ca. 1760).

At **Hampton Plantation State Park** (off U.S. 17, 15 mi south of Georgetown, tel. 803/546–9361) you can tour mansion, rice fields, and grounds.

Hopsewee Plantation (off U.S. 17, 12 mi south of Georgetown, tel. 803/543–7891), a 1740 rice plantation, has tours year-round.

Murrells Inlet. At *Brookgreen Gardens* (U.S. 17, tel. 803/237–4218), a sculpture garden and wildlife zoo, more than 500 works by the likes of Augustus Saint-Gaudens, Daniel Chester French, and Frederic Remington are displayed amid formal English landscaping. *Huntington Beach State Park* (U.S. 17, tel. 803/237–4440), south of town, is home to alligators and other wildlife. Besides camping, fishing, hiking, and beachcombing, you can tour Atalaya, the 30-room Moorish-style mansion.

Myrtle Beach. The *Myrtle Beach Pavilion* (9th Ave. N and Ocean Blvd., tel. 803/448–6456), a cluster of amusements, shops, and restaurants, is the heart of the Grand Strand. It has a pipe organ with figures that move, an antique merry-go-round, and Big Eli, the Ferris wheel. *Ripley's Believe It or Not Museum* (N. Ocean Blvd. at 9th Ave., tel. 803/448–2331) has more than 750 oddities. *Myrtle Beach National Wax Museum* (1000 N. Ocean Blvd., tel. 803/448–9921) displays animated wax figures of renown.

Pawleys Island, south of Murrells Inlet, originally a summer retreat of wealthy rice planters, is one of the last vestiges of the Strand's old days. Scattered amid marsh and dunes are elegantly shabby cottages and a handful of inns—places where going barefoot is still okay. The 4-mile island, said to be haunted, is famous for its hand-tied hammocks.

Restaurants

On the Strand seafood is king. At the clusters of restaurants in Calabash, just across the North Carolina line, and in Murrells Inlet, where the fishing boats come in, it is served any way you like it, but the most popular is "Calabash-style," lightly battered and deep-fried. **The Sea Captain's House** (3002 N. Ocean Blvd., Myrtle Beach, tel. 803/448–8082), in a former bed-and-breakfast on the ocean, has the best fresh seafood on the Grand Strand. **Marina Raw Bar** (U.S. 17, North Myrtle Beach, tel. 803/249–3972), a casual eatery, offers fresh oysters, clams, and other seafood. At Myrtle Beach's north end, where U.S. 17 divides, is Restaurant Row. For elegant dining here, try **Chesapeake House** (9918 N. Kings Hwy., tel. 803/449–3231) or **Chestnut Hill** (9922 N. Kings Hwy., tel. 803/449–3984). **Rice Planters** (6707 N. Kings Hwy., tel. 803/449–3456) serves fresh seafood, quail, and steaks grilled to order in a homey, candlelit setting. In Pawleys Island, **Frank's** (U.S. 17, tel. 803/237–3030) serves reputedly the best Southern dinners on the coast. A few hundred yards away, **Tyler's Cove** (The Hammock Shops, U.S. 17, tel. 803/237–4848) churns out such unusual Low Country fare as fried Carolina alligator and spicy Cajun chicken with a jalapeño honey dressing. At the **Rice Paddy** (408 Duke St., Georgetown, tel. 803/546–2021), local solons settle in at lunchtime for homemade vegetable soup, garden-fresh salads, and sandwiches; dinners are memorable, too. Overlooking the Sampit River, Georgetown's other top eatery, the **River Room** (801 Front St., tel. 803/527–4110), specializes in char-grilled fish, seafood pastas, and steaks. For lunch try the shrimp and grits.

Nightlife

Southern Country Nights (301 U.S. 17, Surfside Beach, tel. 803/238–8888), *The Dixie Jubilee* (701 Main St., North Myrtle Beach, tel. 803/249–4444), *Alabama* (4750 U.S. 17, Barefoot Landing, North Myrtle Beach, tel. 803/272–1111 or 800/342–2262), and *The Carolina Opry* (8901 U.S. 17, Myrtle Beach, tel. 803/449–6779) are live shows in flourishing music halls. Dolly Parton's *Dixie Stampede* (8901-B U.S. 17 Business, Myrtle Beach, tel. 803/497–9700) is a music show and four-course "country" dinner. *Studebaker's* (U.S. 17 at 21st Ave. N, tel. 803/448–9747) is the place in Myrtle Beach to shag and listen to beach music. In North Myrtle Beach try *Duck's* (229 Main St., tel. 803/249–3858), *Harold's* (2301 N. Ocean Blvd., tel. 803/249–5601), or *The Spanish Galleon* (100 Main St., tel. 803/249–1047). Shagging contests are popular; each spring and fall thousands attend the Society of Stranders reunion in Myrtle Beach.

Tourist Information

Georgetown County Chamber of Commerce and Information Center (102 Broad St., Box 1776, Georgetown, SC 29442, tel. 803/546–8436 or 800/777–7705). **Myrtle Beach Area Chamber of Commerce and Information Center** (1301 N. Kings Hwy., Box 2115, Myrtle Beach, SC 29578–2115, tel.

803/626–7444 or 800/356–3016, ext. 132). **Pawleys Island Chamber of Commerce** (U.S. 17, Box 569, Pawleys Island, SC 29585, tel. 803/237–1921).

Chesterfield Inn

To stay at the Chesterfield Inn, built more than half a century ago, is to get a sense of Myrtle Beach in the old days. (The inn's motel rooms, though they have oceanfront balconies, lack authenticity.)

The long, three-story brick building facing the ocean appeals to the type of beachcombers who enjoy being with family and friends—the ones who aren't looking for bright lights and glamour. The lobby, with a fireplace, has changed very little over the years and is the perfect place for reading, playing board games, and working puzzles. Guests sit on the verandas to catch the ocean breezes and play on the grassy area between the inn and the beach. Golf and entertainment packages are available.

The history of the Chesterfield Inn dates to 1937, when the Chapman family and some friends bought an existing house and opened it to guests. The Chapmans bought out the others and in 1946, after the end of World War II, built the present inn, adding the motel block of rooms about 30 years ago. The inn is now owned by Bob Chapman and his daughter Julia. It was instantly popular, being the second hotel on the beach to have private baths and phones. By today's standards, the guest rooms, with their varied, old-fashioned furnishings, are simple and plain, but that doesn't deter the families who have been coming here for five generations. The rooms all have two double beds, and the ones in the main inn are wallpapered.

The food at the Chesterfield is dependable, and most guests choose the Modified American Plan. Meals are served family style on starched white tablecloths in the paneled dining room overlooking the ocean; the same waiter will serve you throughout your stay. The dining room is open to the public; the traditional Southern menu features beef, poultry, pork, and a different variety of fish each evening. Breakfast is one of the best bargains on the beach.

Address: *700 N. Ocean Blvd. (Box 218), Myrtle Beach, SC 29578, tel. 803/448–3177 or 800/392–3869, fax 803/626–4736.*
Accommodations: *31 double rooms with baths in old section, 26 doubles with baths in new section (6 with kitchenettes).*
Amenities: *Air-conditioning, cable TV and phones in rooms; pool, shuffleboard.*
Rates: *$71–$99, breakfast extra; $107–$132, MAP. AE, D, MC, V.*
Restrictions: *No pets, closed Dec.–Jan.*

Sea View Inn

I n the morning you can put your feet on the lye-washed hardwood floor and rush to the window to catch a breath of the fresh air that filters through the starched curtains. You might wander out to drink your early morning coffee on the big screened-in porch, or you may take it into the living room, where there's always a fire on cool days. This is the seaside as it was meant to be— unadulterated by air-conditioning, neon, and such citified comforts as wall-to-wall carpeting. Built in the 1930s and rebuilt in the 1950s after being devastated by Hurricane Hazel, the Sea View is a no-frills two-story beachside boardinghouse with long porches. There is also a six-room air-conditioned cottage on the marsh.

Page Oberlin, who once ran a large restaurant, took over as innkeeper about 18 years ago. A stay at her "barefoot paradise," though certainly not for everyone, is a very special experience (in high season, the minimum stay is a week). Don't expect any programming here, unless you're attending one of the annual painting workshops or wellness retreats (which feature meditation, yoga, massage, health foods, and guest speakers). Meals, served family style—with grits, gumbo, crab salad, pecan pie, and oyster pie—are really the only scheduled events. The time is yours—to read, collect shells, walk on the beach, or just do nothing. This is life on Pawleys Island.

Each guest room has pickled cypress walls and is simply furnished with a dresser, a double bed and a twin covered with handmade bedspreads from Guatemala, and art from the spring workshop. Each room has a half-bath; showers are down the hall (and also outside for ocean swimmers). All the rooms have a view of the ocean or the marsh, and the design of the building always guarantees a cross breeze. Your program for getting your life in order won't be disturbed here; though the inn has a well-stocked library, the tube is nonexistent, and there's only one phone. There are sailing, golf, and tennis nearby, plus arts-and-crafts shops. And you can always go ghost hunting among the moss-draped live oaks; you might encounter Alice, searching for her engagement ring in the marshes, or the Gray Man, who warns people about approaching storms.

Address: *Myrtle Ave., Pawleys Island, SC 29585, tel. 803/237–4253.*
Accommodations: *Main house: 14 rooms with 1/2 baths; cottage: 4 doubles with 1/2 baths, 1 double and 1 single share 1 bath.*
Amenities: *Phone on back porch.*
Rates: *$140–$170; American Plan. No credit cards.*
Restrictions: *No pets, 2-night minimum May and Sept.–Oct., 1 week minimum June–Aug., closed Nov.–Apr.*

Brustman House

This Colonial-style house in a quiet neighborhood two blocks from the ocean is probably the most restful accommodation in high-energy Myrtle Beach. Innkeeper Wendall Brustman makes you feel at home. He'll pick you up at the airport, chat with you over afternoon sweets, and cook you a gourmet breakfast—the 10-grain pancakes are unforgettable. Wendall, a psychologist, has provided the house with Scandinavian furniture from a store he once owned in his native Minnesota. Goose-down comforters are used on all the beds. One room has rosewood furniture; another is done in Laura Ashley fabrics. The two-bedroom housekeeping suite is nicest of all, its furnishings patterned exactly after those of the King and Queen of Sweden.

A philosophy of health, wholeness, and well-being pervades. You can stroll through the rose garden, borrow the bicycles for a quick ride along the Strand, or just sit and read a book in the gazebo; evenings are devoted to reading, playing the piano, watching TV, and socializing.

Address: *400 25th Ave. S, Myrtle Beach, SC 29577, tel. 803/448–7699 or 800/448–7699, fax 803/626–1500.*
Accommodations: *3 double rooms with baths, 1 housekeeping suite.*
Amenities: *Air-conditioning, phones, and ceiling fans in rooms, TV with VCR in lounge and suite; badminton, croquet.*
Rates: *$65–$80; full breakfast, afternoon refreshments. No credit cards.*
Restrictions: *No smoking, no pets.*

DuPre House

Mike and Roberta Streppone opened this inn to cater to families. Planning a romantic night on the town? Your hosts will gladly baby-sit with a little notice. There's a playground and basketball hoop out back, a large pool, a games and TV room, and reproduction antique furniture that's as sturdy and practical as it is elegant. Roberta is a school principal, while Mike, former director of food and beverage at the Waldorf Astoria, runs the B&B. Both are chatty and enthusiastic, willing to help out but unobtrusive. Walking through the immaculate rooms, with shiny, hardwood floors, plush blue carpeting, and crisp white walls, it's hard to believe the house dates to 1734. Bedrooms are new and neat. Two have gas fireplaces, and all have ceiling fans and queen-size four-

posters. The third-floor rooms, which have pitched ceilings, are coziest. One of the second-floor rooms opens onto a large porch. Breakfast includes omelets made to order, French toast, and fresh fruit and juices. For an extra cost, picnic lunches and dinners can be arranged.

Address: *921 Prince St., Georgetown, SC 29440, tel. 803/546–0298 or 800/921–3877.*
Accommodations: *4 double rooms with baths.*
Amenities: *Air-conditioning, TV in lounge; bicycles, yard games.*
Rates: *$70–$90; full breakfast, afternoon refreshments. MC, V.*
Restrictions: *No pets.*

King's Inn at Georgetown

Marilyn Eckerdt, a decorating wizard, has single-handedly transformed what was a dilapidated but stunning Federal home—occupied during the Civil War by a Yankee commandant and later run as a boardinghouse—into an elaborate inn with formal, Empire furnishings. In Georgetown's historic district, the inn hardly resembles the simple four-plan Federal that was built in 1825. Long piazzas were added in the 1840s, elaborate French plaster molding in the 1850s, and entire rooms since. Outgoing Marilyn, who hails from Missouri, has searched for the perfect fabrics and furniture. Long, flowing drapes and lace curtains bracket many windows; walls are painted in striking hues, such as lavender and lemon yellow; and many rooms are anchored by Empire antiques: credenzas, settees, and crystal tear-drop chandeliers and sconces. The large bedrooms contain gilt-framed paintings, canopy beds, and Oriental rugs over the authentic heart-pine floors. An art deco room is for those who miss the 20th century. Only the breakfast room, with a porch, latticework walls, and a gas fireplace, is informal. Breakfast treats include pecan French toast and a piping-hot sausage soufflé.

Address: *230 Broad St., Georgetown, SC 29440, tel. 803/527–6937.*
Accommodations: *7 double rooms with baths.*
Amenities: *TV in lounge; lap pool.*
Rates: *$75–$115; full breakfast. AE, D, DC, MC, V.*
Restrictions: *No smoking, no pets.*

Litchfield Plantation

One of the most photographed plantations in the state, Litchfield offers an authentic inn experience and resort amenities. Missing are innkeepers; you show up, get your key from the gatekeeper, proceed past gnarled live oaks to this dramatic Georgian mansion, and let yourself in. The sensation that you've broken into somebody's home fades in about an hour.

Once the region was the rice capital of North America; almost half the nation's rice was produced here in the mid-19th century. The house, built with rice money, sits a couple of miles off Pawleys Island's golden seashore on the interior banks of the Wacca-maw River, whose dikes and canals once cross-stitched these fields. Suites are luxurious and quite large. The Ballroom Suite has a fireplace, Jacuzzi, long and stately living room fashioned out of the old ballroom, and compact kitchen. Shelves are packed with art and history books. Because the house is on the property of, though hidden from, the major resort of the same name, the amenities entail full use of a beach club, tennis courts, a pool and cabana, and a fine restaurant. Golf is nearby.

Address: *River Rd. (Box 290), Pawleys Island, SC 29585, tel. 803/237–4286 or 800/869–1410.*
Accommodations: *4 suites.*
Amenities: *Air-conditioning, cable TV, and phones in rooms.*
Rates: *$155–$190; Continental breakfast. AE, MC, V.*
Restrictions: *No smoking, no pets.*

Mansfield Plantation

As you drive up the tortuous, bumpy road to the 760-acre plantation, past slave quarters and under the requisite canopy of moss-draped live oaks, you sense what a plantation must have looked like 200 years ago. The original 1812 "big house," where breakfast is served, is actually rather small but still imposing. It has fine Federal detailing and a tile roof. Guest accommodations are spread among three historic redbrick outbuildings: the north guest house, the old kitchen, and the former schoolhouse. Rooms have hardwood floors, detailed molding, excellent reproduction period antiques, and walk-in closets. Some have nonworking coal fireplaces, too. Except for air-conditioning, the tone is rustic; there are no phones or TVs, and the bathrooms are simple and

small. This is not the Ritz-Carlton passing itself off as a plantation but as close to a real pre–Civil War experience as is possible. The property backs onto the Black River, which fueled phenomenal rice production. A variety of outdoor activities can be arranged, and a beach is nearby. Dinner and evening refreshments cost extra.

Address: *U.S. 701 (Rte. 8, Box 590), Georgetown, SC 29440, tel. 803/546–6961 or 800/355–3223.*
Accommodations: *8 double rooms with baths.*
Amenities: *Air-conditioning in rooms.*
Rates: *$75–$95; full breakfast. MC, V.*
Restrictions: *No smoking indoors, pets allowed by arrangement only.*

Serendipity, An Inn

Toronto natives Terry and Sheila Johnson have been visiting Myrtle Beach for more than 20 years. When Cos and Ellen Ficarra, who built Serendipity, retired in 1994, the Johnsons took over this Spanish villa–style inn about 300 yards from the beach. Their daughter, Debra, handles much of the day-to-day operations; her first few months were spent sprucing up the lovely gardens and keeping the already clean rooms spotless. New fixtures and a few new furnishings have been added, but the characterful decor of wrought-iron birdcages, wooden statuary, and quirky bric-a-brac remains. And no, the Johnsons have no plans to install those irksome contraptions known as telephones. Each room is tied to a particular period (e.g., the art deco Roaring '20s Room).

Guests gravitate to the Garden Room, the gathering place for breakfast and conversation. You can munch on boiled eggs, muffins, homemade banana bread, and fresh fruit salad before dashing off to any of the Strand's myriad amusements.

Address: *407 71st Ave. N, Myrtle Beach, SC 29572, tel. 803/449–5268 or 800/762–3229.*
Accommodations: *12 double rooms with baths, 2 housekeeping suites.*
Amenities: *Air-conditioning, TV and refrigerators in rooms; pool, hot tub, ping-pong, shuffleboard.*
Rates: *$67–$110. Continental breakfast. AE, MC, V.*
Restrictions: *No smoking in breakfast room, no pets.*

1790 House

Transplanted Californians Patricia and John Wiley bought this restored house in the historic district in 1992. Built just after the Revolutionary War, it suits those who appreciate the feel of staying with old friends and those seeking privacy. For the latter, the detached cottage has a brick floor and private brick patio, Oriental rugs, a small refrigerator and dry bar, and a huge bathroom with Jacuzzi. In the main house a cozy suite has a pitched roof and dormer windows; with a daybed in a separate room, it's perfect for families. One room has a working fireplace, and several have nonworking ones. Fine craftsmanship is revealed throughout, from heart-pine floors to hand-carved dentil work and moldings. Furniture is a mix of Victorian and Colonial antiques and reproductions. Now retired, John was a printing executive and Patricia was a legal administrator. They will happily offer ideas for local jaunts or will leave you alone. Breakfasts such as apple Dutch baby (a rich soufflé) and oven-baked French toast spiked with orange peel and Triple Sec are for sweet tooths.

Address: *630 Highmarket St., Georgetown, SC 29440, tel. 803/546–4821.*
Accommodations: *4 double rooms, 1 suite, 1 cottage.*
Amenities: *Air-conditioning, TV in rooms on request; bicycles.*
Rates: *$70–$115; full breakfast. AE, D, MC, V.*
Restrictions: *Smoking on veranda only, no pets, 2-night minimum holiday weekends.*

Charleston and the Low Country

At first glimpse, historic Charleston and Beaufort (the state's second-oldest town), in South Carolina's storied Low Country, appear stopped in time. But make no mistake: Both cities bustle with 20th-century purpose, past and present meshing gently.

Founded in 1670 by eight English lord-proprietors and named for Charles II, Charleston has over the centuries endured the Civil War, fires, earthquakes, and hurricanes. Mariners still use Charleston's church spires to find their way to port. Along the Battery (pronounced Bah-try in Charlestonese), handsome balconied mansions line the point of a narrow peninsula bounded by the Ashley and Cooper rivers. Here one of the nation's largest historic districts preserves scores of house museums, churches, private houses, and commercial and municipal buildings. During the spring and fall historic house tours, you can get a glimpse of the past, as you're welcomed into the homes and gardens of the sixth- or seventh-generation descendants of the original owners. In late May and early June, Charleston hosts the international Spoleto Festival USA, founded in 1977 by Gian Carlo Menotti, featuring concerts, dance, theater, and the visual arts.

In this mild climate, you can play golf virtually year-round, at public courses like Oak Point, Charleston Municipal, and Shadowmoss, as well as at some resort courses on a space-available basis, including Wild Dunes and Kiawah Island. Public beaches are open from mid-April through most of October; there's surf fishing at most of them and deep-sea fishing charters at Charleston Marina and Wild Dunes.

From Charleston, U.S. 17 winds south through the heart of the Low Country, where seaside islands are separated from the mainland by extensive salt marshes and meandering estuaries. Rivers with lyrical Indian names like Edisto,

Ashepoo, Combahee, Coosaw, and Coosawatchie flow through the coastal plains and empty into the Atlantic Ocean. Indigo and rice were once the mainstays of this region; then came Sea Island cotton, followed by produce crops. Now Beaufort (pronounced Bew-furt) and nearby towns are centers of the oyster, shrimp, and crab industry.

Once called "the wealthiest, most aristocratic, and cultivated town of its size in America," Beaufort was established in about 1710. The handsome mansions of wealthy planters and merchants still line its streets, contributing to a delightful 19th-century ambience. As word has spread, increasing numbers of vacationers have begun to visit serene, sunny Beaufort, and many of them have chosen to settle here, as have personnel from nearby military bases, making Beaufort something of a retirement center.

Places to Go, Sights to See

Beaches. There are public beaches at Beachwalker Park on Kiawah Island, at Folly Beach on Folly Island, and at Sullivan's Island.

Beaufort Museum (713 Craven St., tel. 803/525–7077). Housed in a 1795 neo-Gothic arsenal, the museum displays prehistoric relics, Indian pottery, Revolutionary War and Civil War artifacts, and regional decorative arts.

Charleston Museum (360 Meeting St., tel. 803/722–2996). The nation's oldest municipal museum (1773), now in a handsome contemporary $6 million building, features South Carolina decorative arts, along with natural history, archaeology, and ornithology exhibits.

Charleston's formal gardens explode with azaleas, camellias, daffodils, wisteria, and dogwood from late March into April. *Cypress Gardens* (U.S. 52, 24 mi north of Charleston, tel. 803/553–0515) was created as a freshwater reserve for Dean Hall, a 160-acre rice plantation with moss-draped cypress trees. *Magnolia Plantation and Gardens* (Ashley River Rd., 10 mi west of Charleston, tel. 803/571–1266) was acquired in 1676 by the Draytons, whose 10th-generation descendants still occupy it. The manor house depicts plantation life after the Civil War. The landscaped gardens at *Middleton Place* (Ashley River Rd., 14 mi west of Charleston, tel. 803/556–6020) date to 1741, and the manor house has collections of family silver, furniture, paintings, and historic documents. In the plantation stableyards, Low Country rural life is depicted through displays of tools, artifacts, and crafts demonstrations.

Charleston's historic houses date from the early 1700s and represent a variety of architectural styles. *Drayton Hall* (Ashley River Rd., 9 mi west of Charleston, tel. 803/766–0188), built in 1738–42, is considered the nation's finest example of Georgian Palladian architecture; the *Heyward-Washington House* (87 Church St., tel. 803/722–0354), a 1772 building, has the city's only restored 18th-century kitchen that's open to visitors. The *Joseph Manigault House* (350 Meeting St., tel. 803/723–2926) is the city's first Federal residence. The *Nathaniel Russell House* (51 Meeting St., tel. 803/724–8481) is headquarters of the Historic Charleston Foundation.

Charles Towne Landing State Park (1500 Old Towne Rd., Charleston, tel. 803/852–4200). The idyllic 663-acre site of the original "Charles Towne" settlement has replicas of fortifications, a reconstructed village, beautiful English gardens with bicycle trails and walkways, a large animal park, a hands-on museum about the coastal region, and a replica of a 17th-century trading vessel.

The **Dock Street Theatre** (135 Church St., Charleston, tel. 803/720–3968) combines a reconstructed early Georgian playhouse and the Old Planter's Hotel (ca. 1809), built around the ruins of the nation's first theater building.

Fort Sumter National Monument (Charleston Harbor; boat tours from Patriots Point, Mount Pleasant, and from Municipal Marina, 17 Lockwood Blvd., Charleston, tel. 803/722–1691). Confederate forces captured this massive fort on April 13, 1861, after a 34-hour siege, and its occupation became a symbol of Southern resistance until the end of the Civil War in 1865. The magnificently restored National Park Service site offers historic displays and dioramas, plus guided tours.

Gibbes Museum of Art (135 Meeting St., Charleston, tel. 803/722–2706). The notable American art collection includes 18th- and 19th-century portraits of Carolinians and more than 400 exquisitely detailed miniature portraits.

Market Hall (188 Meeting St., Charleston, tel. 803/723–1541). Home of a Confederate museum run by the Daughters of the Confederacy, this 1841 building was modeled after the Temple of Nike in Athens. The adjacent *Old City Market* contains restaurants and shops, along with old-time vegetable and fruit vendors, a bustling flea market, and the Mount Pleasant craftswomen who are so famous for their handmade sweet-grass baskets.

Old Point, part of Beaufort's 304-acre historic district, is a National Historic Landmark. Some of its many private antebellum houses are open during the spring and fall house-and-garden tours. Two outstanding ones are the *George Elliott House* (1001 Bay St., tel. 803/524–8450), a Greek Revival mansion of 1840, and the *John Mark Verdier House* (801 Bay St., tel. 803/524–6334), a Federal mansion of 1790, where the Marquis de Lafayette was entertained in 1825.

Patriots Point Naval and Maritime Museum (U.S. 17, Mount Pleasant, tel. 803/884–2727). Board the aircraft carrier *Yorktown*, the World War II submarine *Clamagore,* the cutter *Ingham,* and the destroyer *Laffey.*

The **War Memorial Building Museum** (Parris Island U.S. Marine Corps Recruit Depot, tel. 803/525–2951) has collections of vintage uniforms, photographs, and weapons. Visitors may watch actual recruit training on guided or self-guided tours.

Restaurants

Charleston is known for its great restaurants. At **Carolina's** (10 Exchange St., tel. 803/724–3800), a local favorite, you might try the Carolina quail with goat cheese, sun-dried tomatoes, and chutney. **Anson** (12 Anson St., tel. 803/577–0551), a couple of hundred feet north of the Old City Market, serves Thai-influenced American fare in a gilt-trimmed dining room framed by about a dozen magnificent French windows. The hot, new restaurant in town is **Slightly North of Broad** (192 E. Bay St., tel. 803/723–3424), a high-ceilinged haunt with some seats looking directly into the exposed kitchen; the inventive Low Country dishes include sautéed quail filled with herbed chicken mousse and corn-and-crab soup with spinach ravioli. Wonderful meals are also had at **Louis's Charleston Grill** (224 King St., tel. 803/577–4522), where the food is "local, not too fancy," and entrées match a variety of grilled meat and fish fillets with such exotic sauces as pear-walnut conserve and warm cumin vinaigrette. For casual dining and great harbor views, try **California Dreaming** (1 Ashley Pointe Dr., tel. 803/766–1644) for the broiled seafood, barbecued chicken, or Texas-smoked ribs. **Gaulart and Maliclet Cafe Restaurant** (98 Broad St., tel. 803/577–9797) is a fast French eatery featuring soups, salads, and sandwiches. **Shem Creek Bar & Grill** (508 Mill St., tel. 803/884–8102), across the Cooper River in Mount Pleasant, is a great place to sample oysters and fresh local seafoods in a laid-back setting. In Beaufort, guests and nonguests swear by the dinners at the **Rhett House Inn** (*see below*). Also consider **The New Gadsby Tavern** (822 Bay St., tel. 803/525–1800), overlooking the water, which has three dining rooms serving everything from formal Continental meals to tapas and selections from the raw bar.

Tourist Information

Beaufort County Chamber of Commerce (1006 Bay St., Box 910, Beaufort, SC 29901, tel. 803/524–3163). **Charleston Trident Convention and Visitors Bureau** (Box 975, Charleston, SC 29402, tel. 803/577–2510).

Reservation Services

Charleston East Bed and Breakfast League (1031 Tall Pine Rd., Mount Pleasant, SC 29464, tel. 803/884–8208). **Historic Charleston B & B** (60 Broad St., Charleston, SC 29401, tel. 803/722–6606).

Kings Courtyard Inn

If you're a shop-till-you-drop person, you'll love staying at the Kings Courtyard. The inn is wedged between the city's best antiques shops and fashionable boutiques on King Street, one of Charleston's oldest shopping thoroughfares, and is a block from the Old City Market's souvenir shops, restaurants, and crafts vendors. But you don't have to be a shopper to enjoy the Kings Courtyard Inn's universal appeal. The sophisticated traveler will quickly recognize the ambience, service, and respect for privacy that are characteristic here: The inn is much like a small European hotel.

Designed by architect Francie D. Lee and built in 1853, the two structures that compose the Greek Revival inn have the appearance of being only one because of their exterior stucco, which was added after the great earthquake of 1886. The buildings were restored in 1983 by Richard T. Widman, and converted into an inn, which had been their original use. Prior to the Civil War, plantation owners and shipping magnates stayed here when they did business in Charleston. The rooms are furnished with 18th-century reproductions, including canopy beds and French armoires, and decorated in elegant, traditional fabrics, with Oriental rugs, which look wonderful on the original heart-pine floors. There are guest rooms on all three stories. Many of them have pressed-tin ceilings, and 14 have gas-burning fireplaces. Most of the rooms open onto the courtyard; the rest overlook King Street.

Off one of the two inner courtyards is a small formal room where guests can relax and have cocktails—complimentary wine and sherry are always available here, as is brandy after dinner. Guests may have breakfast here, too, or may choose to eat in their rooms or in the breakfast room; a full meal is available upon order. Breakfast comes with a morning newspaper, and the nightly turndown service includes brandy and chocolates.

Address: *198 King St., Charleston, SC 29401, tel. 803/723-7000 or 800/845-6119, fax 803/720-2608.*
Accommodations: *44 double rooms with baths, 2 suites.*
Amenities: *Air-conditioning, cable TV, and phones in rooms, small meeting room; outdoor whirlpool bath.*
Rates: *$130-$200; Continental breakfast. AE, MC, V.*
Restrictions: *No smoking in 2nd-floor rooms, no pets.*

Rhett House Inn

This 1820 Greek Revival mansion was the home of Thomas Rhett, a rich planter, who lived here with his wife, Caroline Barnwell, and their children. The house exemplifies the rich and lavish lifestyle of prosperous Southern planters prior to the War Between the States, and nowhere in the South was wealth flaunted more than in Beaufort. The three-story square, white building has black shutters and double-decker verandas on the second and third floors supported by 14 fluted Doric columns. It stands on the edge of Craven Street, with a huge live oak hung with Spanish moss directly in front and its gardens to the side and the rear.

The mansion was looking somewhat sad when Steve and Marianne Harrison, executives in New York's garment industry, first spied it on a vacation trip in 1988. But it was love at first sight. So Steve quit his job as president of Anne Klein, and Marianne gave up her knitwear company so they could move to Beaufort and become innkeepers. The Harrisons completely renovated the mansion and filled it with their own antiques and art. Though elegant, the inn is warm and friendly with a country look; guests feel comfortable in sweaters and tennis shoes, and boaters on the Intracoastal Waterway (only a block away) often drop in. The most famous guests to date have been Barbra Streisand and Nick Nolte, when they were filming *Prince of Tides.*

There's a great variety of accommodations. Some rooms have private entrances and are fully accessible to persons with disabilities. Two rooms have working fireplaces, and the lavish honeymoon suite has a whirlpool bath. Each room has a full-length mirror, a double bathroom vanity, four pillows, and a comforter.

The inn acquired a liquor license recently and now offers dinner Wednesday through Saturday to both guests and the public; reservations are required. The cuisine is a representation of such tasty Low Country and Continental favorites as leek-and-goat-cheese tarts, seared veal chops in green peppercorn sauce, and chicken fricassee with quenelles. The full breakfast of fresh fruit, pancakes, and French toast is also quite tempting. Picnics can be arranged on request.

Address: *1009 Craven St., Beaufort, SC 29902, tel. 803/524–9030, fax 803/524–1310.*
Accommodations: *9 double rooms with baths, 1 suite.*
Amenities: *Air-conditioning, ceiling fans, cable TV, and phones in rooms, pool table; bicycles.*
Rates: *$125–$175; full breakfast, afternoon refreshments. MC, V.*
Restrictions: *No smoking indoors, no pets, 2-night minimum weekends.*

Two Meeting Street

You know this is a special place the minute you step through the iron gates onto a walk lined with flowers and shrubs. The landscaped gardens are manicured to perfection; the curved verandas, with their arched columns and balustrades, are freshly painted. The sparkle of the beveled glass and the polished brass on the heavy wooden door add to the welcome of the innkeeper's official greeting.

You enter the foyer, a large open room with richly carved oak paneling, stained-glass windows, and a heavy stairway over which hangs a huge crystal chandelier. The reception rooms are also paneled, and the house has seven stained-glass windows in all, two of them Tiffanys. The formal parlors, off the foyer, are furnished with overstuffed Victorian love seats and chairs, and the formal dining room has a dazzling crystal chandelier and silver that is polished like mirrors.

Each guest room has its own personality, and all are furnished with antique four-poster and canopy beds and Oriental rugs. The two honeymoon suites have working fireplaces and French doors that open to the outside, creating a feeling of privacy. The rooms on the first and second floors are the most sought after, but those on the third floor are just as appealing except that you must climb the stairs.

This Queen Anne Victorian, built in 1892, is one of the most beautiful houses in the city's Historic District and is usually included in spring and fall house tours. Its location, overlooking the Battery and the harbor, makes it convenient to all of Charleston's pleasures. In 1931, it was turned into an inn, and it eventually passed to Jean and Pete Spell. Their daughter, Karen Spell Shaw, the official innkeeper, formerly worked on Capitol Hill for the Senate Budget Committee and for a Charleston congressman. The Spell family has made the house a showplace, one of the city's most popular lodgings, and raised innkeeping to an art. Karen says the profession is in her blood.

The staff members at Two Meeting Street go out of their way to make each stay memorable. Guests are treated to afternoon sherry and snacks and given advice on what to see, where to go, and the best places to eat.

Address: *2 Meeting St., Charleston, SC 29401, tel. 803/723-7322.*
Accommodations: *9 double rooms with baths.*
Amenities: *Air-conditioning and TV in rooms.*
Rates: *$115–$205; Continental breakfast, afternoon refreshments. No credit cards.*
Restrictions: *No smoking, no pets, 2-night minimum weekends, closed Dec. 24–26.*

John Rutledge House Inn

This commanding Georgian Colonial town house, built in 1763 by prominent statesman and signer of the Constitution John Rutledge, sparkles in the historic Broad Street district. Ornate ironwork was added in the 1850s, and Lowcountry Hospitality, Inc. bought and restored the inn in 1989. The attention to 18th- and 19th-century architectural details—original plaster moldings, inlaid floors, hand-carved Italian marble fireplaces, 14-foot ceilings—is impressive. The most popular rooms are in the main inn, including three 850-square-foot suites, two with whirlpools and one opening on a balcony. Although decor in the carriage houses (one authentic, the other built recently to match it) resembles that of the main house, the historic ambience is comparatively lacking. A simple Continental breakfast is delivered to your room; more substantial fare costs extra. Afternoon tea, held in the dramatic second-floor ballroom—where George Washington is said to have met with Rutledge—is a lavish affair.

Address: *116 Broad St., Charleston, SC 29401, tel. 803/723–7999 or 800/476–9741, fax 803/720–2615.*
Accommodations: *16 double rooms with baths, 3 suites.*
Amenities: *Air-conditioning, TV, phones, and refrigerators in rooms, turndown service, concierge.*
Rates: *$170–$285; Continental breakfast, afternoon tea. AE, MC, V.*
Restrictions: *Smoking in one carriage house only, no pets.*

Maison DuPré

Around a quiet courtyard facing George Street in Charleston's Ansonborough district (a 15-minute walk to the Battery) is the walled enclave that is the Maison DuPré. Open since 1987, the inn is a complex of three restored houses and two carriage houses, some of them moved to the site of the original 1801 Federal house.

This Charleston inn is owned by Robert and Lucille Mulholland and their children and managed by son Mark. It is furnished in period antiques, including Charleston rice beds and four-poster canopied affairs. Each room is decorated around one of Lucille's paintings, with silk floral arrangements and fresh flowers contributed by daughter Teri.

The Mulhollands serve daily Low Country tea, with sandwiches, cakes, cookies, cheeses, wine, and coffee. They give complimentary tickets to the Nathaniel Russell house and do nightly turndowns with chocolates. They will even take care of dinner reservations and carriage rides.

Address: *317 E. Bay St., Charleston, SC 29401, tel. 803/723–8691.*
Accommodations: *12 double rooms with baths, 3 suites.*
Amenities: *Air-conditioning, cable TV and phones in rooms, cribs and bassinets.*
Rates: *$85–$200; Continental breakfast, afternoon tea. AE, MC, V.*
Restrictions: *No smoking indoors, no pets.*

TwoSuns Inn

This Neoclassical Revival inn overlooking the Beaufort River was restored by Ron and Carroll Kay for the Fall Tour of Homes in 1990. The sand-colored house, with wraparound verandas, was built in 1917, with every modern convenience: The Roman heat distribution system, steam radiators, skylight ventilation, and rare circular brass body shower all are operational again. The Kays did the decorating with furniture they already had and Victorian pieces bought at antiques shops and flea markets. Carroll made the draperies and bedspreads and does weaving on the loom in the parlor. Ron is a talented graphics artist.

The Kays put their hearts and souls into running the inn; they have a Tea and Toddy hour every afternoon, help with dinner reservations, give directions for walking tours, and serve a full breakfast every morning. They will even serve private champagne breakfasts and pack picnic baskets for an additional fee.

Address: *1705 Bay St., Beaufort, SC 29902, tel. or fax 803/522–1122 or tel. 800/532–4244.*
Accommodations: *5 double rooms with baths.*
Amenities: *Air-conditioning, ceiling fans, cable TV, and phones in rooms, small business center, bicycles.*
Rates: *$99–$109; full breakfast, afternoon refreshments. AE, MC, V.*
Restrictions: *No smoking indoors, no pets.*

Victoria House Inn

This Romanesque-style redbrick town house on King Street, Charleston's antiquing hub, opened in 1992, providing a more intimate alternative to the Kings Courtyard Inn, owned by the same management company. Its location just south of Market Street puts you a stone's throw from the Old City Market, East Bay and Meeting streets' many shops and restaurants, and the College of Charleston. The inn's European ambience sets it apart from the city's other small, Southern hotels. For example, a Continental champagne breakfast is delivered to your bedside by your chambermaid, who's never far should you need extra pillows or turndown service. All but two rooms, which face brick walls, have views of this historic area. A few have magnificent bay windows overlooking King Street. All contain understated Victorian antiques and reproductions, one king-size or two double beds, honor bars, and fully modern bathrooms, but each differs from the others in configuration and color scheme. Suites have large whirlpools, gas fireplaces, and sitting areas.

Address: *208 King St., Charleston, SC 29401, tel. 803/720–2944 or 800/933–5464, fax 803/720–2930.*
Accommodations: *14 double rooms with baths, 4 suites.*
Amenities: *Air-conditioning, cable TV, phones, and refrigerators in rooms.*
Rates: *$125–$190; Continental breakfast. AE, D, DC, MC, V.*
Restrictions: *Smoking in 4 bedrooms only, no pets.*

Thoroughbred Country and the Old 96

The Sandhills region with its moderate climate first lured the wealthy to western South Carolina in the 1890s. They settled in and around Aiken, wintering in stately mansions, throwing lavish parties, and spending their time on hunting and racing. Many of their palatial vacation "cottages" (often surrounded by walls or hedges) are preserved in Aiken's three Winter Colony historic districts.

Among the top race horses that have been stabled and trained here are Kentucky Derby champion Pleasant Colony and Summer Squall, a Preakness winner. In late March and early April, people come to Aiken for the Triple Crown: three successive weekends of steeplechasing, Thoroughbred trials, and harness racing. Polo matches are held at Whitney Field on Sunday afternoons from September through November and March through July. On Saturday mornings, guided tours will take you to some of the local stables; at several you can ride and take lessons.

Golf is also popular; most of the year you can play any of two-dozen nearby courses. In April, the tour of homes welcomes spring, and in May, the Strawberry Festival celebrates a luscious local product. Aiken's Makin' heralds autumn with arts-and-crafts demonstrations and displays, and then comes the Christmas Crafts Show.

History buffs interested in the Colonial and antebellum eras, the American Revolution, or the Civil War should explore some nearby towns in the Old Ninety Six District, 30 miles or so northwest of Aiken. At Abbeville, the Southern Cause was born and died. In 1860, the first organized secession meeting was held here, and scarcely less than five years later, Confederate President Jefferson Davis convened his last Council of War. In more recent times, Abbeville was the location for the filming of Sleeping with the Enemy, *and it has a number of antiques stores and boutiques.*

In Greenwood, founded by Irish settlers in 1802, Andrew Johnson, the 17th president, ran a tailor shop at Courthouse Square before migrating to eastern Tennessee. In mid-July, the city hosts the South Carolina Festival of Flowers at the Park Seed Company, with home-and-garden tours, live entertainment, and a beauty pageant. Anglers, swimmers, and boaters head for nearby Lake Greenwood's 200-mile shoreline.

Along a Native American trade route near Greenwood is the little community of Ninety Six, located that number of miles from the Cherokee village of Keowee in the Blue Ridge Mountains. Two miles south, at the Ninety Six National Historic Site, South Carolina's first Revolutionary War battle was fought in 1775. Also commemorated is a more significant engagement in 1781, which pitted General Nathaniel Greene against a force of British Loyalists.

Places to Go, Sights to See

Abbeville County Museum (215 Poplar St., tel. 803/459–2696). Historic memorabilia and a log cabin are housed in an old 1850s jail designed by Robert Mills, architect of the Washington Monument.

Abbeville Opera House (Town Sq., tel. 803/459–2157). Built in 1908, the structure has been restored to its original grandeur, and current productions range from contemporary comedies to Broadway musicals.

The **Aiken County Historical Museum** (433 Newberry St. SW, Aiken, tel. 803/642–2015), in a wing of *Banksia,* an 1860 estate, depicts the area's early history, with rooms furnished to reflect late 18th- and early 19th-century lifestyles, a firearms collection, and Native American artifacts. On the grounds stand an 1890 one-room schoolhouse and an 1808 log cabin thought to be Aiken County's oldest building.

The **Burt-Stark House** (306 N. Main St., Abbeville, tel. 803/459–4297), site of Jefferson Davis's last Council of War, is open for tours Friday and Saturday or by appointment.

George W. Park Seed Co. (Rte. 245, 7 mi north of Greenwood, tel. 803/941–4213). Colorful experimental gardens and greenhouses put on vivid displays in summer. There are guided tours, and you may buy seeds and bulbs in the company's store.

The **Greenwood Museum** (106 Main St., tel. 803/229–7093) has more than 7,000 items in eclectic displays: Native American artifacts, natural history and geology exhibits, and a replica of a turn-of-the-century community.

Hickory Knob State Resort Park (7 mi southwest of McCormick via U.S. 378, tel. 803/391–2450) has a pool, nature trails, tennis courts, an equestrian center, and an 18-hole championship golf course. There's a lake where you can fish, rent sailboats and motorboats, and go waterskiing.

Hopelands Gardens/Aiken Racing Hall of Fame (Dupree Pl. and Whiskey Rd., tel. 803/642–7630). The gardens have seasonal plantings, summer concerts and plays, and a Touch and Scent Trail lined with plaques in Braille. The hall of fame honors champion Thoroughbreds from Aiken.

Montmorenci Vineyards (U.S. 78, east of Aiken, tel. 803/649–4870) produces 10 varieties of wine, including several award winners. Tours of the family-operated winery are available by appointment with two weeks' notice.

The **Ninety Six National Historic Site** (Rte. 248, 2 mi south of Ninety Six, tel. 803/543–4068) has a reconstructed fort, a frontier settlement, and a trading post. National Park Service archaeological digs and historic restorations continue. A visitor center displays relics and has exhibits.

Restaurants

The elegant **Pheasant Room of the Willcox Inn** (100 Colleton Ave., Aiken, tel. 803/649–1377) serves salmon steak and stuffed baked trout, and a lavish Sunday brunch. The **West Side Bowery** (151 Bee La., Aiken, tel. 803/648–2900), a popular casual spot, serves sandwiches, seafood, steaks, and poultry. On mild days, ask for a table on the sunny terrace. Across the street from the Bowery's rear entrance, **Up Your Alley** (222 In the Alley, Aiken, tel. 803/649–2603) offers steaks, seafood, and healthful alternatives. **No. 10 Downing St.** (241 Laurens St., Aiken, tel. 803/642–9062) offers upscale dining in an early 19th-century cottage. **Yoder's Dutch Kitchen** (U.S. 72, Abbeville, tel. 803/459–5556) has a daily lunch buffet and an evening smorgasbord and sells pies, Dutch bread, apple butter, and salad dressings to go.

Tourist Information

Greater Abbeville Chamber of Commerce (104 Pickens St., Abbeville, SC 29620, tel. 803/459–4600). **Greater Aiken Chamber of Commerce** (400 Laurens St. NW, Box 892, Aiken, SC 29802, tel. 803/641–1111). **Greenwood County Chamber of Commerce** (Box 980, Greenwood, SC 29648, tel. 803/223–8431). **Ninety Six Chamber of Commerce** (Box 8, Ninety Six, SC 29666, tel. 803/543–2900).

Annie's Inn

You won't be a stranger at this inn very long. Before you know it, you'll be sipping coffee by the wood cook stove and getting acquainted with the other guests (usually businesspeople during the week and couples on weekends). The experience is a lot like going to Grandma's because of the friendly, at-home atmosphere that pervades Scottie Peck's kitchen.

Scottie and her late husband bought the house several years ago, and after his death, she turned it into a bed-and-breakfast inn, the oldest B&B in town. The nearly 200-year-old farmhouse in the rural community of Montmorenci, just outside Aiken, stood at one time on a 2,000-acre cotton plantation. The crop is still grown nearby, but only 2 acres of the original tract remain with the house.

There were originally three floors, but the top floor was hit by a cannonball during the Civil War and subsequently removed. A doctor had his practice in the house for a time and used it as a hospital; the resident ghost is a child who cries.

The house's most distinguishing features are its big front porch and second-floor balcony. It has a central hallway, with formal rooms on either side, the kitchen to the back, and bedrooms upstairs. Scottie has furnished it in elegant French and English country style, combining antiques, handmade quilts, area rugs,

and lace. Small bathrooms with showers were carved out of existing space so that each guest room has one. Guests who are staying for a long time usually choose one of the two completely equipped housekeeping cottages behind the house.

Scottie serves breakfast in the kitchen or in the dining room (when she has a full house). Because she is from Colorado, she doesn't serve grits but offers such entrées as waffles with fresh steamed apples on top, popovers served with locally produced honey, and eggs Benedict.

On nice days, guests gather at the swimming pool, play croquet, or pitch horseshoes, and Scottie always has plenty of books, magazines, and games on hand for rainy days.

Address: *U.S. 78 E (Box 300), Montmorenci, SC 29839, tel. 803/649–6836.*
Accommodations: *5 double rooms with baths, 2 housekeeping cottages.*
Amenities: *Air-conditioning, ceiling fans, cable TV in cottages and common rooms.*
Rates: *$45–$75; full breakfast. AE, D, DC, MC, V.*
Restrictions: *No smoking indoors, no pets.*

Belmont Inn

This slightly tattered-looking three-story hotel, with its long, arched double veranda, planted on one corner of Court Square, has played a prominent role in the history of the town. Built in 1903 and called The Eureka, it was the resort of famous statesmen, lawyers and judges during court sessions, drummers, and vaudeville actors in its heyday. The hotel went through hard times, eventually closed in 1974, and was reopened in 1984 after a complete restoration. It's been run since 1993 by a management firm out of Columbia, and efforts are currently under way to spruce things up.

Since its rebirth, the Belmont has developed quite a following. Its guests like to combine a visit with a couple of nights at the Opera House, following the example of such as Jimmy Durante, Fanny Brice, Sarah Bernhardt, and Groucho Marx, who made overnight stops in Abbeville. The town calls itself the "birthplace and deathbed of the Confederacy," and there is a Confederate memorial in the town square.

Guest rooms are furnished in period reproductions, with four-poster beds and armoires; the bathrooms are strictly functional. Though the heart-pine floors are original, the fireplaces are now only decorative. The best lodging in the house, the John C. Calhoun Room, has a four-poster bed and French doors opening onto the second-floor balcony. Public rooms are also furnished in reproductions, along with some period antiques. The lobby exudes a turn-of-the-century atmosphere; a registration desk is in the middle of the room, and sitting areas and separate parlors are off to the side.

The Heritage Room restaurant, serving pasta, seafood, and traditional American chicken and beef dishes, offers all meals plus Sunday brunch, and light fare is served in the Curtain Call Lounge on the basement level. The meeting rooms, also on this level, were originally used by traveling salesmen to display their merchandise.

Address: *Court Sq., 106 E. Pickens St., Abbeville, SC 29620, tel. or fax 803/459–9625.*
Accommodations: *25 double rooms with baths.*
Amenities: *Air-conditioning, cable TV, and phones in rooms; parking.*
Rates: *$67–$87; Continental breakfast. AE, D, DC, MC, V.*
Restrictions: *No pets.*

Willcox Inn

Were it not for the white paint on this three-story classic inn, you would hardly notice the building amid the trees and shrubbery in Aiken's historic district. But it's right there with the elaborate estates and horse farms belonging to the winter people, who come from everywhere each year for the riding, racing, and hunting.

Frederick Sugden Willcox, an Englishman, came to Aiken around 1891 with his Swedish wife, Elise, and soon started the inn. Response was so great that he had to enlarge it several times. Winston Churchill, Elizabeth Arden, Averill Harriman, and other luminaries slept here, and it's said that no room could be found for the Duke of Windsor during a Masters Golf Tournament (Augusta, Georgia, is 16 miles away). The Willcox family managed the inn until 1957, and, after other owners, Grand Heritage Inns, which manages many prestigious small hotels, took over in 1993.

Second Empire and Colonial Revival in architectural style, the weather-board inn has a front porch supported by six Doric columns, over which there is a balcony. The rosewood-paneled lobby has heart-pine floors, a stone fireplace at either end, and a smaller fireplace on the second landing, which was the original dining room. The Pheasant Dining Room serves nouvelle-inspired regional fare—possibly the best food in

Aiken—and a simpler menu is offered in the Wren's Nest, a new dining room on the rear second-floor balcony. The Polo Lounge, with dark paneling and leather chairs, is a perfect setting for the horsey set during racing season. The light, spacious guest rooms have reproduction antiques and bright floral wallpapers with complementary fabrics. The Winston Churchill Suite, in shades of blue, has a separate sitting room, a private entrance, two fireplaces, and a porch. Room 106, on the back side, is cool and quiet; its large bathroom has a claw-foot tub.

Though small, the inn has a friendly, service-oriented staff. You can get room service during the day, and the staff can arrange golf games, historic tours, and carriage rides. There are golf and honeymoon packages as well as popular gourmet weekends, which begin with champagne and chocolates.

Address: *100 Colleton Ave., Aiken, SC 29801, tel. or fax 803/649–1377 or tel. 800/368–1047.*
Accommodations: *24 double rooms with baths, 6 suites.*
Amenities: *Air-conditioning, cable TV and phones in rooms, meeting room, turndown service; free use of nearby health club.*
Rates: *$75–$105; breakfast extra. AE, DC, MC, V.*
Restrictions: *No pets.*

Constantine House

The Constantine House, opened in 1991, is Aiken's most elegant bed-and-breakfast. Completed in 1935, the white stucco Georgian mansion sits on 6½ acres on the highest point between Atlanta and Columbia. It is perfectly symmetrical, with elaborate friezes, four columns, and four chimneys (though only one fireplace). In back there's a terrace and a screened loggia on the second floor. The house was designed for entertaining; there are formal rooms on each side of a central hallway and a spiral stairway in the middle.

Anne S. Smith, who also owns the Four Generations antiques shop in Aiken, has filled the house with treasures and fine accessories. One bedroom has burgundy walls, jewel-tone fabrics, and an Oriental rug; the peach-colored room has a four-poster bed and an 1830 chest; and the white room opens onto the loggia.

Anne serves breakfast to guests along with a morning newspaper in their room, on the loggia, or in the formal dining room.

Address: *3406 Richland Ave., Aiken, SC 29801, tel. 803/642–8911 or 803/641–7477.*
Accommodations: *3 double rooms with baths.*
Amenities: *Air-conditioning, cable TV, and phones in rooms.*
Rates: *$69; full breakfast. AE, MC, V.*
Restrictions: *No pets.*

Greenleaf Inn

Charming Camden, with its horsey history and grand Southern Colonial homes, is a bit reminiscent of Aiken. As in Aiken, Camden's fanciest roads are left unpaved for horses. Because General Sherman spared the town, most of its antebellum homes still stand, and the inn, which opened in 1993, is its prize accommodation.

Alice Boykin, whose name is to Camden what Carnegie's name is to Pittsburgh, runs the inn—though you're just as likely to be greeted by her daughter of the same name. The B&B compound, on several parklike acres, comprises three buildings: a main inn (ca. 1810), which has four rooms on the second floor, above a small restaurant; a nearby carriage house (ca. 1810); and a guest cottage, which sleeps four. Rooms are done in classic Victoriana. Many have four-poster beds, wide-plank uneven floors, Oriental rugs, and period wallpapers. They're spacious, and all have modern baths and ceiling fans. You won't find a better value in the region. Continental breakfast, consisting of fresh-squeezed orange juice, fruit salad, and pastries, is brought to your room.

Address: *1308 Broad St., Camden, SC 29020, tel. 803/425–1806 or 800/437–5874.*
Accommodations: *8 double rooms with baths, 3 suites, 1 cottage.*
Amenities: *Phones in rooms; free use of nearby health club.*
Rates: *$65–$75; Continental breakfast. AE, D, MC, V.*
Restrictions: *No pets.*

Inn on the Square

G reenwood's most elegant lodging, the Inn on the Square was created out of an old warehouse and opened by Tom Fischer in 1986. The progression of the restoration project is highlighted in photographs displayed in the lobby. The new layout is spacious and modern and has all the components of a small luxury hotel, including a formal lobby, dining room, lounge, and meeting space. The building's central focus is the large lobby, with its reception and formal sitting areas. The inn's only flaw is its location on busy and built-up U.S. 25.

All the guest rooms are configured in typical hotel fashion, but the 18th-century reproduction furniture is a cut above the ordinary; there are four-poster beds, large writing desks, and armoires.

Guests receive a small bottle of wine and snacks in their rooms. Golf privileges can be arranged at Stoney Point Golf Club on Lake Greenwood.

Address: *104 Court St., Greenwood, SC 29648, tel. 803/223-4488 or 800/231-9109, fax 803/223-7067.*
Accommodations: *48 double rooms with baths.*
Amenities: *Restaurant, lounge, room service, air-conditioning, cable TV and phones in rooms; pool.*
Rates: *$60–$76; breakfast extra. AE, D, DC, MC, V.*
Restrictions: *No pets.*

New Berry Inn

M ary Ann and Hal Mackey took over this 1924 Colonial Revival inn in 1993, and despite working full-time jobs, they have no regrets. In an old, prestigious Aiken neighborhood, the inn feels like a private home—complete with a white picket fence. The Mackeys, however, live off the premises. The clientele is a mix of businesspeople and golfing and riding enthusiasts, many of whom have been wintering in Aiken for decades. There are four bedrooms upstairs and one, accessible to the disabled, on the ground floor. Victorian antiques and Colonial reproductions fill the rooms, which have large and stately armoires. A few have four-poster beds and antique pedestal sinks. There are two fireplaces in common rooms and two in bedrooms. It's basically function over form here, and antiques aficionados will be happier elsewhere. A breakfast of homemade bread, baked ham, eggs, granola, yogurt, and cereal is set out each morning, buffet style. The wisteria-wrapped, redbrick sun porch is the perfect place to savor iced tea on sleepy afternoons.

Address: *240 Newberry St. SW, Aiken, SC 29801, tel. 803/649-2935, fax 803/642-5840.*
Accommodations: *5 double rooms with baths.*
Amenities: *Cable TV and phones in rooms, meeting room; free use of nearby health club.*
Rates: *$60; full breakfast, afternoon refreshments. AE, D, DC, MC, V.*
Restrictions: *No smoking, no pets.*

Georgia

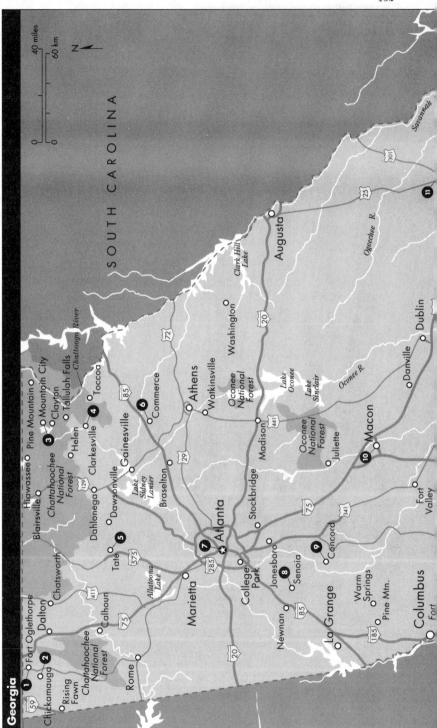

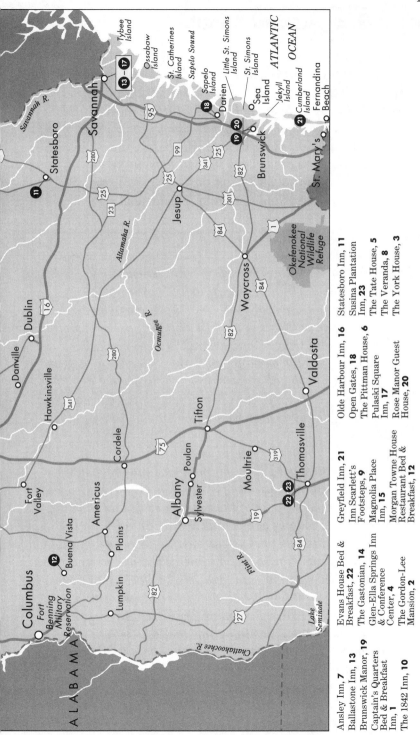

Ansley Inn, **7**
Ballastone Inn, **13**
Brunswick Manor, **19**
Captain's Quarters
Bed & Breakfast
Inn, **1**
The 1842 Inn, **10**

Evans House Bed &
Breakfast, **22**
The Gastonian, **14**
Glen-Ella Springs Inn
& Conference
Center, **4**
The Gordon-Lee
Mansion, **2**

Greyfield Inn, **21**
Inn Scarlett's
Footsteps, **9**
Magnolia Place
Inn, **15**
Morgan Towne House
Restaurant Bed &
Breakfast, **12**

Olde Harbour Inn, **16**
Open Gates, **18**
The Pittman House, **6**
Pulaski Square
Inn, **17**
Rose Manor Guest
House, **20**

Statesboro Inn, **11**
Susina Plantation
Inn, **23**
The Tate House, **5**
The Veranda, **8**
The York House, **3**

North Georgia and Atlanta

No other part of Georgia is as diverse in temperament and appearance as the area that encompasses Atlanta and stretches northward. Cosmopolitan Atlanta seems a world away from the rural mountain areas steeped in the lore of the Cherokees and dotted with Civil War battle sites. The region's rich heritage dates back to the 1700s, when adventurous pioneers moved from the crowded coastal settlements into the untamed upland territories.

Though Atlanta is deservedly known as "the city of trees," development has drastically altered the state capital and its environs. Today steel-and-glass skyscrapers—many designed by John Portman, a Georgia Tech graduate— punctuate the city's downtown and northern perimeters. A lingering presence of the area's earlier history is found only outside these populated centers, where the high-rise silhouettes fade into the distance and are replaced by quaint town squares and lush valley pastures. Then, almost as suddenly as they appeared, the open green spaces lining highways and side roads give way to the smoky blue peaks of the mountains.

Atlanta, which catapulted into the international spotlight when it was named the host city for the 1996 Olympic Games, is the undisputed boomtown of the Southeast. It has such big-city pleasures as the tony shops and restaurants lining the streets of upscale Buckhead and the quirky art scene found in Little Five Points. It also has a six-block underground mall and a pavilion with an unparalleled collection of Coke memorabilia. Just outside the city at Stone Mountain is the nation's largest Civil War monument, carved into a granite cliff. Driving east from Atlanta brings visitors to the charming town of Athens, site of the state's botanical garden and its largest university as well as the birthplace of alternative music groups like REM. Picture Mayberry meets MTV. The rural appeal of the country north of Athens is

*epitomized by the year-round presence of roadside apple-
cider, vegetable, and crafts stands along the winding back
roads and highways. In Dahlonega, in the uplands northeast
of Atlanta, panning for gold is a favorite pastime, as are
kayaking and river rafting along the Chattooga River's
white-water rapids. Popular resorts rim the shores of
pristine Lake Rabun and Lake Burton. Both lakes are
reputed among weekend visitors and vacation-home
residents to be the "in" spots for the pursuit of fishing,
waterskiing, or dockside cocktails.*

*Annual crafts and cultural festivals, county agricultural
fairs, and weekly markets are year-round attractions. The
ideal time for a visit to Atlanta is spring, when azaleas and
dogwood trees are in full bloom and temperatures are mild.
The mountains draw visitors all year long, but especially in
summer for their coolness and in autumn for their
spectacular red and gold foliage.*

Places to Go, Sights to See

Amicalola Falls State Park (16 mi northwest of Dawsonville via Rte. 183,
tel. 706/265–8888) is where the state's highest waterfalls are found, and
where the Georgia portion of the Appalachian Trail begins.

Athens. This small town is the northern gateway to the state's Antebellum
Trail. It is also home of the nation's oldest state university, whose buildings
date back to the early 1800s, and the *State Museum of Art* (North University Campus, tel. 706/542–3254). *The State Botanical Garden* (2450 S.
Milledge Ave., tel. 706/542–1244) is a few miles from downtown.

Atlanta Botanical Garden (1345 Piedmont Ave., tel. 404/876–5859). On 60
acres of Atlanta's Piedmont Park are 5 acres of formal gardens, a 15-acre
hardwood forest, a Japanese garden, and a conservatory for unusual and
flamboyant tropical, desert, and Mediterranean plants.

Atlanta Cyclorama (800 Cherokee Ave., tel. 404/658–7625). A panoramic
battle painting, over a century old and 350 feet in circumference, is the focal
point of this Civil War museum complex. A guided tour and short film are
also provided.

Brasstown Bald. Often referred to as the "top of Georgia," this 4,784-foot
peak is the state's highest point. Georgia, Tennessee, and the two Carolinas
can be seen from here on a clear day.

Château Élan Winery (100 Tour de France, Braselton, tel. 404/932–0900 or 800/233–WINE). Vineyards surround this elegant château and spa, complete with casual and formal restaurants, an art gallery, and wine tastings. The manicured grounds also include a golf course, an equestrian center, and tennis courts.

Chattooga River. A first-class white-water river, the Chattooga annually draws over 100,000 visitors eager to ride its rapids. For information about river outfitters, contact the U.S. Forest Service's Tallulah Ranger District (tel. 706/782–3320).

Chickamauga National Military Park (U.S. 27, Fort Oglethorpe, tel. 706/866–9241). The historic clash of Union and Confederate troops here in 1863 resulted in 34,000 casualties. Today, visitors can take an 11-mile self-guided tour following the battle's stages and see a display of weapons in the visitor center.

Chief Vann House (Rte. 7, Chatsworth, tel. 706/695–2598). This house was built by Cherokee chief James Vann in 1804; it's now a showplace of Cherokee culture.

Cloudland Canyon (Rte. 2, Rising Fawn, tel. 706/657–4050). This scenic park, which straddles a deep gorge on the western side of Lookout Mountain, has waterfalls and dramatic land formations.

Dahlonega Gold Rush Museum (Public Sq., tel. 706/864–2257). The first American gold rush happened in Georgia, not California. Ore samples, early photographs, and mining tools are displayed in the former Lumpkin County Courthouse. Visitors can pan for gold in nearby mines.

Ft. Mountain Park (181 Ft. Mountain Park Rd., east of Chatsworth, tel. 706/695–2621). Ft. Mountain's origins are unknown, but this man-made prehistoric rock wall, extending 875 feet, is believed to have been a Native American religious site.

Helen. This mountain town reinvented itself as a Bavarian alpine village and steeps itself in Germanic traditions with an annual Oktoberfest. Souvenir shops filled with European imports, Christmas ornaments, and local crafts line its main streets.

Kennesaw Mountain National Battlefield (U.S. 41 and Stilesboro Rd., tel. 404/427–4686). This 2,900-acre park outside Atlanta commemorates one of the Civil War's most decisive battles and offers 17 miles of hiking trails.

Lake Burton. The largest of five state reservoirs has breathtaking scenery along its 62 miles of shoreline.

Lake Hartwell. This lake's thriving populations of largemouth bass, catfish, and crappie make it a fisherman's paradise.

Lookout Mountain (off Rte. 189, south of Rock City, tel. 706/398–3541). Hang gliders take off from this mountain's McCarty Bluff, but you can simply stop at the overlooks to get the view of the surrounding mountains and patchwork of farmlands and forest.

Marietta. Well-preserved homes, churches, a renovated business district, the Big Shanty Museum, and a national cemetery are some points of interest along this town's extensive walking and driving tour.

New Echota (Rte. 225 NE, 1211 Chatsworth Hwy., Calhoun, tel. 404/629–8151). Indian mounds and restored buildings represent the history of the Independent Cherokee Nation, which resided here from 1825 until the Cherokees were removed to Oklahoma in 1838.

Nightlife. In Atlanta, blues dominates at *Blind Willie's* (tel. 404/873–2583), while jazz is found at *Dante's Down the Hatch* (tel. 404/266–1600). For country, try the *Buckboard Country Music Showcase* (tel. 404/955–7340) and the *Crystal Chandelier* (tel. 404/436–5006). The hottest dance club in Atlanta is *Axys* (tel. 404/607–0922). Big-band sounds and danceable pop tunes are heard nightly at *Rupert's* (tel. 404/266–9834) in the Buckhead district.

Stone Mountain Park (U.S. 78, Stone Mountain Fwy., tel. 404/498–5690) is a 3,200-acre recreation and amusement park centered on a massive Civil War relief sculpture. Also here are an antebellum plantation, a paddle-wheel riverboat, restaurants, and recreational sports.

Tallulah Gorge (Terrora Visitors Center, Tallulah Falls, tel. 404/754–3276), which plunges to 1,100 feet, provides some of the best hiking in the Southeast, as well as magnificent fall foliage. The visitor center has exhibits on the area's natural resources and pioneer past.

Traveler's Rest (Jarrett Manor, U.S. 123, Toccoa, tel. 404/886–2256). This two-story frame house was a stagecoach inn and plantation home; it is furnished with locally crafted antiques.

Underground Atlanta (50 Alabama St., tel. 404/523–2311) comprises six redeveloped city blocks on the site of the old Atlanta railroad terminus. It is filled with shops, restaurants, and entertainment.

World of Coca-Cola Pavilion (55 Martin Luther King Dr., Atlanta, tel. 404/676–5151). This building's dazzling architecture is nearly as compelling as its spectacular collection of memorabilia related to the Atlanta-based soft drink's history.

Restaurants

Burton's Grill (tel. 404/525–3415) in Atlanta's Inman Park is a soul-flavored bastion of Southern breakfasts and lunches. **Cooley's Café** (tel. 404/607–7736), a block from the Fox Theatre in downtown Atlanta, carries comfort

food like fried catfish and jalapeño hush puppies. **The Horseradish Grill**
(tel. 404/255–7277), across from Chastain Park in Atlanta, has a witty menu
of nouvelle Southern cooking—and valet parking. The **Dillard House** (tel.
404/746–5348 or 800/541–0671), north of Clayton, offers family-style meals of
country ham, chicken, and vegetables plus a panoramic view of the
Nachoochee Valley. **Moon Valley** (tel. 706/746–2466), near Lake Rabun,
serves the area's finest gourmet cuisine. **The Trolley** (tel. 706/754–5566), on
the square in Clarkesville, is a throwback to soda fountain days and offers a
modern American menu. **La Prade's Fishcamp** (tel. 706/947–3312), north of
Clarkesville, is a family-style eatery, serving homegrown vegetables and
fried chicken from April through November. **Cohutta Lodge** (tel. 706/695–
9601) sits on top of Ft. Mountain and serves up three meals daily and a
terrific view. The **Smith House** (202 S. Chestatee St., tel. 706/864–3566) is a
legendary all-you-can-eat institution in Dahlonega.

Tourist Information

Atlanta Committee for the Olympic Games (250 Williams St., Suite 6000,
Atlanta, GA 30303, tel. 404/224–1996). **Atlanta Convention and Visitors
Bureau** (233 Peachtree St., Atlanta, GA 30043, tel. 404/521–6628). **Blue
Ridge Visitors Center** (Historic Depot, Blue Ridge, GA 30513, tel.
706/632–5680). **Calhoun Welcome Center** (300 S. Wall St., Calhoun, GA
30701, tel. 706/625–3200). **Dahlonega-Lumpkin County Chamber of
Commerce** (Box 2037, Dahlonega, GA 30533, tel. 706/864–3711). **Gainesville
Tourist & Convention Bureau** (Box 374, Gainesville, GA 30503, tel.
404/536–5209). **Greater Rome Convention & Visitors Center** (Box 5823,
Rome, GA 30161, tel. 706/295–5576). **Marietta Welcome Center** (4 Depot St.,
Marietta, GA 30060, tel. 404/429–1115). **Rabun County Welcome Center**
(U.S. 441, Clayton, GA 30525, tel. 706/782–5113).

Reservation Services

Atlanta Hospitality (2472 Lauderdale Dr., Atlanta, GA 30345, tel.
404/493–1930). **Bed and Breakfast Atlanta** (1801 Piedmont Ave., Atlanta,
GA 30324, tel. 404/875–0525 or 800/967–3224, fax 404/875–9672).

Ansley Inn

The Ansley Inn is in the heart of Midtown, a handsome landscape of park-lined streets that's one of Atlanta's oldest neighborhoods. The English Tudor yellow brick mansion trimmed with green shutters was built early in this century by a local philanthropist and converted into a bed-and-breakfast in 1987. It is managed by a professional staff.

The front desk is overseen round-the-clock by a concierge. Before breakfast you'll find the morning papers stacked on a table in the main hallway. In the formal dining room, light buffet breakfasts are served. The living room, where afternoon appetizers and drink setups are laid out, has a massive marble fireplace and comfortable seating. Original impressionistic art, crystal chandeliers, and period pieces from Chippendale, Queen Anne, and Empire add to the luxurious ambience.

The well-equipped guest rooms range in size from spacious suites with four-poster beds to cozy double rooms—individually decorated in a variety of paisleys and chintzes, flowers and stripes. The house is furnished with numerous dark mahogany reproductions: tables, bureaus, and armoires based on formal 18th-century designs. Botanical and hunt prints echo the English club theme. Three of the rooms have fireplaces and seating areas, and a two-bedroom cottage has a fireplace and a kitchenette.

Renovation of an additional home next door, scheduled for completion in July 1995, will add 21 rooms. A conference room with a fireplace on the first floor can be reserved for business meetings of up to 10. Health club privileges are offered at a nearby fitness center, and in 1994, the inn opened its own heated outdoor pool. There is no restaurant, but the staff can order catered meals and serve them in your room. The house is within walking distance of the High Museum; Atlanta Botanical Gardens; Piedmont Park, Atlanta's answer to Central Park, replete with a stunning skyline view; and Woodruff Arts Center, where the city's award-winning symphony and theater company perform.

Address: *253 15th St., Atlanta, GA 30309, tel. 404/872–9000 or 800/446–5416, fax 404/892–2318.*
Accommodations: *11 double rooms with baths, 1 suite, 1 housekeeping cottage.*
Amenities: *Air-conditioning; cable TV, phones, wet bars, and whirlpool baths in rooms; laundry and dry-cleaning service; off-street parking.*
Rates: *$85–$500; Continental breakfast, afternoon refreshments. AE, D, DC, MC, V.*
Restrictions: *Small pets only.*

Glen-Ella Springs Inn & Conference Center

G len-Ella Springs Inn, a rambling 100-year-old hideaway just outside Clarkesville, was lovingly renovated in 1987—after years of neglect—by Barrie and Bobby Aycock. The small hotel, listed on the National Register of Historic Places, sits by a gravel road on 17 acres of meadows and gardens laced with nature trails.

At first glance the Glen-Ella, which has heart-of-pine floors, walls, and ceilings, appears down-home, but its uptown flair soon becomes evident. The front lobby, filled with chintz and antiques, serves as a parlor, and fires are lit here against the cool night air. From wide double porches you enter the guest rooms, where quilts, Oriental and hooked rugs, and primitive antiques warm the painted pine-paneled interiors.

The hotel's dining room, with a fireplace, is the realization of Barrie's original dream: to own her own restaurant. She approaches the business of food with a no-excuses attitude. Her kitchen is the source of the sweet baked goods—blueberry muffins and oat scones—served at breakfast; the salads, sandwiches, and chili enjoyed at lunch; and the American Creole cuisine served at dinner. The food here has so enhanced the inn's reputation that it has become a culinary hot spot for Atlantans, who will drive the two hours for the sumptuous meals.

Special pursuits, such as wine tastings, mystery weekends, and herb-gardening conferences, are listed at the lobby desk. Or you can relax by the pool on the large sun deck surrounded by flower gardens. Sports lovers will find excellent hiking at nearby Tallulah Falls. Golf (as well as tennis) is found at the Orchard, a brand-new course within a few miles of the inn. Kayaking and white-water rafting on the Chattooga River are also popular, and the inn arranges horseback riding. To top it off, when you're done exerting yourself, you can get a massage.

During the week, the basement conference center is frequently booked by Fortune 100 companies.

Address: *Bear Gap Rd. (Rte. 3, Box 3304), Clarkesville, GA 30523, tel. 706/754-7295 or 800/552-3479, fax 706/754-7295.*
Accommodations: *14 double rooms with baths, 2 suites.*
Amenities: *Air-conditioning and phones in rooms, whirlpool baths and fireplaces in suites, cable TV in lobby.*
Rates: *$80–$155; full breakfast. AE, MC, V.*
Restrictions: *No smoking in dining room, no pets.*

The Tate House

This pink marble mansion, in woods that frame a picturesque view of the foothills of the Blue Ridge Mountains, is a beacon of civility along a winding mountain road. The elegant interiors, luxurious accommodations, and formal gardens of the striking Tate House would surely have made Rhett and Scarlett feel at home.

Completed in 1926 by Colonel Sam Tate, the marble baron who supplied the stone for the Lincoln Memorial in Washington, DC, the house sat empty for more than 25 years until Ann and Joe Laird painstakingly restored and opened it in 1985. They furnished the house in the ultimate of formal decor, with an impressive collection of antiques that includes a John Adams sideboard, an antique baby grand player piano, and a sparkling dining room chandelier that matches one hanging in Graceland, Elvis Presley's home in Tennessee.

Many of the decorative elements you might expect in a house on the National Register of Historic Places can be found just inside the front door: marble floors, a hand-painted mural, and a winding staircase. The suites are outfitted with heavy tapestry draperies, plush rugs, fireplaces, late Victorian bedsteads and furnishings, and chandeliers. One suite contains an antique game table for checkers, backgammon, and roulette. The property also offers country-style accommodations in nine cabins with sleeping lofts behind the main house; all have oversize hot tubs, working fireplaces, and wet bars.

During the week, when the inn is the site of business conferences, Continental breakfast is served in the sun room overlooking the landscaped gardens. On weekends, when rooms are largely occupied by couples seeking a romantic getaway, suite guests receive two splits of champagne, and all guests are treated to a traditional Southern breakfast.

Guests have free run of the property's 27 acres, including the terrace dining areas, formal gardens, tennis and shuffleboard courts, and heated swimming pool. There's also horseback riding on trails through 700 acres just opposite The Tate House. Nearby are rafting on the Chattooga River and hiking at Amicalola Falls.

Address: *Rte. 53 (Box 33), Tate, GA 30177, tel. 404/735–3122 or 800/342–7515 in GA, fax 404/735–4730.* **Accommodations:** *4 suites, 9 cabins.* **Amenities:** *Air-conditioning, cable TV and phones in rooms; gift shop.* **Rates:** *$120–$125; Continental or full breakfast. AE, D, MC, V.* **Restrictions:** *No smoking, pets allowed in cabins only, closed Dec. 25.*

Captain's Quarters Bed & Breakfast Inn

The Captain's Quarters is one of 15 stately homes outlining Fort Oglethorpe's manicured grassy common. With white, lattice-trimmed twin porches and a quaint front sitting room, this captivating 1902 Greek Revival inn has all the charm of a satin and lace–trimmed dollhouse. The airy sitting room has an appealing Laura-Ashley-meets-country-Victorian flair, with overstuffed armchairs, wicker settees, and floral borders.

After traveling through New England and staying in bed-and-breakfasts, sisters Pam Humphrey and Ann Gilbert bought the house in 1987 and opened it in 1988. A small breakfast room at the end of the second-floor hall overlooks the old fort's parade field. From the back of the inn, you can see Chickamauga National Battlefield. You can have breakfast here or on old Country Roses china and lace tablecloths in the dining room downstairs. Lookout Mountain is 15 minutes away.

Address: *13 Barnhardt Cir., Fort Oglethorpe, GA 30742, tel. 706/858–0624 or 800/710–6816.*
Accommodations: *6 double rooms with baths.*
Amenities: *Air-conditioning; ceiling fans, cable TV and ironing boards in rooms, phone in snack room.*
Rates: *$55–$100; full breakfast. AE, D, MC, V.*
Restrictions: *No smoking indoors, no pets.*

The Gordon-Lee Mansion

The Gordon-Lee Mansion in Chickamauga, the nation's oldest and largest military park, was made a national historic site, and rightly so—the Greek Revival house survived the ravages of the war that raged near here more than a century ago. The mansion sits in the middle of 7 acres, containing formal English and Southern vegetable gardens.

Built in 1840–47 by James Gordon, an early Scottish settler, the house was used by the Union Army as a headquarters and hospital. A wide driveway lined with oaks and maples frames the grand Doric columns on the front veranda as you approach. A stroll across the shade-dappled lawn takes you to a brick slave cabin, which sleeps three in two rooms, and then into the heart of the small mountain town. The mansion's well-preserved rooms have 10- and 12-foot ceilings and are furnished with English, American, and French period antiques. Frank Green, a retired dentist, and his wife, Maria, opened the house to the public in the late 1980s. They live on the grounds nearby, as does the manager, Richard Barclift.

Address: *217 Cove Rd., Chickamauga, GA 30707, tel. 706/375–4728.*
Accommodations: *4 double rooms with baths, 1 cabin.*
Amenities: *Air-conditioning, cable TV in rooms, phone in front hall.*
Rates: *$70–$95; Continental breakfast. MC, V.*
Restrictions: *No smoking indoors, no pets.*

The Pittman House

This 1890s-vintage Colonial-style house—in a small town outside Athens and 2 miles from the sprawling Tanger Factory Outlet Mall—is owned by Tom and Dot Tomberlin, longtime antiques dealers from Atlanta, who bought and restored the house in 1988. Dot works full-time in a chemical plant, so Tom became the daytime manager. He can typically be found next door tending their antiques store, Granny's Old Things, or carving wood figures; he specializes in Old World Santas. Tom runs the inn with an inviting warmth based on the old Southern saying, "If you ain't at home, you ought to be."

The house is just on the edge of the commercial district, but what it lacks in scenery it makes up for in homey comforts. In order to make guests "be at home," they are given the run of the downstairs parlor, the kitchen, and the dining room. The bedrooms are decorated with a potpourri of turn-of-the-century antiques and Oriental and hooked rugs. Old armoires are filled with antique quilts. In the afternoon, guests congregate in the rocking chairs on the front porch, in the sitting area on the landing, or in the sun room, furnished with comfortable wicker.

Address: *81 Homer Rd., Commerce, GA 30529, tel. 706/335–3823.*
Accommodations: *2 double rooms with baths, 2 doubles share 1 bath.*
Amenities: *Air-conditioning, cable TV in common area.*
Rates: *$55–$65; full breakfast. MC, V.*
Restrictions: *No smoking indoors, no pets, no alcohol.*

The York House

This old inn, listed on the National Register of Historic Places, nestles at the base of Rabun Bald Mountain and gives guests the luxury of some of North Georgia's best hiking and rafting. In the winter, skiers take advantage of nearby Sky Valley, the southernmost ski resort in the country. The original log cabin is today a two-story structure with double porches built in an L shape around a towering stand of trees. Now owned by Jim and Phyllis Smith and run by resident managers, it has operated as an inn since 1896.

Guest rooms are simply furnished with assorted vintage pieces and have small sitting rooms with gas fireplaces and Victorian couches. Breakfasts are served on a silver tray here each morning. Each room has a small, private bathroom supplied by natural springs of the Blue Ridge Mountains. Most have balcony entrances. Stacks of current magazines and newspapers cover the tops of bureaus and chests on stairway landings. Mountain breezes cool the house.

Address: *York House Rd. (Box 126), Mountain City, GA 30562, tel. 706/746–2068.*
Accommodations: *13 double rooms with baths, 1 suite.*
Amenities: *Ceiling fans in all rooms, air-conditioning and cable TV in some rooms, phone in parlor; shuffleboard.*
Rates: *$55–$79; Continental breakfast. AE, D, MC, V.*
Restrictions: *No smoking indoors, no pets, 2-night minimum in Oct. and on holiday weekends.*

Middle Georgia

When Margaret Mitchell modeled Tara and its surroundings in Gone with the Wind *on the Jonesboro part of Clayton County, she immortalized the piedmont of Georgia. The landscape here has remained relatively undisturbed since the days when cotton was king. You can drive for hours past flat fields planted in razor-straight rows of soybeans, tobacco, tomatoes, corn, peanuts, cotton, and the famous Vidalia onions and, of course, groves of peach trees. The daily rhythm of rural life has been colorfully captured in works by native writers: Flannery O'Connor's irony-laden short stories, the Uncle Remus tales by Joel Chandler Harris, and* The Color Purple *and other books by Alice Walker. You may have glimpsed the charm of the area on the critically acclaimed TV series "I'll Fly Away," which was set in Madison.*

Many antebellum estates, Federal-era plantation houses, and Victorian bungalows have been handsomely restored and stand as reminders of bygone years. Well-marked driving trails bearing names like Peach Blossom and Antebellum take you through small historic towns dotted with homes of architectural distinction and past lushly landscaped gardens. In Macon (once dubbed Queen City of the South), crowds gather annually in March for the cherry blossom festival; it has almost 200,000 of the Japanese trees, surpassing even Washington, DC. The sheer beauty of Madison, a "cultural and aristocratic town," protected it from destruction by General Sherman on his march to the sea. Augusta, founded in 1736 and the state's second-oldest city, is called the Garden City of the South. Its six historic districts can be viewed from a trolley or on foot. Of particular interest are Broadstreet; Riverwalk; Oldetown, one of the largest neighborhoods of Victorian homes in the state; and Summerville, known as "the Hill," a summer retreat built by John D. Rockefeller. Bike trails along the Savannah River provide a pleasant way to enjoy the wildlife—blue herons, river otters, and wild turkeys—that abounds.

Places to Go, Sights to See

Ashley Oaks (144 College St., Jonesboro, tel. 706/478–8986). Built between 1879 and 1880, this Jonesboro mansion remains the town's most elegant residence. It is renovated, furnished with period pieces, and open for tours by appointment.

Augusta. This beautiful port city hosts golf's Masters Tournament each spring. A five-block area with stores, restaurants, entertainment, and *The Shoppes of Port Royal* shopping center hugs the banks of the Savannah River. Antiques stores line *Broad Street* in the walkable historic district. Augusta has the state's second-oldest opera, a symphony, and a ballet company, all of which perform in the gilded Romanesque-style *Sacred Heart Cultural Center* (1301 Greene St., tel. 706/826–4700).

Callaway Plantation (U.S. 78, 5 mi west of Washington, tel. 706/678–2013). This 56-acre working farm has been under the control of the same family since the late 18th century and today shows how the area's early settlers lived. Tour a circa 1869 Greek Revival house, a log cabin, and a two-story Plain-style house, open daily March–December.

Hawkinsville Historic Opera House (100 N. Lumpkin St., tel. 912/783–1717). The original turn-of-the-century glamour of this elaborately decorated performance hall has been restored, and cultural events, concerts, and plays are presented here once more.

The **Jarrell Plantation** (Rte. 1, Juliette, tel. 912/986–5172), outside Macon, consists of 20 historic buildings dating between 1847 and 1940, including a three-story barn, a beekeeping house, a gristmill, a cane mill, smokehouses, and an extensive collection of domestic artifacts of the period.

Macon, incorporated in 1823, has three national historic districts, which have large garden squares and wide streets lined with Greek Revival mansions and Victorian bungalows. *Pleasant Hills Historic District,* one of the first black neighborhoods on the National Register of Historic Places, and the *Harriet Tubman Museum* (340 Walnut St., tel. 912/743–8544) are dedicated to the preservation of black history. The *Ocmulgee National Monument* (1207 Emery Hwy., tel. 912/752–8257) commemorates 12,000 years of Southeast Indian culture with a museum, a film, and exhibits from the excavated Indian mounds. *Hay House* (934 Georgia Ave., tel. 912/742–8155), a spectacular 24-room Italian Renaissance Revival mansion (ca. 1855–60), was built with an elevator, a secret room, and an early ventilating system. Today it is filled with the art and antiques collections of the Georgia Trust for Historic Preservation. *Woodruff House* (988 Bond St., tel. 912/744–4187) is a Greek Revival mansion built in 1863, owned and operated by Mercer

University. It was the scene of a ball for Winnie Davis, daughter of Confederate President Jefferson Davis.

In **Madison,** often called "the town Sherman refused to burn" on his fiery march to the sea, stringent restoration codes have preserved the city's architectural heritage. Federal and Victorian mansions, churches, and public buildings make it the state's antebellum showcase. Good walking-tour maps and audiotapes are available at the Madison-Morgan County Chamber of Commerce (*see* Tourist Information, *below*).

Male Academy Museum (30 Temple Ave., Newnan, tel. 706/251–0207). In a restored 1883 schoolhouse, Coweta County's history is interpreted through education, industry, architecture, and costume, from pre-settler days through the late 19th century. Civil War and *Gone With the Wind* collections are displayed with rotating exhibits.

Massee Lane Gardens (Rte. 49, outside Fort Valley, tel. 912/967–2358) is the home of the American Camellia Society. The 9 acres of gardens are in full bloom from November to March; azaleas, banksia roses, daylilies, and other bulbs take their turn in season.

Monastery of the Holy Spirit (2625 Rte. 212, 8 mi southwest of Conyers, tel. 706/483–8705). The grounds offer a pastoral spot for picnics and contain a greenhouse where bonsai trees are sold and a gift shop that sells baked goods.

Museum of Aviation at Robins Air Force Base (7 mi from I–75 at Exit 58, outside Perry, tel. 912/923–6600). This collection on 43 acres contains more than 70 historic airplanes, an original Norden bombsight, and an SR–71 Blackbird spy plane.

Panola Mountain State Conservation Park (2600 Rte. 155 SW, Stockbridge, tel. 706/389–7801), in Henry County, has hiking trails, picnic areas, covered shelters, and playgrounds.

Robert Toombs House (216 E. Robert Toombs Ave., Washington, tel. 706/678–2226). This completely restored downtown house was built in 1794. Once the home of Confederate General Robert Toombs, secretary of the Confederacy, it is now a state park, whose exhibits tell the story of the fiery planter and lawyer.

Senoia. You can pick up a pamphlet at city hall or the town library that outlines a driving tour around the national historic district. It covers 24 houses that date from antebellum days through the late 19th century.

Washington Historical Museum (308 E. Robert Toombs Ave., tel. 706/678–2105). Elegant antebellum furnishings, Civil War mementos, and a Native American collection are on display in this historic house.

Restaurants

Another Thyme (tel. 404/678–1672), in Washington's historic Fitzpatrick Hotel, serves Continental breakfast, lunch, and dinner. **Beall's 1860** (tel. 912/745–3663), a Greek Revival mansion in a historic district in Macon, serves prime rib and daily specials at lunch and dinner. **Fincher's Barbecue,** (tel. 912/743–5866 and 912/742–2220), with two Macon locations, has been serving pit-cooked pork, ribs, chicken, and Brunswick stew for over 50 years. **Len Berg's** (tel. 912/742–9255), in Macon, serves fresh vegetables, fried oysters, macaroon pie, and other Southern delights. **The Raines Room** (tel. 912/489–8628), in the Statesboro Inn, serves Continental cuisine Tuesday through Saturday nights. In a renovated Victorian town house in Augusta is the **White Elephant Café** (tel. 706/722–8614). Daily specials have tongue-in-cheek names like Bubba's Delight. Rutledge's **The Yesterday Café** (tel. 706/557–9337), a revamped turn-of-the-century drugstore, has photos dating from the Civil War and is famous for blueberry pancakes and buttermilk biscuits.

Tourist Information

Clayton County Convention & Visitors Bureau (8712 Tara Blvd., Jonesboro, GA 30237, tel. 706/478–4800). **Macon-Bibb County Convention and Visitors Bureau** (Terminal Station, 300 Cherry St., Macon, GA 31201, tel. 912/743–3401). **Madison-Morgan County Chamber of Commerce** (115 E. Jefferson St., Box 826, Madison, GA 30650, tel. 706/342–4454). **Monroe County Chamber of Commerce** (Box 811, Forsyth, GA 31029, tel. 912/994–9239). **Newnan-Coweta Chamber of Commerce** (23 Bullsboro Dr., Box 1103, Newnan, GA 30264, tel. 404/253–2270). **Peach County Chamber of Commerce** (Box 1238, Fort Valley, GA 31030, tel. 912/825–3733). **Perry Area Convention & Visitors Bureau** (Box 1619, Perry, GA 31069, tel. 912/988–8000). **Washington-Wilkes Chamber of Commerce** (104 E. Liberty St., Box 661, Washington, GA 30673, tel. 706/678–2013).

The 1842 Inn

This imposing Greek Revival mansion stands in the heart of Macon's historic neighborhood, a few blocks from Mercer University, a five-minute drive from downtown, and practically next door to the acclaimed Beall's 1860 restaurant.

The medium-size inn, named for the year its oldest portion was built, was enlarged around the turn of the century, was professionally restored in 1986, and has earned many preservation awards. It was bought in 1991 by Philip Jenkins, a Georgia native and fund-raising consultant, and his silent partner Richard Meils, a Michigan physician. Philip or one of the friendly staff members will show you to a spacious, well-appointed guest room in the main house or in the Victorian cottage, which was saved from demolition by being cut in half, moved to the property, and installed in back, past the brick courtyard.

The grand, white-pillared front porch—dramatically lit at night— opens to the traditional center hall found in many Southern houses. In the quietly elegant bedrooms, ceiling fans whirl overhead. Brass or four-poster beds are made up with eyelet-trimmed linens, and breakfast is served along with the morning paper in your bedroom's sitting area. Fresh flowers perfume the rooms, and evening turndown service includes gourmet chocolates. Guests can also have overnight shoe shining. Six of the rooms have working fireplaces, and four have whirlpool baths.

High tea is served on the grand porch each Saturday and Sunday afternoon when weather permits, and cocktails and hors d'oeuvres are available in the library after 5:30 each day. The end of each week is celebrated at the cocktail hour with live jazz on Thursday and Friday.

Address: *353 College St., Macon, GA 31201, tel. and fax 912/741–1842 or 800/336–1842.*
Accommodations: *12 double rooms with baths in house, 9 doubles with baths in cottage.*
Amenities: *Air-conditioning, cable TV, and phones in rooms.*
Rates: *$95–$125; Continental breakfast, afternoon refreshments. AE, MC, V.*
Restrictions: *No pets.*

The Veranda

Two oak trees canopy the walk leading up to The Veranda's wraparound front porch, and rows of green rockers and shutters are outlined against the white paint. The two-story Neoclassic house, on the National Register of Historic Places, was built in 1906 as the Holbury Hotel. Senoia, which contains 113 sites on the National Register of Historic Places, is near both Callaway Gardens and the Little White House in Warm Springs, 20 miles south of Atlanta.

The quality of this inn's hospitality, cuisine, and charm has earned it several "inn of the year" awards. Jan Boal, a college mathematics professor, and his wife, Bobby, an extraordinarily good cook, run the place as if every guest is a cherished friend. You are greeted in the foyer by a board printed with your name and room assignment. For breakfast, Bobby prepares fruit cups topped with sorbets, freshly baked cinnamon rolls, and three-cheese omelets. On weekends it's Belgian waffles cooked to order, fresh fruit, and a hot buffet. Breakfast in bed is even brought to one room. Promptly at 7, Bobby serves five-course, home-cooked dinners (for an extra charge) with, for example, French onion soup, sourdough brown bread, broccoli and chicken casserole, shrimp mousse, and raspberry layer cake. You'll go off to bed with an armload of children's books, because, having written one,

Jan believes they're just right for bedtime reading. In your room you'll find magazines and goodies cushioned on each pillow.

Guest rooms have themes, like bird-watching, or the Civil War, or butterflies, and are equipped accordingly, with binoculars, an army drum—even a group of walking sticks. Fresh-cut flowers and homemade quilts decorate the rooms, too. The hallways are also full of curiosities: antique tools and an old portable record player.

Downstairs in the parlor, which doubles as a gift shop, you'll find an old pump organ and the Boals' huge collection of kaleidoscopes for sale. Throughout the comfortable inn are Victorian furnishings, some of which came with the house; family memorabilia; and games and puzzles.

Address: *252 Seavy St. (Box 177), Senoia, GA 30276, tel. 404/599–3905.*
Accommodations: *9 double rooms with baths.*
Amenities: *Air-conditioning, TV and phone in common area, whirlpool bath in 1 room.*
Rates: *$85–$105; full breakfast. AE, MC, V.*
Restrictions: *No smoking indoors, no pets, BYOB.*

Inn Scarlett's Footsteps

This Greek Revival, white-columned plantation house was built at the turn of the century by C.T. Smith, owner of one of the largest nurseries in the South. In 1993, K.C. and Vern Bassham bought it and modeled a B&B after *Gone with the Wind*. Songs from the movie soundtrack greet you from the wide front porch, surrounded by magnolias and oaks. With great care, K.C. has assembled an impressive and valuable collection of GWTW memorabilia. One room serves as a museum for the bulk of the collection. The Basshams play their roles to the hilt, even dressing in period costumes. For dinner, they'll direct you to nearby General Wheeler's Mess Tent, which serves Civil War–era cuisine. For shopping, you'll be sent to Saks, which sells Civil War memorabilia, or you can look in their gift shop, in the original carriage house.

Queen Anne furnishings and period antiques adorn the house, which has hardwood floors throughout. Each of the bedrooms is named for a different GWTW character and is decorated accordingly. Civil War buffs enjoy an annual reenactment nearby, and at Christmas there's a barbecue and ball on the stately grounds.

Address: *138 Hill St., Concord, GA 30206, tel. 706/495-9012.*
Accommodations: *4 double rooms with baths, 1 suite.*
Amenities: *Cable TV and phone in library.*
Rates: *$55–$85; full breakfast. MC, V.*
Restrictions: *No smoking, no pets.*

Statesboro Inn

This large cream-colored Neoclassical frame house with shaded verandas was built in 1903. It was renovated and opened as a B&B in 1981, equipped with such modern luxuries as whirlpools and such simple old-fashioned pleasures as rocking chairs on the front porch.

The Garges family purchased the inn in 1993. Michele, Tony, and their daughter, Melissa, share the duties entailed in hosting guests. Bedrooms have brass beds, love seats, and country charm, and some have private porches. Four bedrooms and three common rooms have working fireplaces. In a restored cabin behind the house, Willie McTell wrote "Statesboro Blues," a hit song for the Allman Brothers Band. The Raines Room, the inn's public dining room, is known for casual but elegant dining. The 50-seat, award-winning restaurant cooks up such specialties as shrimp Cancún. A conference facility accommodates 100.

Located in a quiet downtown area, the inn is 1 mile from Georgia Southern and its botanical gardens. Savannah is a day trip away.

Address: *106 S. Main St., Statesboro, GA 30458, tel. 912/489-8628 or 800/846-9466.*
Accommodations: *13 double rooms with baths, 2 suites.*
Amenities: *Cable TV and phones in rooms; off-street parking.*
Rates: *$65–$90; full breakfast. AE, D, DC, MC, V.*
Restrictions: *No pets.*

Coastal Georgia

*Sandy white beaches and saltwater marshes rim the state's
100 miles of coast, from the mouth of the Savannah River at
the South Carolina border south to the St. Marys River. The
islands (called the Golden Isles) and mainland towns that
dot this coastline attracted Colonial settlers and later became
the winter retreats of Carnegies, Rockefellers, and
Vanderbilts. All were lured, as visitors are today, by the
balmy winters, the promise of escape on sun-drenched
beaches, and calm afternoons spent drifting along winding
tidal creeks. Along with these timeless pleasures come
exciting Independence Day celebrations, rowdy beach music,
wonderful seafood, and jazz and art festivals. The area's
diverse pursuits and sunny climate combine to make it a
year-round vacation spot.*

*Historic Savannah boasts a Colonial setting with cobble-
stone squares and parks draped with Spanish moss. The
city's River Street waterfront gift shops and jazz bars bustle
with visiting crowds, and the annual St. Patrick's Day
parade is one of the country's largest. Travelers seeking a
more informal setting can continue south toward St. Simons
Island for swimming, fishing, golf, and tennis.*

*Little of urban America is evident in these rural, coastal
areas, but glimpses of the lavish lifestyle of the 19th-century
rich and famous remain on Jekyll Island in Millionaire's
Village, where stately Victorian and shingled manses rim the
waterway compound. Cumberland Island National
Seashore's protected forests and 16 miles of pristine white-
sand beaches and dunes offer isolated serenity. Inland near
the Georgia-Florida state line lies the 700-square-mile
Okefenokee Swamp, whose black waters are dotted with water
lilies and inhabited by alligators.*

*During the off-season, before Memorial Day and after Labor
Day, the crowds leave these seashore communities, and the*

already remote beaches become virtually private play-grounds. If you visit at this time of year, you discover what locals already know: that the humid temperatures and the insects leave with the crowds.

Places to Go, Sights to See

Cumberland Island. A national seashore, this island is distinguished by an undisturbed landscape. Accessible only by boat, the island is a sanctuary for wild horses, deer, and bobcats. It is popular for day trips and overnight camping, and the park service (tel. 912/882–4335) operates a ferry service on a limited, reservations-only schedule.

Darien. The British *Ft. King George* (tel. 912/437–4770), 19th-century houses, and historic churches (including the smallest one in the United States) are some of what you'll see in Georgia's second-oldest planned town.

The Green-Meldrim House (1 W. Macon St., Savannah, tel. 912/232–1251), a Gothic Revival mansion with wraparound wrought-iron balconies, was built in 1850 for cotton merchant Charles Green. General Sherman stayed here during his occupation of Savannah; it was later occupied by a Judge Peter Meldrim and is now the parish house of St. John's Episcopal Church. The house, in its original condition, is furnished with period antiques (some original to the house) and is open for tours.

Hofwyl-Broadfield Plantation (Rte. 2, Darien, tel. 912/264–9263), estab-lished in the early 1800s, was one of the few that functioned around the turn of the 20th century. Visitors can tour the 1858 plantation house and walk along the canals that were used to flood the rice fields lining the riverbanks.

Jekyll Island (tel. 912/635–3636). Named for Sir Joseph Jekyll, the largest contributor to Georgia's colonization, the island is reached from Brunswick by causeway. It offers 63 holes of golf, 10 miles of Atlantic Ocean beach-front, and a historic district that was a turn-of-the-century private winter playground for the Rockefellers, Cranes, Pulitzers, and Vanderbilts. Many of their brick, shingle, and tabby manses stand today as architectural landmarks of a bygone era.

Little St. Simons Island is a private getaway resort, accessible by small plane or by boat from St. Simons Island. The 12,000-acre island is even more secluded than Cumberland, and if you plan to stay over, reservations must be made well in advance (Box 1078, St. Simons Island, GA 31522, tel. 912/638–7472).

Okefenokee Swamp Park (Rte. 177, off U.S. 1, 8 mi south of Waycross, tel. 912/283–0583). This wildlife sanctuary is at the north end of the Okefenokee Swamp National Wildlife Refuge, one of the country's most acclaimed wilderness areas. Guided boat tours highlight the swamp's flora and fauna, and a network of bridged walkways allows visitors to penetrate the park on foot.

The **Owens-Thomas House** (124 Abercorn St., Savannah, tel. 912/233–9743), built in 1817, was architect William Jay's first Regency mansion in Savannah and is still the city's finest example of that style. In 1825 the Marquis de Lafayette bade Savannah good-bye from the house's wrought-iron balcony. Daily tours highlight its architectural details and priceless antique furnishings.

St. Simons Island. This seashore haven, connected to the mainland by a causeway, is the most developed of the Golden Isles. Its southern tip is rimmed by white sand beaches and dotted with souvenir shops, gift boutiques, and restaurants; a network of bike paths extends across the marshlands into the center of the island. Historic sites established by early settlers include *Ft. Frederica* (tel. 912/638–3639) and *St. Simons Lighthouse* (tel. 912/638–4666).

Sapelo. After the Creek Indians, Spanish missionaries, British soldiers, and rice planters came tobacco magnate R.J. Reynolds, who bought this barrier island in the 1930s for his own agricultural projects. Today the island is a state-owned protected area, which operates as an institute for the study of marine life and marshland. It's accessible only by boat, and the Department of Natural Resources (tel. 912/437–4192) conducts tours three days each week.

Tybee Island, east of Savannah on Victory Drive (U.S. 80), is a popular, commercialized seashore escape for families; seafood restaurants, shops of the salt-water taffy ilk, and summer cottages crowd the island.

Restaurants

Elizabeth's on 37th (tel. 912/236–5547), in Savannah, is famed for regional specialties. In Savannah's historic district, **Mrs. Wilkes Boarding House** (tel. 912/232–5997) serves Southern breakfasts and lunches in an appealing elbow-to-elbow family-style setting, while **Bobbie's** (tel. 912/238–2443), a vintage diner, offers burgers and fries. **The Fourth of May** (tel. 912/638–5444) on St. Simons Island and Savannah's **45 South** (tel. 912/233–1881) offer gourmet regional cuisine in cozy, contemporary settings. The **Crab Trap** (tel. 912/638–3552), a casual spot on St. Simons, serves fried and broiled seafood entrées caught locally. **Speeds Kitchen** (tel. 912/832–4643), amid the odd collection of house trailers and shingled buildings in Shellman's Bluff, outside Darien, is considered by many locals to have the area's best fried seafood.

Tourist Information

Jekyll Island Convention and Visitors Bureau (901 Jekyll Island Causeway, Jekyll Island, GA 31520, tel. 912/635–3636). **St. Simons Chamber of Commerce** (Neptune Park, St. Simons Island, GA 31522, tel. 912/638–

9014). **Savannah Visitors Center** (301 W. Broad St., Savannah, GA 31499, tel. 912/944–0455).

Reservation Services

RSVP Savannah (9489 Whitfield Ave., Box 49, Savannah, GA 31406, tel. 912/232–7787 or 800/729–7787). **Savannah Historic Inns** (147 Bull St., Savannah, GA 31401, tel. 912/233–7660 or 800/262–4667).

The Gastonian

Two blocks from Savannah's Forsyth Park and 12 from River Street stands The Gastonian. A pineapple, a symbol of hospitality, is engraved on the brass sign at the entry, a hint of the comforts within. Californians Hugh and Roberta Lineberger bought the two adjacent Regency Italianate mansions that compose the inn in 1985. The couple has transformed the pair—constructed for two prosperous merchants after the Civil War—into one of the South's most captivating inns.

Roberta spent months selecting authentic Georgian and Regency-period antiques and original Savannah colors to recall the 19th-century ambience. In the front parlor and formal dining room, the antiques have the patina that comes from being well loved and from much polishing. Sideboards and tabletops are laden with heirloom crystal, silver, and fine china. Yet the inn doesn't have the museum feel that can make some historic homes uncomfortable. Guests are encouraged to lounge in the coral upholstered wing chairs on either side of the drawing room fireplace or pick out tunes on the antique baby grand piano that dominates the front parlor. Scalamandre's Savannah collection wallpapers adorn the hallways. Of the bedrooms, one is decorated in rustic country and contains ladder-back cane chairs and antique trunks; another is reminiscent of Colonial America, with crewel draperies and bedspreads; and

still another is all British formality, dressed in chintz and damask upholstery. Most have rice poster or Charleston canopy beds. The baths are well lit and luxurious. Directly behind the main house is the carriage house suite. Guests are greeted with fruit and a split of wine, and turndown service includes fresh pecan pralines and peach schnapps.

A sumptuous Southern breakfast is served in the large country kitchen or the dining room. Late risers can opt for a Continental breakfast delivered bedside on a silver tray along with the local paper. An elevated sundeck with chaise longues, a wisteria- and jasmine-draped pergola, and a large hot tub makes for a pleasant spot to laze away the afternoon. The concierge has plenty of suggestions for terrific restaurants and will arrange for transport by horse-drawn carriage. March, April, May, and October are the inn's busiest times, so call well in advance.

Address: *220 E. Gaston St., Savannah, GA 31401, tel 912/232-2869 or 800/322-6603, fax 912/232-0710.*
Accommodations: *10 double rooms with baths, 3 suites.*
Amenities: *Cable TV, phones, and gas fireplaces in rooms; off-street parking.*
Rates: *$125–$275; full breakfast, afternoon tea. AE, MC, V.*
Restrictions: *No smoking, no pets.*

Greyfield Inn

The only hotel on Cumberland Island, Greyfield Inn is a symbol of civility in the wilds. The island is accessible only by ferry or other boat or by private plane. Round-trip transportation aboard the *Lucy R. Ferguson* is free to inn guests. The imposing house with wide colonnade porches stands by itself in the 1,300-acre, primitive landscape. Built in 1901 by tycoon Thomas Carnegie for his daughter, the two-story, glinty white, Victorian house retains much of its original glory. The inn is operated by Mitty Ferguson, Carnegie's great-great-grandson, and his wife, Mary Jo, who carefully preserve ties to the past. They furnished the inn as if it were still a private residence, with dark, heavy, late-19th-century furniture; family photographs; tabletop collections of seashore memorabilia; and antique rugs. The formal dining room is typically decorated with freshly cut greenery—vines and berries collected on the island. Mantelpieces are lit by candelabras.

The inn's enthusiastic staff is dedicated to making guests feel comfortable. The bedrooms are spacious, the linens crisp, and the hardwood floors burnished to a glossy shine. The spit-and-polished bathrooms (shared by four rooms) have antique tubs, and there's an enclosed backyard shower house that is another full bath. The best times to visit are in spring and early autumn, when the insect population and level of humidity remain low. In winter, guests can go on beach excursions and guided Jeep tours of the island's historic ruins.

All meals are included in the rates. Breakfast is an informal affair of baked apples, ginger flapjacks, sausages or bacon, and coffee. Hors d'oeuvres are served at the cocktail hour, and afternoon tea is a winter ritual. The ring of a bell announces the formal evening meal, which often includes tasty soups, pasta and shrimp dishes, and always wonderful desserts. The staff's tradition of dressing for dinner transforms the nightly ritual into a festive occasion, but the inn's atmosphere is still relaxed. Lunches are left in picnic baskets in the old-fashioned kitchen. The Fergusons let you follow your own agenda or help plan a day's activities: shelling, fishing, clam digging, swimming, hiking, or beachcombing.

Address: *Cumberland Island, GA (Drawer B, Fernandina Beach, FL 32034), tel. 904/261-6408.*
Accommodations: *3 double rooms with baths, 3 doubles and 1 suite share 3 baths, outdoor shower house.*
Amenities: *Air-conditioning in dining room; shuttle to ferry, bike rentals, guided nature tours.*
Rates: *$275–$315; American Plan, afternoon refreshments. MC, V.*
Restrictions: *No smoking indoors, no pets.*

Open Gates

Abrick-and-white-picket fence outlines the perimeter of Open Gates bed-and-breakfast, the home of Carolyn Hodges. The white frame Victorian, plantation-plain house with gray shutters and a red front door was built in 1876. It is tucked beneath a canopy of Spanish moss cascading from live oaks and is on the corner of Vernon Square, a national historic district, three blocks from the Altamaha River, historic Darien's major thoroughfare.

Founded in 1736, the town was a shipping center for cotton and a busy lumber port. It is now a jumping-off point for boat tours to Sapelo (a nearby barrier island), a shrimping port, and a center of domestic caviar production. It was profiled in the nonfiction best-seller *Praying for Sheetrock*, by Melissa Fay Green.

Carolyn Hodges, an avid preservationist and nature lover, eagerly shares her knowledge with interested visitors. She pulls a vintage fishing boat behind her vintage Mercedes-Benz for the bird-watching expeditions she conducts.

In a sunny den, a game table is set for chess or backgammon, and shelves are filled with books on coastal history, including the diary of the English actress Fanny Kemble, who recorded her controversial stand against slavery while living in the area briefly. Carolyn delights in engaging guests in a literary pop quiz over a breakfast of plantation pancakes, served with an assortment of jams in her collection of fruit-shaped jam pots.

One guest bedroom, in Savannah blue, has a sleigh bed and a display of old doll clothes and children's books; another, done in peach and blue, has twin beds; and an upstairs room, painted dark green, has wooden floors and framed botanical illustrations. A room above the garage with a private entrance has natural wood walls adorned with antique quilts.

A canoe standing on the back porch, the aquarium gurgling away in the den, and the baby grand, family portraits, and photographs in the deep-orange front parlor remind you that this is a family's home.

Address: *Vernon Sq. (Box 1526), Darien, GA 31305, tel. 912/437–6985.*
Accommodations: *2 double rooms with baths, 2 doubles share 1 bath.*
Amenities: *Air-conditioning, TV and phone in common area; large pool.*
Rates: *$45–$53; full breakfast. No credit cards.*
Restrictions: *No smoking indoors, no pets.*

Ballastone Inn

This handsome stucco inn converted from an antebellum mansion was built for a well-to-do Savannah shipping magnate, later became home to a bank president, and today is run by Timothy Hargus. Its central location along Savannah's Oglethorpe Avenue in the historic district puts you on the main bus line, a quick walk from the Civic Center. It also makes the first-floor rooms a bit noisy.

The Ballastone has Old World flair. It's not as lavish as The Gastonian; the linens are not as fine and the guest rooms are smaller. Many of the rooms have rice poster and canopy beds and are decorated with antiques from the Regency period and Victorian era. A town house next door has 6 suites.

Tea, coffee, and Southern pastries are set out in the genteel parlor, done in authentic Savannah color schemes. Breakfast is served in the parlor each morning, and evening nightcaps are mixed in guest rooms or out in the courtyard in nice weather.

Address: *14 E. Oglethorpe Ave., Savannah, GA 31401, tel. 912/236–1484 or 800/822–4553, fax 912/236–4626.* **Accommodations:** *17 double rooms with baths, 9 suites.* **Amenities:** *Air-conditioning, cable TV with VCR and phones in rooms, fireplaces and whirlpools in some rooms, video library, 24-hr concierge, elevator; off-street parking.* **Rates:** *$135–$185; Continental breakfast, afternoon tea and nightcaps. AE, MC, V.* **Restrictions:** *No pets.*

Brunswick Manor

The ticktock of a collection of antique clocks from around the world resounds through the handsomely renovated interior of Brunswick Manor, a stately 1886 Victorian in the historic district. Claudia and Harry Tzucanow, whose enthusiasm for sailing brought them to the Georgia coast, opened the inn in 1989.

In a setting of oaks and palmettos, with a sweeping veranda graced with a wicker porch swing and settee, the house lets visitors sample an aristocratic lifestyle. The fine Victorian reproductions and antiques complement the ornate oak staircase, high ceilings, and beveled glass mirrors of the house. Deluxe frills are the trademark of this B&B: plush robes and fresh flowers in each room and,

at extra cost, sailing aboard the owners' 51-foot ketch or trawler. The sleeping quarters are typically Southern, dressed up with ornate antique bedsteads, bureaus, and decorations, and both the suite and one double have small kitchenettes. A simply decorated housekeeping cottage that sleeps four is ideal for groups traveling together.

Address: *825 Egmont St., Brunswick, GA 31520, tel. 912/265–6889.* **Accommodations:** *3 double rooms with baths, 1 housekeeping suite, 1 housekeeping cottage.* **Amenities:** *Air-conditioning, phone in common area.* **Rates:** *$55–$100; full breakfast. No credit cards.* **Restrictions:** *No smoking indoors, pets in cottage only.*

Magnolia Place Inn

After passing through the front yard gate, you climb steep steps softly carpeted with moss to reach the freshly painted Magnolia Place. Striking two-story verandas wrap around the front of this 1878 Savannah house, where poet Conrad Aiken was born. There's a sophisticated elegance to the well-proportioned house, but inside you'll find that the front parlor has been sacrificed for bedrooms, giving the inn a claustrophobic feeling. The rose-hued back parlor, furnished in Colonial style (except for the glow of a clock radio), is the only reception room.

Though the guest rooms aren't as well decorated as those in the other historic houses, the antiques are English and well cared for. Eleven rooms are equipped with fireplaces, and six have oversize whirlpool baths. Breakfast is served on fine china either in the parlor, in the garden, on the veranda, or bedside. What the Magnolia lacks in ambience it makes up for in its unbeatable location, overlooking the lush landscaping of Forsyth Park.

Address: *503 Whitaker St., Savannah, GA 31401, tel. 912/236-7674 or 800/238-7674.*
Accommodations: *13 double rooms with baths.*
Amenities: *Air-conditioning, cable TV with VCR and phones in rooms; off-street parking.*
Rates: *$90–$195; Continental breakfast. AE, MC, V.*
Restrictions: *No pets, closed mid-Jan.–mid-Feb.*

Olde Harbour Inn

The Olde Harbour Inn, in a converted three-story warehouse built in 1892, has been open as an inn since 1987. It offers prime access to the many gift shops, restaurants, and bars lining the city's popular River Street district.

The inn's white-on-white interiors may lack the flavor of the historic mansions, but they do have a clean, crisp appeal and contemporary conveniences: Each bedroom is carpeted, has a fully equipped kitchen, and is individually decorated with period antiques.

You can reserve a two-room suite or a deluxe suite on the fourth floor, which has a sleeping loft overlooking two entertaining rooms. Some suites have a spacious riverfront balcony. Light breakfasts are served in the downstairs Marine Room, where wine, cordials, and cheese are set out in the late afternoon. At night guests are treated to turndown service and a dish of homemade ice cream.

Address: *508 E. Factors Walk, Savannah, GA 31401, tel. 912/234-4100 or 800/553-6533, fax 912/233-5979.*
Accommodations: *24 suites.*
Amenities: *Cable TV with HBO and phones in rooms, concierge; off-street parking.*
Rates: *$95–$165; Continental breakfast, afternoon refreshments. AE, D, DC, MC, V.*
Restrictions: *Smoking in bedrooms only, no pets.*

Pulaski Square Inn

Designed in 1853 by the Colonial architect William Jay, the Pulaski Square Inn retains the grandeur of the city's early days. The stucco building stands as one of the city's finest examples of town-house architecture. J.B. and Hilda Smith, the current proprietors, are, according to available records, only the third owners of the house, which they opened as a bed-and-breakfast in 1984.

The entire inn is beautifully restored and finished with the finest touches, from the polished heart-of-pine floors and period antiques to the bathrooms' Oriental rugs and gold-plated fixtures. Chandeliers hang from 11-foot ceilings, illuminating the bedrooms. Each floor has a separate living room, and the main-floor parlor can be rented with an adjacent bedroom as a suite. Beyond the garden courtyard is a carriage house that's a two-bedroom suite with a Japanese-style tiled bath.

Address: *203 W. Charlton St., Savannah, GA 31401, tel. 912/232–8055 or 800/227–0650.*
Accommodations: *5 double rooms with baths, 2 doubles share 1 bath, 1 suite, 1 carriage house.*
Amenities: *Air-conditioning, cable TV and phones in rooms, elevator; off-street parking.*
Rates: *$48–$196; Continental breakfast. AE, MC, V.*
Restrictions: *Smoking in bedrooms only, no pets.*

Rose Manor Guest House

Hanover Square in Old Town Brunswick is an appropriate setting for the old-fashioned charm of Rose Manor. A steeply pitched tin roof shades the white-columned porch of this pale pink bungalow surrounded by beautiful English gardens. Rachel Rose converted the entire downstairs of her family's circa-1885 home into guest quarters. She and her family reside on the second floor.

Rachel's love of old textiles and floral prints shines through in Rose Manor's comfort and nostalgic decor. Small but comfortable guest rooms have designer sheets; heirloom linens; cushy, pastel, upholstered sofas; and antique bedsteads. Bathrooms have claw-foot tubs and tiled showers.

Afternoon tea is served in the parlor or garden, and later, sherry, fresh fruit, and tea are set out on the porch so you can watch the sun set across the marsh.

Address: *Hanover Sq., 1108 Richmond St., Brunswick, GA 31520, tel. 912/267–6369.*
Accommodations: *4 double rooms share 3 baths.*
Amenities: *Cable TV and phones in public rooms; croquet, badminton.*
Rates: *$65–$95; full breakfast, afternoon tea, sherry. No credit cards.*
Restrictions: *Smoking on porches and in sun room only, no pets.*

The Southwest

Though it's steeped in Civil War history, landscaped with lush gardens, and rich in plantation lore, this corner of Georgia is frequently overlooked. A hundred years ago, however, the southwest's low-key charm developed a following among the celebrated and wealthy, and the area is associated with two American presidents. Franklin D. Roosevelt's Little White House in Warm Springs, the only home he ever owned, is now a museum, preserved as it was on the day he died there. When Jimmy Carter was elected president, the small town of Plains, west of Americus, became instantly famous.

Columbus, on the Chattahoochee River, is the region's largest city. Surrounded by the huge Fort Benning Military Reservation, it was the home of John Pemberton, the inventor of Coca-Cola, and is the site of the PGA Southern Open Golf Tournament. North of Columbus, in the Appalachian foothills, are Franklin D. Roosevelt State Park and Callaway Gardens, a resort development on 14,000 acres comprising woodlands, lakes, gardens, and wildlife that's the center of the spring Azalea Festival and an annual November steeplechase.

Near the Florida border lies Thomasville, a town of architectural grandeur, where the turn-of-the-century elite built hunting lodges and plantations and spent the winters entertaining. Many of the sporting retreats are still occupied, and a few are open to the public.

The southwest corner of Georgia also has good outlet shopping, camping, hunting, and white-water rafting. At the Andersonville National Historic Site, Civil War buffs can delve into the past. Those intrigued by Native American culture should explore Kolomoki Mounds State Historic Park, which contains seven mounds built during the 12th and 13th centuries by some of the most advanced tribes in the United States.

Places to Go, Sights to See

Andersonville National Historic Site (Rte. 49, 10 mi north of Americus, tel. 912/924–0343). In 14 months between 1864 and 1865, 13,000 Union prisoners died in the Confederate prison on this site. The reconstructed portion of the stockade is open for tours, and the museum chronicles prisoners of war in all the American conflicts from the Revolution to Vietnam. A nearby village comprises a log church, prison officials' quarters, a pioneer farm, and crafts and antiques stores.

Bellevue (204 Ben Hill St., La Grange, tel. 706/884–1832). This Greek Revival house, famous for its Ionic columns, portico, and upstairs balcony, was built in the early 1850s.

Callaway Gardens (U.S. 27, Pine Mountain, tel. 706/663–2281 or 800/282–8181). Spread across 14,000 acres of woodlands, lakes, and gardens near La Grange, this excellent family resort has four golf courses, soft and hard tennis courts, swimming, waterskiing, sailing, quail hunting, and the *Cecil B. Day Butterfly Center* (tel. 706/663–5102).

The **Chattahoochee Valley Art Association** (112 Hines St., La Grange, tel. 706/882–3267), in a restored Victorian house, displays a permanent collection of regional and local artists' works Tuesday through Sunday and puts on special monthly exhibits.

Columbus may have more museums than any other Georgia town. It also boasts a downtown historic district with well-preserved residential and commercial buildings that you can see on a walking tour. At the *Columbus Museum* (1251 Wynton Rd., tel. 706/322–0400), a multimillion-dollar expansion completed in 1989 houses an outstanding regional history section, a fine arts area, and a hands-on exhibit for children. The museum also has an excellent folk-art collection. The *Confederate Naval Museum* (202 4th St., tel. 706/327–9798), on the riverfront, contains the remains of two Confederate warships, the *Muscogee* and the *Chattahoochee.*

Cordele. This small town established in 1888 by the Americus Investment Company grew from the junction of two railroads and was the state capital during the final stage of the Civil War. The Chamber of Commerce runs walking tours of the turn-of-the-century downtown, which is on the National Register.

The **Fort Benning National Infantry Museum** (Baltzell Ave., Fort Benning Reservation, tel. 706/545–2958) traces the evolution of the infantry from the French and Indian War to the present.

Jimmy Carter National Historic Site (Main St., Plains, tel. 912/824–3413). The 39th president's first campaign headquarters, in his hometown, houses a museum, informative collections of pictures, and memorabilia from his boyhood.

Little White House (Rte. 85W and U.S. 27A, Warm Springs, tel. 706/655–3511). Franklin D. Roosevelt, afflicted with infantile paralysis, built this small house in Warm Springs as a vacation retreat during the early 1900s, so he could be near the beneficial waters. It's open daily for tours.

Providence Canyon (30 mi south of Columbus, tel. 912/838–6202), a natural wonder of spectacular color and shape, was formed entirely by rainwater erosion. There's an interpretive center, picnic areas, and hiking trails.

Thomasville. This storybook town in a scenic setting was a booming winter resort during the late 19th and early 20th centuries. The rich and famous invested in its development by buying acreage and building mansions. Today, 71 plantations still stand (on 300,000 acres), many still owned by original-family descendants. One of them, the *Lapham-Patterson House* (626 N. Dawson St., tel. 912/225–4004), a landmarked Queen Anne 20-room cottage, is an architectural tour de force without a single right angle. It is open for tours, as is *Pebble Hill Plantation* (U.S. 319S, tel. 912/226–2344), a former hunting retreat. Memorabilia from the 1800s is displayed in the *Thomas County Museum* (725 N. Dawson St., tel. 912/226–7664).

Trebor Plantation (Macon Rd., Andersonville, tel. 912/924–6887). In the 1840s, one of Sumter County's earliest settlers built this white frame house with double galleries, home to the same family for five generations. It is nicely restored, has furnishings of the period, with a few original pieces, and is open for tours.

Westville (S. Mulberry St., Lumpkin, tel. 912/838–6310). This living-history museum south of the town square depicts 19th-century Georgia life with its authentically restored buildings and daily crafts demonstrations.

Restaurants

Blue Willow Café (tel. 706/655–2195) in Warm Springs serves home-style Southern entrées. **Daphne Lodge** (tel. 912/273–2596), nestled in a pine grove setting near Lake Blackshear outside Cordele, is renowned for catfish, seafood, steaks, and melt-in-your-mouth biscuits. The cafeteria-style **Deutsche House** (tel. 912/472–2024), outside Montezuma, is famous for its authentic Mennonite cuisine and the adjacent bakery.

Tourist Information

Albany Local Welcome Center (225 W. Broad St., Albany, GA 31701, tel. 912/434–8700). **Americus–Sumter County Chamber of Commerce** (Box 724, Americus, GA 31709, tel. 912/924–2646). **Andersonville Local Welcome Center** (Old Railroad Depot, Andersonville, GA 31711, tel. 912/924–2558). **Columbus Convention & Visitors Bureau** (Box 2768, Columbus, GA 31902, tel. 706/322–1613). **Plains Visitors Information Center** (U.S. 280, Plains,

GA 31780, tel. 912/824–7477). **Thomasville–Thomas County Local Welcome Center** (401 S. Broad St., Thomasville, GA 31792, tel. 912/226–9600).

Reservation Service

Quail Country Bed and Breakfast, Ltd. (1104 Old Monticello Rd., Thomasville, GA 31792, tel. 912/226–7218).

Evans House Bed & Breakfast

This tidy yellow and white Victorian built in 1898 is across the street from the 27 acres of historic Paradise Park, in the heart of Thomasville, an elegant and affluent small town 60 miles from Albany. Leverne Puskar, whose husband, John, is a hotel executive, runs the house with a polished professionalism that stems from a wealth of experience and insight accumulated over the years. She seems to anticipate every need, providing such luxuries as crisply pressed linens, fresh flowers, plates of homemade cookies at bedtime, and made-to-order breakfasts served on china in the country kitchen.

The bedrooms—three of which are decorated with antique beds dating from the 1880s—are isolated from one another and from the Puskars' quarters. All have 11-foot ceilings, well-cared-for antiques and reproductions, and the convenience of modern baths. The suite's bath has the house's original footed tub. Both hosts are well versed in the area's history; they will arrange plantation tours or direct you to nearby antiques shops.

Address: *725 S. Hansell St., Thomasville, GA 31792, tel. 912/226–1343 or 800/344–4717, fax 912/226–0653.*
Accommodations: *3 double rooms with baths, 1 suite.*
Amenities: *Air-conditioning, cable TV with VCR and movie library in living room; guest kitchen; bicycles.*
Rates: *$45–$85; full breakfast, afternoon refreshments, evening sherry. No credit cards.*
Restrictions: *No smoking indoors, no pets.*

Morgan Towne House Restaurant Bed & Breakfast

In a bid to make this sleepy town of 2,200 the Branson of the Southeast, local entrepreneur Mike Moon has opened a National Country Music Hall of Fame, an Elvis Presley museum, a rodeo arena, and two music halls. Nevertheless, guests come to this B&B, a block from the town square, to escape the big city. Nightlife is sitting on the wraparound porch watching lightning bugs. The imposing Victorian home was built in 1880 and opened as an inn in 1993. On the National Register of Historic Places, it features the ornate woodwork and stained-glass windows that were common in its era. The rooms contain period antiques, fireplaces, and large baths with claw-foot tubs and hand-held showers. The inn is run by Richard and Claudine Morgan. (Claudine's ancestors settled the county.) The entire downstairs is a restaurant that seats 100, where groups can arrange for a special menu. In fact, personalized service is the signature for overnight guests as well. The Morgans fill such requests as ironing and serving breakfast in bed.

Address: *Church St. and 4th Ave. (Box 522), Buena Vista, GA 31803, tel. 912/649–3663.*
Accommodations: *3 double rooms with baths.*
Amenities: *Air-conditioning, TV with VCR in rooms, phone by stairs.*
Rates: *$50; full breakfast. MC, V.*
Restrictions: *No smoking, no pets.*

Susina Plantation Inn

Time stops as you enter the 115 acres of lawn and woodlands on your way to this inn, originally the great house of an 8,000-acre cotton plantation. Magnificent magnolias and centuries-old live oaks drip with Spanish moss. The 1841 Greek Revival house is owned by Anne-Marie Walker, who came from Sweden, via California, determined to have the area's most upscale inn. She has succeeded, and guests have included Paul Newman and Joanne Woodward.

Guests have the run of the house, which has an Old World feeling: large, antiques-filled public rooms and high-ceilinged bedrooms furnished with heavy Empire mahogany and opening onto screened verandas. Instead of television, there is a well-stocked bookcase. Lavish country-style breakfasts and five-course dinners with optional wine are served beneath the glow of a crystal chandelier.

If the tennis court, pond stocked with bream and bass, walking trails, croquet court, and pool don't keep you busy, you can go antiquing or take a plantation tour in Thomasville.

Address: *Meridien Rd. (Box 1010), Thomasville, GA 31792, tel. 912/377-9644.*
Accommodations *8 double rooms with baths.*
Amenities: *Restaurant, air-conditioning, phone in common area.*
Rates: *$175; MAP. No credit cards.*
Restrictions: *No smoking, no pets.*

Alabama

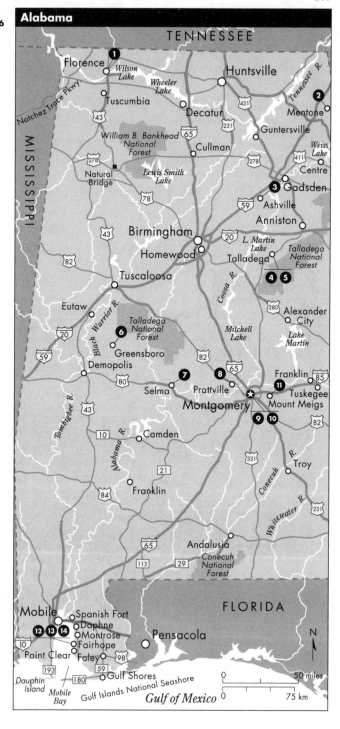

The Highlands

From a tourist's point of view Alabama, like all Gaul, can be divided into three parts: the upland country from Birmingham north, the belt of black earth where the plantations grew, and the Gulf Coast. The rocky and mountainous land in the northern section, called the Highlands, has none of the expected flavor of antebellum life. The region is made up of unproductive small farms, which sell their produce in charmless towns that look like the poor relations of other communities that are moving ahead.

The largest of the latter is Huntsville, home of the Redstone Arsenal (forerunner of NASA), the world's largest space museum, and in its Twickenham section, more pre–Civil War houses than anywhere in the state, many dating from 1814. The most sophisticated city in Alabama, Huntsville has many foreigners, the space and rocket scientists who have added considerable panache to the community and who have even made it possible to find restaurants that do not serve collard greens.

There are nine covered bridges left in this part of the state, as well as a number of state and national parks that offer recreation and interesting sights. The longest natural bridge east of the Rockies is near Haleyville; in DeSoto State Park there's the 110-foot DeSoto Falls in the beautiful Little River Canyon. Russell Cave National Park has the remains of Native American tribes dating back 8,000 years.

Farther south, set in a valley amid rolling hills, is Birmingham, the state's largest city and in the '20s and '30s the South's major industrial area. Atop Red Mountain on the city's south side is a huge statue of Vulcan, symbol of the iron and steel industry, on which the city's wealth was founded. Though the steel mills are now closed, one is used as an outdoor theater for summer concerts, its enormous furnaces rising against the skyline. The city now dedicates itself to medicine instead of steel and is one of the country's leading centers of medical care and study. An impressive fine-arts museum that specializes in Oriental and French art hosts traveling exhibitions from national galleries and contains a scholarly library.

Places to Go, Sights to See

The **Birmingham Botanical Gardens** (2612 Lane Park Rd., tel. 205/879–1227) comprise 67 acres in which a Japanese garden, a rose garden, and fern and rock gardens are intermingled with fountains and plantings of azaleas, camellias, and dogwoods.

Birmingham Museum of Fine Arts (2000 8th Ave. N, tel. 205/254–2565 or 205/254–2566) has the S. H. Kress collection of Oriental porcelains and bronzes, paintings, and silver and the Hitt collection of 18th-century art and decorations.

Depot Museum (320 Church St., Huntsville, tel. 205/539–1860) is in one of the country's oldest surviving railway stations, built in 1860. The museum covers the history of the region's transportation. It is closed Monday.

Ivy Green (300 W. North Commons, Tuscumbia, tel. 205/381–0570) is the birthplace of Helen Keller, the house where her teacher, Anne Sullivan, taught her to communicate despite her deafness and blindness. It is complete with Keller's furniture, schoolroom, and clothes.

Museum of Art in Huntsville (700 Monroe St., tel. 205/535–4350) has changing exhibits and permanent collections of American paintings, sculpture, and Japanese netsuke. It is closed Monday.

Sloss Furnaces National Historic Landmark (between 1st Ave. and University Blvd., Birmingham, tel. 205/324–1911). In this open-air concert hall, converted from a steel mill, rock, symphonic, and popular music performances are held—also festivals and picnics. It is closed Monday.

Space and Rocket Center (1 Tranquility Base, Huntsville, tel. 205/837–3400 or 800/637–7223). The largest space museum in the world depicts the development of space exploration through 60 exhibits. You can see the 354-foot *Saturn V* moon rocket, experience the effects of weightlessness, and look at a piece of moon rock.

Vulcan State Park (20th St. at Valley Ave., Birmingham, tel. 205/328–6198) surrounds a huge statue of Vulcan, the god of metalworking, which sits atop Red Mountain overlooking the city. A small booth at the foot of the statue has information on the museums of Birmingham.

Restaurants

In Birmingham, at the moderately priced **Highland Bar & Grill** (2011 11th Ave. S, tel. 205/939–1400), a chef with Cordon Bleu training serves extraordinary French food. **Botega** (2240 Highland Ave., tel. 205/939–1000) offers fine northern Italian food, good wine, and luscious bread.

The **Irondale Cafe** (1906 Irondale Ave., Irondale, tel. 205/956–5258), the inspiration for novelist Fannie Flagg's Whistlestop Cafe, serves infamous fried green tomatoes.

The **Victoria Inn** (1604 Quintard Ave., Anniston, tel. 205/236–0503) serves seafood, steaks, and chicken, as well as domestic and imported wines at very reasonable prices.

Muffins Café (U.S. 411 just outside Centre, tel. 205/927–2233) is the place for home cooking; there are three meats and 23 vegetables at every meal. **Shelley's Irongate Restaurant** (402 Johnston St. SE, Decatur, tel. 205/350–6795) is a homey restaurant in a restored Victorian house, where everything served is made from scratch, including unusual desserts.

Like its sister restaurant, Ol' Heidelberg, **Cafe Berlin** (505 Airport Rd., Huntsville, tel. 205/880–9920) cooks up good German food, especially cakes and other desserts. It's owned by children of the "bomb-brought team," scientists who came to town to work at the Space and Rocket Center.

Tourist Information

Birmingham Convention and Visitors Bureau (2200 9th Ave. N, Birmingham, AL 35203–1100, tel. 205/458–8000 or 800/458–8085).

Mentone Inn

ookout Mountain in northeastern Alabama forms the backdrop for the Mentone Inn, a building perfectly suited to its setting. Stone steps, dark wood, flagstone paths, flowers, and evergreens show you the way to the entrance. A stone foundation supports screened or glassed-in porches, set with rocking chairs and small tables where breakfast can be served. Striped awnings over most of the bedroom windows confirm the impression that this is a house from the early days of the century. And rolling hills and valleys provide dark-green views on all sides and in fall are ablaze with foliage too dramatic to seem real.

Amelia Kirk has owned the inn since 1976. It's open April through November, since, she says, it's impractical to try to heat the 1927 building. Many of Kirk's guests flock to these parts for the festivals and crafts shows that take place during the summer and autumn.

The living room is paneled in natural-colored old pine. There is comfortable beige furniture, a grandfather clock, a plate rack circling the room, and a stone fireplace. Here guests play dominoes or bridge; then for a change they sit on the porch and spin tall tales as they rejoice in not being back home in the heat. In the glassed-in dining area, more plate racks and more paneling surround one long table and six or seven smaller ones, all with views of the mountains. There's complimentary coffee in the kitchen. Everything feels the way a relaxed country inn should.

A handsome staircase made of pale wood leads upstairs. All the walls in the house are wood-paneled, some painted, some left the natural color. The bedrooms are full of furniture from the 1920s. One has a bookcase with glass doors, a tall oval mirror on a stand, walls painted a pale blue, and a blue-and-white flowered bedspread. In the corner is a flowered washbowl with matching towels and soap. Rooms have either one queen-size or two double beds, with multicolored matching spreads and curtains, and most have Art Deco night tables.

Several yards behind the house, backed by a grove of trees, is a wooden deck, weathered a soft gray, which holds lounge chairs and small tables.

Address: *Rte. 117 (Box 284), Mentone, AL 35984, tel. 205/634-4836.*
Accommodations: *12 double rooms with baths.*
Amenities: *Air-conditioning, cable TV in living room.*
Rates: *$50-$55; full breakfast. No credit cards.*
Restrictions: *Smoking on porches only, no pets, BYOB, closed Dec.-Mar.*

Wood Avenue Inn

This three-story Queen Anne house lifts square and octagonal towers high above its garden on a tree-lined street in this college town. Built in 1889, it is pure, concentrated Victorian, with 14-foot ceilings, multipane leaded windows, and an assortment of nooks, crannies, and bay windows—the deepest of which, in one of the drawing rooms, holds a large piano.

The owners are Alvern and Gene Greeley. They have both worked in various fields, he as a clergyman turned auto-parts salesman, she as the dean of a Bible college and then as a real estate agent. With her radiant smile and enveloping warmth, Alvern makes innkeeping an art form. Since she likes to pamper people, she is doing what comes naturally in running a bed-and-breakfast, and she delights in making home-cooked delicacies for her guests. The zucchini bread served at breakfast is unsurpassed in the world of cookery.

The house has an inviting porch with green wicker furniture and begonias growing in flower boxes. Two formal parlors open off the wide central hall, which bisects the two lower floors. One drawing room has dark-green walls with gleaming white woodwork, a red velvet sofa 150 years old, and a cabinet in a corner whose rosewood shelves have held someone's china for over a century. But it's the bric-a-brac that sets the tone. Arranged among and around the furniture are enough figurines, artificial flowers, bows, wreaths, footstools, and ruffled cushions to stock a theatrical warehouse. Five minutes in that room and you know exactly how the well-to-do characters in a Dickens novel live.

Fireplaces are in every room, even the bathrooms, two of which have narrow tubs resting on claw feet. Beside the tub a table holds a bottle of sparkling cider and two silver-wrapped chocolates. After a good soak, you climb into a huge bed, its pale-rose-colored satin spread topped by matching pillows against the 19th-century-look wallpaper.

Outside the back door, wisteria climbs over an arbor, and a black carriage handmade by the Amish stands under a protective roof. Not far away a winding path leads to the bridal cottage and to other accommodations kept readied for guests who want to reserve for longer stays.

Address: *658 Northwood Ave., Florence, AL 35630, tel. 205/766–8441.*
Accommodations: *6 double rooms and 2 singles with baths, 2 suites.*
Amenities: *Special catering on request, air-conditioning in rooms, cable TV in lounge, ping-pong, badminton, horseshoes.*
Rates: *$50–$85; full breakfast. MC, V.*
Restrictions: *Smoking on porches only, no pets, BYOB.*

Roses and Lace

Roses and Lace sits beside a rose garden on 11 acres of farmland in the historic town of Ashville, where in front of the county courthouse stands a statue of a Confederate soldier, trying to look fierce in spite of his teenage softness.

On the wraparound porch, large clay pots hold ferns, spreading their greenness among the wicker furniture. The pinkish mauve Queen Anne Victorian house retains its stained-glass windows, fireplaces, wide-board floors, and crystal chandeliers hanging from 12-foot ceilings. Innkeeper Shirley Sparks makes quilts, and her husband, Mark, is a cabinetmaker, so, along with Mark's father and Shirley's brother, they decided to restore the house themselves, spending two years on the downstairs alone. Though lace curtains hang at the windows and lace cloths cover tables, the rooms don't look cluttered in the classic Victorian way. One bedroom holds a headboard 8 feet high, a fireplace, a carved walnut wardrobe, and a china pitcher and basin for rinsing upwardly mobile mustaches.

Address: *Box 852, Ashville, AL 35953, tel. 205/594-4366.*
Accommodations: *2 double rooms with baths, 2 doubles share 1 bath.*
Amenities: *Air-conditioning, ceiling fans, TV in 2 rooms and cable TV in common room.*
Rates: *$55-$75; full breakfast. MC, V.*
Restrictions: *No smoking, no pets.*

Plantation Country

The Plantation Country, called the Black Belt because of its rich black soil, runs through the center of Alabama from the Mississippi line to the area around Montgomery. This is the land that produced King Cotton and that until the Civil War supported immensely rich plantations. It's a flat, gentle land, wooded with oak, hickory, sweet gum, and beech trees, magnolias, sycamores, and semitropical bay trees and palmettos. Most of the large holdings have become cattle farms.

On the eastern edge of Plantation Country lies Tuskegee, an extraordinary community, where in 1881 Booker T. Washington founded a university for blacks. Here, in a largely black town, the university provides an intellectual and educational haven and carries on the research begun by George Washington Carver, whose work with peanuts and sweet potatoes helped to change the life of Southern farmers.

The Black Belt now provides a background for little old towns like Selma, Franklin, Demopolis, and Greensboro, full of antebellum houses and cemeteries—the one in Selma holds the grave of Abraham Lincoln's sister-in-law. Many of these homes are in a fine state of preservation and look as though Scarlett O'Hara should come strolling through the white columns on their encircling porches. Some of them are open to the public during spring festivals and pilgrimages, for a few weeks allowing visitors to relive the dear dead days when Great-great-grandmother's silver teapot was used regularly and had no need to be hidden from the Yankee soldiers.

Montgomery, the state capital and center of both Civil War recollections and the civil rights movement, is, with its historic Old Town district, a quintessential Southern city, where people who moved here 30 years ago are still considered outsiders. Martin Luther King, Jr., preached here regularly from the pulpit of the Baptist church on Dexter

Avenue. The church is almost cheek by jowl with the state capitol, where the Confederate flag is kept flying and the bronze star where Jefferson Davis stood to be sworn in as president of the Confederacy is still kept brightly polished. The Montgomery bus boycott began here, and the Selma march ended here, not far from the First White House of the Confederacy.

Places to Go, Sights to See

Alabama Shakespeare Festival (1 Festival Dr., Montgomery, tel. 205/271–5353 or 800/841–4273) comprises two theaters, with a professional repertory company that presents classical and modern plays from December to August.

Alabama State Capitol (Bainbridge St. at Dexter Ave., Montgomery, tel. 205/242–3184). The long-neglected neoclassical building has been fully restored to antebellum magnificence. The double curving staircase without supports is one of only a few left in the United States.

Civil Rights Memorial (400 Washington Ave., Montgomery, tel. 205/264–0286). Designed by Maya Lin, who did the Vietnam Memorial in Washington, this one of black granite and flowing water honors those people killed in the struggle for black equality.

Dexter Avenue King Memorial Baptist Church (454 Dexter Ave., Montgomery, tel. 205/263–3970), where Dr. King was pastor during his early civil rights struggles, has a large civil rights mural in the basement. It is open to the public weekdays. To visit on holidays and weekends, call two weeks in advance.

Tuskegee Institute, a national historic site on the campus of Tuskegee University, is managed by the National Park Service. The *Carver Museum* (Tuskegee campus, tel. 205/727–3200) has artifacts, photo displays, and films on the institute and on George Washington Carver's research with peanuts and sweet potatoes. Park rangers conduct guided tours of *The Oaks* (1212 Old Montgomery Rd., tel. 205/727–3200), home of Booker T. Washington. Built in 1899, it is a fine example of Queen Anne Victorian architecture and was designed and built by blacks. Its furnishings are suitable to the period and include a few Washington family pieces.

Victoryland Greyhound Park (off I–85, Shorter, tel. 205/727–0540 or 800/688–2946), east of Montgomery, is open year-round; races are held in the afternoon and evening. The minimum age is 19.

Restaurants

In Montgomery, try **Le Bistro** (1059 Woodley Rd., tel. 205/269–1600) for imaginative French cooking, an adequate wine list, and faultless service. Reservations are necessary, and a coat and tie will make you feel more comfortable. At the moderately priced **Vintage Year** (405 Cloverdale Rd., tel. 205/264–8463), you'll get luscious Provençal-style food, crunchy bread, and a large wine list. The even less expensive **Kat & Harri's Nice Place** (1061 Woodley Rd., tel. 205/834–2500) is something of a landmark and specializes in local cuisine such as fried catfish.

In Demopolis, at **The Red Barn** (905 U.S. 80, tel. 205/289–0595), you'll find reasonably priced Southern cooking: steaks, catfish, hush puppies, and chicken. The elegant **GainesRidge Supper Club** (Rte. 10, tel. 205/682–9707), 2 miles east of Camden in a 19th-century house, serves 13 entrées, gumbo, and homemade hot rolls at very reasonable prices from Wednesday to Saturday. At the **Cotton Patch** (Exit 42 off I–59, tel. 205/372–4235), in Eutaw,there's homespun Southern cooking, with fried chicken, barbecue, and hot biscuits.

Just outside Tuscaloosa, in the picture-postcard town of Northport, **The Globe** (430 Main Ave., tel. 205/397–0949) is a trendy eatery decorated with theatrical paraphernalia. It serves adventurous Mexican dishes and sinful desserts.

Tourist Information

Alabama Bureau of Tourism & Travel (410 Adams Ave., Montgomery, AL 36103–4309, tel. 205/242–4169 or 800/252–2262).

The Colonel's Rest

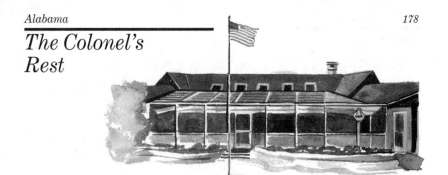

On the northeastern outskirts of Montgomery, just 15 minutes from downtown, is this 80-acre property. The brick and cedar central building is long and low, wrapping in a wide U shape around a patio with a pool. There's a duplex cabin, an A-frame with one bedroom, the neat one-bedroom Cedar House, and the Carriage House—a large hall for dinners, receptions, and wedding rehearsals. In front of the main house, surrounded by bushes, lies a large open field with spaces for 50 recreational vehicles. When the area is full of RVs, it can get a little crowded and noisy.

The four rooms in the main house face the patio, where azaleas and camellias are spaced on paths around the pool and a fountain's music soothes guests at breakfast. A brick fireplace warms the cedar living room, lit by a huge, sparkling chandelier and full of soft chairs. Each bedroom is decorated in a different style. The Oriental Room has grass-paper wall covering, pagoda paintings, and black lacquer furniture with black and white accessories. The Captain's Quarters is white and blue, with a striped bedspread, sea gull wallpaper, white rattan furniture, and two ship's wheels over one door. In the Early American Room, a cannonball bed is set against dark wainscoting, and an oak chest has Victorian gingerbread. The Cedar House is a small rough-wood cabin, with pine parquet floors,

tall bookshelves packed with tomes, spacious leather chairs, a full kitchen, twin beds, and, best of all, the gentle scent of cedar in every corner.

The property was developed by Jim and Jane Watson, he a retired Army colonel, she a gifted musician. They can produce a seated meal for 100 in the Carriage House, which has a professional kitchen and a barbecue large enough to roast an ox. The inn looks out on fields and heavily forested areas. Stargazing, bird-watching, and walks in the woods are especially enchanting during Alabama's early spring. The Watsons encourage extended stays on a weekly or monthly basis. Several repeaters have been snowbirds from Canada, who find wearing only a sweater in January little short of miraculous. And then, of course, there's redeye gravy and grits, considered by most Southerners to be one of civilization's highest achievements.

Address: *11091 Atlanta Hwy., Mount Meigs, AL 36057, tel. 205/215–0380.*
Accommodations: *8 double house-keeping rooms with baths.*
Amenities: *Restaurant, air-conditioning, cable TV in rooms, TV with VCR in public area, fax machine, copier, laundry; 2-acre pond.*
Rates: *$53 ($150/week, $350/month); full breakfast. MC, V.*

Grace Hall

Among the stately homes of Selma is Grace Hall, built in 1857 and also known as the Ware-Baker-Jones House, after the three families who lived here for more than 110 years. The mansion became run-down apartments and then a grungy boardinghouse, but today, resplendent again, with many original antiques, it shines as brilliantly as ever. The owners are Coy and Joey Dillon, he a former steel executive, she a designer. Since the age of 16, when Joey bought her first antique (an oval mirror for $10), she has been interested in old buildings. She jumped at the chance to buy and restore Grace Hall. The Dillons drifted into B&B management when the mayor of Selma asked them to put up a visiting dignitary.

The house is a certified restoration of a Victorian home, an interesting alternative to the slew of Federal-style mansions in the area. It is stunningly beautiful and contains double parlors, a pressed-tin ceiling in the study, red-stained glass, Romantic portraits in the hallway, heart-of-pine floors throughout, and windows 10 feet tall. The dining room has its original mahogany pedestal table, seating 12, and there's a smaller room behind for the three-course breakfast. Solid brass chandeliers light the house; on the south porch overlooking the manicured garden and its huge live oak is original wicker furniture. The large bedrooms in the main house have marble fireplaces, where fires are lit as soon as guests arrive; step-up, antique, carved rosewood beds; oak desks; Oriental rugs; and hand-painted enameled clocks. Wallpapers are copies of 19th-century designs; in one bedroom, the Brighton pattern fits perfectly with a four-poster bed flanked by brother-and-sister walnut chests. TV sets are concealed in cabinets. Leading off the back is a latticed, galleried wing, whose porches, facing the garden, provide open-air sitting space for three more, smaller but just as charming, bedrooms. Fitting the Southern surroundings, an overhead fan turns lazily above a large bowl holding branches full of cotton bolls. The Dillons offer occasional house tours to the public, and, though they are discreet, guests may find this somewhat discomforting.

Address: *506 Lauderdale St., Selma, AL 36701, tel. 205/875-5744, fax 205/875-9967.*
Accommodations: *6 double rooms with baths.*
Amenities: *Air-conditioning, cable TV and phones in rooms, complimentary house tour.*
Rates: *$65–$90; full breakfast, evening refreshments. AE, MC, V.*
Restrictions: *No smoking indoors, no pets.*

Oakwood

Oakwood, on the National Register of Historic Places, was commissioned in 1847 by the first mayor of Talladega. Painted white, with green shutters, tall columns, chimneys, and a freestanding balcony, it is the quintessential Federal-style Southern mansion. It has a garden full of azaleas and dogwoods and faces a pretty street lined with carefully tended houses and yards. Naomi and Al Kline, the owners, have agreed to a perfect division of labor: The house is in her name, but Al does all the work. He's chef, gardener, and singing waiter, for he was a professional tenor. When not sweeping the front porch, he teaches voice, piano, and organ; conducts the Talladega Community Chorus; and tells daring tales of his operatic exploits across Europe and North America. Naomi commutes to Birmingham, where she is a registered nurse. In the well-equipped recording studio, guests may play the organ or piano, lift up their voices in deathless song, and preserve for posterity their performances.

Oakwood is done on a large scale: The rooms are 20 by 20 feet, the ceilings are 11 feet, and the windows almost as tall. The original heart-pine floors have been redone, adding a special gleam. In the wide entrance hall, a broad staircase invites you upstairs and contributes an air of welcome and elegance. Throughout the house, the wallpapers have been copied from original designs. They make a fitting background for the original furniture, most of it English Victorian, with some delicate French pieces. One nice touch is a table from an English pub; its brass hinges allow it to unfold to seat eight hungry or thirsty people. The centerpiece of the dining room is a great oak table with plush leather chairs that date from the 1830s, all surrounded by busts of famous baroque and classical composers and a hanging collection of pewter and glass goblets. One bedroom has a spool bed, the others four-posters. In two you will find English armoires, washstands, 1895 dressers, cast-iron chandeliers, and (in one) a strange hand-carved curio cabinet. One room was decorated as if for the Klines' youngest daughter, with light, floaty curtains; old white wicker chairs and sofas; family portraits; and an antique doll propped against cushions. Everywhere else, the long sweeps of draperies at the windows are copies of fabrics of the period. Out back, Al has built a large, plain, treated-wood deck that has an arbor, a swing, and benches.

Address: *715 E. North St., Talladega, AL 35160, tel. 205/362–0662.*
Accommodations: *4 double rooms share 2½ baths.*
Amenities: *Air-conditioning, TV in common area; horseshoes, croquet.*
Rates: *$55–$65; full breakfast. No credit cards.*
Restrictions: *No smoking, no pets.*

Orangeva Plantatio

Four miles south of Talladega stand the remaining 150 acres of Orangevale, which was once a 3,000-acre cotton plantation. Built in 1854, the main house is unashamedly Greek Revival, complete with six 25-foot pillars and a gleaming white exterior. Next to the main building, the Old Kitchen has been restored and turned into guest accommodations, as have two log cabins. Orangevale is run by the charming Billy Bliss and her husband, Richard, a doctor. What sets it apart is that it's on a functioning farm. The Blisses, along with their sons, who live in houses nearby, manage to maintain Hereford cattle, sheep, horses, ducks and geese, an orchard and berry farm, cornfields, a fish pond, and a vineyard. Guests can stroll the nature trail and enjoy this agricultural theme park.

Inside the main house, the hallway gives an immediate taste of what's to come throughout the house; original gaslights (now wired for electricity) hang from a fine plaster medallion, and a French Empire wood-and-leather desk sits atop a large Oriental rug. The Blisses live downstairs and pretty much leave the upstairs, which has its own living room area, to the guests. In typical antebellum fashion, the two bedrooms here open off a central hall, and, though these rooms have their own bathrooms, you have to tiptoe down the hall to reach them. Both bedrooms have four-poster beds

with huge down comforters, Sheraton chests, large windows overlooking the property, and brick fireplaces. The little white clapboard Old Kitchen has a kitchenette, walk-in closets, a brick fireplace, queen-size bed, and a bathroom accessible for disabled guests. Cabin interiors carry the sweet aroma of old pine logs, and both manage to appear rustic while being exceptionally comfortable. The one farthest from the house overlooks the orchard. Each of its two rooms, connected by a dogtrot, has a queen-size and single bed. Also inside are a freestanding brick chimney, wicker rocking chair, and walls and ceiling made of rough-hewn wood. A 1932 GE refrigerator purrs away on the porch and still keeps root beer perfectly chilled.

There is always plenty of fresh fruit and produce, but beware of calories. Richard likes to cook up a storm in his barbecue pit, which, he boasts, is big enough to roast a whole hog.

Address: *1400 Whiting Rd., Talladega, AL 35160, tel. 205/362–3052.*
Accommodations: *2 double rooms with baths, 1 cottage, 2 cabins.*
Amenities: *Air-conditioning, TV in common area of house, cottage, and cabins; complimentary tour of house and grounds.*
Rates: *$85; full breakfast. No credit cards.*
Restrictions: *No smoking, no pets.*

The Plantation House

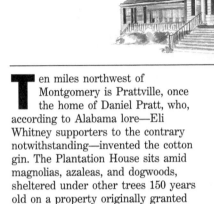

Ten miles northwest of Montgomery is Prattville, once the home of Daniel Pratt, who, according to Alabama lore—Eli Whitney supporters to the contrary notwithstanding—invented the cotton gin. The Plantation House sits amid magnolias, azaleas, and dogwoods, sheltered under other trees 150 years old on a property originally granted by President Andrew Jackson. The 2½-story white-and-green, clapboard-over-brick house, its columns rising past a freestanding balcony, is an example of Greek Revival at its best.

Before John and Bernice Hughes bought and rebuilt the house after a fire, she worked for the state of Alabama, and he was a businessman. The idea of a B&B was suggested by her son. They are talkative, knowledgeable, walking examples of Southern hospitality.

You enter the spacious hall under a spreading fanlight, which shows up the gleam of the wide marble floor. The house, built in 1832, is supported on joists a foot and a half thick that contain enough lumber to build a small bungalow. Walls throughout are painted off-white. On both floors, dark mahogany paneling adds coolness to the decor. There are nine fireplaces, eight of them original. A portrait of Jenny Lind when she sang in Prattville, hangs in the dining room. In the formal parlor with its 11-foot ceiling, a crystal chandelier once hung from the enormous plaster medallion, molded in Birmingham (the one in England, that is); however, the chandelier proved too heavy for the much more interesting medallion, so it was removed. The furniture is easy, comfortable modern blended with many period pieces from John Hughes's mother. There's a lady's love seat wide enough for hoopskirts, a chair whose back is carved in delicate swirls, and an early 19th-century rosewood piano. The upstairs hall leads to bedrooms lit by tall windows. There are four-poster beds, white chenille spreads, and pale ruffled curtains. Guests may have breakfast in a small sitting room with white wicker furniture if they prefer not to go downstairs to the dining room. Every bedroom has a fireplace; in front of one sits a tiny antique child's rocking chair. The largest room also boasts a Jacuzzi, an oak washstand, and a bed so tall you must climb up a set of narrow steps.

Address: *752 Loder St., Prattville, AL 36067, tel. 205/361–0442.*
Accommodations: *1 double room with bath, 2 doubles share 1 bath.*
Amenities: *Air-conditioning, cable TV and phones in rooms, VCR in 1 room; nature trail.*
Rates: *$50–$75; Continental breakfast. No credit cards.*
Restrictions: *No smoking, no pets.*

Blue Shadows

Isolated on 320 acres of fields and woods, this white frame house backs onto a 2-mile nature trail to a bird sanctuary, wildflower preserve, orchard, and old barn. Its undistinguished 1930s exterior belies the glowing interior, from the living room's apricot hues to the foyer's burnished grass-cloth walls. Thaddeus May, a retired pilot, has always lived here. His wife, Janet, an artist and decorator, opened the B&B as a hobby that soon became a passion. Bedrooms have antique beds with ruffled pillows, silver-plated and Florentine iron chandeliers, French provincial mirrors, and Janet's prints and drawings. The bathroom has bright-blue wallpaper and matching towels that look a foot thick. The small guest sitting room, with 10-foot windows, is a quiet haven. In the comfortable but blandly furnished three-bedroom apartment, guests can eat goodies from the fridge. Janet leaves champagne for guests celebrating an anniversary, and on fine days she often serves sherry on the lawn. For privacy, you can take a small boat on the 12-acre fish pond.

Address: *Rte. 2 (Box 432), Greensboro, AL 36744, tel. 205/624–3637.*
Accommodations: *2 double rooms share 1 bath, 1 apartment.*
Amenities: *Air-conditioning, TV with VCR in apartment.*
Rates: *$65; full breakfast for rooms only, afternoon tea. No credit cards.*
Restrictions: *No smoking indoors, no pets.*

The Lattice Inn

Follow the aroma of freshly baked cookies through Montgomery's historic garden district to this turn-of-the-century craftsman bungalow. Proprietor Michael Pierce bakes more than 1,400 cookies a month and even slips a bag of them into your suitcase as you depart. The renovated house is set among wild gardens with oak and pine trees, an ornamental fish pond, and lots of flowers. The shady front porch has just enough of the eponymous lattice to provide privacy, while an intricately designed multilevel deck overlooking the pool is great for sitting and dozing. Spacious bedrooms contain brick or cement wood-burning fireplaces, high coffered ceilings, stained-glass windows, and antique furnishings. One bathroom contains a 19th-century claw-foot tub, a porcelain basin mounted on an antique chest, and original art. The wine-colored walls and mahogany paneling in the living room add to the dark and serene mood. The cottage's plain pink wooden exterior conceals a kitchen, living-room area, bathroom, and queen-size, single, and sofa beds.

Address: *1414 S. Hull St., Montgomery, AL 36104, tel. 205/832–9931 or 800/525–0652, fax 205/264–0075.*
Accommodations: *4 rooms with baths, 1 cottage.*
Amenities: *Air-conditioning, cable TV in library.*
Rates: *$50–$70; full breakfast. AE, MC, V.*
Restrictions: *Smoking on porches only, no pets.*

Red Bluff Cottage

Built to accommodate guests, this raised cottage sits high above the Alabama River and has public rooms on the second floor and bedrooms below. The lower level's porch has an unusual swinging bed that invites a snooze.

Mark Waldo, a retired Episcopal rector, is tall, slim, and intellectually gray. His wife, Anne, is gardener, chef, and an accomplished musician.

The public rooms have Oriental rugs, a fireplace, and the kind of soft lamplight that makes you want to sit down and tell someone the story of your life. Guests may play an ancient harpsichord in the baroque music room, where Bach sheet music and wooden recorders are scattered about. Breakfast is served at a mahogany table, on family china and silver, under a crystal chandelier; on the porch amid hanging baskets of pansies; or in a white lattice gazebo in the garden. The bedrooms are full of light, thanks to large windows hung with light net curtains. Old carved cherry pieces are arranged among framed photos of ancestors taken against sepia backgrounds. One room is really a suite, with a small attached room suitable for children.

Address: *551 Clay St., Montgomery, AL 36104, tel. 205/264–0050.*
Accommodations: *3 double rooms with baths, 1 suite.*
Amenities: *Air-conditioning, TV in living room, games, laundry.*
Rates: *$55–$85; full breakfast, prebreakfast coffee. MC, V.*
Restrictions: *No smoking, no pets.*

Gulf Coast Delta

*The southwestern part of Alabama, the Gulf Coast Delta, is
dominated by water: by the rivers and streams of the delta,
draining into Mobile Bay, and by the Gulf of Mexico, whose
beaches have sand so gleaming white it looks as though it has
been scooped up from the streets of paradise. The flat and
uninteresting area approaching the coast, however, has no
distinctive features but heat, insects, and high humidity.
Throughout much of the region large trees support gray-
green curtains of Spanish moss that festoon their branches,
hanging down 10 or 15 feet in irregular clusters and adding
an air of mystery to the silent, motionless landscape.*

*Mobile, with its active shipping industry, is Alabama's only
important port. The French settled it in 1711, and many of
the older parts of the city hold fast to bits and pieces of their
French ancestry. Live oaks, 100 years old and riotous, and
exploding stretches of azaleas turn the town into fairyland
in early spring.*

*Strung along the eastern shore of Mobile Bay is a scattering
of small towns with evocative names: Point Clear, Fairhope,
Daphne, Montrose, and Spanish Fort. Point Clear has one of
the South's most famous hostelries, the 140-year old Grand
Hotel, whose half-moon dining rooms overlook the bay and
whose sweeping lawn is so manicured guests are almost
afraid to walk on it.*

Places to Go, Sights to See

Bellingrath Gardens (1241 Bellingrath Gardens Rd., Theodore, tel.
205/973–2217), on 800 acres 20 miles south of Mobile, are famous for their
imaginative landscaping with traditional Southern flowers, shrubs, and trees.
The house contains a collection of Boehm porcelains.

At **Dauphin Island,** a gateway to Mobile Bay, regattas and fishing
tournaments take place, notably the Deep-sea Fishing Rodeo, which has been
held every July for 50 years.

Fairhope, the most interesting village on Mobile Bay, was settled about 1900 by a group of high-minded Midwesterners, who established the country's oldest and largest single-tax colony. It was based on the taxation theories of Henry George, a 19th-century American economist, who believed the only tax should be on the land itself. The system remains in operation in Fairhope and is studied by economists worldwide. The village is a growing art colony with 20 antiques shops and several potteries and is also a center for fishing, boating, and marine services.

The **Grand Hotel** (U.S. 98, Point Clear, tel. 205/928–1149), originally built in 1847, housed Confederate soldiers during the Civil War. It was destroyed by fire in 1870 and then rebuilt in its current splendor. Its decadent architecture is Southern and proud of it.

Mobile. The *Cathedral of the Immaculate Conception* (Dauphin at Claiborne St., tel. 205/432–6684) is a Greek Revival masterpiece built in 1835, with German art-glass windows. Three museums featuring city life in the 19th century—the *Carlen House,* the *Phoenix Fire Museum,* and the *City Museum*—are in the center of town, all within walking distance of one another. The Museum Office (tel. 205/434–7569) provides information about all three. Moored offshore in Mobile Bay is the USS *Alabama* (Battleship Pkwy., tel. 205/433–2703), which was called "the hero of the Pacific." The ship is a popular tourist attraction, but during the summer months it's likely to be full of crowds dripping ice cream and perspiration.

Restaurants

At **The Gift Horse** (209 W. Laurel Ave., Foley, tel. 205/943–3663), reasonably priced Southern cooking (but no wine) is served buffet style in an elegant house built in 1912. In the dining room of Point Clear's **Marriott Grand Hotel** (U.S. 98, tel. 205/928–9201), the French cuisine tries to be light and nonfattening, but the desserts are sinfully tasty. At **Old Bay Steamer** (312 Fairhope Ave., Fairhope, tel. 205/928–5714), you can enjoy the framed quotes of famous people that adorn the walls while you sample the eastern shore's best grilled and steamed seafood. Just south of Mobile, right on the water, is **Nan Seas** (4170 Bayfront Rd., tel. 205/479–9132); one could write paeans to the seafood fresh from Mobile Bay.

Tourist Information

Fort Condé Welcome Center (150 S. Royal St., Mobile, AL 36602, tel. 205/434–7304). **Mobile Chamber of Commerce** (Box 2187, Mobile, AL 36652, tel. 205/433–6951).

Bay Breeze

Within walking distance of downtown Fairhope, a winding white-shell driveway takes you through a beautifully landscaped camellia and azalea garden to this stucco and wood guest house. Owners Bill and Becky Jones live in their own wing, while guests enjoy the main house area and the nearby white-pine cottages. Becky has a fondness for ducks. (A sketch of Donald Duck drawn by a Disney artist who stayed here hangs proudly in the kitchen.) She has populated the grounds with many varieties and is occasionally found in the kitchen tending to an orphan duckling. The real star, however, is Mobile Bay, and the house overlooks the stretch of water where the Yankee ironclad *Tecumseh* still lies along with the remains of 116 sailors. The Joneses' private 460-foot pier stretches into the bay. At the end is a fully equipped kitchen, where Bill often cooks up Saturday breakfasts or a seafood barbecue. Fortunate guests may find themselves here for Jubilee—a natural phenomenon that washes hordes of crab, shrimp, snapper, and other fish on shore.

A large front lawn area has a stone fountain and pine benches. Inside, a large living room has unusual pecan-wood floors, and furniture is family hand-me-downs. Collections of china and rare books stand in a cabinet next to a musket from the War of 1812. The adjoining Bay Room has white wicker chairs facing large French windows and the water beyond. A cozy sitting room hides an old upright piano and a sturdy brick fireplace. Breakfast is served in the open kitchen; a view of ducks and bay enhances the meal. Becky keeps a wide selection of ice cream for hungry guests to snack on at any hour.

The three bedrooms in the main house are small but comfortable. They have wooden floors, brass double beds, old family portraits, large windows, antique furnishings, and, unfortunately, thin walls. The two cottages, however, are models of privacy. Cathedral ceilings rise above big windows, oak armchairs, original Morris reclining chairs, an old chest with a very modern TV, brass double beds, and an extra-large sofa bed. The cottages are perfect for two couples or small groups. Bay Breeze was Becky's family home, and she loves to sit at the end of the pier and tell tales of days that are no more.

Address: *742 S. Mobile St. (Box 526), Fairhope, AL 36533, tel. 205/928–8976.*
Accommodations: *3 double rooms share 2 baths, 2 cottages.*
Amenities: *Air-conditioning, TV in rooms, games.*
Rates: *$85–$95; full breakfast. AE, MC, V.*
Restrictions: *No smoking, no pets.*

Church Street Inn

This early 20th-century, white stucco house, on the National Register, has housed some of Fairhope's finest citizens, including a local schoolteacher—Becky Jones's mother. Becky and her husband, Bill, now run it as their second B&B while they live at Bay Breeze, so guests usually have the place to themselves. The Joneses intrude only to answer queries, restock the ice cream, and serve breakfast. There are five generations of family antiques and heirlooms. Elegant portraits of Becky's relatives adorn the dining room, where a huge glass case displays fine china. In the bay window of the living room a "memory book" tells of Becky's mother's life. Included are love letters and her first teaching contract, dated 1926, for $40. Mahogany tables and Tiffany lamp shades abound downstairs. The three bedrooms are named after Becky's grandchildren; those downstairs have similar furnishings—four-poster beds, oak rocking chairs, lace curtains, and brass ceiling fans. Upstairs is a large attic room with dark pine floors, a walk-in closet, and an adjoining original bathroom with claw-foot tub. All have queen-size beds.

Address: *51 S. Church St. (Box 526), Fairhope, AL 36533, tel. 205/928–8976.*
Accommodations: *3 double rooms with baths.*
Amenities: *Air-conditioning, TV in rooms.*
Rates: *$85; Continental breakfast. MC, V.*
Restrictions: *No smoking, no pets.*

The Guest House

This low, clapboard, turn-of-the-century structure has been added to and subtracted from several times. It's saved from blandness by fresh pink paint, a wraparound porch, and a church door of antique leaded glass with glass side panels. Its location is noisy but near Fairhope, with pleasant places to walk. The owner, Betty Bostrom, was in real estate and now operates not only her B&B but also a conference and reception center. A staff of 13 keeps both running smoothly.

The living room has attractive traditional decor, including a Chinese rug and big chairs perfect for a snooze. But the lounge looks somewhat bare and cramped. The three upstairs bedrooms are decorated in pink and gray candy stripes with wicker furniture, or yellow floral prints on curtains and beds. The downstairs Garden Room is larger and has bleached pine floors, bay windows overlooking the fish pond, and an iron four-poster. A neat little carriage house has a living room area with old wicker furniture and double plus sofa beds. Breakfast is often served in the brick courtyard, as are afternoon tea, wine, and cheese.

Address: *63 S. Court St., Fairhope, AL 36532, tel. 205/928–6226.*
Accommodations: *2 double rooms with baths, 2 doubles share 1 bath, carriage house.*
Amenities: *Air-conditioning, TV with VCR in lounge.*
Rates: *$75–$85; full breakfast, afternoon refreshments. AE, MC, V.*
Restrictions: *No smoking, no pets.*

Mississippi

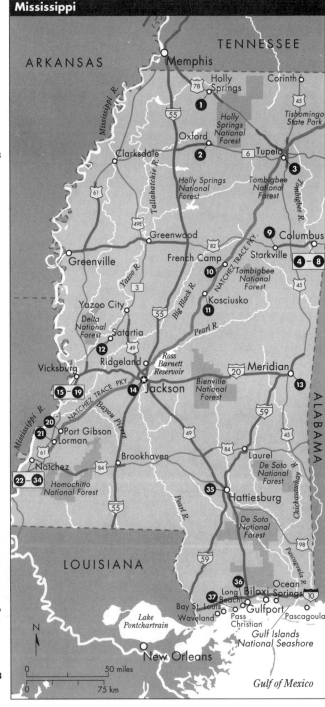

North Mississippi Hill Country

*Though Oxford and Holly Springs are within an hour or so
of Memphis, Tennessee, they are very much a part of the
rural Deep South. This "big woods" region was introduced to
the world by Oxford native William Faulkner, who won the
1949 Nobel Prize in literature for his depictions of small-
town life. Faulkner fans may recognize his mythical
Yoknapatawpha County when they visit Lafayette County. In
its seat, Oxford, is the University of Mississippi (Ole Miss),
which has excellent museums, one with an extensive
collection of Greco-Roman antiquities. The university also
maintains Faulkner's home, Rowan Oak.*

*Even before Faulkner made Holly Springs famous, the
Union soldiers who were bivouacked there during the Civil
War were quite enamored of it. Rumor has it that because of
certain blandishments of local women determined to save
their homes, the Yankees chose not to burn the town. Today,
those private houses are open for the Pilgrimage tour in late
April, and some by appointment. The entire Courthouse
Square, with its neat box of shops and offices, is on the
National Register of Historic Places.*

*Two other pretty towns, Corinth and Columbus, are steeped
in yet more Civil War history—and herstory. In 1866, the
women of Columbus helped to heal the nation by placing
flowers on the graves of both Confederate and Union soldiers
at Friendship Cemetery. "Decoration Day," initiated by
those genteel ladies, evolved into the nation's Memorial Day.
In 1884, the first state-supported college for women was
founded here. Corinth, a town of tree-canopied streets and
quiet, historic neighborhoods, was of strategic importance
during the Civil War because the railroads met and crossed
here. It changed hands more than once, and the Battle of
Corinth cost thousands of lives. The major Battle of Shiloh
occurred just across the state line in Tennessee.*

Between the two towns, along the northern stretches of the Trace, is Tupelo, which offers museums, mall shopping, and Elvis Presley's birthplace/museum. Nearby are several state parks and lakes.

Starkville, west of Columbus, is the home of many museums and Mississippi State University, where SEC (Southeastern Conference) sports offer year-round activities.

Places to Go, Sights to See

Agricultural Laboratory Tours (Food and Enology Lab, Mississippi State University, Starkville, tel. 601/325–3200). Those who appreciate wine and wine making will enjoy the excellent tour of the lab.

Antebellum Home Tours (Columbus, tel. 601/329–3533 or 800/327–2686). The town opens at least three of its antebellum mansions—with period antiques—for tours every day, year-round.

Blues Archives (Farley Hall, University of Mississippi, Oxford, tel. 601/232–7753). See how singin' the blues evolved from Mississippi Delta roots. B. B. King's collection of memorabilia and recordings is exhibited, as are the works of other blues musicians.

The **Center for the Study of Southern Culture** (Barnard Observatory, University of Mississippi, Oxford, tel. 601/232–5993) examines the region's music, folklore, and literature.

The **Cobb Institute of Archaeology** (Mississippi State University, Starkville, tel. 601/325–3826) has North American Indian artifacts and much more.

Corinth National Cemetery (tel. 601/286–5782), once a major battlefield, is now the gravesite of 6,000 Civil War soldiers.

Elvis Presley Birthplace and Museum (306 Elvis Presley Dr., Tupelo, tel. 601/841–1245). The museum is called "Times and Things Remembered" and has a collection of unique Elvis memorabilia.

The **Kate Freeman Clark Art Gallery** (292 E. College Ave., Holly Springs) exhibits more than 1,000 paintings by the Holly Springs native who left her home in the 1890s to study with William Merritt Chase at the Art Students League in New York. By choice, she never sold a painting.

Marshall County Historical Museum (220 E. College Ave., Holly Springs, tel. 601/252–3669) is full of interesting artifacts and artful conversation.

Natchez Trace Parkway Visitor Center (milepost 266, Natchez Trace Pkwy., tel. 601/680–4025), open every day but Christmas, has exhibits, a hands-on area for children, a bookstore, and the "Official Map and Guide," which opens to 4 feet and lays out the Trace mile by mile.

The **Northeast Mississippi Museum** (204 4th St., Corinth, tel. 601/286–3120) has Native American relics and artifacts and Civil War maps and battle plans.

Rowan Oak (Old Taylor Rd., Oxford, tel. 601/234–3284) is writer William Faulkner's antebellum home. His outline of the prizewinning story, *A Fable*, is still written on the wall of his study.

Tupelo City Museum (Ballard Park, tel. 601/841–6438) has permanent and traveling exhibits that range from the arts to astronauts to remembrances of Elvis Presley.

Waverley Plantation (between Columbus and West Point, tel. 601/494–1399) is a spectacular mid-1800s showplace built around an octagonal rotunda.

Restaurants

Harvey's, in Tupelo, Columbus, and Starkville, specializes in mesquite-grilled fish, steak, and chicken, and dressed-up hamburgers and salads. All locations are relaxed and casual, and the service is unusually good. In Tupelo, **Jefferson Place** (tel. 601/844–8696) serves the finest cuts of beef and lighter fare— sandwiches, salads, and burgers. **The Front Porch** (tel. 601/842–1591) is known for the best Mississippi catfish, with hush puppies and cole slaw. And yes, it actually has a front porch with rocking chairs.

Tourist Information

Columbus Convention & Visitors Bureau (Box 789, Columbus, MS 39703, tel. 601/329–1191 or 800/327–2686). **Corinth Chamber of Commerce** (Box 1049, Corinth, MS 38834, tel. 601/287–5269). **Holly Springs Chamber of Commerce** (Box 12, Holly Springs, MS 38635, tel. 601/252–2943). **Oxford Tourism Council** (Box 965, Oxford, MS 38655, tel. 601/234–4651). **Starkville Visitors & Convention Council** (Box 2720, Starkville, MS 39759, tel. 601/323–3322). **Tupelo Convention & Visitors Bureau** (Box 1485, Tupelo, MS 38802, tel. 601/841–6521 or 800/533–0611).

Reservation Services

Columbus Historic Foundation (Box 46, Columbus, MS 39703, tel. 601/329–3533) can make reservations at five houses in Columbus. **Lincoln, Ltd. Bed & Breakfast Mississippi Reservation Service** (Box 3479, Meridian, MS 39303, tel. 601/482–5483 or 800/633–6477).

The Mockingbird Inn

Jim and Sandy Gilmer decided to leave the corporate world and strike out on their own. So in addition to starting a recycling business, they found a spacious old home on a shady street corner and transformed it into a B&B. Because there was no available history on the original occupants, the Gilmers named the circa 1923 two-story house The Mockingbird Inn, after the state bird—a symbol of hospitality. It's only fitting that one appears at the porch windows periodically.

It's also only fitting that people who have seven favorite places in the world and seven rooms to decorate should re-create those places in the rooms', and the bathrooms', decor. You can almost hear gondolas gliding across a canal in the Venice Room. Rich, dark colors call attention to the old Venetian tapestry on the wall and the ecru lace coverlet on the bed. The Mackinac Island Room transports you to a wonderful whitewashed lakeside cottage. It is light and airy, with pickled wood, and has the furnishings and decor you'd expect to find in an upscale summer house. It also has a wheelchair ramp and a bathroom designed for those with physical disabilities. A pewter wedding canopy bed and chaise longue are two of many elements that leave no doubt as to the inspiration for the Paris Room. Greek columns are perfectly at home in the large Athens Room; a plus is the L-shaped whirlpool for two. Even

Isak Dinesen would feel at home in the Africa Room, where wooden African carvings, faux jungle-animal skins, and mosquito netting around the bed set the scene. Pastels and seashells make the Sanibel Island Room as authentic as possible; add the verdigris iron bed and wicker furniture, and you're practically basking in the Florida sun. And in the Bavaria Room, lots of knotty pine, a sleigh bed, antique skis, and typical lace-trimmed windows bring southern Germany to northern Mississippi.

Guests enjoy the living room, with plush white sofas and chairs, lots of greenery, and a few antiques, and they linger on the indoor porch, complete with wicker furniture and coffee and tea makings. The inn is popular with businesspeople who attend one of the two Tupelo furniture markets and with tourists, especially those of the rock 'n' roll persuasion, who like to look across at the school where Elvis Presley attended sixth and seventh grades.

Address: *305 N. Gloster St., Tupelo, MS 38801, tel. 601/841–0286, fax 601/840–4158.*
Accommodations: *7 double rooms with baths.*
Amenities: *Air-conditioning, cable TV and phones in rooms.*
Rates: *$65–$95; full breakfast, afternoon refreshments. D, MC, V.*
Restrictions: *No smoking, no pets.*

The Amzi Love House

In the town of Columbus, where women have made a mark, one of the many antebellum homes was built for a woman, and her descendant, Sid Caradine, now runs it as a bed-and-breakfast. Built in 1848 for the bride of Amzi Love, the Italian-style villa in the historic district is much the way it was originally, because seven generations have intentionally preserved its unique character. In fact, Sid tells his guests that it's like a journey back in time, complete with original Empire and Victorian furnishings and such accessories as the crocheted bed-spreads and needlepoint done by Amzi Love's five daughters.

Sid returned to his birthplace in 1989, after deciding that writing poetry was preferable to working in the stock market. He has made the house more appealing to guests by providing extra amenities like bicycles and lush terry-cloth robes for use after bathing. He offers beverages upon arrival and serves lunch and dinner on request.

Address: *305 7th St. S, Columbus, MS 39701, tel. 601/328–5413 or 601/329–3533.*
Accommodations: *3 double rooms with baths, 1 suite.*
Amenities: *Air-conditioning, phones in rooms.*
Rates: *$85–$100; full breakfast, welcoming refreshments. MC, V.*
Restrictions: *No smoking in bedrooms, no pets.*

Carpenter Place

After driving down a long, narrow road through a pecan orchard, amid rolling hills and fields, you come to a rambling old house. You might not think that in this country setting you'd find modern amenities, but indeed you will. This, the county's oldest home (ca. 1835), has won awards for its astute restoration, updating the house while maintaining architectural integrity. The two-story plantation-style house now sports original interior colors— sunny light yellow in most areas—and is filled with fine old linens and lace, antiques, and family treasures. It was the birthplace and boyhood home of Roy Carpenter, the great-great-grandson of the builder. With his wife, Lucy, he now owns and manages it as a B&B, keeping it in mint condition. Roy teaches at a local university, and Lucy, a former educator, contributed much of the interior design expertise. It is she who planned the English gardens, where something is always in bloom. Explore the approximately 120 acres, and fish in the pond if you wish. The hosts are happy to show the house's treasures or explain its Civil War history.

Address: *1280 Rte. 25 S, Starkville, MS 39759, tel. 601/323–4669.*
Accommodations: *2 double rooms with baths in main house, 1 suite in carriage house.*
Amenities: *Air-conditioning, TV in suite and kitchen, phone in suite.*
Rates: *$65–$150; full plantation breakfast. MC, V.*
Restrictions: *No smoking, no pets.*

The Cartney-Hunt House

This 1828 house is thought to be the oldest brick structure in north Mississippi, but it is still light and airy. That has as much to do with the young owners as with the decor. Vicky Hicks Hardy, a teacher, and her CPA husband, Kirk, treat guests hospitably. They are pleased to share the history of the community and their residence, in Columbus's Southside Historic District, and know other heritage houses as well—Vicky's family home is Rosewood Manor, a Greek Revival mansion a few blocks north.

The house was completely restored in 1982–83, with all historic stipulations observed, and so has won coveted restoration awards. It is not ornate; rather, it exhibits the no-nonsense Federal style of the period. The blue, formal parlor is small and furnished with Victorian and period pieces, while the bedrooms are spacious and have a pleasing mix of antiques. Pastel colors highlight the warm woods. A shaded brick patio and wrought-iron furniture let you enjoy the pleasant climate, and the house is near downtown shops and restaurants.

Address: *408 7th St. S, Columbus, MS 39701, tel. 601/329–3856 or 601/328–7313.*
Accommodations: *3 double rooms with baths.*
Amenities: *Air-conditioning, TV in den, phones in rooms.*
Rates: *$85; full breakfast. MC, V.*
Restrictions: *No pets.*

Hamilton Place

Cotton money built lavish Southern homes, and this is a case in point. It was built in 1838 as a grand three-story Greek Revival mansion with massive columns. During the Civil War, Mrs. Carrington Mason, mistress of the house, is said to have saved Holly Springs by giving piano "concerts" with Union General B.H. Grierson. According to legend, after getting to know the intelligent, cultivated townspeople, Grierson could not destroy the town. The house was not so lucky in 1923, when a fierce storm demolished the third story and the columns. The facade was converted to a Louisiana-style raised cottage, though the proportions remain grand and the high ceilings, ornate moldings, and original interior design elements are still in place.

The only B&B in town, Hamilton Place is home to Jackson and Linda Stubbs—he with the Social Security Administration, she a dietitian. Among their treasures are a Mallard tester bed and exquisite blue-and-gold antique French twin beds. They've combined inherited pieces with collected items to furnish the main house and a carriage house, where there is an antiques shop.

Address: *105 E. Mason Ave., Holly Springs, MS 38635, tel. 601/252–4368.*
Accommodations: *4 double rooms with baths.*
Amenities: *Air-conditioning, TV in sitting room; pool, hot tub, bicycles.*
Rates: *$75; Continental breakfast. MC, V.*
Restrictions: *No pets.*

Liberty Hall

his 1832 planter's home is still inhabited by descendants of the builder. Some of their ancestors now grace the halls and walls in fine old oil paintings, while others, including a South Carolina senator of the early 1800s, lie in the wrought-iron-enclosed family burial plot. Though Liberty Hall is only 6 miles from Columbus, its split-rail fence and tall timbers recall a distant time. The white, two-story Greek Revival house boasts tall columns, a gallery, and plenty of room to roam. A lovely wooded path leads to a clear, bubbling creek. Inside, this old house, on the National Register of Historic Places, is an antiques-lover's delight. Many furnishings are original to the home. Empire pieces adorn the formal parlor, while the other parlor is more comfortable. In the dining room, outstanding French country scenes were painted on upper panels before the Civil War and left unfinished.

The W. S. Fowler family is close-knit and traditional. There's still a big family dinner each Sunday. Guests can arrange dinner with advance notice and an additional fee.

Address: *Armstrong Rd., Columbus, MS 39701, tel. 601/328–4110 or 601/329–3533.*
Accommodations: *3 double rooms with baths.*
Amenities: *Air-conditioning; pool.*
Rates: *$85; full breakfast. MC, V.*
Restrictions: *No smoking indoors, no pets.*

Puddin Place

ince 1992, when Ann and Guy Turnbow decided to turn an 1892 house near the Ole Miss campus into a Victorian B&B, its name has piqued the interest of guests. Puddin Place was named for a former resident, Miss Mary "Puddin" Sims, a dear friend of the owners. The general consensus, though, is that it is "a puddin' of a place," to use an old Southern phrase.

Because the same family owned the house until 1980, it didn't go through multiple changes imposed by multiple owners. The current owners have made it very comfortable, while maintaining the home's early character through colors and decor. The suites are furnished with antiques and collectibles, and they all have open fireplaces and ceiling fans. In addition to the tangible reminders of yester-year, there's an unhurried pace here. Guests can let the porch swing lull them into a nap on a summer day. Those who relish more activity can find, within a short walk, the University Museums, the downtown square, and the William Faulkner home. Some folks come to Oxford hoping to catch a glimpse of local writer John Grisham, of *The Firm* fame.

Address: *1008 University Ave., Oxford, MS 38655, tel. 601/234–1250.*
Accommodations: *2 suites, game room can be converted to guest room.*
Amenities: *Air-conditioning, cable TV in rooms, phone in common room.*
Rates: *$85–$125; full breakfast. No credit cards.*
Restrictions: *No smoking, no pets.*

Temple Heights

This aptly named house has 14 towering Doric columns on three sides; it sits high on a hill with a view of Alabama, about 10 miles to the east. Built in 1837 in a combination of Federal and Greek Revival styles, the house has four stories, with a hall and two large rooms on each floor. It is listed on the National Register of Historic Places and the Historic American Building Survey and is a Mississippi Landmark.

Owners Carl and Dixie Butler, educators and historians, bought the house as newlyweds back in the early '70s and have since restored the structure originally built by Richard T. Brownrigg. They welcome guests to their warm and comfortable home and proudly show the fine antiques they've collected over the years.

Colors, design elements, and furniture (consisting of Empire and Restoration pieces) are as true to the period of the home's construction as research can make it. Many original items remain, such as hall door locks, which were manufactured in England in the 1830s and bear the symbol of King William IV. You might also find other interesting historical tidbits, among them the name "Anne" scratched in a sidelight, supposedly by a resident during the Reconstruction.

Address: *515 9th St. N, Columbus, MS 39701, tel. 601/329–3533.*
Accommodations: *2 double rooms share 1 bath.*
Amenities: *Air-conditioning.*
Rates: *$85; full breakfast. MC, V.*
Restrictions: *No smoking, no pets.*

White Arches

Nestled on a quiet tree-lined street in one of Columbus's prettiest neighborhoods, this appealing antebellum mansion, built in 1857, is a focal point among many historic treasures in the area. Local architects have dubbed its design "Columbus Eclectic" because it gracefully and creatively combines the prominent styles of its day: Gothic, Greek Revival, and Italianate. Of particular interest is a central octagonal tower with an observatory. Four double doors lead from the tower's second floor onto a balcony surrounded by a cast-iron railing. Interior colors are warm and vivid, and period antiques are used throughout. A favorite of designers is the floor-to-ceiling built-in walnut bookcases in the library; in fact, the woodwork is superb throughout. An anteroom for the downstairs bedroom, supposedly once used for storing hoop skirts, is now a child's room.

Owners Ned Hardin and his wife are pleased to share their home and its history. They are both retired, he from the appliance business and she from teaching. White Arches is a Pilgrimage tour home and is on the National Register.

Address: *122 7th Ave. S, Columbus, MS 39701, tel. 601/329–3533.*
Accommodations: *5 double rooms with baths.*
Amenities: *Air-conditioning, TV and phone in common area, microwave, iron, refrigerator.*
Rates: *$85; full breakfast. MC, V.*
Restrictions: *No smoking indoors, no pets.*

Near the Natchez Trace

*The two-lane paved road crossing Mississippi from
southwest to northeast, connecting Natchez to Nashville,
Tennessee, has had a long and colorful past. It began about
8,000 years ago, when a path was "traced out" by buffalo and
Native Americans. By 1800, the well-worn Old Trace was the
route used by post riders, settlers, outlaws, peddlers, and
"Kaintucks," or boatmen, from all points north. They came
down the Mississippi River to New Orleans, sold their goods
and boats, then headed home via the Trace, hoping not to
encounter hostile tribes, bandits, or wild animals on the way.
Those who could spare a few pennies slept inside—often on
the floor—at inns (called "stands") scattered along the Trace,
sharing "mush and milk" with other wayfarers pleased to
have the simple luxury of hot food and a roof over their head.*

*After the late 1820s, when steamboats began to offer better
accommodations and shorter trips, the wilderness path to the
new frontier fell into disuse. The Old Trace had been taken
over by weeds when, in about 1909, the Mississippi chapter of
the Daughters of the American Revolution waged a
campaign to mark it. Their exemplary efforts resulted in the
450-mile, limited-access Natchez Trace Parkway, a long, thin
park running from Natchez to Nashville.*

*Travelers today who seek historic places and a slower pace
choose this road. The Trace is safe, scenic, and impeccably
maintained by the National Park Service and has been
landscaped to open up peaceful vistas in the dense woodland.
Uniformed rangers patrol it, enforcing the 50 mph speed
limit, and commercial vehicles and outdoor advertising are
prohibited. You can drive the Trace from Natchez to Tupelo
in seven hours, but to appreciate fully its beauty and history
requires a more leisurely approach—perhaps a weeklong
odyssey.*

Expect to see abundant tall timber, historic markers, wild game, and nature trails, but plan to leave the Trace for restaurants, shopping, and city sights. They're available in Natchez, Jackson, and Tupelo (see North Mississippi Hill Country, above), right on your way, and in Vicksburg, on the Mississippi River, 15 miles west.

In Natchez, one of the South's favorite destinations, many antebellum houses are open for daily tours throughout the year, and travelers today catch a glimpse of the way things were in the Old South.

Near Jackson, swaying pines and moss-draped oaks are replaced by sailboats and the glistening waters of the Ross Barnett Reservoir. Jackson is the best choice for restaurants, museums, and entertainment.

Places to Go, Sights to See

French Camp Log Cabin (milepost 180.8, tel. 601/547–6657) is a "dogtrot" cabin. (A center hall, open on both ends, separates the two sides.) Built in the early 1800s, it contains Native American and French artifacts and has an operating sorghum mill.

Jackson, Mississippi's capital, is the place to stop for cultural events and tours of historic sites and old government buildings. You can see the *Governor's Mansion* (300 E. Capitol St., tel. 601/359–3175) on 30-minute tours Tuesday through Friday. The *Old Capitol* and *State Historical Museum* (100 S. State St., tel. 601/359–6920) are open daily for self-guided tours. The *Jackson Zoological Park* (2918 W. Capitol St., tel. 601/352–2580) is open year-round, and the *Russell C. Davis Planetarium* (201 E. Pascagoula St., tel. 601/960–1550) gives multiscreen space and nature shows Tuesday through Sunday. The *Mississippi Museum of Art* (201 E. Pascagoula St., tel. 601/960–1515) contains continuing and changing exhibits, often international in scope, and a gallery for children with interactive high-tech exhibits. At the *Mississippi Agricultural and Forestry Museum* (1150 Lakeland Dr., tel. 601/354–6113), which has farm buildings and exhibits on the state's agrarian roots, you can see an orientation film and a re-created small town, circa 1920, complete with farm animals and living-history enactments. Juried works and native crafts are sold here at the *Chimneyville Crafts Gallery* (tel. 601/981–2499 or 601/981–0019).

Mississippi Crafts Center (Ridgeland, just north of Jackson, tel. 601/856–7546), a quaint log cabin with front porch rockers, sells local crafts, including quilts, baskets, and jewelry.

The **Mississippi Delta**—known only as the Delta in these parts—is a good drive, but it's worth it. West of the Trace on U.S. 82, it's a land of mood and mystique where vast, flat fields seem to go on forever. This is the heart of the state's cotton country. The rich Delta soil spawned numerous writers and artists and the unique music of hot days and hard times—the inimitable Delta blues. You can hear the blues throughout the Delta, on front porches and in juke joints, at festivals and church socials.

Mount Locust Inn, at milepost 15.5, is the only remaining example of a frontier "stand," or inn. Built around 1780, it is furnished accordingly and is closed during January and February.

Natchez's grand mansions attest to the former wealth of this old and colorful river town, recalling a time when lavish entertaining was de rigueur for the landed gentry. About 30 of the more than 500 mansions are on parade during the spring and fall "pilgrimages." A carriage ride through the historic district is a memorable way to see the houses and hear their stories. The riverboats *Delta Queen* and *Mississippi Queen*—calliopes playing, flags flying, passengers cheering—make regular stops at Natchez Under-the-Hill, the riverbank area that was the former hangout of rowdy boatmen and gamblers.

Port Gibson features quaint churches, historic houses of varying architectural styles, and the towering columns at the *Windsor Ruins,* remnants of another time. In contrast, you can take a tour of the *Grand Gulf nuclear plant*, a futuristic facility.

At **Tishomingo State Park** (milepost 302.8, tel. 601/438–6914), in northeast Mississippi, the Appalachian Mountains begin. The park has nature trails, canoe trips, and beautiful rustic settings.

Vicksburg, on the Mississippi, approximately 25 miles west of the Trace, is a lively and appealing river town known for its Civil War significance. Its historic antebellum houses are open for tours year-round. The *Vicksburg National Military Park* (3201 Clay St., tel. 601/636–0583) encompasses more than 1,800 acres of hills, fortifications, monuments, and the USS *Cairo,* a Union gunboat.

Restaurants

In Jackson, **Nick's** (1501 Lakeland Dr., tel. 601/981–8017) is the choice of Jacksonians and guests for fine dining. It's known for great seafood, pasta, and an exceptional wine list. The casual **Amerigo** (6592 Old Canton Rd., tel. 601/977–0563) serves grilled seafood, steaks, veal, and pasta. A local favorite, **Hal & Mal's** (200 S. Commerce St., tel. 601/948–0888), in a 1920s warehouse, serves such good Mississippi cooking it's sure to be packed. The prime rib and Gulf seafood at **Primo's** (4330 N. State St., tel. 601/982–2064) are a Jackson tradition.

In Natchez Under-the-Hill, try the casual **Cock of the Walk** (200 Broadway, tel. 601/446–8920), in an old depot on a bluff overlooking the river, for catfish, shrimp, and gumbo or **Natchez Landing** (61 Silver St., tel. 601/442–6639) for catfish and barbecue. **Pearl Street Pasta** (105 S. Pearl St., tel. 601/442–9284) specializes in fresh pasta dishes and fillet of beef. The food at **Brothers** (209 Franklin St., tel. 601/442–1777) has an unmistakable New Orleans flavor. Locals and visitors alike rave about both the quality and presentation of the contemporary regional cuisine at the new **Liza's** (657 S. Canal St., tel. 601/446–6368).

Among Vicksburg's popular restaurants are the rather formal **Delta Point** (4155 Washington St., tel. 601/636–5317), overlooking the Mississippi River and serving a variety of good food, from Cajun to Continental; **Tuminello's** (500 Speed St., tel. 601/634–0507), a tradition since 1899 for seafood, steaks, and veal, and also near the river; and **Walnut Hill** (1214 Adams St., tel. 601/638–4910), where everyone passes the down-home food—including fresh vegetables galore and, some say, the best fried chicken in the South—around the table.

Tourist Information

Greenville Convention & Visitors Bureau (410 Washington St., Greenville, MS 38939, tel. 601/453–9197 or 800/748–9064). **Greenwood Convention & Visitors Bureau** (Box 739, Greenwood, MS 38930, tel. 601/453–9197 or 800/748–9064). **Jackson Convention & Visitors Bureau** (Box 1450, Jackson, MS 39215, tel. 601/960–1891 or 800/354–7695). **Mississippi Department of Economic Development,** Division of Tourism Development (Box 22825, Jackson, MS 39205, tel. 601/359–3297 or 800/647–2290). **Natchez Convention & Visitor Bureau** (311 Liberty Rd., Natchez, MS 39120, tel. 601/446–6345 or 800/647–6724). **Natchez Pilgrimage Tours** (Box 347, Natchez, MS 39121, tel. 601/446–6631 or 800/647–6742). **Port Gibson Chamber of Commerce** (Box 491, Port Gibson, MS 39150, tel. 601/437–4351). **Vicksburg Convention & Visitors Bureau** (Box 110, Vicksburg, MS 39180, tel. 601/636–9421 or 800/221–3536). **Yazoo County Convention & Visitors Bureau** (Box 186, Yazoo City, MS 39194, tel. 601/746–1815).

Reservation Services

Lincoln, Ltd. Bed & Breakfast Mississippi Reservation Service (Box 3479, Meridian, MS 39303, tel. 601/482–5483 or 800/633–6477). **Natchez Pilgrimage Tours Bed & Breakfast Reservations** (Box 347, Natchez, MS 39121, tel. 601/446–6631 or 800/647–6742).

The Briars

One of Mississippi's prettiest and most serene B&Bs, The Briars is quietly tucked away on a bluff high above the Mississippi River. The Federal-style house, built around 1818, with its 80-foot veranda, dormer windows, and fanlight doorways, is one of the finest examples of Southern plantation-style architecture extant and one of the state's most historically significant houses. In the mid-1800s it was the home of the Howell family, whose beautiful Varina was called "the Rose of Mississippi." In the parlor of The Briars in 1845, Varina Howell married a dashing young graduate of West Point, Jefferson Davis, who was to become a Mexican War hero, a member of the Senate, Secretary of War under U.S. President Pierce, and, in 1861, President of the Confederate States of America. The Briars is listed on the National Register of Historic Places.

Interior designers Robert E. Canon and Newton Wilds purchased the house in 1975, and since that time, their talents have produced a retreat as grand as it is gracious. Each bedroom has a different color scheme and fabric, and as one would expect of a house done by designers, it is a showplace, although not so design perfect as to be uncomfortable. On the contrary, it's a warm and congenial place with lots of special features. It contains an enclosed gallery supported by arches and

fluted columns, unusual fan-shaped windows, and walk-in closets in some rooms. In the pretty and spacious guest rooms, antiques and reproductions are amicably mixed and there's a choice of king-size, queen-size, or extra-long twin beds. Many guests enjoy early morning coffee on the veranda or in their rooms.

From an observation point on the grounds, you can see the flatlands of Louisiana and many miles of the busy Mississippi River, where there's always something going on, from tugboats pushing barges to festive riverboats up from New Orleans. The flowering plants and foliage offer almost as nice a view as the river. The pavilion dining room, where guests are served breakfast, is another choice spot for outstanding views. The Briars is, understandably, one of eight Mississippi properties given a Four-Diamond rating by the American Automobile Association.

Address: *31 Irving La. (Box 1245), Natchez, MS 39120, tel. 601/446-9654 or 800/634-1818, fax 601/445-6037.*
Accommodations: *13 double rooms with baths.*
Amenities: *Air-conditioning, cable TV and phones in rooms; pool.*
Rates: *$135-$145; full breakfast. AE, MC, V.*
Restrictions: *Smoking in foyer and on porches only, no pets.*

The Burn

The name of this impressive Greek Revival house dates to 1836, when owner and Natchez mayor John Walworth chose the Scottish word for "small brook" to commemorate the one that once meandered through the property. Though it's only a punny coincidence, Loveta Byrne and her children are in residence now.

The house was built in 1832 as a pure Greek Revival cottage, and from the street, it does not appear to be the three-story mansion that you find upon closer inspection. Doric columns support the portico; as you enter through the transomed and sidelighted Grecian doorway, the first thing you see is the unique spiral staircase with its delicate spindle banisters. Dramatic red and green Natchez Collection wall covering and fabric by Schumacher are used in the music room, and in the formal dining room Schumacher wallpaper and draperies draw attention even when the Empire table is set with the 1820 Old Paris china. Outstanding woodwork and plaster moldings enhance the quality you note at The Burn.

Guest rooms in the main house are downstairs in the original house-servants' quarters, where quiet and comfort prevail. Bedrooms boast Mallard furniture, pastel walls, and exquisite Belgian fabrics on windows and beds. The Pink Room is elegantly furnished in Rococo Revival style, which was a Natchez favorite in the mid-1800s; in fact, The Burn is a treasure trove of 19th-century European antiques and accessories throughout. The house retains its Old South charm while offering modern conveniences. Guest-room TVs in the main house are discreetly hidden in antique armoires. There are additional guest rooms across the courtyard in the dependency, a building formerly used as servants' quarters.

A free tour of the house shows off the impressive antiques and architecture, and Loveta encourages guests to explore the lush and lovely grounds. Though it is located in the city, The Burn has a country feel about it. The property is on a rise, surrounded by tall trees and flowering shrubbery, except for the clearing of the pool and courtyard areas.

Address: *712 N. Union St., Natchez, MS 39120, tel. 601/442–1344 or 800/654–8859.*
Accommodations: *2 double rooms with baths in main house, 4 doubles with baths in dependency.*
Amenities: *Air-conditioning.*
Rates: *$82.50–$137.50; full breakfast. AE, MC, V.*
Restrictions: *No smoking indoors, no pets.*

Canemount Plantation

This 6,000-acre working plantation near Port Gibson, just off the Natchez Trace, is nestled quietly among vast forests and fields, flowing streams, and hills, welcoming guests to an idyllic escape. Listed on the National Register of Historic Places, Canemount was built in 1855 in the Italianate Revival style. It is much as it was then, except that the butler's pantry has been converted to a small kitchen for the owners, Ray John and Rachel Forrest and their son John. When it was built, the kitchen was out of doors, as is today's cozy, wood-paneled kitchen with a brick fireplace, where guests gather for meals.

Canemount, in all its Spanish moss–draped glory, is a haven for wildlife. The Forrests, formerly of Morganza, Louisiana, initially purchased it in 1981 as a retreat for their hunting club, but according to Rachel, they "fell in love with the place and decided to stay here permanently." White-tailed deer are so plentiful that the place was selected for a Mississippi State University study of their life span. Meandering paths and trails offer opportunities to see deer, Russian boar, and wild turkey. Areas are designated for wildlife photography, and guides are available for hiking or as drivers of four-wheel-drive vehicles.

Guests are greeted with a complimentary wine and cheese tray upon arrival, are invited to have dinner with the Forrests at no extra charge, and are treated to a tour of the antiques-filled main house. Accommodations are in nearby, private, restored antebellum structures: Rick's Cottage, with brick walls, original wood floors, and a tester bed draped with mosquito netting; the Grey Cottage, which has a Jacuzzi; and the Pond House, with a whirlpool tub. Each cottage is furnished with a mixture of antiques and contemporary pieces, contains a wood-burning fireplace or stove, and is wonderfully quiet except for the sounds of birds and running deer.

The plantation acreage also includes the historic Windsor Plantation, where the haunting ruins—23 towering Greek columns—still stand, though the massive house was destroyed by fire in 1890. The Persnickety Pig dining area, also on the plantation, is in a converted dairy. It's where fun and festive Cajun pig roasts are held for groups.

Address: *Rte. 552 W (Rte. 2, Box 45), Lorman, MS 39096, tel. 601/877–3784 or 800/423–0684.*
Accommodations: *3 cottage suites.*
Amenities: *Air-conditioning, TV in rooms and common area, phone in common area; heated pool, ponds.*
Rates: *$145–$165; MAP, welcoming refreshments. MC, V.*
Restrictions: *No smoking indoors, no pets.*

Dunleith

Dunleith is one of the South's most beautiful houses, from the colonnaded galleries that encircle it to the superior antiques within and the 40 acres of landscaped grounds, wooded bayous, and green pastures without. It is constantly photographed, often written about, and occasionally appears in films. Dunleith is also a National Historic Landmark on the National Register of Historic Places.

The palatial mansion (ca. 1856) is owned by William Heins III of Natchez. A resident manager and staff run the business of daily tours and lodging, and it is, quite noticeably, a business. Fortunately, the magnificence of Dunleith's architecture and interiors neutralizes the regimented recitations of the staff and their curt responses to questions. The grandeur of the place prevails.

Among the elegant furnishings are the dining room's French Zuber wallpaper from 1855 woodblocks that were hidden in a cave in France during World War I. The V'Soske carpet in the front parlor determined the color scheme for the room's walls, draperies, and upholstery; the greenish-gold walls and draperies perfectly complement the peachy pinks and gold tones in the carpet. A Louis XV ormolu-mounted mahogany Linke table is in a prominent place in the front parlor.

Three of the guest rooms at Dunleith are in the main house, and eight are in the former servants' wing. The rooms are quiet and private and are well decorated in mid-19th-century style, with a mixture of reproductions and antiques. All of them have working fireplaces.

Another nice feature is that the grounds are subtly lighted at night so that guests can stroll in the "moonlight" or enjoy the romantic views from wicker rockers on the galleries.

Old brick and warm woods set the stage for the big plantation breakfast served in the restored poultry house. Exposed beams, lots of windows, and wooden floors add a homey touch that guests may have missed in the elaborate, museumlike main house.

Address: *84 Homochitto St., Natchez, MS 39120, tel. 601/446–8500 or 800/433–2445.*
Accommodations: *11 double rooms with baths.*
Amenities: *Air-conditioning, TV in rooms, phones in common area.*
Rates: *$85–$130; full breakfast. AE, D, MC, V.*
Restrictions: *No pets.*

Millsaps Buie House

Though its location in Mississippi's busiest city keeps it from being just another moss-and-magnolia bed-and-breakfast inn, the Millsaps Buie House in Jackson is grand and historic and filled with antiques. It's actually an elegant Victorian mansion, built in 1888 in the heart of downtown. Everything about the house says "quality," from exterior construction to interior details like the hand-molded plaster frieze work, bay windows, and other elements of the Queen Anne influence.

Once the home of Major Reuben Webster Millsaps of the Confederate Army, banker, financier, and founder in 1892 of the distinguished Millsaps College, the house has been in the same family for five generations. It has been a B&B since 1987 and is described as "a 19th-century urban retreat for the 20th-century traveler." One might add "business traveler," for although the house contains priceless heirlooms, each room has a telephone with computer dataport and a small, unobtrusive bedside radio, and TVs are concealed in old armoires. For health-conscious guests, a fitness center is nearby.

Guests are encouraged to relax in the drawing room, parlor, or library before retiring to their room for the evening. Pier mirrors in the parlor reflect the grand piano and a French "courting bench," as the house as a whole reflects the style and taste of the distinguished interior designer who also refurbished the Governor's Mansion, the New State Capitol, and Florewood Plantation in Greenwood.

Bedrooms are furnished in a pleasing mixture of period antiques and reproductions, including tester or canopy beds, rosewood chairs, and marble-top tables. Original mantelpieces add detail and interest, while old family portraits add authenticity. The rich, pleated draperies in one of the rooms are made of solid fabric in a shade matching the dominant color in the flowered wallpaper; carpet color matches the draperies.

The staff members here are truly gracious, unlike those efficient but impersonal people at some other inns. The Millsaps Buie House won AAA's Four-Diamond Award.

Address: *628 N. State St., Jackson, MS 39202, tel. 601/352–0221, fax 601/352–0221.*
Accommodations: *11 double rooms with baths.*
Amenities: *Air-conditioning, cable TV in rooms.*
Rates: *$95–$165; full breakfast. MC, V.*
Restrictions: *Smoking on porches only, no pets.*

Monmouth

The massive Monmouth (ca. 1818) may lack the delicate lacelike ornamentation of some other Natchez homes, but it is no less interesting in monumental architecture and Victorian furnishings. Its sturdy appeal inspired a daughter of the house to write this in her diary in 1868: "Dear old Monmouth, within whose substantial weather-beaten walls it used to seem to my childish imagination that care and trouble could never come."

Staying at Monmouth still evokes such feelings of security and well-being, and touring the house is a treat. Perhaps the children of owners Ron and Lani Riches will someday write such tributes, though the Riches actually live in Los Angeles, where he is a land developer. A resident manager and full staff keep the inn ready for guests.

The Riches bought Monmouth in 1978, then spent two years restoring it, recapturing the grandeur it knew in earlier days. The interior mood is formal, with the blue-silk-covered Rococo Revival furniture in the double parlor made even prettier by the glow of a Waterford crystal chandelier. The windows are done with fanciful swags, valances, fringes, and lace. The "courting chair" in the parlor, a major conversation piece, is a three-cornered contraption just suited for a couple and a chaperone. The bedrooms in the main house are

a decorator's dream. The peach bedroom, a favorite, features peach walls and fabrics, including magnificent draperies on the windows and the canopy bed.

Monmouth's Greek Revival portico was added in 1853, at which time the original brick was covered with eggshell stucco and scored. The grounds, all 26 acres, are immaculate, and there's always something in bloom. Though the interior of the main house is designer perfect, the four garden cottages, the carriage house, and the servants' quarters are great to stay in, too. They are cozy and intimate, and far removed from the hustle and bustle of the house, with its tours and gift shop.

Monmouth is a member of the prestigious Small Luxury Hotels of the World and is an AAA Four-Diamond property.

Address: *36 Melrose Ave., Natchez, MS 39120, tel. 601/442–5852 or 800/828–4531.*
Accommodations: *6 double rooms with baths and 1 suite in main house, 11 doubles with baths and 1 suite in outbuildings.*
Amenities: *Restaurants, air-conditioning, TV and phones in rooms.*
Rates: *$90–$160; full breakfast. AE, D, MC, V.*
Restrictions: *No smoking indoors, no pets.*

Mount Repose

While Natchez is often busy entertaining guests, the surrounding countryside is so quiet you can almost hear the Spanish moss gently swaying in the breeze. Though only 7 miles from downtown, the aptly named Mount Repose seems to be a world away. This roomy, rambling plantation house listed on the National Register of Historic Places is a perfect spot in which to rest and regroup. Mount Repose has high ceilings, lots of doors, tall windows, and fireplaces in every room; it is not delicately ornate but "country comfortable," the way planters' homes were meant to be.

The house was built in 1824 in the Federal style, with a central 2½-story facade. When the Greek Revival style became popular in Natchez in the 1830s, one-story wings were added to each side, resulting in a carefully planned and pleasingly eclectic building. Square columns across the front support double-tiered galleries; matching doors with oval fanlights and sidelights open onto both galleries, where porch swings wait to be used. In front you'll see magnolias and dogwood trees, rows of centuries-old live oaks draped with Spanish moss, a circle of azaleas, and perhaps a fat bullfrog resting on the rim of the brick lily pond. The back porch, shaded by a big ginkgo tree, offers views of rolling hills, woods, and a lake, as well as glimpses of a plethora of birds, squirrels, maybe even a wild turkey or two. Mount Repose is indeed a country place.

William Bisland built the house, and it has been occupied since by Bisland descendants. The walls are filled with portraits of ancestors, and many of Mount Repose's original furnishings are still in place, among them tester beds by Mallard, the New Orleans cabinetmaker; armoires; and dressers. Various Bisland descendants have added such items as an Italian palace chair and rare porcelains from Paris.

Off the front bedroom, which has Mallard furniture, an Oriental carpet, and rose-flowered wallpaper, is the children's room and nursery, where old christening gowns, porcelain dolls, and first-edition children's books are displayed. Bathrooms have recently been updated to luxury status, and the old doctor's office adjoining the house has been restored.

Address: *1733 Martin Luther King, Jr., Rd., Natchez, MS 39120, tel. 601/446–6631 or 800/647–6742.*
Accommodations: *3 double rooms with baths.*
Amenities: *Air-conditioning, phones in rooms.*
Rates: *$110–$135; full breakfast. AE, MC, V.*
Restrictions: *No smoking indoors, no pets.*

No Mistake Plantation

When John William N.A. Smith purchased 12,000 acres of wild virgin timber for $1.50 an acre back in 1833, he made no mistake—hence the name. Those who stay at this B&B near Satartia make no mistake, either. Its remaining 700 acres of great trees and flowers, its lake, and its wonderful solitude are 30 miles north of Vicksburg on Route 3. Today, the plantation is owned by descendants of the original Mr. Smith, Earl and Kathryn Barfield, who inherited the place from Earl's aunt Ethel Smith. Aunt Ethel was a noted horticulturist best known for her exquisite daylilies. In fact, No Mistake remains a daylily farm that hybridizes, cultivates, and sells daylilies commercially. Spring and early summer are the peak blooming seasons for azaleas, dogwoods, wisteria, magnolias, and daylilies.

Guests may never want to leave the peaceful, shady grounds where colorful peacocks strut, but more treasures await inside. Family heirlooms are featured in every room of the two-story Greek Revival–style house, but even with fine antiques all around, No Mistake has managed to maintain its livability and warmth. It is country elegant rather than city stuffy, and not at all commercial. It's not unusual to see a peacock peering in through the tall porch windows.

The Barfields want guests to enjoy the home and some privacy. The Barfields live in the original log portion of the house, connected to the main house by an arbor, so guests have the house to themselves. So that guests aren't disturbed by ringing telephones, there are no room phones, though they are available elsewhere. Guests especially appreciate the freedom to explore the plantation and the candlelit plantation dinner, served on the best china and old sterling. Dinner is included, since the nearest good-size town is Yazoo City, about 20 miles north.

This part of the state borders the Delta, so the surrounding countryside is primarily vast, flat fields of cotton and soybeans. No Mistake itself is a working plantation, though a shady 7-acre garden complex is reserved for guests, who may wish to photograph the flowers and wildlife. A picture of Canada geese swimming on the dark still water of the pond has graced several magazine covers.

Address: *Rte. 3, Satartia, MS 39162, tel. 601/746–6579.*
Accommodations: *4 double rooms with baths in main house, 1 housekeeping cabin.*
Amenities: *Air-conditioning, TV in den and some rooms, phone in den.*
Rates: *$100–$110; MAP. AE, MC, V.*
Restrictions: *No smoking, no pets.*

Anchuca

Time seems to have stood still at Anchuca. It may be the most authentic—in style, decor, and attitude—of Vicksburg's antebellum bed-and-breakfasts. The owner, May Burns, is about as Southern a belle as you'll find, for she hails from the Mississippi Delta, upriver from Vicksburg. Anchuca (ca. 1830) was the first Vicksburg B&B, and in the more than 10 years since it began, guests have experienced the South the way it must have been in the pre-1860 days. It has consistently earned the AAA Four-Diamond rating.

You step into the music parlor, where the Knabe grand piano shares billing with a pair of exquisite watermelon-colored recamiers, on which many a belle probably swooned over men and music. Though the master suite with its pink tufted furniture can be reserved, most guests are put up in an original dependency formerly used by house servants or in a turn-of-the-century guest cottage. Antiques and period reproductions are used throughout the guest rooms.

Address: *1010 1st East St., Vicksburg, MS 39180, tel. 601/636–4931 or 800/262–4822.*
Accommodations: *9 double rooms with baths, 3 suites.*
Amenities: *Air-conditioning, TV and phones in rooms; pool*
Rates: *$75–$125; full breakfast. AE, D, MC, V.*
Restrictions: *No smoking in main house.*

Annabelle

John Alexander Klein built Annabelle for his son in 1868, just 10 years after he completed Cedar Grove. Luckily for the old Victorian Italianate house, George and Carolyn Mayer came up from New Orleans and purchased it in 1992. The Mayers have traveled extensively, spent years in the hospitality industry, and understand the expectations and needs of travelers. George is European and bilingual, and languages spoken at Annabelle include German, Portuguese, some Spanish, and American South, ya'll.

Located in the historic River View Garden District, Annabelle sits just east of the Mississippi River bed. It's bordered by magnolia and pecan trees and is reminiscent of the New Orleans French Quarter. A brick patio adjoins the house and is a great place to relax prior to or after exploring Vicksburg. Inside, period Victorian antiques are set off by bright colors, but best of all, the house lacks the fussiness often found in early Victorian houses. Two bedrooms in the cottage can be converted to a suite.

Address: *501 Speed St., Vicksburg, MS 39180, tel. 601/638–2000 or 800/791–2000.*
Accommodations: *6 double rooms with baths.*
Amenities: *Air-conditioning, TV with movie channels in rooms.*
Rates: *$80–$100; full breakfast. MC, V.*
Restrictions: *No smoking indoors, no pets.*

Cedar Grove

A house of eclectic design, though predominantly Greek Revival, this "grand antebellum mansion" is a National Historic Landmark on the National Register of Historic Places. The four-story house, in all its stucco glory, has round columns and wings and is on a very grand scale. It was built in 1840 and still has a Union cannonball from the Battle of Vicksburg lodged in a parlor wall. Amazingly, the original heavy furnishings made for the house remain in the master bedroom and the children's rooms. Many of Prudent Mallard's dark, massive pieces are in evidence, including a specially made king-size bed. All rooms are spacious and colorful, and they feature elaborate moldings, woodwork, wallpaper borders, gaslit chandeliers, gold-leaf pier mirrors, Italian marble mantels, and rich draperies. The house also boasts a grand ballroom and many choice spots from which to view the river. The staff goes to great lengths to meet guests' needs. The Garden Room Restaurant, with piano bar, serves a gourmet candlelit dinner.

Address: *2300 Washington St., Vicksburg, MS 39180, tel. 601/636–1000 or 800/862–1300.*
Accommodations: *13 double rooms with baths, 12 suites.*
Amenities: *Air-conditioning, TV in rooms, phones in most rooms; pool, hot tub, croquet.*
Rates: *$110–$160; full breakfast. AE, MC, V.*
Restrictions: *Smoking in designated rooms only, no pets.*

The Corners

The Corners has had a happier history than many other Vicksburg dwellings. No cannonballs are lodged in the walls, and there are no stories of the siege, just interesting anecdotes about the house. The Corners sits almost in the shadow of Cedar Grove, because John Klein, Cedar Grove's builder, presented the smaller and more intimate two-story brick house to his daughter as a wedding gift.

The late Greek Revival/early Victorian house was built in 1873 and bought by Texans Bettye and Cliff Whitney in 1986. It was not a planned purchase but a fortuitous happening: On a trip, the Whitneys saw the delightful house and bought it the same day. Today you can enjoy the river sights and sounds from the 68-foot front gallery.

All the guest rooms are furnished with antiques, each with a different color combination. The master bedroom is "on the mauve side," with a canopy bed (ca. 1842) and a river view. The Corners is a AAA Four-Diamond Award winner and is on the National Register of Historic Places.

Address: *601 Klein St., Vicksburg, MS 39180, tel. 601/636–7421 or 800/444–7421.*
Accommodations: *6 double rooms with baths, 1 suite, 2-bedroom housekeeping cottage.*
Amenities: *Air-conditioning, TV and phones in rooms, Jacuzzis in 2 rooms.*
Rates: *$75–$95; full breakfast. AE, MC, V.*
Restrictions: *Smoking on veranda only, no pets.*

The Duff Green Mansion

Times were good when Duff
Green built a house for his bride,
Mary, back in 1856—a grand
Palladian-style house with elaborate
cast-iron grillwork on the second- and
third-floor galleries. A few years
later, however, Confederate Vicksburg
was under siege by Union forces. The
Green family joined other local
citizens and moved to the safety of
nearby caves, where Mary gave birth
to a son she named Siege. The house
survived and later served as a
hospital with Confederate wounded
downstairs, it is said, and Union
wounded upstairs.

The Duff Green Mansion stands tall
and proud, a little heavier with
cannonballs, but as elegant and
graceful as ever. The interior
proportions are grand, with outstanding millwork and plaster ornamentation, solid cypress doors, and exquisite Waterford chandeliers. Fifteen
fireplaces still keep the house warm
and cozy. Owners Alicia and Harry
Sharp bought the house in 1985 and
restored it. The original wall and trim
colors were duplicated; the furnishings are of the period, but none are
original to the house.

Address: *1114 1st East St., Vicksburg,
MS 39180, tel. 601/636–6968,
601/636–6662, or 800/992–0037.*
Accommodations: *4 double rooms
with baths, 3 suites.*
Amenities: *Air-conditioning, phones
in rooms; pool.*
Rates: *$75–$150; full breakfast. AE,
MC, V.*

French Camp Bed and Breakfast Inn

The settlement on the Natchez
Trace called French Camp got
its name when Louis le Fleur
built an inn here back in 1812. Le
Fleur, a French Canadian, married a
Choctaw woman; their son changed
his name to Greenwood Leflore and
became a Choctaw chief, a state
senator, and a colorful figure in
Mississippi history. Today, Leflore's
ornate carriage is on display at
French Camp Academy, a small
secondary school begun in 1885.

Sallie and Ed Williford, both associated with the school (she teaches
algebra and tutors math; he is
director of development), manage the
academy's nearby bed-and-breakfast.
The inn on the Natchez Trace (ca.
1850) is intentionally rustic; it is made
from two log cabins now joined
together, each more than 100 years
old. Rich, warm wood, chinked log
walls, antiques, iron beds, and
handmade quilts give the B&B the
right touch of Old World charm mixed
with its 20th-century conveniences.
Big windows with forest views plus
Sallie's bread and jams are a bonus.

Address: *1 Bluebird La., French
Camp, MS 39745, tel. 601/547–6835.*
Accommodations: *4 double rooms
with baths.*
Amenities: *Air-conditioning.*
Rates: *$60; full breakfast. MC, V.*
Restrictions: *No smoking indoors.*

Governor Holmes House

Walk through the historic door at the "Governor's House" and hear marvelous Mozart extending a melodious welcome. Built in 1794, the Federal brick town house was the residence of David Holmes, the last governor of the Mississippi Territory and the first governor of the state of Mississippi. The house is also rumored to have been owned by Jefferson Davis, president of the Confederacy.

Perhaps these high-powered former occupants inspired the present owners when they set about making the remarkably well-preserved house reflect its history and happenstance; it is now a National Historic Landmark. In the Governor's Suite, beamed ceilings and ecru walls provide a perfect background for the colorful Oriental carpet and canopies that cover the two double beds. The fabric is by Scalamandré. Leather wing chairs positioned beside the fireplace are inviting. Owners Rivet Hedderel (an interior designer who owns an antiques shop in New Orleans), Bob Pulley, and Hermann Stenz have put their time, talents, and expertise to good use.

Address: *207 S. Wall St., Natchez, MS 39120, tel. 601/442–2366.*
Accommodations: *3 double rooms with baths, 1 suite.*
Amenities: *Air-conditioning and TV in rooms.*
Rates: *$85–$115; full breakfast. MC, V.*
Restrictions: *No pets.*

The Guest House Historic Hotel

This small hotel in the heart of Natchez's downtown historic district was built around 1840. It has tall Greek columns across the front and a wide porch on two sides, an inviting spot to enjoy morning coffee or a late-afternoon beverage. The Guest House is within walking distance of many historic tour homes, fine antiques shops, and restaurants. Actually, it's in a prime location, whatever your plans.

Each guest room is individually decorated with antiques—including tester beds in some rooms—and excellent reproductions. Good quality is notable in the fabric used on beds and windows, in lots of dark woods, and in the print wallpaper. A room in this small, friendly property feels more like it's in a private home than a hotel. Southern hospitality begins with complimentary wine upon arrival.

Listed on the National Register of Historic Places and a AAA Three Diamond–rated hotel, the Guest House is locally owned. It's a favorite place for meetings, corporate retreats, family reunions, and weddings. Children are welcome.

Address: *201 N. Pearl St., Natchez, MS 39120, tel. 601/442–1054 or 800/442–1054, fax 601/442–1374.*
Accommodations: *18 double rooms with baths.*
Amenities: *Air-conditioning, cable TV, phones, small refrigerators, stocked minibars, and coffee makers in rooms.*
Rates: *$95; Continental breakfast, welcoming beverage. AE, MC, V.*

Hope Farm

All the bed-and-breakfasts in Natchez are old, but Hope Farm is surely the oldest. The original portion, now the B&B wing, was built of heavy cypress around 1775. Don Carlos de Grand Pré, the Spanish commandant of the Natchez District, bought the house in 1789, built the main house, and commenced to entertain distinguished guests. Perhaps he set the precedent for the lavish entertaining that is still part of the Natchez lifestyle.

Hope Farm is now owned by Ethel Banta, a Natchez native who moved to New York after graduating from Sweet Briar College. She "came home" in 1986; bought the house, 15 acres of land, and the furnishings as well; and became the fifth owner of Hope Farm. One of the many treasures is a Duncan Phyfe dining room table, which is often set with Old Paris china and exquisite Gorham silver. The cream-colored parlor is dressed with early American Empire furniture; the guest rooms are furnished with some plantation-made pieces, a chair designed by Thomas Jefferson, and other important antiques.

Address: *147 Homochitto St., Natchez, MS 39120, tel. 601/445–4848 or 800/647–6742.*
Accommodations: *4 double rooms with baths.*
Amenities: *Air-conditioning, house tour.*
Rates: *$80–$90; early coffee on the porch, full breakfast, welcoming refreshments.*
Restrictions: *No pets.*

Lansdowne

The entrance to Lansdowne leads down a quiet country road through thick woods and foliage. Then the house appears. It is civilized isolation in its purest form and a marvelous country retreat for city dwellers. Lansdowne was built in 1853 by George Marshall. His descendants are still in residence, and so are many of the original furnishings. The style is Greek Revival, with fine accent work, pale pink brick, and dark-green shutters, reminiscent of the Italianate style. All is contained on one floor and two dependencies, which used to be the governess's room and school-rooms.

Lansdowne's guest rooms are quiet and comfortable, furnished with antiques and reproductions, but plain in comparison with the main house and its treasures. High ceilings emphasize the plaster medallions and chandeliers, though it is the outstanding Rococo Revival parlor furniture that catches the eye. The exquisite old family silver in the formal dining room is a treat for guests to see at breakfast, and so are the old wood-graining and marbleizing, which have been preserved.

Address: *1323 Martin Luther King, Jr., Rd., Natchez, MS 39121, tel. 601/446–9401 or 800/647–6742.*
Accommodations: *2 double rooms with baths.*
Amenities: *Air-conditioning, TV in rooms.*
Rates: *$90; full breakfast. AE, MC, V.*
Restrictions: *No smoking, no pets.*

Linden

Linden's ornately carved Federal-style doorway may be familiar to movie fans, because it was copied for the doorway to Scarlett O'Hara's Tara in *Gone with the Wind.* The house was built around 1800 and sold in 1818 to the first U.S. senator from Mississippi. Linden is a sprawling, two-story house with wings on each side, known for its 98-foot front gallery and for the Federal furniture found inside. Hepplewhite, Sheraton, and Chippendale are well represented at Linden; other treasures include three original paintings by Audubon and a portrait of Jenny Lind.

The guest rooms are furnished in antiques and some heirlooms, for one family's descendants have been in residence here since 1849. The east-wing bedrooms open onto a back gallery that overlooks the garden and courtyard. The owner, Jeanette Feltus, a former teacher, conducts free tours of the house and joins guests for breakfast. The house is listed on the National Register of Historic Places and is also a AAA Three-Diamond property.

Address: *1 Linden Pl., Natchez, MS 39120, tel. 601/445–5472 or 800/647–6742.*
Accommodations: *7 double rooms with baths.*
Amenities: *Air-conditioning.*
Rates: *$90; full breakfast. AE, MC, V.*
Restrictions: *No pets.*

Oak Square

Port Gibson's massive white-frame Greek Revival–style Oak Square (ca. 1850), whose white columns support a second-story porch, was built as the town home of a cotton planter who apparently wanted his family to enjoy culture as well as comfort. The house features a foyer/ballroom with a wide stairway leading to a "minstrel gallery." The gentility of the old house (a AAA Four-Diamond Award winner) has been retained by owners Martha and William Lum, former retail merchants in Port Gibson. Both the Lums inherited massive antiques from old family plantations, and their treasures are now on display at Oak Square.

Elaborate crown moldings and ornate plasterwork adorn the ceilings, and Empire and Rococo Revival furniture fills all 30 rooms in the mansion. Guest rooms are in the Guest House and the French House, both adjoining the property and both completely furnished with family antiques and treasures.

Address: *1207 Church St., Port Gibson, MS 39150, tel. 601/437–4350 or 800/729–0240.*
Accommodations: *10 double rooms with baths.*
Amenities: *Air-conditioning, TV and phones in rooms.*
Rates: *$75–$95; full breakfast. AE, MC, D, V.*
Restrictions: *No smoking indoors, no pets.*

Pleasant Hill

T he name fits: This is one of the most pleasant and cheerful B&Bs in the South. The "raised cottage" is an elegant three-story house elevated from a fully raised basement. A wide central hall separates the formal parlor and dining room from the library and a bedroom, with a gracefully winding stairway at the end. On the National Register of Historic Places, the circa 1835 house is known for its well-planned space and high-quality Greek Revival trim.

Everything here is superb—from the custom-made Stark carpet and the Italian marble mantels to the mostly Empire, Federal, and Victorian antiques. Particularly noteworthy are a Boston recamier from 1815 and a New York breakfast table, possibly a Duncan Phyfe. Furnishings are in turn set off by glowing shades of peach and terra-cotta, bordered by rich cream. Guests gather in the glass-enclosed garden room or the sitting room around which the bedrooms are situated. Owner Eliza Sharp also owns Natchez's newest upscale restaurant, Liza's.

Address: *310 S. Pearl St., Natchez, MS 39120, tel. 601/442-7674 or 800/621-7952.*
Accommodations: *4 double rooms with baths.*
Amenities: *Air-conditioning, TV and phone in common area.*
Rates: *$95–$125; full breakfast. MC, V.*
Restrictions: *Smoking on porches only, no pets.*

Ravenna

V isitors will remember Ravenna for its remarkable elliptical stairway, which gracefully spirals from the first to the third floor. A magnificent hallway arch sets the stage for the stairway and the other architectural elements of the interior. The Greek Revival house was built in 1835 for a prominent cotton broker who spared no expense, and people still look in awe at the staircase.

Ravenna, the home of Catherine Morgan and her family, is furnished mostly in period antiques and family heirlooms; it has a nice "lived-in" appeal. The guest rooms, with old armoires and tester beds, are restful and gracious, and their decor matches the age and style of the house, with no unnecessary adornment. Catherine is known for her culinary talent, and each morning she serves up Southern delicacies with all the trimmings.

The gardens are lush and lovely at any time of year, with foliage so thick the house appears to peek from behind the leaves and Spanish moss. In springtime, azaleas and dogwoods provide a haven of color.

Address: *S. Union at Ravenna La., Natchez, MS 39121, tel. 601/446-9973 or 800/647-6742.*
Accommodations: *2 double rooms with baths, 1 housekeeping cottage.*
Amenities: *Air-conditioning, TV and fireplace in cottage; pool.*
Rates: *$85–$100; full breakfast. AE, MC, V.*
Restrictions: *Smoking in designated areas only, no pets.*

Redbud Inn

The Redbud Inn is as pretty as the name sounds, and the 1885 Victorian house has other attractions, too. A popular restaurant on the first floor that serves lunch to the public will prepare private candlelit dinners for B&B guests, if requested in advance. The inn is also an antiques shop where English and Victorian antiques may be admired or purchased.

Owners Rosemary Burge, an interior designer, and Maggie Garrett, a teacher, have done wonderful things with the Redbud Inn in the years they've owned it. Each room is decorated with period antiques and individual colors and appointments. The Peach Room, for example, features a big Victorian bed so tall it has antique steps beside it. Flowers and accessories complement the decor. The Dogwood Room boasts a balcony.

This B&B, right in the heart of Kosciusko, is a fine example of Queen Anne architecture and is listed on the National Register of Historic Places. It is within walking distance of the town square and other charming Victorian houses.

Address: *121 N. Wells St., Kosciusko, MS 39090, tel. 601/289–5086.*
Accommodations: *4 double rooms with baths.*
Amenities: *Restaurant; air-conditioning, TV, and phones in rooms.*
Rates: *$75–$100; full breakfast. MC, V.*
Restrictions: *Smoking on porches only, no pets.*

Weymouth Hall

For a stunning and uninterrupted view of the mighty Mississippi, this is the place. High on a bluff, this H-shaped, cupola-topped, Greek Revival mansion (ca. 1855) probably would be in the river by now if owner Gene Weber had not shored up the bluff with 500,000 yards of hauled-in dirt, terraced it, and planted it with grass to stop the erosion. The house is now regally watching the river run rather than being threatened by it.

Recessed porches front and back are great getaways if it's peace and quiet you seek. Actually, the location itself provides solitude, for no other house is close by on either side; the river is in front and the National Cemetery is behind. Watching the meandering river traffic is about as relaxing a pastime as you'll find anywhere.

Weymouth Hall still has the look and feel of the mid-1800s. It's not as commercialized as some historic homes, and it is furnished with rare antiques, including pieces by John Belter and Prudent Mallard. A collection of fine porcelain includes Old Paris, Meissen, and Dresden. Gene or his sister Nancy Weber will acquaint guests with Weymouth Hall's history upon arrival.

Address: *1 Cemetery Rd., Natchez, MS 39120, tel. 601/445–2304.*
Accommodations: *5 double rooms with baths.*
Amenities: *Air-conditioning.*
Rates: *$85; full breakfast, welcoming beverage. MC, V.*
Restrictions: *No smoking indoors, no pets.*

Mississippi Gulf Coast Region

Despite its late-17th-century beginnings as the region's first permanent European settlement, the Mississippi Gulf Coast region has few vestiges of the French and Spanish period. Today, the international influence in this seaside resort area comes from workers in the seafood business, which, along with tourism, ranks as the leading industry. A drive along scenic U.S. 90 reveals palatial beach "cottages" and a 26-mile strip of man-made beach, said to be the world's longest. It's hard to tell one coastal town from the next, but whether you're in Biloxi, Gulfport, Long Beach, Pass Christian, or Bay St. Louis, a stop at any one of many restaurants will turn up the coast's specialty: fresh seafood. Daily excursions can be made to the barrier islands, where water is blue and beaches are white; there are scheduled departures on daily cruise ships, and West Ship Island can be reached by passenger ferry. Charter boats go out deep-sea fishing, and 14 golf courses attract players year-round.

Inland from the Gulf but considered somewhat coastal in attitude and climate are Hattiesburg and Laurel. Hattiesburg is a shopping hub for south Mississippi, and the site of the University of Southern Mississippi. There's a plethora of university-related activities: theater, art galleries, and SEC sports, and Hattiesburg hosts the popular Deposit Guaranty Golf Classic, on the PGA tour, each April. Outdoor recreational areas and water parks abound along the nearby Pat Harrison Waterway. Laurel has one of the country's best small museums, the Lauren Rogers Museum of Art. The privately endowed museum, set in a neo-Georgian building and known for the quality of its exhibits and permanent collections, is a surprise and a delight.

Still farther inland lies Meridian, whose Highland Park has a museum for country-music legend Jimmy Rodgers and a

one-of-a-kind antique carousel. Meridian's downtown is
much as it was in the 1940s and appears to be thriving.

Places to Go, Sights to See

Beauvoir (224 Beach Blvd., Biloxi, tel. 601/388–1313). This beachfront
dwelling was the last home of Jefferson Davis, president of the Confederate
States of America. The 1854 house museum contains Civil War artifacts and
Confederate memorabilia.

Biloxi Lighthouse (U.S. 90, tel. 601/435–6294). This 65-foot cast-iron
structure, built in 1848, is the area's major landmark. The base holds a
permanent exhibit of the lighthouse's history.

De Grummond Children's Literature Research Collection (University of
Southern Mississippi, Hattiesburg, tel. 601/266–4345). More than 1,100
authors and illustrators are included in this extensive collection of original
children's works.

Dentzel Carousel (Highland Park, Meridian, tel. 601/485–1801). Painted
ponies and other hand-carved animals on this antique carousel, one of three
in the United States, have thrilled children and adults since 1892.

Fort Massachusetts (West Ship Island, tel. 601/875–9057) was built in 1858,
captured by Union forces, and used as a prison for Confederate soldiers and
civilians. The ferry trip takes 1 hour and 15 minutes and costs $11 for
adults, $5 for children.

Grand Opera House (2208 5th St., Meridian, tel. 601/693–5239). The state's
grand lady of opera has been restored. See the stage where Lillian Gish, the
Barrymores, Sarah Bernhardt, and others performed after 1890.

Gulf Islands National Seashore (3500 Park Rd., Ocean Springs, tel.
601/875–9057). The National Park Service runs this 400-acre park on the
mainland (with a visitor center, campground, and nature trail). It offers
fishing and, in summer, free bayou excursions and ferry trips to West Ship
Island, 12 miles out in the Gulf, where there are unspoiled beaches and blue
water, bathhouses, umbrellas, and food stands.

Jimmy Rodgers Museum (Highland Park, Meridian, tel. 601/485–1808).
Rodgers, called the "father of country music," was the first inductee into the
Country Music Hall of Fame.

J.L. Scott Marine Education Center & Aquarium (115 Beach Blvd., Biloxi,
tel. 601/374–5550). The 26 aquariums and other exhibits serve as an
introduction to the sea life of the region.

John C. Stennis Space Center (Rte. 70, Bay St. Louis, tel. 601/688–3390)
offers a guided tour, a look at space shuttle testing, and films on space.

Lauren Rogers Museum of Art (5th Ave. at 7th St., Laurel, tel. 601/649–6374) shows works by John Singer Sargent, Jean-François Millet, Winslow Homer, and "Grandma" Moses. It houses 19th- and 20th-century American landscapes, European salon paintings, a Georgian silver collection, and over 600 baskets of Native American and other cultures.

Magnolia Hotel/Mardi Gras Museum (119 Rue Magnolia, Biloxi, tel. 601/432–8806). Mardi Gras is a big celebration on the Gulf Coast, complete with parades and festive costumes. It warrants its own museum, which is located in the only remaining pre–Civil War hotel on the Gulf.

Old Spanish Fort & Museum (4602 Fort Dr., Pascagoula, tel. 601/769–1505). Built by the French in 1718, the oldest building in the Mississippi Valley has thick walls made of oyster shell, mud, and moss. The museum has a varied collection of 18th-century items and a children's hands-on exhibit.

Seafood Industry Museum (Point Cadet Plaza, Biloxi, tel. 601/435–6320). A tribute to the industry that helps to keep the coast afloat, the museum features tools of the trade and even an architectural exhibit called "The houses that seafood built."

Restaurants

For an authentic coast atmosphere and great gumbo, try **McElroy's Harbor House Seafood Restaurant** (Biloxi Small Craft Harbor, tel. 601/435–5001), overlooking the Gulf. The **Blue Rose Restaurant & Indigo Lounge** (120 W. Scenic Dr., Pass Christian, tel. 601/452–9402), a legend along the coast as far as New Orleans, has great food and a grand view of the Gulf. **Germaine's** (U.S. 90, Ocean Springs, tel. 601/875–4426), formerly Trilby's, is another coast tradition, with steaks and seafood much in demand. The famous **Mary Mahoney's Old French House** (138 Rue Magnolia, Biloxi, tel. 601/374–0163) is in one of the oldest houses in America, built in 1737, and has served two U.S. presidents with seafood and steaks. **Lil' Ray's Po-Boys** (500-A Courthouse Rd., Gulfport, tel. 601/896–9601) is a coast favorite for piled-up sandwiches and fresh seafood. **Weidmann's** (210 22nd Ave., Meridian, tel. 601/693–1751) has served fresh vegetables and Gulf seafood since 1870, to the delight of Mississippians and travelers, too.

Tourist Information

Meridian-Lauderdale County Tourism Commission (Box 5866, Meridian, MS 39302, tel. 601/483–0083). **Mississippi Beach Convention & Visitors Bureau** (Box 6128, Gulfport, MS 39506, tel. 601/896–6699 or 800/237–9493).

Reservation Service

Lincoln, Ltd. Bed & Breakfast Service (Box 3479, Meridian, MS 39303, tel. 601/482–5483 or 800/633–6477).

Harbour Oaks Inn

An hour's drive from New Orleans is a home with an outstanding view of the Pass Christian Yacht Harbor and the Gulf of Mexico. Harbour Oaks has welcomed guests since it was built in 1860 and named Live Oak House. It later became the Crescent Hotel, perhaps named for the Crescent City because so many New Orleanians came for sun and surf. Tony and Dianne Brugger, owners since 1991, are restoring the old home, on the National Register of Historic Places, with guidance from the Mississippi Department of Archives and History. Formerly with American Airlines, the Bruggers found that the gigantic registered live oaks with swaying Spanish moss and the old New Orleans–style structure pulled at their heartstrings. Their labor of love has come a long way, and their aim is to keep the atmosphere "mellow, gracious, and congenial."

The inn has three stories, with covered porches on the first and second floors. French doors open onto the porches from all rooms facing the Gulf. Some antiques are used in the decor, some old and not-so-old pieces. The house is within walking distance of antiques shops and art studios.

Address: *126 W. Scenic Dr., Pass Christian, MS 39571, tel. 601/452–9399.* **Accommodations:** *9 double rooms with baths.* **Amenities:** *Air-conditioning, kitchen and game room privileges.* **Rates:** *$75–$95; full breakfast. MC, V.* **Restrictions:** *No pets.*

Lincoln, Ltd.

For those who want complete privacy in a bed-and-breakfast suite with no owners around, Lincoln, Ltd. is just the place. The house is a 1905 cottage in Meridian's historic district that serves a dual purpose. The front portion is the office of Lincoln, Ltd. Bed & Breakfast Reservation Service, where B&B pro Barbara Hall and her staff work. They have all the answers to questions concerning B&Bs and inns in Mississippi, plus a few listings in adjoining states. Their office closes at about 5 PM; from then until 9 AM or so, guests have the charming house to themselves.

The back suite has a private entrance, use of the kitchen, a carport, and other comforts of home. The suite's living room is cheerful, with pretty plaid sofas, nice woodwork and accessories, and, in the connecting bedroom, walls of a restful, light sea green with rich cream-colored trim and cream curtains. A fireplace, a rocking chair, and flowered chintz cushions and spread enhance the antique walnut bed and chest. The adjoining bathroom has a footed tub and plenty of storage space.

Address: *2303 23rd Ave. (Box 3479), Meridian, MS 39303, tel. 601/482–5483 or 800/633–6477.* **Accommodations:** *1 suite.* **Amenities:** *Air-conditioning, TV, phone.* **Rates:** *$65; Continental breakfast. AE, MC, V.* **Restrictions:** *No pets.*

Red Creek Colonial Inn

When guests are asked their favorite things to do at the Red Creek Colonial Inn, just 5 miles from the Gulf of Mexico, they invariably say, "Swinging on the front porch and walking through the woods," according to innkeeper Christina Smith. She adds that guests who come for one night either end up staying longer or wish they could.

Built around 1899, the three-story brick-and-frame raised cottage boasts a 64-foot front porch, six fireplaces, and interesting antiques like an electric pump organ and a working Victrola. Better still, the inn sits on 11 lush acres, with 300-year-old trees registered with the Live Oak Society.

The inn is the brainchild of owner Karl Mertz, from Atlanta, who grew up on the Mississippi Gulf Coast. He and Claudia, his wife, have spent the past few years collecting and restoring antiques and decorations for the inn, and their efforts have paid off in a homey atmosphere that pleases most everyone. Rooms are clean, cozy, and comfortable rather than lavishly done in heavy antiques.

Address: *7416 Red Creek Rd., Long Beach, MS 39560, tel. 601/452–3080 or 800/729–9670.*
Accommodations: *3 double rooms with baths.*
Amenities: *Air-conditioning, TV in den, portable phone.*
Rates: *$44–$64; Continental breakfast. No credit cards.*
Restrictions: *No smoking, no pets.*

Tally House

Hattiesburg is a town that officially got its start in the late 1800s; thus it is fitting that the only bed-and-breakfast inn in town should be a Victorian-style, red-roofed white frame building. In fact, the Tally House is pure turn of the century, complete with dormers and a double-tiered porch wrapping around three sides, from which to admire the flower borders, well-manicured lawn, and brick walkway.

The house was built in 1907 and since that time has welcomed three Mississippi governors as overnight guests. The 13,000-square-foot two-story house contains 11 fireplaces and a nice collection of well-displayed antiques and artifacts. The house is listed on the National Register of Historic Places.

Overnight guests of the Tally House are greeted by the owners, Mr. and Mrs. C. E. Bailey, and are offered a mint julep made with mint grown in the Baileys' herb garden. The bedrooms are done with Victorian furniture and accessories and decorated with fresh flowers. In the morning, breakfast is served with homemade jellies and jams.

Address: *402 Rebecca Ave., Hattiesburg, MS 39401, tel. 601/582–3467.*
Accommodations: *4 double rooms with baths.*
Amenities: *Air-conditioning.*
Rates: *$50–$75; Continental breakfast, welcoming beverage. MC, V.*
Restrictions: *No smoking, no pets.*

Louisiana

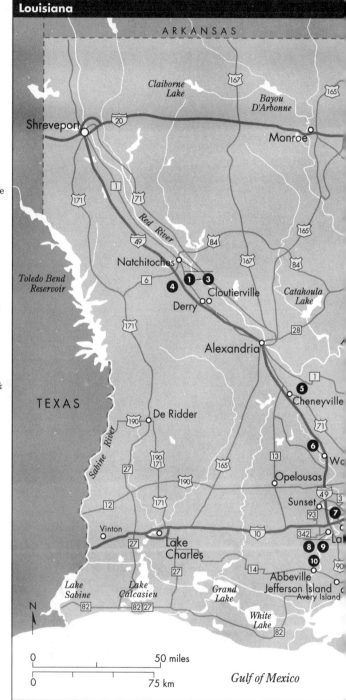

Louisiana

165

165

133

20

65

15

MISSISSIPPI

Ferriday
84

Mississippi River

Pearl River

la

Red River

15

1

eyville

71

Atchafalaya R.

1

12 Clinton

13 14

15 St. Francisville

Jackson

New Roads

False River

61 67

Washington

190

Baton Rouge

10

Bogalusa

55

Folsom

29 30

Covington

Madisonville

12

Slidell

31

49 31

t

3 7 Henderson

Breaux Bridge

0 Lafayette 11

White Castle

Plaquemine

1 16

Darrow

Lake Maurepas

Lake Pontchartrain

Burnside

44

Reserve

18 Kenner

St. Martinville

New
Iberia

land
y Island

329

Franklin

Patterson

Donaldsonville

18 Edgard

Vacherie

Napoleonville

17

20 24

90

Houma

57 56

55

Destrehan

New
Orleans

19 – 28

Chalmette

Lake Salvador

Mississippi River

23

Gulf of Mexico

1

90 31

90

0

9

0

10

Greater New Orleans

Internationally known for its fine French Creole cuisine and great jazz, New Orleans basks in the sun smack on the Mississippi River about 110 miles inland from the Gulf of Mexico. The city is something of a paradox: It's a major convention city and one of the world's largest ports; some 8 million visitors come to call annually; and Mardi Gras is but the best known of dozens of annual festivals (New Orleanians do love to party)—all of which means there is a great deal of activity here. And yet, this is a very laid-back, Caribbeanesque city that much prefers to operate on "island time." Not for naught is it called The Big Easy. The Crescent City (another sobriquet) is unlike any other American city; certainly it is different from other Southern cities. It has been promoted as "America's European Masterpiece"—yet there is nothing quite like it in Europe, either. It is, in a word, unique.

Within the city proper, the French Quarter is the prime tourist target. Comprising about a square mile, the Quarter is an easily walkable, perfect grid. Its narrow streets are lined with picturesque, pastel-painted buildings garnished with fanciful ironwork or dollops of gingerbread. It is both a carefully restored living museum whose structures date from the 18th and 19th centuries and a residential district with about 3,500 somewhat smug inhabitants. Most of the famed French Creole restaurants are in the Quarter, and Bourbon Street is lined with music clubs of every description. This is a 24-hour town, which means there is no legal closing time. At almost any hour of the day or night, you can stroll down Bourbon and hear the syncopated rhythms of Cajun, rhythm and blues, gutbucket (that's low-down, mean blues), Dixieland, rinky-dink piano, ragtime, and even Irish music. The heartbeat of the Quarter is Jackson Square, a pedestrian mall where stately St. Louis Cathedral soars like a hymn over a riotous scene of Dixieland bands, red-nosed clowns, sidewalk artists, costumed kooks, tap dancers and break

*dancers, fire-eaters, bongo players, unicyclists, nonchalant
New Orleanians, and curious tourists.*

*Almost as much activity, frivolous as well as serious, takes
place in the Central Business District (CBD), adjacent to the
Quarter. The Foot of Canal Street, as it's known to locals,
boasts several splashy attractions. From the downtown area,
the St. Charles Streetcar, a National Historic Landmark,
makes a jolly rumble upriver via St. Charles Avenue. It
chugs through the Garden District, a residential area in
which posh, palatial mansions are surrounded by luxuriant
gardens, and on past pretty Audubon Park, which has
magnificent live oaks dressed in Spanish moss and a
wonderful zoo. Lake Pontchartrain drapes for 40 miles over
the northern border of the city, and the lakefront area is a
favorite summertime playground for locals. There are
several marinas, sailboats to be rented, and a plethora of
funky restaurants frequented by hard-core, no-nonsense
seafood eaters. The metropolitan area extends to the piney
woods on the north shore of the lake, where fishing and
boating are popular and bed-and-breakfasts abound.*

*Six miles east of the city lies Chalmette National Historical
Park, on whose rolling green fields Andy Jackson whipped
the Brits in the 1815 Battle of New Orleans. And to the west
of town, the Great River Road, which follows the meandering
Mississippi from New Orleans to Baton Rouge, is decorated
with handsome, restored antebellum plantation homes.
Many are open to the public, and several companies offer
tours to plantation country. If you fly into New Orleans,
you'll note that dry land seems to sort of fizzle out the closer
you get to the city. These flat marshlands are laced with
waterways, and swamp tours, which sneak into erstwhile
pirates' lairs and give you a tempting taste of Cajun Country
to the west, are extremely popular outings.*

Places to Go, Sights to See

Carriage Rides. Decatur Street at Jackson Square is lined with fringed
carriages drawn by mules in silly hats. The lively raconteurs at the reins

dispense a wealth of misinformation but give a pleasant half-hour overview of
the Quarter.

Cemeteries. Reminiscent of Père Lachaise in Paris, New Orleans's
aboveground cemeteries are usually high on visitors' must-see lists. The
oldest, *St. Louis No. 1,* lies on the fringes of the Quarter; the largest, and
most photographed, is *Metairie Cemetery.* Many of these Cities of the Dead
are in high-crime areas; visitors should not venture into them alone. For a
group tour on Sunday, contact Save Our Cemeteries (tel. 504/588–9357).

City Park. Home of the *New Orleans Museum of Art* (Lelong Ave., tel.
504/488–2631), this is one of the nation's largest city parks. Within its 1,500
acres are golf courses, tennis courts, baseball and softball diamonds, lagoons
and boat rentals, botanical gardens, and, for the little ones, Storyland and an
amusement park with a delightful antique carousel.

Foot of Canal Street. If you keep on going toward the river on Canal
Street, you'll drive right off dry land and onto the commuter ferry (free
outgoing, $1 returning) that sidles across the Mississippi to the neighborhood
of Algiers on the West Bank. Smack at the river and the CBD, there are
several diversions. A good place to get your bearings is *Viewpoint* (2 Canal
St., tel. 504/581–4888), a glass-enclosed observation deck on the 31st floor of
the World Trade Center. The *Aquarium of the Americas* (Canal St. and the
river, tel. 504/861–2537), which boasts four major exhibits and a plethora of
sea creatures, sits in the handsomely landscaped Woldenberg Riverfront
Park. *Riverwalk,* sprawling upriver from the ferry landing, comprises
Spanish Plaza—a broad, open expanse with mosaic pavement and a huge
fountain—and a festival marketplace with some 200 specialty shops and
restaurants. Several of the sightseeing boats dock at Riverwalk. On Lundi
Gras (the Monday night before Fat Tuesday), the city tosses a huge, free-to-
the-public masked ball on Spanish Plaza, replete with live music, fireworks,
and much merriment. The face of the Foot, so to speak, will change
dramatically with the 1995 opening of *Harrah's New Orleans* (Canal St.), a
250,000-square-foot casino across the street from the World Trade Center. A
temporary casino in Municipal Auditorium (Armstrong Park) will operate
until then.

House Museums. Several restored homes (almost all in the Quarter) provide
a glimpse of old New Orleans. *Pitot House* (1440 Moss St., tel. 504/482–0312)
is a West Indies–style house typical of those built by early planters. *Gallier
House* (1118–32 Royal St., tel. 504/523–6722) was designed and built by noted
19th-century architect James Gallier, Jr., as his family home. The *Hermann-
Grima House* (820 St. Louis St., tel. 504/525–5661) is an 1831 mansion in
whose outbuildings Creole cooking demonstrations (and tastings) are held on
Thursdays, October–May. *Beauregard-Keyes House* (1113 Chartres St., tel.
504/523–7257), a Greek Revival raised cottage, was home to Confederate
General P.G.T. Beauregard and, much later, to novelist Frances Parkinson
Keyes. *Longue Vue House & Gardens* (7 Bamboo Rd., tel. 504/488–5488), set
on 8 acres of manicured gardens in Mid-City, resembles an English country
estate and is filled with priceless French, American, and Oriental antiques.

Nightlife. *Tipitina's* (501 Napoleon Ave., tel. 504/895–8477), laid-back and with a loyal following, is arguably the city's most popular club. Live reggae, rock, rhythm and blues, and Cajun music entertain a dressed-down crowd. Tip's may be in for strong competition from Dan Aykroyd's *House of Blues* (225 Decatur St., tel. 504/529–2624), which opened with a blast in 1994. Local and nationally known artists perform in the appropriately funky venue, complete with a recording studio, restaurant, and shop in addition to an awesome sound system. *Michaul's* (840 St. Charles Ave., tel. 504/522–5517) offers live Cajun music, Cajun food, and free Cajun dance lessons nightly. The *Maple Leaf Bar* (8316 Oak St., tel. 504/866–9359) features live music seven nights a week. The dance floor is the proverbial postage-stamp size, and the dancing often overflows out onto the street. For great traditional jazz sans dancing (and creature comforts), *Preservation Hall* (726 St. Peter St., tel. 504/522–2238 or 504/523–8939) is the place to hear the city's jazz legends. Next door, *Pat O'Brien's* (718 St. Peter St., tel. 504/525–4823)— perhaps the world's most famous bar and birthplace of the now ubiquitous Hurricane—features a raucous sing-along piano bar that roars long after the fat lady has sung. *Pete Fountain's Club* (Hilton Hotel, 2 Poydras St., tel. 504/523–4374) is home base for the world-famous New Orleans clarinetist, and *Jelly Roll's* (501 Bourbon St., tel. 504/568–0501) is the venue for trumpet player Al Hirt. Many of the city's best jazz and rhythm and blues musicians perform regularly at the *Palm Court Jazz Café* (1204 Decatur St., tel. 504/525–0200). The popular *Napoleon House* (500 Chartres St., tel. 504/524–9752) and *Lafitte's Blacksmith Shop* (941 Bourbon St., tel. 504/523–0066) are marvelous, musty old bars in buildings that date from the 1700s.

Riverboats. Frilly riverboats kicking up froth on the mighty Mississippi offer a variety of excursions. Among the most popular are the *Steamboat Natchez* (tel. 504/586–8777) and the *Creole Queen* (tel. 504/524–0814), both of which operate evening dinner/jazz cruises as well as daytime outings. Floating casinos have joined the parade of riverboats. The *Star Casino* (1 Star Casino Blvd., Lake Ponchartrain, tel. 504/243–0400 or 800/504–7827 outside New Orleans); the *Boomtown Belle Casino* (4132 Peters Rd., Harvey, tel. 504/366–7711), on the Harvey Canal on the West Bank; and Hilton's *Queen of New Orleans* (Poydras St. Wharf at Riverwalk, tel. 504/587–7777 or 800/587–5825 outside New Orleans) are all awash with gaming tables, video poker, and one-armed bandits.

Restaurants

The city's most famous restaurant, **Antoine's** (713 St. Louis St., tel. 504/581–4422), established in 1840, serves fine French Creole cuisine in several grand, Old World dining rooms. **Arnaud's** (813 Bienville St., tel. 504/523–5433) and **Galatoire's** (209 Bourbon St., tel. 504/525–2021) are two other venerable and fashionable French Creole restaurants. **Commander's Palace** (1403 Washington Ave., tel. 504/899–8221), in a splendid Victorian mansion in the Garden District, is a great favorite for its innovative French-American menu and weekend jazz brunches. For Cajun cooking, try **K-**

Paul's Louisiana Kitchen (416 Chartres St., tel. 504/942–7500), bastion of celebrity chef Paul Prudhomme.

On the north shore of Lake Ponchartrain, about an hour's drive from central New Orleans, **La Provence** (U.S. 90, Lacombe, tel. 504/626–7662) serves French provincial cuisine in an atmosphere evocative of a fine tavern in the French countryside.

Tourist Information

Greater New Orleans Tourist & Convention Commission (1520 Sugar Bowl Dr., New Orleans, LA 70112, tel. 504/566–5011).

Reservation Services

Bed & Breakfast, Inc. (1021 Moss St., Box 52257, New Orleans, LA 70152–2257, tel. 504/488–4640 or 800/749–4640). **New Orleans Bed & Breakfast** (Box 8163, New Orleans, LA 70182, tel. 504/838–0071, fax 504/838–0140).

Note: The rates quoted below do not apply during special events. Prices skyrocket for Mardi Gras, Sugar Bowl, Jazz Fest, and Super Bowl; also, in addition to three- to five-day minimums, inns sometimes request full payment in advance. On the other hand, when summertime temperatures soar, rates can plunge much lower than those quoted, and attractive packages are often available.

Hotel Maison de Ville and Audubon Cottages

The Maison de Ville is tucked behind an etched-glass door, a half-block off the French Quarter's bawdy Bourbon Street. It's easy to stroll right by it; only a discreet coat-of-arms sign heralds the three-story European-style hotel, which dates from the late 1700s.

To the rear of the small lobby is a sedate parlor, with a fireplace and marble mantel. The parlor opens onto one of the city's prettiest courtyards, which has a tiered fountain, banana trees, and flowers. Two-story, balconied former slave quarters extend from the rear of the main house and border the courtyard.

Rooms in the main house are small, but all are done in 18th- and 19th-century French and American antiques, with four-posters, marble fireplaces, swagged draperies, and matching quilted spreads. The small marble baths have brass fittings. The slave-quarter rooms are more rustic and contain beamed ceilings and small fireplaces. (Tennessee Williams once lived in No. 9.) It's necessary to draw the draperies for privacy, which darkens the rooms. The hotel can be noisy. Light sleepers should avoid the front rooms overlooking Toulouse Street.

More luxurious (and pricier) are the one- and two-bedroom Audubon Cottages, two blocks from the main building. They are so named because

John James Audubon lived in Cottage No. 1 in 1821. Set behind a high stucco wall, the quiet, secluded cottages have kitchens and walled private patios. They're clustered around a landscaped patio, with statuary and a pool (which is available to all hotel guests). The spacious rooms have slate or brick floors, antique furnishings, and a French country flavor.

Breakfast, served on a silver tray and accompanied by the morning paper and a rose, can be taken in your room or in the courtyard.

Despite its corporate ownership and noisy location, the hotel maintains the ambience of a small country inn.

Address: *727 Toulouse St., New Orleans, LA 70130, tel. 504/561–5858 or 800/634–1600, fax 504/561–5858.*
Accommodations: *14 double rooms with baths, 2 suites, 7 housekeeping cottages.*
Amenities: *Restaurant; air-conditioning, cable TV, phones, and minibars in rooms; turndown and overnight shoe-shine services; concierge.*
Rates: *Hotel $145–$240, cottages $325–$405; Continental breakfast; afternoon port, sherry, and tea. AE, DC, MC, V.*
Restrictions: *No pets, 3-night minimum during Mardi Gras and Jazz Fest.*

Melrose Mansion

This splendid Victorian Gothic on the fringe of New Orleans's French Quarter was built in 1884. It has a turret, dormers, stained-glass windows, a steeply pitched roof, Corinthian columns, and a guest list that includes Lady Bird Johnson. The former first lady attended the grand opening of the bed-and-breakfast in 1990 and was the first person to sign the register.

Each of the large, high-ceilinged rooms is furnished differently, but all feature handsome 19th-century Louisiana antiques, including canopy beds and four-posters. The usual amenities include down pillows, fine-milled soaps, monogrammed robes and towels, coffeemakers, and small refrigerators stocked with mineral water, soft drinks, and a split of complimentary champagne. Fresh flowers and a decanter of Courvoisier are placed in each suite, where there are also wet bars, private balconies, and whirlpool baths.

The star is the Donecio Suite, in the turret, with its 18-foot ceiling, chandelier of brass and etched glass, and ecru-and-ivory lace touches. All the mansion's baths are sumptuous affairs, but in this suite the whirlpool bubbles in the turret, a huge window overlooks the French Quarter, and a frosted silver ice bucket containing a bottle of champagne is within easy reach.

Melrose's owners, Melvin Jones and Sidney Torres, bought the building in 1976 from New Orleans entertainer Chris Owens. It was an apartment house then and remained so for more than 10 years. Melvin, a general contractor, spent more than two years in extensive renovations, and his wife, Rosemary, did the interior decoration.

Guests can take breakfast in their room, around the heated pool, or in the formal dining room. An astonishing array of hors d'oeuvres is served with afternoon cocktails.

The Melrose is not in an entirely safe neighborhood; guests should avoid walking around the area at night.

Address: *937 Esplanade Ave., New Orleans, LA 70116, tel. 504/944–2255, fax 504/945–1795.*
Accommodations: *4 double rooms with baths, 4 suites.*
Amenities: *Air-conditioning, library, 1 meeting room, fitness center, turndown service; complimentary airport limousine.*
Rates: *$225–$425; full breakfast, afternoon refreshments. AE, MC, V.*
Restrictions: *No pets, 4-night minimum during Mardi Gras, Jazz Fest, and Sugar Bowl.*

Salmen-Fritchie House

The little town of Slidell, on the Pearl River, about 35 minutes from downtown New Orleans, is the casting-off place for several swamp tours. It is also home to one of the state's showplaces, which is also a B&B. Owners Sharon and Homer Fritchie live upstairs, and all 12 rooms on the main floor are for use by overnighters. Listed on the National Register of Historic Places, the 1895 white mansion, which has a high-pitched roof, broad front porch, porte cochere, and beveled-glass door, basks on a spacious lawn. Its front walk is lined with flowering plants. Immediately upon stepping inside the central hall, you'll notice a white Italian-marble sculpture on a table and an elaborate burgundy jardiniere, both original to the house. Nearby stands an 18th-century Chippendale long-case clock. A tour of the mansion and its priceless antiques is included.

The mansion boasts 12-foot ceilings, wood-burning fireplaces with intricately carved mantelpieces, expanses of cypress paneling, and an 85-foot-long by 25-foot-wide central hall. Within that ample space are a sitting area (with console TV and VCR) and a grand piano, on which are displayed miniature family photographs. To the right of the hall is the library. The twin Queen Anne sofas came from Linden in Natchez, Mississippi, and the bookcase holds contemporary novels and volumes of the Encyclopaedia Britannica. In chilly weather, it's fun to read by the fireplace. (Additional heating throughout the house is courtesy of old-fashioned steam-heat radiators.)

Each of the five guest rooms is furnished in period style. The Mallard Bedroom features the hand-carved work of Prudent Mallard, a well-known 19th-century New Orleans furniture maker. Another room has a half-tester bed, chairs upholstered in needlepoint, and a fringed, rose-colored lampshade, and yet another contains twin beds with satin comforters. Three of the guest rooms have wood-burning fireplaces, and two can be combined to create a suite. Baths are spacious and modern. Early morning coffee can be brought to your room. Breakfast, served at a long table in a many-windowed breakfast room, may take the form of pecan waffles, French toast stuffed with fruits, or cheese, chive, and mushroom omelets with bacon.

Address: *127 Cleveland Ave., Slidell, LA 70458, tel. 504/643-1405 or 800/235-4168, fax 504/643-2251.*
Accommodations: *5 double rooms with baths.*
Amenities: *Air-conditioning, phones in 2 rooms, portable phone for others.*
Rates: *$75-$95, 2-bedroom suite $125; full breakfast. AE, MC, V.*
Restrictions: *No smoking indoors, no pets, closed Jan. 1, Thanksgiving, Dec. 25.*

Soniat House

The two 1830s town houses that comprise the Soniat House were among the first Greek Revival houses in New Orleans. The green shutters across the front are kept closed for privacy and security, which gives the building a some- what austere look despite its lacy ironwork galleries. But behind the shutters a graceful flagstone carriageway leads from the street to a small landscaped courtyard with a lily pond, a softly gurgling fountain, and a profusion of gardenias, night-blooming jasmine, and banana plants. The courtyard is particularly romantic at night, when it's lit by candles. The tiny office and the elegant First Empire parlor that adjoins it are just off the courtyard.

Rodney and Frances Smith have furnished their French Quarter guest house with English, French, and Louisiana antiques gathered during 25 years of world travel. Rooms are uncluttered and have a starkly elegant look. Each is decorated differently, right down to the colors of the paint and custom-made fabrics. Four-poster and canopy beds are complemented by framed contempo- rary paintings, some of them on loan from the New Orleans Museum of Art. The polished hardwood floors are covered with thick Oriental rugs. All the rooms have fireplaces except one. Beds are made with luxurious 200- count cotton percale bed linens and goose-down pillows (extra ones for

reading in bed). The baths are large and well appointed, all with bathside phones and most with whirlpools.

A private elevator takes guests to the secluded third-floor rooms, which offer even more peace and privacy, but the second-floor rooms require a long haul up a graceful but steep spiral staircase. Small and intimate though it is, the Soniat House has a sophisticated business center with fax and photocopying machines and a modem for personal computers.

A breakfast of plump, hot biscuits, homemade strawberry jam, freshly squeezed orange juice, and chicory coffee on a silver service can be taken in your room or on white-clothed tables in the courtyard.

Address: *1133 Chartres St., New Orleans, LA 70116, tel. 504/522–0570 or 800/544–8808, fax 504/522–7208.*
Accommodations: *14 double rooms with baths, 3 singles with baths, 5 suites.*
Amenities: *Room service, honor bar, air-conditioning, TV and phones in rooms, VCRs in suites, 1 meeting room, business center, concierge.*
Rates: *$135–$350, 2-bedroom suite $525; Continental breakfast extra. AE, MC, V.*
Restrictions: *No pets, 3-night minimum weekends, 5-night mini- mum during Mardi Gras, Jazz Fest, and Sugar Bowl.*

Terrell House

From the outside, the Terrell House—with its tall French doors, shutters, and frilly iron galleries—looks much like any other Greek Revival house in the lower Garden District. But it contains one of the city's most extensive and impressive collections of antiques.

Built in 1858 by a cotton merchant, the house is currently owned by the Nicaud family, whose collections of gaslight fixtures and lamps, European and Louisiana antique furniture, Oriental rugs, and antique carnival memorabilia are displayed everywhere. The furnishings are true to the style and period of the house, and many are Nicaud family heirlooms. Some of the ornate beds and armoires were hand-carved in the studio of Prudent Mallard.

A glass case in one of the twin parlors displays miniature carved antique furnishings, while in the hallway there's a full set of 1850 doll furniture in the Mallard style. A Waterford crystal chandelier sparkles in the formal dining room, where breakfast and cocktails are served.

Guest rooms in the main mansion are original bedrooms of the house and have balconies overlooking a landscaped courtyard with a fountain and an ancient crape myrtle tree. Rooms 1 and 3 contain Mallard armoires, washstands, and marble-top tables and dressers. (No. 3 is a two-bedroom

suite with half-tester beds and a sitting room.) There are two attic rooms with sloping ceilings and queen beds. Room 10, in the servants' quarters, has twin white-iron beds with half testers and crocheted coverlets. The four rooms in the carriage house have balconies or patios opening onto the courtyard.

Harry Lucas, the affable manager, operates Terrell House in laid-back style. He began at the guest house as a gardener and still loves landscape gardening. Harry's wife, Alma, occasionally comes in to cook special dinners for guests; she gets raves for her crawfish étouffée, bread pudding, and other regional dishes.

Operation Comeback, an ongoing project, is restoring the lower Garden District to its former grandeur and creating safer streets.

Address: *1441 Magazine St., New Orleans, LA 70130, tel. 504/524–9859 or 800/878–9859.*
Accommodations: *8 double rooms with baths, 1 2-bedroom suite.*
Amenities: *Air-conditioning, cable TV and phones in rooms.*
Rates: *$70–$130; Continental breakfast, afternoon cocktails. AE, MC, V.*
Restrictions: *No pets, 3-night minimum during Jazz Fest and Sugar Bowl, 5-night minimum during Mardi Gras.*

The Chimes

If you're wondering about the name, you have but to stand for a moment on the front porch of Charles and Jill Abbyad's home and listen to the soft tinkling of the wind chimes. The house, built in 1875, is on a quiet residential street just upriver from the Garden District, three blocks from the St. Charles Streetcar.

Accommodations are in cottages built around the rear courtyard; rooms and baths vary in size and decor. There is a mix of four-posters, twins, and white-iron beds. One of the largest rooms has slate floors, an overstuffed sofa, and a spiral stair that leads to a loft with a big white-iron bed. One of the baths has an old-fashioned claw-foot tub, another a shower but no tub, and a modern tile bath is graced with a skylight. Each room has a coffee-

maker, teapot, tea and coffee makings, and spring water. Just off the courtyard, tucked into a closet, is a full-size refrigerator for guests' use, as well as an ironing board and iron. The Abbyads welcome children and well-behaved pets; however, they discourage drop-in guests.

Address: *1146 Constantinople St., New Orleans, LA 70115, tel. 800/228–9711.*
Accommodations: *4 double rooms with baths.*
Amenities: *Air-conditioning; TV, phones, minifridges, and stereos in rooms.*
Rates: *$68–$96; full breakfast. No credit cards.*
Restrictions: *No smoking indoors.*

Girod House

This historic house was built in 1833 as a town house for François Girod, son of New Orleans's mayor. It is owned and operated by Rodney and Frances Smith, proprietors of the nearby Soniat House. The complex of apartments surrounds a brick courtyard that's decorated with a green trellis, flowering plants, and tables for alfresco breakfasting. As with the Soniat House, the Girod House has pieces from the Smiths' collection of French and English antiques and such amenities as Crabtree & Evelyn toiletries and 200-count cotton percale bed linens.

Apartments have full kitchens or kitchenettes, which have coffeemak-ers, cutlery, china, and glassware. Apartments 4-D and 3-C are duplex-

es: A living room, dining room, and powder room are downstairs, while upstairs each has a spacious bedroom with double closets, a large marble bath, exposed beams, and balconies overlooking tree-shaded Esplanade. Daily maid service and a 24-hour switchboard are available.

Address: *835 Esplanade Ave., New Orleans, LA 70116, tel. 504/522–5214 or 800/544–8808, fax 504/522–7208.*
Accommodations: *6 apartments.*
Amenities: *Air-conditioning, cable TV and phones in apartments; limited off-street parking.*
Rates: *$85–$185; Continental breakfast. AE, MC, V.*
Restrictions: *No pets, 3-night minimum weekends, 5-night mini-mum during Mardi Gras, Jazz Fest, and Sugar Bowl.*

Josephine Guest House

A block from St. Charles Avenue is the home of Jude Daniel Fuselier and his wife, Mary Ann Weilbaecher. The large Italianate mansion dates from 1870, and Mary Ann calls the furnishings "Creole baroque"; indeed, cherubs and angels decorate virtually everything. The most elaborate piece is a massive ebony bed inlaid with ivory and bone. Dutch marquetry daybeds are a focal point of the downstairs guest room. The couple's passion for antique-collecting is everywhere apparent; French Empire and English Gothic are among the periods represented. There is a Gothic refectory table in the cluttered country-style kitchen and an 18th-century mahogany banquet table in the formal dining room.

Dan and Mary Ann are eager to acquaint their guests with the "real New Orleans." Mary Ann, a former home economics teacher, makes the fresh breads that accompany morning café au lait and juice. Breakfast is served on Wedgwood china.

Address: *1450 Josephine St., New Orleans, LA 70130, tel. 504/524–6361 or 800/779–6361.*
Accommodations: *6 double rooms with baths.*
Amenities: *Air-conditioning, cable TV in some rooms.*
Rates: *$85–$145; Continental breakfast. AE, MC, V.*
Restrictions: *Smoking in courtyard only, 4-night minimum during Sugar Bowl, 5-night minimum during Mardi Gras and Jazz Fest.*

Lafitte Guest House

S mack in the middle of the French Quarter, the Lafitte Guest House is a restored French manor house that dates from 1849. The red and gold Victorian parlor is resplendent with velvet chairs, matching swag curtains, fringed lamp shades, and an Oriental rug. Public areas are adorned with art from the private collection of owner Dr. Robert Guyton.

For the most part, guest rooms are large and bright, and some have private balconies. Most are done in early 19th-century Louisiana antiques—four-poster, canopy, and tester beds; crystal chandeliers; carved wooden armoires. The room on the fourth floor has beamed ceilings and wicker furnishings, and the suite has a splendid view of the Quarter.

Tucked away behind the courtyard is the former carriage house, with a parlor, a bedroom, and a bath that was cleverly converted from a coal bin.

Address: *1003 Bourbon St., New Orleans, LA 70116, tel. 504/581–2678 or 800/331–7971.*
Accommodations: *13 double rooms with baths, 1 suite.*
Amenities: *Air-conditioning, TV and phones in rooms, 1 small meeting room.*
Rates: *$59–$165; Continental breakfast, afternoon refreshments. AE, MC, V.*
Restrictions: *No pets, 3 night minimum during Jazz Fest and Sugar Bowl, 4-night minimum during Mardi Gras.*

Riverside Hills Farm

If you had a mind to—and a boat—you could arrive at the 14-acre Riverside Hills Farm via the Tchefuncte River, on which this erstwhile turkey farm sits. Sans boat, you approach it via a long driveway that runs between sky-high pines and lush shrubbery in the countryside near Covington.

The three-bedroom B&B cottage was once the caretaker's quarters. The pine-paneled living room has hardwood floors, traditional furnishings, and displays of colorful patchwork quilts, as well as plenty of books. The large early American kitchen comes with dishwasher, coffeemaker, full-size refrigerator, and owner Sandra Moore's collection of basketry, cookbooks, and Italian dishes. The side porch has rocking chairs, a swing, and a splendid view of the river. One of the bedrooms has twin beds, another a white-iron queen bed, and the other an interesting four-poster made of mimosa painted to look like white birch. With only a bath and a half, the cottage is let solely to people traveling together.

Address: *96 Gardenia Dr., Covington, LA 70433, tel. 504/892–1794, fax 504/626–5849.*
Accommodations: *1 housekeeping cottage.*
Amenities: *Air-conditioning, cable TV, and phone in cottage; boat launch, fishing rods, nature trails.*
Rate: *$80; Continental breakfast. No credit cards.*
Restrictions: *Smoking on porch only, no pets.*

St. Charles Guest House

Joanne and Dennis Hilton describe their guest house as "simple, cozy, and affordable." It comprises four 19th-century buildings in the lower Garden District, a block from the St. Charles streetcar line. Rooms vary; some are large enough for a family of four, and some are small "backpacker" rooms with no air-conditioning and shared baths. (All the rooms with private baths are air-conditioned.) None of the rooms are grand; they are all functionally furnished, clean, and well maintained. A breakfast room with a large picture window overlooks the pool and sun deck. In the morning, guests help themselves to rolls and doughnuts, juice, and paper cups of coffee.

The Hiltons provide guests with a "survival manual," containing safety hints and suggestions for inexpensive dining. And they sometimes treat their guests to a crawfish boil or special meals of other regional specialties.

Address: *1748 Prytania St., New Orleans, LA 70130, tel. 504/523–6556.*
Accommodations: *22 rooms with baths, 4 rooms share 1 bath.*
Amenities: *Air-conditioning in most rooms, pay phones in lobby.*
Rates: *$35–$75; Continental breakfast. AE, MC, V.*
Restrictions: *No smoking indoors, no pets, 5-night minimum during Mardi Gras, Jazz Fest, and Sugar Bowl.*

Sully Mansion

Most of the Garden District's fine mansions are private houses, but one—a huge Queen Anne with wraparound veranda, dormers, turrets, and frilly trim—is a B&B. New Orleans architect Thomas Sully built it, and it's now Maralee Prigmore's home. In the spacious foyer, sunlight filters through original stained-glass windows and falls on a grand piano. An ornate carved staircase spirals up to the second floor. The house has 12-foot coved ceilings, 10-foot cypress doors, and heart-of-pine floors covered with Oriental rugs. Swagged, floor-length draperies hang from tall windows. Porcelain figurines are displayed on the fireplace mantels. A 1993–94 remodeling produced larger guest rooms, huge modern tile baths, and many new furnishings. An upstairs room has 1950s French provincial–style furnishings, while the downstairs bedroom/sitting room has a handsome four-poster, damask draperies, and upholstered sofa and chairs. There are scores of books and magazines to browse through, and a gathering room is the place to chat, watch TV, or play board games.

Address: *2631 Prytania St., New Orleans, LA 70130, tel. and fax 504/891–0457.*
Accommodations: *5 double rooms with baths.*
Amenities: *Air-conditioning, cable TV and phones in rooms.*
Rates: *$85–$150; Continental breakfast. MC, V.*
Restrictions: *2-night minimum Jazz Fest weekends.*

Woods Hole Inn

Seven miles from downtown Covington on the north side of Lake Pontchartrain, a long tree-shaded drive takes you to the home of Mike and Bea Connick. (He's the uncle of crooner Harry Connick, Jr.) Their B&B—separate from their house—is a rustic one-bedroom cottage with private entrance and driveway. It's set in a veritable forest of tall trees and greenery.

The living room/dining room has a wood-burning fireplace, hardwood floors, hooked rugs, and cushioned, upholstered furniture. Walls are hung with patchwork quilts, and the vaulted ceiling has exposed wooden beams. In the dining area there is a coffeemaker, small microwave, and minirefrigerator stocked with fresh juices and milk for coffee.

The bedroom, with its huge four-poster, opens onto a shaded courtyard, where a wrought-iron table and chairs make a fine place for breakfasting in pleasant weather. The bath is enormous and contains a tub with brass claw feet, a separate shower with sliding glass doors, stained-glass windows, an ample vanity with brass fittings, and a small black-and-white TV (in addition to the TV in the living room).

Address: *78253 Woods Hole La., Folsom, LA 70437, tel. 504/796–9077.*
Accommodations: *1 cottage.*
Amenities: *Air-conditioning, cable TV, and phone in cottage.*
Rates: *$80; Continental breakfast. No credit cards.*
Restrictions: *No smoking indoors, no pets.*

Plantation Country

From north to south, the state of Louisiana is graced with fine old plantation homes, but the area officially designated Plantation Country begins with a reservoir of grand houses north of Baton Rouge and stretches all the way down the Mississippi River to New Orleans.

As the crow flies (or I–10 runs), Plantation Country is over 100 miles long, though wherever you go you won't be far from the bright lights of a big city. As the river flows—and twists and curves—the going is much slower. The romantic-sounding Great River Road (U.S. 61) follows its serpentine meanderings between Baton Rouge and New Orleans, but unfortunately, it is less scenic than the interstate—huge industrial and chemical plants line the road and the river. The stretch of Route 1 between Baton Rouge and Donaldsonville on the west bank is an alternative.

This is the proverbial moonlight-and-magnolias country; there are more mint juleps sipped on sweeping verandas than you can shake a swizzle stick at. Homes with sky-high ceilings are filled with such 19th-century necessities as petticoat mirrors, hoopskirt chairs, courtship settees, and fire screens. The hostesses and docents tell tales of Union gunboats, Yankee soldiers, the valorous men and women of the Confederacy, and the tons of silver that were buried to keep the Bluebellies from stealing it. Ghosts are also favorite topics; it seems that almost every mansion is haunted—by a tiny child, an entire massacred family, or a wild-eyed murderer dragging around chains.

The terrain north of Baton Rouge—rolling hills, high bluffs, deep valleys, and piney woods—is much more akin to North Louisiana than to South Louisiana. So, too, is the culture: The East and West Feliciana parishes, which compose the instep of this boot-shaped state, roll eastward from the Mississippi (the river) to Mississippi (the state). The

*Felicianas were settled by the English, many of whom came
from Virginia, and the people of this area, which includes the
towns of St. Francisville, Jackson, and Clinton, proudly
cling to their English heritage.*

*St. Francisville, less than a half-hour north of Baton Rouge,
has been described as "2 miles long and 2 yards wide." Much
of the long, skinny little city is listed on the National
Register of Historic Places. In the early 19th century, West
Feliciana Parish, in which it lies, was the seat of government
for the short-lived Republic of West Florida. Antique-seeking
is popular here; the Feliciana towns are loaded with
wonderful old poke-around places.*

*But a ferry ride across the Mississippi puts you in a pocket
of South Louisiana that has a definite Gallic flair. Not yet
Cajun Country, which is farther west, this area was settled
by French Creoles. Though it is cloaked in a Southern
disguise of white columns and Spanish moss, Pointe Coupee
Parish preserves the culture of the Creoles who settled here in
the 18th century. The parish "capital" is the tiny town of New
Roads, which snoozes on the banks of False River—an oxbow
lake left behind long ago when the Mississippi changed its
course. The large number of fishing cabins attests to the
quality of False River's fishing and boating.*

*As the Mississippi nears New Orleans, the land flattens out
and becomes marshy. Stark cypress trees poke up through the
swamplands, and pirogues bob lazily on sluggish bayous.
You can almost hear Cajun fiddles tuning up to the west and
Dixieland bands stomping off to the east, but much of the
charm of Plantation Country is in . . . well, sipping mint
juleps on the veranda and listening to tales of carpetbaggers,
scalawags, and Yankees.*

Places to Go, Sights to See

Audubon State Commemorative Area (Rte. 956 near St. Francisville, tel.
504/635–3739). In 100 wooded acres, you can tour *Oakley Plantation*, where

John James Audubon created many of the paintings for his *Birds of America* series.

Catalpa Plantation (3½ mi north of St. Francisville, tel. 504/635–3372), reached by an elliptical oak alley, has been in the same family since the 18th century and contains fine antiques, silver, and family heirlooms.

Houmas House (Rte. 942, Burnside, tel. 504/473–7841), a large white Greek Revival house, was the setting for the Gothic thriller *Hush, Hush, Sweet Charlotte,* starring Bette Davis and Olivia DeHaviland.

Oak Alley Plantation (3645 Rte. 18, near Vacherie, tel. 504/265–2151) is a Greek Revival mansion on whose splendid grounds scenes from the Tom Cruise film *Interview with the Vampire* were shot.

Parlange Plantation (Rte. 1, just north of Rte. 78, New Roads, tel. 504/638–8410) is a working plantation built in 1750 and operated by the eighth generation of the founding family. It is open by appointment.

Plaquemine Lock (downtown at the Mississippi River, tel. 504/687–0641), built in 1909 and no longer in use, has the original lock house and an interpretive center with displays and exhibits that examine the history of the river and its boat traffic.

The **Port Hudson State Commemorative Area** (756 W. Plains–Port Hudson Rd., south of St. Francisville, tel. 504/654–3775) encompasses part of the Port Hudson battlefield, a Civil War site that saw the longest siege in American military history. There are an interpretive center and a picnic area, as well as 6 miles of hiking trails on the 650 acres.

Republic of West Florida Historical Museum (E. College St., Jackson, tel. 504/634–7155) is a sprawling indoor/outdoor facility whose displays include an antique, computerized Wurlitzer organ; antique cars, including a replica of Henry Ford's first auto, built in 1896; a working cotton gin; a general store; a blacksmith's forge; a Civil War room; and a diorama of the Port Hudson battlefield.

Rosedown Plantation House and Gardens (U.S. 61 at Rte. 10, St. Francisville, tel. 504/635–3332), a restored 1835 mansion with original furnishings, on 28 acres of landscaped gardens, is one of the state's most impressive houses.

Restaurants

Lafitte's Landing (Sunshine Bridge Access Rd., Donaldsonville, tel. 504/473–1232) features South Louisiana specialties in a quaint raised Acadian plantation house. **Joe's "Dreyfus Store"** (Rte. 77, Livonia, tel. 504/637–2625) is a rustic old-time general store transformed into one of the state's best restaurants, featuring creative seafood concoctions, steaks, charbroiled pork tenderloin, stuffed quail in port wine sauce, plus burgers, soups, and sandwiches. **The Coffee House** (124 W. Main St., New Roads, tel. 504/638–7859) is a handsome restaurant whose walls are decorated with art. The chef specializes in updated versions of Old-World French Creole recipes.

Tourist Information

Baton Rouge Area Convention & Visitors Bureau (Drawer 4149, Baton Rouge, LA 70821, tel. 504/383–1825 or 800/527–6843). **Greater New Orleans Tourist & Convention Commission** (1520 Sugar Bowl Dr., New Orleans, LA 70112, tel. 504/566–5011). **West Feliciana Tourist Commission** (Box 1548, St. Francisville, LA 70775, tel. 504/635–6330).

Reservation Service

Southern Comfort Bed & Breakfast Reservation Service (Box 13294, New Orleans, LA 70185, tel. 504/861–0082 or 800/749–1928, fax 504/861–3087).

Butler Greenwood

Shaded by huge live oaks dripping tangled tendrils of Spanish moss, Anne Butler's home—a two-story frame house with a wraparound veranda, dormers, and gables—was built in the early 1800s. Still a working plantation, the property, about 2 miles north of St. Francisville, has been in her family since 1796. A tour of the house is included with an overnight stay.

The Victorian parlor contains a 12-piece set of scarlet-upholstered rosewood furniture, a massive gilded pier mirror, full-length windows topped with elaborate lambrequins, floral Brussels carpet, oil paintings, and a marble mantel. All are original to the house.

The bed-and-breakfast accommodations are in five cottages sprinkled around a large pond, which is home to geese and ducks. Each of the cottages has either a full kitchen or kitchenette—stocked with a coffeemaker, toaster oven, fresh juice and croissants in the refrigerator, cereal, and fruit—so you can prepare breakfast at your leisure. Each cottage has remote-control cable TV, plenty of books and magazines, and good lamps for reading.

Anne found three 9-foot stained-glass church windows in an antiques shop and designed the Gazebo cottage around them. It has a king-size metal four-poster, wicker furnishings, and a kitchenette. The Cook's Cottage, which dates from the 1800s, has a working fireplace, brick walls, a porch with rocking chairs, and an old-fashioned bath with claw-foot tub. Another charmer is the Old Kitchen, built in 1796, which has exposed beams, old brick walls, and skylights, as well as piles of old *National Geographic* magazines to browse through. The largest cottage, decorated with gingerbread trim, can sleep six in two Victorian double beds and a sleeper sofa.

Each guest is given a copy of Anne's *A Tourist Guide to West Feliciana Parish.* Anne has been a writer and journalist for more than 25 years; she has written children's books, books on the criminal justice system, and a cookbook that includes vintage Feliciana photographs and anecdotes.

Address: *8345 U.S. 61, St. Francisville, LA 70775, tel. 504/635–6312 or 800/749–1928.*
Accommodations: *5 housekeeping cottages.*
Amenities: *Air-conditioning, phones on request and clock radios in cottages; pool, guided nature/bird-watching walks.*
Rates: *$75; Continental breakfast. No credit cards.*

Cottage Plantation

The country road to Cottage Plantation ambles across a wooden bridge and through a splendid wooded area thick with moss-covered live oaks, as well as dogwood, mimosa, and crape myrtle trees. The plantation nestles in 400 such idyllic acres, far from traffic noises and other 20th-century distractions.

Built between 1795 and 1850, Cottage is one of only a handful of antebellum plantations that still have their original outbuildings. The office and one-room schoolhouse, kitchen, tiny milk house, barns, slave quarters, and other dependencies that made up the working plantation are intact, though weathered. One outbuilding is now a rustic restaurant called Mattie's House (open for dinner only); another is an antiques shop.

The well-maintained main building is a long, low yellow frame structure; green shutters outline the gallery and dormer windows. The sloping roof is punctuated with chimneys and dormers from which window air-conditioning units jut anachronistically. A variety of dogs and cats nap or amble around the grounds.

Angling off from the main house is a similar structure—also original to the plantation—which houses the guest rooms. Downstairs rooms open onto the porch and get more light than those upstairs. All have four-posters and baths with modern plumbing and fixtures.

A tap on the door in the morning signals the arrival of a demitasse of coffee, accompanied by a flower. A serious breakfast is later served in the formal dining room, which, like the rest of the house (including guest rooms), is furnished with antebellum Louisiana pieces that might have been in the house when General Andrew Jackson called on the original owners after the 1815 Battle of New Orleans.

The plantation has been in the Brown family since 1951; Harvey and Mary Brown, the present owners, moved to St. Francisville from Miami to take charge in 1984. One of Mary's hobbies is apparent when you see the flower gardens that decorate the grounds near the main building.

Address: *10528 Cottage La., St. Francisville, LA 70777, tel. 504/635-3674.*
Accommodations: *5 double rooms with baths.*
Amenities: *Restaurant, air-conditioning, TV in rooms; pool.*
Rates: *$90; full breakfast. MC, V.*
Restrictions: *Smoking on porch only, no pets, closed Dec. 24-25.*

Madewood Plantation

In a lush country setting about equidistant from New Orleans and Baton Rouge, this handsome 21-room Greek Revival mansion offers a nostalgic glimpse of 19th-century life. Built in 1846 for Colonel Thomas Pugh, the house had fallen into a terrible state of repair when, in 1964, it was bought and restored by the Harold K. Marshall family of New Orleans. It is now owned by the Marshalls' son Keith and his wife, Millie, who will tell you, laughing, that the mansion became a bed-and-breakfast as the result of an exorbitant electric bill. Keith had just seen the bill when the phone rang and a caller asked if Madewood accepted paying guests. He replied, "Yes!" The Marshalls sometimes spend weekends at Madewood, but the resident managers are Janet Ledet and Dave D'Aunoy, who preside at the informal wine-and-cheese gatherings and candlelit Southern dinners served to guests in the main mansion. Thelma Parker, the cook and housekeeper, who's been at Madewood for 25 years, makes a mean pumpkin casserole that's almost always served.

Madewood has spacious rooms with high ceilings, hardwood floors, handsome carved moldings, Oriental rugs, and sparkling crystal chandeliers. In addition to 18th- and 19th-century Louisiana antiques in the mansion and in Charlet House, there are English antiques collected by Keith when he was a Rhodes Scholar.

There are four bedrooms upstairs and one downstairs; the latter has a handsome tester bed. Though all baths are private, those for the two back bedrooms upstairs can only be reached through the hall. Originally dressing rooms, these baths are much more spacious than those that were squeezed in when indoor plumbing became all the rage. The master bedroom, upstairs, has a large canopied four-poster; across the hall is a guest room decorated with antique children's toys. In addition, there are three suites in Charlet House, one of five outbuildings on the property. Its Honeymoon Suite has a working fireplace and a large screened porch. The house has served as a set for films, among them *A Woman Called Moses*, starring Cicely Tyson.

Address: *4250 Rte. 308, Napoleonville, LA 70390, tel. 504/369–7151, 800/749–7151 outside LA, or 800/375–7151 in LA.*
Accommodations: *5 double rooms with baths, 3 suites.*
Amenities: *Air-conditioning, turndown service, free tour of house and grounds.*
Rates: *$165; MAP. AE, D, MC, V.*
Restrictions: *Smoking on porches only, no pets, closed Thanksgiving Eve and Day, Dec. 24–25, Dec. 31–Jan. 1; rooms must be vacated for tours 10 AM–5 PM in the main mansion and noon–3 PM in Charlet House.*

Green Springs Plantation

Ivan and Madeline Nevill opened their bed-and-breakfast in 1991 in the newly built home they had modeled after an 1800s cottage. From the back gallery there is a splendid view of rolling hills; dogwood, oak, and magnolia trees; and the natural spring for which the house is named. The 150 acres surrounding the house have been in Madeline's family for 200 years.

The Nevills live downstairs; all of the upstairs, which in addition to bedrooms, has a common room with a working fireplace and cable TV, is for guests. Though the modern tile baths are large, rooms are average in size and are decorated with a mix of contemporary and antique furnishings. One has a four-poster, another a queen bed tucked under a sloping ceiling. The twin beds in the Iris Room are covered with patchwork quilts; this room and an adjacent "lagniappe room," as Madeline calls it, can be rented as a suite.

You can be assured of a superb breakfast. A fine cook, Madeline is well-known for her Spinach Madeleine, which appears in *River Road Recipes*.

Address: *7463 Tunica Trace, St. Francisville, LA 70775, tel. 504/635–4232 or 800/457–4978.*
Accommodations: *3 double rooms with baths.*
Amenities: *Air-conditioning, portable phone; nature trails.*
Rates: *$85; full breakfast. D, MC, V.*
Restrictions: *Smoking on porches only, no pets.*

Nottoway

This three-story Italianate/Greek Revival mansion built in 1859 is a knockout. The interior, which was restored in 1980, has undergone extensive recent refurbishment, and the exterior now shows off fresh white paint. In a lush country setting, across a quiet road from the Mississippi River levee, it has 22 white columns, 200 windows, and 53,000 square feet of living space.

Guest rooms are in the main mansion (the best are those facing the river) and the overseer's cottage, which overlooks sculpted gardens and a duck pond. Four-posters, testers, brass beds, and armoires are among the 19th-century furnishings; the master bedroom's Rococo Revival furniture, made in New Orleans by McCrackin, is original to the house.

Address: *Rte. 1 (Box 160), White Castle, LA 70788, tel. 504/545–2730 or 504/346–8263 in Baton Rouge.*
Accommodations: *10 double rooms with baths, 3 suites.*
Amenities: *Restaurant, air-conditioning, phones in 11 rooms, free house tour; pool.*
Rates: *$125–$250; wake-up Continental breakfast in rooms, full breakfast, sherry. AE, D, MC, V.*
Restrictions: *Smoking on verandas only, no pets, closed Dec. 24–25, Randolph Suite and Master Bedroom must be vacated for tours 9 AM–5 PM.*

Ormond Plantation

Typical of the houses of early Louisiana planters, Ormond (built sometime prior to 1790) is a two-story West Indies–style home with double galleries, a sloping roof, and attached garçonnières (young men's quarters). It is currently owned by Ken and Dede Elliott, who completed extensive restoration before opening it as a bed-and-breakfast in 1989.

Large, sunny rooms have high ceilings, hardwood floors, and lace-curtained French doors opening onto the galleries. In addition to furnishings representative of Louisiana in the 18th and 19th centuries, the house contains a roomful of adorable antique dolls and carriages, a display of antique guns, and a collection of antique one-armed bandits. From the rocking chairs on the upstairs gallery, you can watch the parade of boats on the Mississippi. Bowls of potpourri and miniature picture hats add warmth. Baths are large and modern, with tub/showers and plenty of vanity space for toiletries.

Address: *8407 River Rd., Destrehan, LA 70047, tel. and fax 504/764–8544.*
Accommodations: *3 double rooms with baths.*
Amenities: *Air-conditioning, free house tour, meeting room.*
Rates: *$125; full breakfast. AE, MC, V.*
Restrictions: *Smoking on veranda only, no pets, rooms must be vacated for tours 9 AM–5 PM.*

Pointe Coupee Bed & Breakfast

Al and Sidney Coffee, who own and operate the European-style restaurant called, appropriately, The Coffee House, are also proprietors of the Pointe Coupee Bed & Breakfast. The two houses that make up the B&B are on a quiet residential street in New Roads, a short walk from their restaurant on False River.

Al and Sidney live in the Hebert House with Angus, a huge black Lab. If you like dogs you'll love Angus. If you've never liked dogs before, he'll steal your heart. The two-story, turn-of-the-century home also houses two of the guest rooms. The Blue Room has a canopy bed, fireplace, and a big bath with claw-foot tub. A Victorian parlor is just off the dining room, where a full breakfast is served.

Right next to the Hebert House, the Samson-Claiborne House is a Creole cottage that dates from 1835. The antiques-filled home has two 2-bedroom suites downstairs. They each have a fireplace and open onto both the front and back porches. Two additional guest rooms are upstairs.

Address: *401 Richey St., New Roads, LA 70760, tel. 504/638–6254 or 800/832–7412.*
Accommodations: *4 double rooms with baths, 2 suites.*
Amenities: *Air-conditioning, TV in 3 rooms and available in others, portable phones, clock radios in rooms.*
Rates: *$55–$75; full breakfast, welcoming cocktail. MC, V.*
Restrictions: *No smoking indoors, no pets.*

Cajun Country

The Cajun craze of recent years has had the whole world two-stepping and tasting such hot-peppery dishes as Cajun chef Paul Prudhomme's blackened redfish. For the residents of South Louisiana, "Cajun" denotes not a passing fad but a way of life that spans almost 400 years. This way of life involves hard work, a strong Catholic faith, devotion to family and friends, plenty of good food, and an exuberant joie de vivre. In these parts, the Cajun motto is Laissez les bons temps rouler *(Let the good times roll). And roll they do; though for the rest of the world fads may come and fads may go, there is still plenty big fun down on the bayous.*

The Cajuns are descendants of the French who settled in what is now Nova Scotia and New Brunswick, Canada; they called their colony l'Acadie. The Acadians ("Cajun" is a corruption of the word) were expelled by the British in the mid-18th century, and a few thousand of them came to South Louisiana. Henry Wadsworth Longfellow's epic poem Evangeline *is based on the true story of Emmeline Labiche and Louis Arceneaux (Evangeline and Gabriel in the poem), the real-life lovers who were separated during the arduous exile—called by the Cajuns* Le Grand Dérangement.

Cajuns speak an antique 17th-century form of French, though they can understand and speak standard French (as well as English). Radio stations sometimes broadcast in French, and French-speaking disc jockeys spin Cajun music. Billboards touting a local fried chicken chain proclaim, "J'aime cette poule!" (Love that chicken!), and at Evangeline Downs, races begin, "Ils sont partis!" (They're off!). Most shops have a sign in their window announcing, "Ici on parle français." Needless to say, this is a great place to brush up on your French.

Not surprisingly, given the Cajun exuberance, festivals pop up almost every 10 minutes in this neck of the bois. *Events* celebrate alligators, crawfish, strawberries, cotton, shrimp, tomatoes, and potatoes—and in between festivals, the Cajuns simply celebrate themselves.

The interstates that race through the region are the quickest routes from there to there, but the best way to savor the scenery is by taking the state and parish roads that follow twisting bottle-green bayous or amble by canebrakes, rice paddies, exotic old plantations, and immense live oak trees whose gnarled boughs are draped with gray shawls of Spanish moss. South Louisiana is sprinkled with salt domes, called "islands," which have nudged up from under the flatlands over a few thousand millennia and look a bit like dry-land islands. There are several picturesque state parks that are ideal for hiking, picnicking, boating, or building castles in the air.

Places to Go, Sights to See

Acadian Village (off Rte. 342 south of Lafayette, tel. 318/981–2364), a rural folk-life museum, is a re-creation of a bayou village. It has a cluster of authentic 19th-century houses, a church, a blacksmith shop, and a general store.

Atchafalaya Basin, east of Breaux Bridge, is 800,000 watery acres, an eerily beautiful place where stark cypress trees dripping with Spanish moss rise from the murky waters. At *Henderson*, where the levee is lined with tour and fishing boats, a host of operators will take you gliding out beneath canopies of trees to find alligators, herons, egrets, beavers, and all manner of critters. Try *McGee's Landing* (tel. 318/228–2384) for pontoon-boat tours or *Angelle's Atchafalaya Swamp Tours* (Whiskey River Landing, tel. 318/667–6135).

Avery Island (on Rte. 329 south of New Iberia, tel. 318/369–6243) boasts both a 300-acre *Jungle Garden* (tel. 318/369–6243), thick with subtropical trees, plants, and flowers, and an aviary fluttering with egrets. Here you can also tour the *Tabasco Sauce factory* (tel. 318/365–8173), where the McIlhenny family still makes the red-hot condiment created by Edmund McIlhenny in the 1800s.

Breaux Bridge, whose chief claim to fame is Mulate's (*see* Restaurants, *below*), draws some 100,000 visitors at its *Crawfish Festival,* held every year.

Chitimacha Indian Reservation (Rte. 326, Charenton, tel. 318/923–4830). Some 300 Chitimacha Indians live on a 280-acre reservation under the auspices of the Jean Lafitte National Historical Park. Besides the tribal center, the reservation has a museum, a trading post, a crafts shop, a park, and picnic areas. The Chitimacha were known for basket weaving, and their colorful crafts can be purchased on the reservation.

Franklin, sitting smugly on the Teche to the south, is a lush little Main Street USA town that boasts a half-dozen antebellum mansions open for tours. Oddly, for this part of Louisiana, Franklin was settled by the English.

Lafayette, a city of some 150,000, which proudly calls itself the capital of French Louisiana, lies less than two hours west of New Orleans. Lafayette's museums and music halls are good places in which to get acquainted with Acadian lore and life. The city is also a hub for exploring the smaller towns and villages in the area. *Cajun Mardi Gras* in Lafayette and environs is second only to its sister celebration in New Orleans. Picture a few hundred masked and costumed horsemen thundering around the countryside during the annual *Courir de Mardi Gras* (Mardi Gras Run). Lafayette is also home to the *Festival International de Louisiane,* which brings musicians, actors, dancers, jugglers, and all sorts of other performers and aficionados from all over the world. *The Lafayette Natural History Museum and Planetarium* (637 Girard Park Dr., tel. 318/268–5544) has an adjunct *Acadiana Park Nature Trail and Station* (E. Alexander St., tel. 318/235–6181), with an interpretive center. It organizes bird-watching walks, hikes, and other field trips. *The Acadian Cultural Center* (501 Fisher Rd., tel. 318/232–0789) is a large, modern facility with audiovisual exhibits that trace the Acadian heritage.

Live Oak Gardens (284 Rip Van Winkle Rd., Jefferson Island, tel. 318/367–3485) was once the winter home of 19th-century actor Joseph Jefferson. It features landscaped grounds, a boat ride on the lake, and tours of Jefferson's lavish three-story house.

New Iberia, proclaiming itself the Queen City of the Teche, is a picturesque town that was settled by Spaniards from the Iberian coast. One of the South's best-known antebellum homes—*Shadows on the Teche* (317 E. Main St., tel. 318/369–6446)—is a perfect example of what went with the wind. The *Conrad Rice Mill and Konriko Company Store* (307 Ann St., tel. 800/551–3245) is the country's oldest rice mill, and *Trappey's* (900 E. Main St., tel. 318/365–8281 or 800/365–8727) turns out red-hot spices. Both are open for tours.

St. Martinville was a major debarkation point for the Acadians. Here, on the banks of Bayou Teche, stands the *Evangeline Oak,* a giant tree that was the legendary last meeting place of the two lovers. It is one of the region's most photographed sights. In the late 18th century, St. Martinville was a haven for French aristocrats who fled from France during the revolution. The town was known then as Petit Paris because of the elaborate balls and operas staged there. St. Martinville is also home to *St. Martin de Tours,* the mother church of the Acadians. In the church square, the *Petit Paris Museum* (103 S. Main St., tel. 318/394–7334) has carnival costumes and historical displays pertaining to Cajun country. And behind the church, where Emmeline Labiche is buried, there is a statue of Evangeline. In 1929, *The Romance of Evangeline,* starring Delores del Rio, was filmed in the town; Ms. del Rio posed for the statue, and it was given to St. Martinville. Just north of town is the *Longfellow-Evangeline State Commemorative Area* (1200 N. Main St., tel. 318/394–3754), a 157-acre park with an interpretive center, an early 19th-century Creole home, an Acadian crafts shop housed in a Cajun cottage, picnic grounds, and a boat launch.

Washington, north of Lafayette, is a historic little town that flourished during the steamboating era. It's home to *Magnolia Ridge* (Prescott St., tel. 318/826–3027), one of the state's grand antebellum mansions, and to *Hinckley House* (405 W. DeJean St., tel. 318/826–3906), which is awash with steamboat memorabilia.

Restaurants

You'd be hard-pressed to find any bad food in this part of the country. Standout Cajun restaurants include **Enola Prudhomme's Cajun Café** (4676 N.E. Evangeline Thruway, Carencro, tel. 318/896–7964) and **Prejean's** (3480 U.S. 167, Lafayette, tel. 318/896–3247), both housed in cypress Cajun cottages; **Mulate's** (325 Mills Ave., Breaux Bridge, tel. 800/422–2586 or 800/634–9880 in LA), a wildly popular dance hall–cum–café with live Cajun music; and **Café Vermilionville** (1304 Pinhook Rd., Lafayette, tel. 318/237–0100), which serves Creole cuisine in a lovely restored 1799 inn. **Lagniappe Too** (204 E. Main St., New Iberia, tel. 318/365–9419) is a good lunch spot for salads, quiches, and sandwiches; the menu goes haute for dinner Friday and Saturday. **The Steamboat Warehouse Restaurant** (Main St., Washington, tel. 318/826–7227), a rustic, restored 19th-century structure, serves great seafood and steaks and has steamboat memorabilia and a dock overlooking Bayou Courtableau.

Tourist Information

Atchafalaya Delta Tourist Commission (Box 2332, Morgan City, LA 70381, tel. 504/395–4905). **Iberia Parish Tourist Commission** (2690 Center St., New Iberia, LA 70560, tel. 318/365–1540). **Lafayette Convention & Visitors Commission** (Evangeline Thruway and Willow St., Box 52006, Lafayette, LA 70505, tel. 318/232–3808, 800/346–1958 in the United States, or 800/543–5340 in Canada).

Reservation Service

Southern Comfort Reservation Service (Box 13294, New Orleans, LA 70185, tel. 504/861–0082 or 800/749–1928, fax 504/861–3087).

A la Bonne Veillée

Off a country road between Lafayette and Abbeville stands A la Bonne Veillée, a two-story Acadian cottage. Moss-draped live oaks shade it, and ducks waddle about a nearby pond. Their quacking and the songs of birds are about the only sounds that can be heard.

Made of hand-cut cypress timbers, the house has a steeply pitched wood-shingled roof through which pokes a chimney made of old brick. Wood for the two fireplaces is stacked neatly on the front porch, where there are rocking chairs. American Empire antiques and plenty of books grace the parlor; adjacent is a master bedroom with a huge tiger maple Sheraton canopy bed and scatter rugs on the cypress floors. The other downstairs rooms are a full kitchen and the only bath (it's almost as big as the bedroom). Steep, unfriendly stairs lead to an attic room with a brass bed, patchwork quilts, a trundle bed, and other pieces "from grand-mother's attic," says owner Carolyn Doerle.

Carolyn and her husband, Ron Ray, who live in the historic LeBlanc House a stone's throw away, saved the cottage from demolition and had it moved to their 30-acre farm. (Ron, a psychotherapist, also raises Gertrudis cattle. Carolyn is CEO of Doerle Food Services, her family's wholesale food concern.) The two love restoring old houses, and the cottage was special. More than 100 years ago it was a *maison dimanche* (Sunday house)—it was customary for prosperous rural plantation owners to keep a town house to use on week-ends.

The cottage is rented only to a family or to two couples traveling together. Breakfast is brought in, and there is an intercom to the main house, which guests may tour; apart from that, they have absolute peace and privacy. (Those who want to pick up the pace can drive to the Cajun dance halls in Lafayette, about 15 minutes away.)

The unusual name of the guest house derives from a Cajun phrase, "Let's go *veiller*." It means to make long evening visits after supper, chatting, gossiping, and telling stories.

Address: *Rte. P-I-21 off Rte. 339 (LeBlanc House, Rte. 2, Box 2270), Abbeville, LA 70510, tel. 318/937–5495.*
Accommodations: *1 housekeeping cottage.*
Amenities: *Air-conditioning and TV in rooms, phones in cottage.*
Rates: *$100; Continental breakfast. No credit cards.*
Restrictions: *No smoking indoors, no pets.*

Camellia Cove

Herman and Annie Bidstrup's 1825 home, listed on the National Register of Historic Places, sits on 2 acres on a peaceful residential street in the little town of Washington. The large, white, two-story house has double porches and lacy Victorian trim. Rocking chairs on the upstairs porch are great for relaxing and enjoying the peace and quiet. On the broad side lawn, the scent of clover in the springtime is delicious.

The Bidstrups bought the house in 1982, spent a year and a half restoring it, and in 1986 moved into it. After living in Scotland and England, where they enjoyed staying in B&Bs, they decided to run one themselves. The two have traveled extensively, and the house is filled with mementos and artifacts, such as the African tribal masks that adorn the dining room wall.

Camellia Cove has a wealth of wonderful memorabilia, in addition to its Louisiana antique furnishings. At the turn of the century, this was the home of Dr. Herbert Kilpatrick. His desk in the parlor remains much as it was when he lived in the house, and displayed on it is his license to dispense opium. In the central hallway, Herman's grandfather's handwritten marriage license, dated 1887, is pressed between the pages of the Bidstrup family Bible. (Herman is of Danish-German ancestry; Annie is French Acadian.)

Three of the upstairs rooms—all of them exceptionally large—are rented to overnight guests. A front room, just off the porch, has Victorian furnishings: a wood-carved bed, washstand, armoire, and dressing table. Its bath, almost as large as the bedroom, has a claw-foot tub with spray shower as well as a marble-topped dresser with a big mirror under a row of makeup lights. (Incidentally, part of the fun here is finding amenities, such as manicure scissors nestled in little porcelain potpourri-filled pots.) One of the guest rooms has two beds; its bath is across the hall. The third guest room does share that bath, but Annie only rents these two rooms to families or people traveling together.

Breakfast is served in the formal dining room. It always includes heaps of homemade biscuits and homemade fig preserves.

Address: *205 W. Hill St., Washington, LA 70589, tel. 318/826–7362.*
Accommodations: *1 double room with bath, 2 doubles share 1 bath.*
Amenities: *Air-conditioning.*
Rates: *$65–$75; full breakfast. No credit cards.*
Restrictions: *Smoking on porch only, no pets, closed Jan. 1, Thanksgiving, Dec. 25.*

Chrétien Point Plantation

I n the early 1930s, a local photographer took pictures of this house and sent them to Hollywood. As a result, the stairway and the window above it were used as a model for those in Scarlett O'Hara's Tara. Then, too, there's the tale of the long-ago lady of Chrétien Point who shot a man on the steps, as Scarlett shot the Union soldier. Owners Jeanne and Louis Cornay will point out the very step on which the man was standing when he was killed.

Of solid brick construction, with six round white columns and double galleries across the front, the two-story house was built in 1831 for Hypolite Chrétien II and his wife, Félicité. During the War Between the States, the house figured in a major battle. There is still a bullet hole in one of the front doors. The last Chrétiens lost the house a few years after the war, and it began to fall into a sorry state.

Louis found the deteriorated mansion while looking for a barn in which to keep his son's horse. Hay was stored in it; chickens, cows, and pigs roamed through it. The Cornays bought the house and restored it to its former grandeur.

The colors used in the house are those of nature's sunsets. Silk wall coverings are in vivid scarlets and pinks; one of the ceilings is painted a cool blue. There are six working fireplaces with imported French Empire marble mantels. The 19th-century Louisiana antiques include a carved armoire and four-poster by Mallard. Two rooms have full-tester beds, one with a pale gold sunburst canopy and crocheted spread, the other with canopy and spread in rich fabrics and bold colors. A downstairs room, formerly the wine cellar, has redbrick floors, pink velvet chairs, a marble-top dresser, and a hand-carved bed. The bins that once held wine are now filled with books.

The only guest room with an adjoining bath is the master bedroom upstairs. Most other rooms have private hall baths.

There is no restaurant, but Louis says that in bad weather they'll rustle up something for hungry guests.

Address: *Rte. 1, Sunset (1108 Johnston St., Lafayette, LA 70501), tel. 318/233–7050 or 318/662–5876.*
Accommodations: *3 double rooms with baths, 2 doubles share 1 bath.*
Amenities: *Air-conditioning, free mansion tour, 1 meeting room; pool, tennis court.*
Rates: *$110–$200; full breakfast. MC, V.*
Restrictions: *Smoking on galleries only, no pets, rooms must be vacated for tours 10 AM–5 PM.*

Bois des Chênes

Beneath the branches of huge live oaks, peacocks preen in a thatch-roofed aviary, while a Labrador and a miniature poodle greet visitors. The setting is so serenely bucolic that it seems to be deep in the woods rather than just off a busy thoroughfare.

This historic plantation is home to Marjorie and Coerte Voorhies, who have restored the mansion and carriage house. All the guest rooms are in the carriage house and have private entrances. Spacious, airy rooms have hardwood floors and Oriental rugs; one of the rooms has cypress beams. Marjorie, a former antiques dealer, furnished the rooms with 18th- and 19th-century American and Louisiana French pieces. Four-posters have patchwork quilts and a crocheted canopy or a filmy mosquito net. Baths are especially well done: large and modern, with brass fittings.

Address: *338 N. Sterling St., Lafayette, LA 70501, tel. 318/233-7816.*
Accommodations: *3 suites.*
Amenities: *Air-conditioning, cable TV, and minifridges in suites; fenced yard and kennel for small pets.*
Rates: *$85-$105; full breakfast, wine. AE, MC, V.*
Restrictions: *Smoking on porch only, closed Dec. 24-25.*

Old Castillo Hotel/Place d'Evangeline

Hard by Bayou Teche, beneath the branches of the Evangeline Oak (which suggests the rooms with the best view), this three-story brick building looks like a "little red schoolhouse." In fact, in its more than 150-year history it has *been* a school, as well as a 19th-century inn (the Castillo Hotel) and a hall for operas and balls.

The Place d'Evangeline restaurant opened in 1987; two years later owners Peggy and Gerald Hulin began restoring the upstairs rooms for overnighters. The restoration is ongoing. Curtains, color-coordinated with the furnishings, have been added, as has a balcony on the front of the building. (Rooms 1 and 4 open onto the balcony.) Peggy plans to plant a rose garden and add fresh flowers in the rooms. The rooms themselves are enormous (ceilings are sky-high) and at present somewhat sparsely furnished with 19th-century Louisiana French antiques. Room 3 is of awesome size, with a four-poster and a book-filled breakfront. Its bath is also large, with double marble vanities. All baths are adjoining and have modern fixtures and vanities complemented by old-fashioned touches like porcelain washbowls and pitchers.

Address: *220 Evangeline Blvd., St. Martinville, LA 70582, tel. 318/394-4010 or 800/621-3017.*
Accommodations: *5 double rooms with baths.*
Amenities: *Air-conditioning.*
Rates: *$75; full breakfast. AE, MC, V.*
Restrictions: *No pets.*

T' Frère's House

A trim white gazebo stands on the spacious lawn of T' Frère's House, which sits well back from a busy thoroughfare. "Little Brother's House," a gabled Acadian cottage, was built about 1880 of cypress and brick. A leaded-glass door opens to a central hallway with a crystal chandelier and ornate gold-leaf mirror. Two guest rooms are to the right of the hall; a formal parlor and dining room are opposite. There are two side porches—one glassed in and the other enclosed in latticework.

The big front room has an 1840s full-tester bed, floor-length draperies with lace valances, a working fireplace, and a whirlpool bath (accessible from the hall). This room is a bit noisy, but better suited for a couple than the smaller room, which has a tiny bath with a footed tub and spray shower. Up the steep stairs is another room, with twin beds and an old-fashioned bath.

Address: *1905 Verot School Rd., Lafayette, LA 70508, tel. 318/984–9347.*
Accommodations: *3 double rooms with baths.*
Amenities: *Air-conditioning and TV in rooms; fireplaces in 1 room, parlor, and kitchen; terry-cloth robes.*
Rates: *$75–$85; full breakfast. D, MC, V.*
Restrictions: *Smoking on porches or in gazebo only, closed Thanksgiving week and Christmas week.*

North-Central Louisiana

*Many people predicted that Interstate 49, to join North
Louisiana and South Louisiana, would never be completed.
Well, the highway has been finished, and the two "states" are
now connected—by car, at least, if not in spirit. Louisiana
has always been a divided state. Natives invariably refer to
North Louisiana and South Louisiana, and even in
conversation you can detect a capitalized distinction. North
Louisiana is Southern, and South Louisiana is not. (New
Orleans, though way down south, has neither a Northern nor
a Southern flavor but is in a class by itself.)*

*Alexandria, in the middle of the state, is Louisiana's own
unofficial but acknowledged Mason-Dixon Line. North of
Alex (or "Elleck," as it's pronounced around here), the
terrain, accents, customs, and cuisine change. Flat
marshlands, moss-draped cypress trees, and gray earth give
way to rolling green hills, pine forests, and rich red clay—
stained, as they say in these parts, by the blood of the
Confederacy. The area around Alexandria has several
notable Civil War sites, including a cemetery and antebellum
houses.*

*Natchitoches (pronounced "nack-i-tish"), about one hour
northwest of Alexandria, is the oldest permanent settlement
in the entire Louisiana Purchase—four years older than the
more highly publicized French Quarter of New Orleans. The
town's restored historic district is a 33-block area containing
fine old homes. Front Street, paved with old brick, stretches
along the pretty Cane River Lake. Created when the Red
River changed its course, Cane River Lake not only
decorates Natchitoches but meanders on down through the
region's plantation country.*

*Natchitoches gained fame as the town of Chinquapin in the
film* Steel Magnolias. *The film, which was shot here in 1988,
has virtually transformed this sleepy little town. You can't*

*walk 2 feet in any direction without encountering someone
who wants to tell about the "part"—on camera or off—he or
she played in the film.*

*In these parts, Natchitoches has long been known for its
Christmas Festival of Lights, now more than 65 years old.
The monthlong festival, which begins the first Saturday of
December, draws about 150,000 people to town. The historic
district, on which the festival centers, is a riot of twinkling
lights, and the first weekend is a continual festival of food
and fun.*

*Another celebrated, though slightly smaller, event is the two-
day Natchitoches Pilgrimage, held in October, which
includes walking tours of the historic district, admission to
some of the landmark homes and plantations, and
candlelight tours.*

*Although I–49 makes the drive easy, you should take the state
and parish roads to explore the backcountry of Louisiana
and visit the house museums and plantations. State Route 1
slips diagonally from the northwest corner all the way to the
Gulf of Mexico. Although the road is substandard along some
stretches, the scenery is prettier, and you'll pick up more
flavor than on the interstate. Routes 494, 119, and 493 are
also picturesque, drifting alongside Cane River Lake
between Natchitoches and Melrose. And the drive through the
Kisatchie National Forest is spectacular.*

Places to Go, Sights to See

Bayou Folk Museum (Cloutierville, tel. 318/352–8072). In the late 1800s,
Kate Chopin, who wrote the book on which the film *The Awakening* was
based, lived in this region. Her home is now a museum containing costumes,
furnishings, and various memorabilia pertaining to her life and times.

Beau Fort Plantation (Rte. 494 south of Natchitoches, tel. 318/352–9580) is
a 265-acre working cotton plantation. A long alley of live oaks leads to the
mansion, which has an 84-foot gallery and the ambience of the Old South.

Cane River Cruises (Natchitoches, tel. 318/352–7093 or 318/352–2577) runs
an easygoing narrated cruise on scenic Cane River Lake—a pleasant way to

while away an hour. Boats leave from Roque House on the downtown riverfront.

Kent House (3601 Bayou Rapides Rd., Alexandria, tel. 318/487–5998), built around 1800, is the oldest known structure still standing in central Louisiana. Its outbuildings—milk house, carriage house, and kitchen—have been preserved, and a variety of activities, including cooking and quilting demonstrations, take place here on a regular basis.

Kisatchie National Forest. South of Natchitoches, a 100,000-acre division of this national forest contains the 17-mile Longleaf Trail Scenic Byway, which crosses a beautiful bayou; an 8,700-acre wilderness with hiking and riding trails; and several strategically placed viewpoints. For further information, write to the District Ranger, Kisatchie Ranger District, Box 2128, Natchitoches, LA 71457.

Magnolia Plantation (Rte. 119, 1 mi north of Derry, tel. 318/379–2221), one of the largest homes in the area, is a 2½-story structure with 27 rooms. The only cotton press in the country still in its original location is housed in a barn behind the house.

At **Melrose Plantation** (Exit 119 of I–49, Melrose, tel. 318/379–0055), tours take in the main mansion, the blacksmith shop, the doctor's office, and the African House, the most famous structure, the second floor of which boasts murals by primitive artist Clementine Hunter. The "black Grandma Moses" lived and painted here till her death in 1988, just short of her 102nd birthday.

Trolley Tours (Natchitoches, tel. 318/352–7093 or 318/352–2577) has an open tram that rattles around town on a Steel Magnolia Tour; a narrator does a colorful commentary on who lived where and what happened here during the filming of the movie. If you're curious about where the stars—Dolly Parton, Shirley MacLaine, Sally Field, Olympia Dukakis, Julia Roberts, and Tom Skerritt—lived, this is the way to find out.

Restaurants

Finding good food is not a problem anywhere in Louisiana. In the Natchitoches/Alexandria area, there are some standouts. People who travel frequently between North and South Louisiana plan things so that at feeding time they'll be near **Lea's Lunchroom** (U.S. 71, Lecompte, tel. 318/776–5178), a big, noisy down-home café that dishes out zillions of plate lunches, sandwiches, and mouth-watering homemade pies. Natchitoches is known for meat pies, and the best place to get them is **Lasyone's Meat Pie Kitchen & Restaurant** (622 2nd St., tel. 318/352–3353). For more formal dining in Natchitoches, **The Landing** (530 Front St., tel. 318/352–1579) is a large bistro-style eatery serving pasta, seafood, steaks, and superb garlic bread and bread pudding.

Tourist Information

Natchitoches Parish Tourist Commission (Box 411, Natchitoches, LA 71458, tel. 318/352–8072). **Rapides Parish Convention & Visitors Bureau** (Box 8110, Alexandria, LA 71306, tel. 318/443–7049).

Reservation Service

Southern Comfort Reservation Service (Box 13294, New Orleans, LA 70185, tel. 504/861–0082 or 800/749–1928, fax 504/861–3087).

Cloutier Townhouse

Adorned with filigreed cast-iron galleries that were assembled in France, the Cloutier (pronounced "cloo-chee") Townhouse sits smack in Natchitoches's historic district. Conna Cloutier's elegant home is one of the only bed-and-breakfasts that offers an unobstructed view of Front Street and Cane River Lake. This is the center of the town's famed Christmas Festival of Lights, when the trees, buildings, and bridges are ablaze. Conna opens her home for group tours (by appointment) during the month of December.

The town house occupies the top two floors of a three-story building that dates from the 1830s. In the European style, the first floor is a commercial establishment—in this case, Le Bistro, a chef John Folse market and deli. A carriageway leads from Front Street to a courtyard paved with old brick. From there, behind an iron gate, steps lead to the broad rear porches, where there are tables and rocking chairs. At both the front and back, French doors open onto the galleries.

In the large open area that contains the foyer, living room, and dining room, polished hardwood floors are covered with Oriental rugs, and paneled walls reach to a 30-foot ceiling. A winding central staircase leads to the part of the third floor where Conna lives. Most of the furnishings are of the American Empire period. An Empire sideboard and a gold-leaf mirror supported by rosewood piano legs on a marble base were made for an early plantation nearby. Bookcases are filled with books, and the walls are hung with oil paintings, one a portrait of the wife of a 19th-century owner of the property.

The front guest room, which has a four-poster bed and other Louisiana antiques, opens onto the gallery and is somewhat noisy; its bath is private, but you have to go out into the hall to reach it. The master bedroom, which opens onto the foyer and the rear gallery, is both larger and quieter. Its focal points are a full-tester bed with an embroidered spread, old-brick walls, and a fireplace with gas logs. Wing chairs and an upholstered settee (with good reading lamps) are tempting places to curl up and read the many books that lie about. Twin dressing areas, each with a spacious marble vanity and ample wall mirrors, are outside a large carpeted bath, which has a platformed whirlpool and a wood-paneled lighted shower stall.

Address: *8 Ducournau Sq., Natchitoches, LA 71457, tel. 318/352–5242.*
Accommodations: *2 double rooms with baths.*
Amenities: *Air-conditioning, cable in 1 room, 2 fireplaces in public rooms.*
Rates: *$65 and $89; full breakfast. MC, V.*
Restrictions: *No smoking indoors, no pets.*

Loyd Hall

oyd Hall is a 640-acre working plantation that grows cotton, corn, and soybeans. Frank Fitzgerald's father bought the land in 1949, unaware that a deteriorated 19th-century mansion was buried beneath a tangle of trees and bushes. Frank and his wife, Anne, now live in the restored house. Frank is a veterinarian, and in addition to chickens, cattle, horses, and other farm critters, a small army of cats and dogs calls Loyd Hall home. A Catahoula hog dog, with one blue eye and one brown eye (a distinguishing feature of the breed), and a pudgy English bulldog make it a point to befriend guests.

Guests have a choice of three accommodations. The first B&B on the property—a replica of a rustic 19th-century Acadian cottage—has a sloping shingle roof, a front porch with rocking chairs, two bedrooms with four-posters and plump comforters, a washer and dryer, and a bath with claw-foot tub/shower and plenty of vanity space. A sleeper sofa in the parlor enables the cottage to sleep six; however, because of its small size, it's rented only to a family or to others who know each other well.

In 1993, the ancient separate kitchen behind the mansion was transformed into an elegant Cinderella that now houses the Camellia Suite and the Magnolia Suite. The former has a full-tester bed, the latter a half-tester; both have brick floors, wing chairs cozied up to an open fireplace, and rocking chairs on the front porch. They can be combined to create a two-bedroom suite.

Frank's mother had an antiques shop, and the cottage and suites are furnished with some of her 19th-century Louisianiana. All three have wood-burning fireplaces and kitchens with modern appliances, including dishwasher, toaster, and coffee maker. They are stocked with a chilled decanter of wine, homemade muffins, milk, juice, and all the ingredients for a bacon-and-eggs breakfast, which guests prepare at their leisure and enjoy in privacy, wrapped in the cushy terry-cloth robes provided.

The plantation is in a quiet country setting, 16 miles south of Alexandria near the intersection of U.S. 167 and 71.

Address: *292 Loyd Bridge Rd., Cheneyville (5119 Masonic Dr., Alexandria, LA 71301), tel. 318/776-5641, fax 318/279-2335.*
Accommodations: *1 housekeeping cottage, 2 suites.*
Amenities: *Air-conditioning, TV with VCR in cottage and suites; pool, bicycles, fishing rods.*
Rates: *$95, 2-bedroom suite $180; full breakfast. AE, MC, V.*
Restrictions: *No smoking indoors, no pets.*

Fleur-de-Lis

The Fleur-de-Lis, opened in 1983, is the granddaddy of Natchitoches bed-and-breakfasts. In 1993, longtime owner Bert Froeba sold his turn-of-the-century house to Tom and Harriette Palmer, who now operate the B&B with help from their friendly golden retriever, Moose. The two-story brown-and-beige frame house has a front porch with a swing and rocking chairs, shaded by a roof that juts out beneath a second-story bay window topped by a gable. Behind leaded-glass doors are a large foyer and stairway. Adjoining the foyer, a cozy family room has a sofa and chairs grouped around the TV. Breakfast is served family-style at a long table in the dining room. Knickknacks and framed family pictures are displayed throughout.

Guest rooms feature four-poster, white-iron, or brass beds and patchwork quilts; some have white wicker furnishings and headboards. The quietest room is the Blue Room, which has a country French flavor. All the baths are tiny but have modern fixtures.

Address: *336 2nd St., Natchitoches, LA 71457, tel. 318/352–6621 or 800/489–6621.*
Accommodations: *5 double rooms with baths.*
Amenities: *Air-conditioning, cable TV in family room; wheelchair ramp.*
Rates: *$65; full breakfast. AE, MC, V.*
Restrictions: *No pets, 2-night minimum during Christmas Festival.*

Jefferson House

The back veranda of Gay and L. J. Melder's contemporary white frame home affords a mesmerizing view of Cane River Lake. Although the house sits on a busy extension of Front Street, within walking distance of the historic district, the weeping willows, herb garden, rocking chairs on the veranda, and pier sneaking onto the lake create a bucolic ambience.

The house is a split-level whose lower floor is hidden from the street. The Melders live on the lower floor; guests occupy the entire street-level floor. Gay, who has an upmarket gift shop, has decorated the house with a blend of exquisite Oriental objets d'art and traditional furnishings. The large, stately parlor has a high, beamed ceiling, a brick fireplace, and

doors opening to the veranda. Bedrooms are done with quilted spreads and matching draperies. The larger room has an adjoining tile bath that's big enough for a fair-size cocktail party! The rooms may be rented as a suite.

Address: *229 Jefferson St., Natchitoches, LA 71457, tel. 318/352–3957 or 318/352–5756.*
Accommodations: *2 double rooms with baths.*
Amenities: *Air-conditioning, large-screen cable TV in living room.*
Rates: *$50–$60, 2-bedroom suite $90; full breakfast, afternoon cocktails. MC, V.*
Restrictions: *Smoking on porch only, no pets.*

Starlight Plantation

ts name conjures up images of white columns, but the plantation that stood in this country setting went with the wind long ago. Susan and Peter Cloutier renovated a cottage on the property as their home and added a rambling cypress deck with tables and chairs, a view of the Cane River, and a hot tub, in which guests can skinny-dip at night in complete privacy.

Opening onto the deck is a two-bedroom suite to which guests are given a key. The front room—spacious and sunny with upholstered rattan chairs and a bed tucked into an alcove—leads into the master bedroom, which has a four-poster and traditional furnishings. The modern tile bath has ample vanity space and plenty of big thirsty towels but is not overly large. Although this is a suite, it seems less well suited to four people than to a couple, as there is not much privacy.

Peter and Susan run things in a laid-back style, being neither intrusive nor reclusive. They're there if you need them; otherwise, guests come and go as they please and even specify what time they'd like to have breakfast.

Address: *Rte. 1 (Box 239), Natchitoches, LA 71457, tel. 318/352–3775 or 800/866–8893.*
Accommodations: *1 suite.*
Amenities: *Air-conditioning, TV with VCR, phone, and clock radio in suite.*
Rates: *$85; full breakfast. MC, V.*
Restrictions: *Smoking on deck only, no pets.*

Tennessee

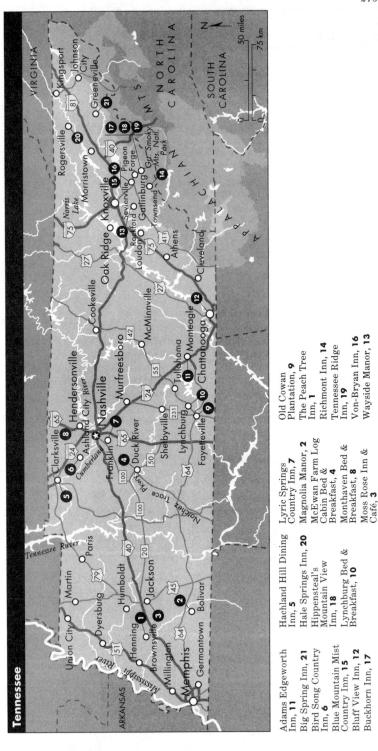

Tennessee

Adams Edgeworth Inn, **11**
Big Spring Inn, **21**
Bird Song Country Inn, **6**
Blue Mountain Mist Country Inn, **15**
Bluff View Inn, **12**
Buckhorn Inn, **17**

Hachland Hill Dining Inn, **5**
Hale Springs Inn, **20**
Hippensteal's Mountain View Inn, **18**
Lynchburg Bed & Breakfast, **10**

Lyric Springs Country Inn, **7**
Magnolia Manor, **2**
McEwan Farm Log Cabin Bed & Breakfast, **4**
Monthaven Bed & Breakfast, **8**
Moss Rose Inn & Café, **3**

Old Cowan Plantation, **9**
The Peach Tree Inn, **1**
Richmont Inn, **14**
Tennessee Ridge Inn, **19**
Von-Bryan Inn, **16**
Wayside Manor, **13**

East Tennessee

High above a patchwork of rolling farmland and forests, the peaks of the Great Smoky Mountains dominate the landscape of East Tennessee. Covered with a dense carpet of wildflowers in spring and ablaze with foliage in autumn, the Smokies—named for the mantle of blue haze that so often blankets them—are a joy to hike or drive through.

The highest and most rugged elevations are in the Great Smoky Mountains National Park, the most visited national park in the United States. The gateway city to the park is Gatlinburg, not too long ago a remote little place with a few hotels and some mountain crafts shops. Now hordes of visitors are attracted here for outdoor recreation. Neighboring Pigeon Forge—site of Dolly Parton's theme park, Dollywood, and numerous other tourist attractions— has become a favorite with family vacationers.

Less commercialized is the Great Smoky Mountains Arts and Crafts Community just outside Gatlinburg. Pretty byways into the national park take travelers far from the crowds to stunning vistas and roadside trailheads that mark the start of tranquil walks. Mountain folkways persist in smaller communities, preserved by artisans who practice age-old crafts and traditional cooks who conjure up hearty meals from surrounding streams, fields, and woodlands. Most bed-and-breakfast inns are located off the beaten path, but within a few miles of the major attractions. City lovers will find urban bustle and diversity at Knoxville and Chattanooga. The latter has become a favorite with tourists since the Tennessee Aquarium opened.

Places to Go, Sights to See

Andrew Johnson National Historic Site (College and Depot Sts., Greeneville, tel. 615/638–3551). The 17th president's home, grave, and simple tailor shop are preserved here in the smallest national park in the country.

Chattanooga Choo-Choo and Terminal Station (1400 Market St., tel. 615/266–5000). This renovated facility commemorating the heyday of railroads has several restaurants, shops, and train exhibits.

The **Dixie Stampede** (3849 Parkway, Pigeon Forge, tel. 615/453–4400 or 800/356–1676). This live dinner-show features barbecue and a musical Wild West rodeo.

Dollywood (700 Dollywood La., Pigeon Forge, tel. 615/428–9400 or 800/DOLLYWOOD). Dolly Parton's popular theme park offers the food, music, and fun of the region in a re-created 1880s mountain village with modern rides and professional entertainment throughout the day.

The **Gatlinburg Sky Lift** (tel. 615/436–4307) offers a bird's-eye view of the town, as does the **Ober Gatlinburg Tramway** (tel. 615/436–5423), which goes to a ski area and mountaintop amusement park. Both leave from 1001 Parkway.

Great Smoky Mountains Arts and Crafts Community (take U.S. 321 east of Gatlinburg and turn left on Glades Rd., tel. 615/436–3301) is an enclave of 70 shops and galleries scattered along back roads only 10 minutes outside Gatlinburg.

At the **Great Smoky Mountains National Park** (tel. 615/436–1200), shared by North Carolina and Tennessee, the Southern Appalachians reach their ultimate grandeur as 16 peaks soar more than 6,000 feet. Highlights of the park include *Clingmans Dome,* which, at 6,643 feet, is the highest point in Tennessee; you can take a spiral pathway to the top of an observation tower here for panoramic views of the Smokies. *Cades Cove* (tel. 615/448–6967) gives a beautiful picture of mountain life more than a century ago. In an isolated valley within the park are farmhouses, barns, churches, and an old gristmill still in operation.

Knoxville Zoological Gardens (Chilhowee Park on Rutledge Pike S, Exit 392, tel. 615/637–5331). Home to more than 1,000 animals, this zoo is famous for breeding big African cats and elephants.

Museum of Appalachia (Rte. 61, 1 mi east of I–75, Exit 122, Norris, tel. 615/494–7680). Three dozen log buildings are preserved in a compound; historical displays and exhibitions are sometimes punctuated by musical hoedowns.

The **Tennessee Aquarium** (1 Broad St., Chattanooga, tel. 615/265–0695), the largest freshwater facility of its kind, drew more than a million visitors in the six months after it opened in 1992. The fish range from 60-pound catfish, which prowl the Mississippi, to the small, mysterious fish that inhabit Japan's Shimanto River. The highlight of this world-class, $45 million aquarium is a spectacular 60-foot canyon, comprising two living forests and 22 tanks.

Restaurants

The **Apple Tree Restaurant** (Parkway and Frances Rd., Pigeon Forge, tel. 615/453–4961) offers a traditional and inexpensive menu of mountain cuisine, including fried chicken and barbecue. The **Green Valley Restaurant** (804 S. Parkway, Pigeon Forge, tel. 615/453–3500), just up the road, has similar fare, offering such dishes as biscuits and gravy with ham as well as seafood in a rough-hewn room with a fireplace.

In Gatlinburg, the **Burning Bush Restaurant** (1151 Parkway, tel. 615/436–4669), decked out with Colonial-era antiques, is a favorite for its sumptuous breakfasts and Continental menu, and the **Smoky Mountain Trout House** (410 N. Parkway, tel. 615/436–5416), aptly named, serves eight trout dishes in a cozy restaurant also known for its country fried chicken and prime rib.

The **Copper Cellar/Cumberland Grill** (1807 Cumberland Ave., Knoxville, tel. 615/673–3411), serving sandwiches and drinks, is a fun place to grab lunch or Sunday brunch.

Chattanooga's **212 Market Street** (212 Market St., tel. 615/265–1212), directly across from the Tennessee Aquarium, is a hip restaurant with a wide-ranging American menu.

Tourist Information

Chattanooga Area Convention and Visitors Bureau (1001 Market St., Chattanooga, TN 37402, tel. 615/756–8687, 800/338–3999 in TN, or 800/322–3344 outside TN). **Knoxville Area Convention and Visitors Bureau** (500 Henley St., Box 15012, Knoxville, TN 37901, tel. 615/523–7263 or 800/727–8045). **Northeast Tennessee Tourism Association** (Box 415, Jonesborough, TN 37659, tel. 615/753–4188 or 800/468–6882). **Smoky Mountain Visitors Bureau** (309 S. Washington St., Maryville, TN 37801, tel. 615/983–2241 or 800/525–6834).

Reservation Services

Bed & Breakfast Adventures (Box 150586, Nashville, TN 37215, tel. 615/383–6611 or 800/947–7404). **Tennessee Bed & Breakfast Innkeepers Association** (Box 120428, Nashville, TN 37212, tel. 615/321–5482 or 800/820–8144).

Adams Edgeworth Inn

Adams Edgeworth Inn is located atop the Cumberland Plateau inside a Victorian community nicknamed "the Chautauqua of the South." It is a Southern hotel in the grand, old-fashioned sense, with a broad wraparound porch and screen doors. Every summer, the Monteagle Assembly, the 96-acre community surrounding the inn, hosts an eight-week program of events that range from literary seminars to classical music concerts. Most of the assembly is vacant during the rest of the year, and guests at the inn are free to wander the enclave of 160 Victorian houses and scenic paths. Originally a boardinghouse, the inn was built in 1896 but was renovated and reopened in 1977; none of its authenticity seems to have been lost in the remodeling. The entire compound is listed on the National Register of Historic Places.

David and Wendy Adams, the owner-proprietors, retired from prominent jobs in Atlanta. Wendy was director of fund-raising for the city's opera and ballet, and David headed the research department at a brokerage firm. They are an outgoing, articulate couple who know the area well. The Edgeworth library boasts some 2,000 volumes, and its art collection ranges from Old-Master paintings to contemporary art and items of antiquity picked up during the Adamses' extensive travels.

A gentle quiet pervades the Edgeworth, where guests read, talk, or play board games. The rooms, which have 12-foot ceilings and a mix of Victorian antiques and modern furniture, are reminiscent of an English manor and border on the luxurious. Some rooms have fireplaces and four-poster beds; others have twin brass beds. The bridal suite has a Jacuzzi. In warm weather, the porch is the perfect place to spend an evening in a rocking chair; in the afternoon, the hammocks are irresistible. Breakfast is served in a cozy dining room, and five-course, candlelit dinners (by reservation) are served on antique china and silver. Wendy graduated from the Culinary Institute of America.

Nearby attractions include the University of the South at Sewanee, a small, well-respected school, and the South Cumberland State Recreation Area, which has some trails. The Monteagle Winery produces a nice selection of sweet German wines.

Address: *Monteagle Assembly, Box 372, Monteagle, TN 37356, tel. 615/924–2669.*
Accommodations: *13 double rooms with baths, 1 suite.*
Amenities: *Air-conditioning, cable TV in 5 rooms, library, and dining room, phone on each floor; pool, gift shop.*
Rates: *$60–$160; full breakfast. AE, MC, V.*
Restrictions: *No smoking indoors, no pets, 2-night minimum weekends and during summer assemblies.*

Big Spring Inn

Up a long drive shrouded by walnut, maple, pecan, and magnolia trees sits Big Spring Inn, a Greek Revival house built in 1905 as a wedding present. Since 1993, it has been owned by Nancy and Marshall Ricker, who worked as a manager of a speech pathology department and an architect, respectively, and traded the beauty of Bend, Oregon, for this dream.

The expansive, newly repaired front porch, outfitted with a white wicker porch swing and other wicker pieces, is welcoming. Inside, the Rickers have filled the rambling inn with English and American antiques and good reproductions, some purchased from a nearby antiques store, one of many. The 1790 Hepplewhite dining table seats 12 at reservation-only dinners for inn guests. The Rickers' taste runs to Laura Ashley prints and accessories, which nicely complement the oak floors; beveled, leaded-glass windows; and original chandeliers. Six chimneys punctuate the unusual roof line, and metal shingles produce a soothing rhythm in the rain. Of the bedrooms, a favorite is the Felice Noell Austin Room, a light, airy room with Victorian Rose wallpaper and a white wrought-iron bed. Its spacious bath has original black and white tiles, a walk-in shower, and a large tub. The Hassie Hacker Doughty Room, the original owners' master bedroom, has a fireplace with mantel,

large bay window, king-size antique brass bed, and oversize bathroom.

The Rickers are gracious yet unobtrusive hosts and provide many special touches. At 6:45 AM a tea cart appears on the second-floor landing for early risers. Rooms have robes, Caswell-Massey toiletries, and homemade pralines in the evenings, and croquet and other lawn games are often played in the well-kept yard.

The inn is in historic Greeneville, a New England–style village settled in 1783, and is a short walk from the burial site and birthplace of President Andrew Johnson. The village is close to plenty of attractions—the brilliant fall colors of the Cherokee National Forest and the Great Smoky Mountains; white-water rafting; the Dixon-Williams Mansion, a pre–Civil War showplace that housed troops from both sides; and storytelling in Jonesborough—but it's far from the crowds and mini–traffic jams that plague Gatlinburg.

Address: *315 N. Main St., Greeneville, TN 37745, tel. 615/638–2917.*
Accommodations: *2 double rooms and 2 singles with baths, 1 suite.*
Amenities: *Air-conditioning, cable TV on request and phones in rooms, Jacuzzi in 1 room; pool.*
Rates: *$70–$120; full breakfast. AE, MC, V.*
Restrictions: *No smoking, no pets.*

Blue Mountain Mist Country Inn

The Blue Mountain Mist Country Inn sits high on a hill amid a 60-acre farm at the foot of the Great Smoky Mountains, and the owners of this Victorian-style inn, Sarah and Norman Ball, have played their vantage point to the hilt. A wraparound porch is well equipped with leather deck chairs and wicker rockers, and a walking trail encircles the farm. In spring, flowers blossom in the yard; by summer, the pond, a short distance from the porch, is abloom with water lilies. Of course, fall, with its brilliant foliage, is the busiest season.

The Balls have deep roots in the area: Their parents grew up in the rugged terrain that is now Great Smoky Mountains National Park (one set lives on another farm across the road), so they know the history and geography of the area. Both were educators by profession—Sarah was an elementary school teacher, and Norm was principal at a vocational center.

Built in 1987, the inn is modeled after local, Victorian-style farmhouses. It's bright and airy and is furnished with family heirlooms, locally made quilts, and country crafts. Old photographs and paintings of the area, by the Balls' daughter and a local artist, hang on the walls, and two rooms are equipped with claw-foot tubs. The Bridal Room has a two-person whirlpool bath in the inn's turret,

which has windows on three sides. It shares a balcony and the mountain view with The Rainbow Falls Room, which has its own hot tub tucked behind a stained-glass partition, and with The LeConte Suite, the most spacious of the rooms. All bedrooms are carpeted.

Common areas upstairs and down have fireplaces and shiny hardwood floors. Each of the five small wooden cottages has a fully equipped kitchen, fireplace, TV and VCR, porch, and large whirlpool tub in the middle of the main room.

The inn, near Little Pigeon River, is on a country road that serves as a back door into both the park and the Great Smoky Mountains Arts and Crafts Community, circumventing much of the local traffic. Pigeon Forge, known for its outlet shopping, is just 4 miles away.

Address: *1811 Pullen Rd., Sevierville, TN 37862, tel. 615/428–2335.*
Accommodations: *12 double rooms with baths, 5 housekeeping cottages.*
Amenities: *Meal service for groups, cable TV with VCR and phone in parlor.*
Rates: *$79–$125; full breakfast, evening dessert. MC, V.*
Restrictions: *No smoking, no pets, 2-night minimum holidays and Oct., inn closed Dec. 23–25, inn and cottages closed last 2 weeks in Jan.*

Buckhorn Inn

The lobby of the Buckhorn Inn, which is on a wooded hillside at the edge of Great Smoky Mountains National Park, commands one of the best views of the local peaks, and several of the rooms have good views as well. Designed to blend in with its surroundings, the inn has a rustic flavor much as it must have had when it was built in 1938. The Buckhorn is in the middle of a lush, 35-acre estate surrounded by pine trees; comfortable fireside chairs in the sitting and dining rooms invite guests to relax with a glass of wine and look out on Mt. LeConte, one of the highest peaks in the Smokies. A Steinway grand piano rests in one niche of the lobby, and a library dubbed the "hikers' corner" is in another spot. This inn, well-loved shabby in decor, appeals to the old-money crowd.

Rooms are small—almost to the point of being cramped—but all are carpeted and furnished with simple but understated grace. The most interesting bedroom is in the inn's original water tower, where bath facilities are on one level and the bedroom is above. It has the feel of a tree house. On all but the warmest days of the year, the scent of wood smoke lingers in the air. In the dining room, breakfast and a six-course gourmet dinner (by reservation only) are served on small tables with green tablecloths. Four cottages and two relatively spacious guest houses are

on the grounds, but the cottages are a cut or two below the inn rooms. Each is equipped with a fireplace and a screened-in porch with a good view, but the carpets are worn, the beds are on the soft side, and the buildings themselves are made of cinder blocks, with concrete decks. The two-bedroom guest houses, one of which can accommodate conferences, have much more room but are not much more comfortable than the cottages.

Nonetheless, this secluded inn with its own ½-mile nature trail and fishing pond remains one of the best in the Smokies. It's 1 mile from the entrance to the national park and about 6 miles northeast of Gatlinburg and its myriad activities. It is in the midst of some 70 shops, galleries, and eateries of the secluded Great Smoky Mountains Arts and Crafts Community.

Address: *2140 Tudor Mtn. Rd., Gatlinburg, TN 37738, tel. 615/436-4668.*
Accommodations: *6 double rooms with baths, 4 cottages, 2 guest houses.*
Amenities: *Air-conditioning, cable TV in cottages, phone in lobby.*
Rates: *$95-125, 2-bedroom guest house $175-250; full country breakfast. MC, V.*
Restrictions: *Smoking on patio and in 2 cottages only, no pets, 2-night minimum holidays, weekends, and Oct.*

Von-Bryan Inn

The Von-Bryan Inn commands what may well be the best mountaintop bed-and-breakfast view in the Smokies. A crooked dirt road climbs to the inn, situated on a knoll with a 360-degree vista of the surrounding mountains. Morning mist typically blankets the patchwork farmlands in Wears Valley below and the wooded dales beyond.

Jo Ann and D. J. Vaughn bought the house from the original owner, who built it in 1986 as a private retreat, and they now run the place with their sons, David and Patrick. Jo Ann, who operated a telephone-answering service in Knoxville, and D. J., a retired corporate accountant, opened the Von-Bryan after traveling extensively in surrounding states to research country inns. They are quiet but amicable people who offer plentiful advice on the area. D. J., a woodworker by hobby, made many of the pendulum clocks in the house and some of the furniture. The inn's builder emphasized wood surfaces and soaring, cathedral-like ceilings. Bright skylights filter in the sunshine, and big windows frame the view.

Every room, furnished in a blend of traditional and country antiques, has a view. The honeymoon suite—one of two with a whirlpool—is appropriately decorated in passionate red hues. A trilevel suite has a canopy bed draped with silk wisteria on the second floor, a bath with a steam shower on the

first, and a reading loft on the third. Three skylights and wraparound windows with a view of the English country garden add to the romance. A plush canopy bed graces another room, two brass beds from the Middle East are in another, and a queen-size spool bed anchors yet another room. Soft jazz is usually on the stereo in the common area upstairs, and a fireplace blazes in the downstairs living room. In summer, the pool is a good place to bask in the sun; the deck out back is open year-round—it's just off the garden room, which has its own hot tub. The inn is aptly equipped with a telescope for a closer look at distant sights. The log cabin chalet, designed for families, has a full kitchen and a television room as well as a living room with a fireplace, three bedrooms (one with a balcony), and two bathrooms. It has a wraparound deck, too, and a whirlpool bath. Gatlinburg, Pigeon Forge, Dollywood, and the entrance to the national park are within 30 minutes.

Address: *2402 Hatcher Mtn. Rd., Sevierville, TN 37862, tel. 615/453–9832 or 800/633–1459, fax 615/428–8634.*
Accommodations: *5 double rooms with baths, 1 suite, 1 chalet.*
Amenities: *Air-conditioning, TV in living room, phone in library.*
Rates: *$80–$125, chalet $160; full buffet breakfast. AE, MC, V.*
Restrictions: *No smoking, no pets.*

Bluff View Inn

This 1928 Colonial Revival mansion hugging a bluff high above the Tennessee River is Chattanooga's best B&B. Owner Charles A. Portera, an oncologist, has spared no expense in restoring it. Within walking distance are the Tennessee Aquarium and the famed Walnut Street Bridge, one of the nation's oldest pedestrian bridges. The nearby River Gallery Sculpture Garden is a pleasant spot to wander.

Tastefully decorated bedrooms have whirlpool baths and fireplaces. The C. G. Martin Room has a firm king-size bed and a private balcony overlooking the river. Glossy hardwood floors, white silk wallpaper, dark walnut paneling, and English, Queen Anne, and Chippendale antiques and fine reproductions dominate the downstairs. Shades of plum and teal add to the richness of the fabrics, and simple dried roses and fresh lilies dot the mantels and tables. The art—mainly glass and pottery—is switched every two weeks and is on sale at the River Gallery, down the street. You can eat in the fine restaurant, which has views of the river to the east, or in the more casual Back Inn Cafe, offering Italian bistro fare.

Address: *412 E. 2nd St., Chattanooga, TN 37403, tel. 615/265-5033.*
Accommodations: *3 double rooms with baths.*
Amenities: *Air-conditioning, cable TV and phones in rooms.*
Rates: *$125–$175; full gourmet breakfast. DC, MC, V.*
Restrictions: *No smoking, no pets.*

Hale Springs Inn

Overnighters here stay in the same rooms that hosted presidents James Polk, Andrew Jackson, and Andrew Johnson. Once an important stop in the nation's westward expansion, Rogersville is now off the beaten path, a Colonial-style burg known mostly for its tranquillity. The town is an hour from the Great Smoky Mountains National Park, and this Federal-style inn is right on its square.

Built in 1824–25 of bricks made from a formula that slaves imported from Virginia, the inn—the oldest continuously operated in the state—was restored in 1981–82. Ed Pace, a retired TVA administrator, is the garrulous manager. The lobby has a friendly, small-town quality about it, and rooms are decorated in the austere fashion of its frontier heyday. Original bent-pine floors and 12-foot ceilings remain, and each bedroom has a fireplace. Central heating takes the chill off the spacious rooms, and the slight mustiness is overshadowed by the air of authenticity. There is a porch off the hallway on each of three levels; a small garden with a gazebo is next door.

Address: *110 W. Main St., Rogersville, TN 37857, tel. 615/272-5171.*
Accommodations: *9 double rooms with baths.*
Amenities: *Restaurant, air-conditioning, cable TV in rooms, phone in sitting room.*
Rates: *$45–$90; Continental breakfast. AE, MC, V.*
Restrictions: *No pets, closed Dec. 25.*

Hippensteal's Mountain View Inn

This rambling, white, three-story New England–style inn is situated in the Great Smoky Mountains Arts and Crafts Community. From the broad-plank wraparound porch, equipped with rockers and ceiling fans, you can see Greenbriar Pinnacle, Mt. LeConte, and Mt. Harrison. The inn is owned by Lisa and Vern Hippensteal—he's one of the area's leading watercolorists, concentrating on local scenes. His work is in evidence throughout the inn.

The grand lobby has black and white tiles and hunter green walls; a fireplace blazes in winter. The great room is decorated with white wicker and English chintz. In the bedrooms, which have whirlpools and fireplaces, romance is on tap. The popular Victorian room has reading chairs and a private, spacious bath, whose whirlpool tub fits two. Though the inn seems far from the madding crowds, Gatlinburg is still convenient. During the holidays, the spot provides an ideal vantage point for Gatlinburg's Million Dollar Smoky Mountain Lights, a popular display. Book well in advance for October.

Address: *Grassy Branch Rd. (Box 707), Gatlinburg, TN 37738, tel. 615/436–5761 or 800/527–8110.*
Accommodations: *8 double rooms with baths.*
Amenities: *Air-conditioning, ceiling fans, TV and phone jacks in rooms.*
Rates: *$115; full gourmet breakfast, evening dessert. AE, D, MC, V.*
Restrictions: *No smoking, no pets, closed Dec. 24–25.*

Richmont Inn

Designed for its mountain setting, this inn looks like a gray cantileverd barn. Opened in 1992 by Susan and Jim Hind, two former corporate executives eager to escape city life, this haven for couples is a short drive from postcard-perfect Cades Cove.

The main living room has beamed ceilings, broad-plank floors, and 18th-century English and American antiques. Crammed bookshelves flank the fireplace in the great room. One bedroom is paneled with old bar boards; others are bathed in light. Some have spa tubs and private balconies. Old family photographs are tastefully mingled with Impressionist paintings, and antiques are a mix of formal and country. Rustic twig furniture and rocking chairs on a stone patio provide a comfortable spot from which to take in the views.

Guests are pampered here. Dessert is served on china by the light of old-fashioned hurricane globes. A single rose and gourmet chocolates are left on down pillows. Classical harp music is piped into rooms, or you can just enjoy the sound of gurgling water from the 40-foot cascade dropping into a man-made pond.

Address: *220 Winterberry La., Townsend, TN 37882, tel. 615/448–6751.*
Accommodations: *10 double rooms with baths.*
Amenities: *Air-conditioning, phone on landing; gift shop, nature trail.*
Rates: *$85–$120; full breakfast, evening dessert. No credit cards.*
Restrictions: *No smoking, no pets.*

Tennessee Ridge Inn

Perched on top of a mountain with a smashing view of 6,500-foot Mt. LeConte is this ultramodern chalet with walls of windows. Gatlinburg is only a five-minute, 1-mile drive below, but you feel far removed from its touristy kitsch. "Noise" here is the occasional drumming of a woodpecker getting breakfast. Nearby are trout fishing, hiking, rafting, and swimming.

Bob and Dar Hullander sampled inns in Europe, the Far East, and the Caribbean before opening their own. They've furnished it with a sleek mix of cool-colored modern pieces—primarily Oriental, and many picked up on their sojourns to distant lands. Most rooms have views facing south, to the grand majesty of the mountains. Four bedrooms have stone fireplaces, and all have private balconies, private baths with two-person whirlpool tubs, and king-size beds. Honeymooners seek out the inn because of the romance, privacy, and view of the mountains with the bright lights of the city glowing below.

Address: *507 Campbell Lead Rd., Gatlinburg, TN 37738, tel. 615/436–4068.*
Accommodations: *5 double rooms with baths.*
Amenities: *Air-conditioning, cable TV in rooms on request, phones in great room and lounge; pool.*
Rates: *$98–$135; full deluxe breakfast. AE, D, MC, V.*
Restrictions: *Smoking on balconies only, no pets, 2-night minimum weekends, 3-night minimum holidays, closed Jan.*

Wayside Manor

Mother-and-daughter team Becky and Abby Koella have made the most of their redbrick, tile-roofed, turn-of-the-century estate, just outside Knoxville. They cater to the corporate crowd with elaborate meals and attention to detail. Becky, who is retired from public relations, grew up in the Smokies. With a little encouragement, she charms guests with lively tales of mountain life.

Victorian lampposts and elaborate wrought-iron benches punctuate the grand lawn, where croquet is often played. A screened porch dominates the front of the house, while the side yard has lighted tennis, basketball, and volleyball courts. A man-made lake comes complete with gazebo and waterfall. Badminton rackets, shuffleboard, bikes, and a hot tub are available as well, and there's fishing, horseback riding, and golf nearby. Baby-sitting is offered. Inside, the plushly carpeted house has high ceilings and French doors. Fresh flowers and old quilts are the centerpieces of an eclectic style mixing modern with antique.

Address: *4009 Old Knoxville Hwy. 33, Rockford, TN 37853, tel. 615/970–4823 or 800/675–4823, fax 615/981–1890.*
Accommodations: *6 double rooms with baths, 2 suites, 1 cottage.*
Amenities: *Air-conditioning, TV with VCR and phones in rooms, Jacuzzis in suites, business center; pool.*
Rates: *$90–$135; full deluxe breakfast. D, MC, V.*
Restrictions: *Smoking on porch only, no pets.*

Middle Tennessee

The sprawling city of Nashville (population more than 1 million) extends over eight counties in the middle Tennessee heartland, a pocket of rolling Cumberland Mountains foothills and bluegrass meadows that's one of the state's richest farming areas. Its impressive skyline, dotted with high-rise office towers, is a vivid reminder that it has been a long time indeed since Christmas Day 1779, when James Robertson and a small, shivering party of pioneers began to build a crude wooden fortress and palisades on the Cumberland River's west bank.

Heralded as the world's Country Music Capital and Music City USA, it also proudly calls itself the Athens of the South. The labels fit, and Nashville is one of the middle South's liveliest cities. Its role as a cultural leader is enhanced by an impressive performing arts center and the many colleges, universities, and medical and technical schools located here, most notably Vanderbilt University.

A rich Southern heritage is evident in the surrounding countryside, where highways meander through farmland punctuated by small towns. Lynchburg, home of the Jack Daniel Distillery, is among the most famous of the outlying communities. Franklin, a restored 19th-century town that historian Shelby Foote calls one of the top three Civil War sites, has excellent antiques shops and art galleries. Columbia, site of the family home of President James K. Polk, is famous for its antebellum architecture. West of Nashville, Clarksville boasts its own vineyards and winery as well as several sites memorializing the colorful past of the Old South, from its frontier heyday to its Civil War pain.

Places to Go, Sights to See

Belle Meade Mansion (110 Leake Ave., Nashville, tel. 615/356–0501). One of the grand old houses of Nashville, this Greek Revival home is set on a 5,300-

acre estate near Centennial Park off West End Avenue. It is known for its Thoroughbred horse stables and a Victorian carriage museum.

Cheekwood (1200 Forest Park Dr., Nashville, tel. 615/356–8000). This verdant estate and Georgian-style mansion, built in the 1920s, is now a fine arts center. It's surrounded by the 55-acre *Tennessee Botanical Gardens,* a showcase picnic ground graced by roses, herbs, and Southern wildflowers.

Country Music Hall of Fame (4 Music Sq. E, Nashville, tel. 615/256–1639). The definitive collection of country music memorabilia is housed here—from Elvis Presley's "solid gold" Cadillac to Kris Kristofferson's songwriting scribbles and Marty Robbins's six-string guitar. The museum ticket is also good for admission to nearby *Studio B,* where Dolly Parton, Elvis, and Roy Acuff—among many others—recorded classic hits.

The District (Nashville). Two blocks off the Cumberland River in the Church Street vicinity is one of the country's best-preserved rows of 19th-century commercial buildings, now transformed into some of the town's best restaurants, nightclubs, and boutiques.

The Hermitage (4580 Rachel's La., 12 mi east of Nashville, tel. 615/889–2941), built by President Andrew Jackson for his beloved wife, Rachel, is in a bucolic setting just beyond the urban sprawl of Nashville. It is the perfect place for a stroll beneath huge live oaks.

Jack Daniel Distillery (¼ mi northeast of Lynchburg on Rte. 55, tel. 615/759–6180). Demonstrations on the art of making Tennessee sourmash whiskey are given on daily tours.

Opryland USA (2802 Opryland Dr., Nashville, tel. 615/889–6611). The musical show park offers performances of 12 different musicals and two dozen rides as well as restaurants and shops. Opryland is also home to the Grand Ole Opry House.

The Parthenon (off West End Ave., Centennial Park, Nashville, tel. 615/862–8431). This exact replica of the Grecian original includes a gigantic statue of the goddess Athena and an art museum.

Restaurants

In Nashville, **The Wild Boar** (2014 Broadway, tel. 615/329–1313) offers fine Continental fare and wild game in a setting resembling an old English hunting lodge. The **Elliston Place Soda Shop** (24th Ave. and Elliston Pl., tel. 615/327–1090), an old-fashioned meat and three near Vanderbilt that is not generally known to tourists, serves wonderful diner-style lunches and malts big enough for two. The **Loveless Café** (8400 Rte. 100, tel. 615/646–9700) continues to draw lovers of Southern food to its almost rural setting for a menu rich in local cuisine; reservations are advised. **The Bluebird Cafe** (4104 Hillsboro Rd., tel. 615/383–1461) is famed for launching songwriters' careers—Garth Brooks was discovered here—and for good American fare.

At **Miss Mary Bobo's Boarding House** (Main St., tel. 615/759–7394), an 1867 white frame home in Lynchburg, chatty hostesses serve a midday all-you-can-eat dinner of country fare every day but Sunday to a usually talkative crowd.

Tourist Information

Nashville Convention & Visitors Bureau (161 4th Ave. N, Nashville, TN 37219, tel. 615/259–4700). **Nashville Tourist Information Center** (I–65 and James Robertson Pkwy., Exit 85, Nashville, TN 37202, tel. 615/259–4747). **Tennessee Department of Tourist Development** (Box 23170, Nashville, TN 37202, tel. 615/741–2158) is good for information on outlying areas.

Reservation Services

Bed & Breakfast Adventures (Box 150586, Nashville, TN 37215, tel. 615/383–6611 or 800/947–7404). **Tennessee Bed & Breakfast Innkeepers Association** (Box 120428, Nashville, TN 37212, tel. 615/321–5482 or 800/820–8144).

Hachland Hill Dining Inn

The his inn is a treat for the traveler in search of a rustic evening beside a fireplace. Forty-five minutes north of Nashville in rural Clarksville, it is surrounded by an 80-acre park full of raccoon, deer, and other wildlife. Trails wander into the woods, and guests wake up to the sound of birds.

Phila Hach is an extraordinary hostess, a worldly woman who was a flight attendant before settling down with her late husband, Adolph Hach, and founding the inn 35 years ago. She appears on local television shows and is the author of eight cookbooks. The dinner menu is laden with fried chicken, Tennessee country ham, and surprises like Moroccan leg of lamb (pricey but worth the splurge), or indulge in the decadent, full Southern breakfast (extra charge). Phila's specialty is catering large events; the grand ballroom seats 300.

Phila designed the inn after Federal-style Cape Cod homes, and on winter nights, soup bubbles in a pot dangling on a fireplace crane. The bedrooms are neat and comfortable, with historic touches: One has a spool bed with a wedding-ring quilt, and many of the furnishings throughout are Early American. Some have Germanic touches, heirlooms from the time when Phila's family emigrated from their North Sea environs. The mantel keystone over the main fireplace is from the long-since-demolished local tobacco exchange (Adolph was a tobacconist). An 1870 cigar store Indian is on the premises, and a 150-year-old, 2,000-piece "postage-stamp" quilt hangs from a wall. The Hachs traveled widely, and items from their sojourns are in evidence: a Japanese print here, a Swiss vase there.

The 1790 House, a cabin connected to the inn by a breezeway, has been transformed into a dormitory space for those taking part in a wedding or reunion. Out back sit a pair of cabins, perfect for either romantic solitude or family lodging. Each cabin has two levels and modern bathrooms and comes with a guarantee of tranquillity; though the cabins are equipped with phones on which guests can dial out, the phones do not ring. The cabins are on a wide, shady terrace, where warm-weather cookouts are held, overlooking a wooded ravine near a pen where a pair of goats live.

Address: *1601 Madison St., Clarksville, TN 37043, tel. 615/647-4084, fax 615/552-3454.*
Accommodations: *7 double rooms with baths, 3 cabins.*
Amenities: *Air-conditioning, TV with VCR in 2 rooms, nonringing phones in rooms, office facilities.*
Rates: *$65; Continental breakfast. AE, MC, V.*
Restrictions: *Closed Dec. 24–25.*

McEwen Farm
Log Cabin
Bed & Breakfast

The McEwen Farm Log Cabin Bed & Breakfast features a trio of buildings for rent on a farm 2 miles from the Natchez Trace, hidden away on a back road. No signs point the way, but it's easy enough to find: just north of the crossroads community of Duck River, named for the slow-moving waterway known for small-mouth bass and catfish as well as canoeing. Bill and Helen McEwen run the place from their house on a hilltop pasture several hundred yards from the well-spaced lodgings, evidently situated with privacy in mind. The farm is a popular stopover for bicyclists traveling the Natchez Trace Parkway, and it attracts visiting joggers and walkers as well to its big, quiet fields.

Helen is a homemaker, and Bill, a community college administrator, raises hunting dogs; the hounds are kept in pens near the barn, their howls occasionally piercing the otherwise quiet night. The McEwens began hosting guests in 1987, after restoring a log cabin that dates back to the 1820s. They designed the cabin on the back of a paper sack with the intention of turning it into a guest house for family and friends, but passersby were drawn to it immediately. The original structure belies its age; its floors and walls are rugged but clean, and the main room, which has a fireplace, leads into a modern kitchen. Outside there is a porch swing; upstairs are three beds. Cabin

No. 2—next to a railroad sign that says, "McEwen Crossing, elevation 607"—is much like No. 1.

Downhill in an adjacent dale is No. 3, which is not a cabin at all but a restored 1879 Victorian passenger train depot from nearby Centerville, where it served the Nashville, Chattanooga, and St. Louis railways. The most secluded of the lodgings, it is completely wrapped by a wooden deck generously furnished with rocking chairs that face a tiny stream. It has two bedrooms, one bath, and a kitchen beneath its original 14-foot ceilings, where fans turn lazily. The ticket window has been turned into a reading nook. Family antiques— country-style tables and sideboards— furnish the cozy cabins.

Guests at McEwen Farm are welcome to meet the hunting dogs or wander the grounds at will. Nashville is 45 minutes away, and—this being Tennessee walking horse country— stables abound.

Address: *Bratton La. (Box 97), Duck River, TN 38454, tel. 615/583–2378.*
Accommodations: *3 cabins.*
Amenities: *Air-conditioning; canoe rental.*
Rates: *$85; Continental breakfast. MC, V.*
Restrictions: *No smoking.*

Monthaven Bed & Breakfast

To meet the host of Monthaven Bed & Breakfast is to encounter something of Nashville's fabled country-music world. Musician Hugh Waddell maintains a record library of 10,000 albums he shows to his guests, and he happily talks about the industry he has come to know through his role as Johnny Cash's publicist. Hugh, an intelligent and witty man whose business cards say "Johnny Cash Sent Me," operates the Greek Revival mansion with panache. The place has been in his family for 32 years. Hugh inherited it from his mother, who opened Monthaven in the early 1980s as a casual lodge for family and friends but gradually accepted other visitors.

Monthaven, decorated with Victorian elements inside and out, was built as a plantation home around 1840 on the site of a former Indian campground and today remains separated by considerable acreage from its closest neighbors. It sits well above a busy highway, maintaining a tranquil air, though it's within 30 minutes of every Nashville attraction. No sign marks the driveway, noted only by an old-fashioned mailbox and a simple stone gate. Old trees ring the mansion, and the 75-acre working farm has horses, goats, and cows, which roam its pastures. The place is rich in history, including a Civil War association that saw it used as a military hospital for both Union and Confederate soldiers.

A guest cabin nearby was reconstructed in 1938 from logs that went into a similar structure almost 200 years ago. Finished inside with white oak and cedar, it is a roomy but romantic building with a big fireplace in the living room. The cabin also has a full kitchen and sports some oddities, such as a ping-pong table and a museum-style glass case that holds local memorabilia running the gamut from old pharmaceuticals to Civil War bullets.

The house itself has two guest rooms—one upstairs and one down—that are far less rustic than the cabin, furnished with antiques and four-poster beds beneath high ceilings. The small library just off the main hall features some striking French provincial parlor furniture, and a hallway chandelier adds to the inn's feel. Animal lovers will appreciate the Monthaven fauna, which includes cats as well as a dog named Johnny Cash. Guests' pets are allowed; a kennel on the property can accommodate large dogs.

Address: *1154 W. Main St., Hendersonville, TN 37075, tel. 615/824–6319.*
Accommodations: *2 double rooms with baths, 1 cabin.*
Amenities: *Air-conditioning, cable TV in library, TV in cabin; pool.*
Rates: *$75–$85; Continental breakfast. AE, D, DC, MC, V.*
Restrictions: *Smoking on porch only.*

Old Cowan Plantation

The Old Cowan Plantation captures some of the genteel charm of the Old South in an 1886 Colonial home beside a country road. Hostess Betty Johnson's ambition was to open an antiques shop in the house, but after deciding there was a glut of such businesses in nearby Fayetteville, she turned the house into an inn and gift shop, filling a void in local lodging. Though it was modernized in 1985, the place clings tenaciously to its farmhouse ambience.

Betty's hobbies show up around the house in various handicrafts, quilts, and cross-stitch items, many of them priced for sale in the gift shop, which doubles as a bedroom when there's no room at the inn. The room has a gas-log fireplace.

One upstairs room has a brass bed and a spacious bath and shower; the other is equipped with a pair of twin beds and uses a bath downstairs with a pedestal tub. The home's original staircase leads to a narrow landing with an antique pie safe that now serves as a linen closet. Breakfast is served at a lace-covered table with a view of the neighboring pasture.

The inn's rural setting is one of its biggest draws. In spring, the yard is full of wildflowers, and a rose garden blooms in June. When snow covers the ground, oak and magnolia trees frame the house in a striking winter scene. Guests usually gravitate to the front-porch rocking chairs, particularly in the early evening, when deer graze across the road and sometimes even wander into the yard.

The Old Cowan Plantation is 2 miles from Fayetteville's town square and 15 miles from the Jack Daniel Distillery at Lynchburg. It is 30 miles from the Space and Rocket Center in Huntsville, Alabama, where you can tour NASA labs and space shuttle test sites and roam through a park full of rockets, visit the center's hands-on museum, or view an Omnimax space film. Fifteen minutes away is Tims Ford Lake, with waterskiing in summer and fishing year-round. The inn is just north of U.S. 64, which has been designated an official scenic highway east almost to Chattanooga and as far west as Shiloh National Military Park, site of a bloody Civil War battle.

Address: *126 Old Boonshill Rd., Fayetteville, TN 37334, tel. 615/433–0225.*
Accommodations: *2 double rooms with baths, 1 apartment.*
Amenities: *Air-conditioning, phones in hall and kitchen.*
Rates: *$42; Continental breakfast. No credit cards.*
Restrictions: *No smoking, pets in fenced backyard only.*

Bird Song Country Inn

At the turn of the century, the Cheek family of Maxwell House coffee fame had a passion for Jackson Hole, Wyoming. In 1910 they re-created the rambling, cedar-log lodge there as a summer home 20 minutes from Nashville. In 1991, current owners Anne and Brooks Parker turned this showplace into a country inn. They are passionate collectors; she previously owned an antiques store in an exclusive Nashville neighborhood. Eclectic antiques range from English country to folk to Empire. The screened-in porch overlooks English perennial gardens. For a respite from the bustle of Music City, there's a heated spa, a hammock under oak trees, or a massage by a registered therapist. You can also arrange canoeing, golf, and horseback riding.

Large bedrooms are stocked with snacks. One has an 1840 Empire sleigh bed with a down comforter and a Persian rug. Another is decked out with a white-iron bed, pre–Civil War caned rocker, and braided rug. Two bedrooms can be combined to make a suite.

Address: *Sycamore Mill, 1306 Rte. 49 E, Ashland City, TN 37015, tel. and fax 615/792–4005.*
Accommodations: *3 double rooms with baths.*
Amenities: *Air-conditioning; pool.*
Rates: *$90–$135; deluxe Continental breakfast, welcoming refreshments. AE, D, MC, V.*
Restrictions: *Smoking on porch only.*

Lynchburg Bed & Breakfast

This cozy, centrally located inn is near the famous Jack Daniel Distillery in Lynchburg, a speck of a town established in 1871 in the farmland of south-central Tennessee. The proprietors, Virginia and Mike Tipps, opened it in 1985. Longtime area residents—Virginia is a former mail clerk and Mike is in quality control at the distillery—they know what to see and do around Lynchburg.

The 1877 two-story house (built for Moore County's first sheriff) is decorated with country antiques. Both of its slightly cramped bedrooms, which have antique walnut washstands, are up a narrow staircase. They can be combined as a suite. The second-floor common area leads to a small balcony that's a good place to

sip morning coffee. From here the distillery's warehouses, where its famous whiskey is aged, are visible. The distillery has tours daily, and visitors won't want to miss midday dinner at nearby Miss Mary Bobo's Boarding House. The tiny town square, a block away, has a handful of antiques and arts and crafts shops centered on a monument to Confederate soldiers.

Address: *Mechanic St. (Box 34), Lynchburg, TN 37352, tel. 615/759–7158.*
Accommodations: *2 double rooms with baths.*
Amenities: *Air-conditioning, cable TV in rooms, portable phone.*
Rates: *$50; Continental breakfast. MC, V.*
Restrictions: *No pets.*

Lyric Springs Country Inn

Nestled in the green, rolling hills of Franklin, a 15-minute drive from Nashville's Music Row, is a real find. Bright and cheery, decorated in 1940s Americana and uptown country antiques, this inn began as a one-room log cabin a century ago and has turned into a sprawling cedar home. Talent agent and hostess Patsy Bruce, who penned the country classic "Mammas, Don't Let Your Babies Grow Up to Be Cowboys," is the perennial Nashville insider. A vivacious woman in her mid-50s, Patsy is full of stories and ideas about where to go. She'll gladly arrange tickets to the Grand Ole Opry—not always easy to come by—but there's also plenty to explore on the property, on foot or horseback, or on Franklin's beautifully restored Main Street.

The large bedrooms are imaginatively decorated and offer privacy. One has framed collections of old linens, while a yellow-and-white checkerboard floor creates a light mood in another. A billiard table in a common room pays homage to the cowboy era. Two chefs oversee the gourmet lunch and dinner (by reservation). If you're visiting Nashville and want a pleasant dose of "the country" to go along with all the country music, Lyric Springs hits the right note.

Address: *7306 S. Harpeth Rd., Franklin, TN 37064, tel. 615/329–3385 or 800/621–7824.*
Accommodations: *3 double rooms with baths.*
Amenities: *Air-conditioning; pool.*
Rates: *$100; full breakfast. MC, V.*
Restrictions: *No smoking.*

West Tennessee

The mighty Mississippi River defines the western boundary of Tennessee, rolling through the fertile plain of the Delta and past the "cradle of the blues" on its way to the sea. Stretching east and north from Memphis, the western plains where cotton was king are interspersed with hardwood forests, wildlife refuges, and state parks. Outdoor types flock to the region's rivers and lakes, including Kentucky Lake, on the Kentucky border, the second-largest man-made lake in the world.

You can hear stories of folk heroes Davy Crockett and Casey Jones, explore the Civil War battlefield at Shiloh National Military Park, and visit the late Alex Haley's hometown of Henning.

The culture of the Mississippi Delta converges in Memphis, a city with a uniquely American music heritage that is well preserved today behind the gates of Elvis's beloved Graceland, on stage at the Beale Street nightclubs, and in the oft-told tales of rockers like Elvis Presley and Jerry Lee Lewis, whose careers were launched at tiny Sun Studio.

The city celebrates the mighty Mississippi with an entertainment park on Mud Island, and The Pyramid, beside the Hernando DeSoto Bridge, is actually the world's third-largest pyramid. The Memphis in May International Festival, scheduled before the arrival of summer's heat and humidity, pays tribute to the city's music and features the open-air World Championship Barbecue Cooking Contest. In November, there's Blues Music Week. Memphis honors the civil rights movement and Martin Luther King, Jr., at the National Civil Rights Museum.

Places to Go, Sights to See

Alex Haley State Historic Site Museum (Haley St., Henning, tel. 901/738–2240). The boyhood home and burial site of the Pulitzer

Prize–winning author of *Roots* is in this charming little river town 50 miles north of Memphis via U.S. 51.

Beale Street Historic District. A restored row of nightclubs and shops pays homage to the Memphis blues. Highlights include the *W.C. Handy Memphis Home and Museum* (352 Beale St., call ahead, tel. 901/527–2583); the *Old Daisy Theatre* (329 Beale St., tel. 901/525–1631), which was built in 1918 and shows continuously running silent short films; and any of 10 nightclubs, whose acts are advertised in the *Memphis Commercial Appeal.* The *Rum Boogie Café* (182 Beale St., tel. 901/528–1050) has one of the best house bands in the city, and *B.B. King's Blues Club* (147 Beale St., tel. 901/527–5464) features appearances by its famous eponym.

The **Casey Jones Home and Railroad Museum** (U.S. 45 Bypass and I–40, Jackson, tel. 901/668–1222), adjacent to an old-fashioned ice-cream shop, houses an excellent collection of train memorabilia.

Chucalissa Archaeological Museum (1987 Indian Village Dr., Memphis, tel. 901/785–3160). At this peaceful, thought-provoking site about 10 miles southwest of downtown, a simple river culture that existed from 1000 to 1500 is immortalized. The 4-acre reconstruction is operated by Memphis State University, and on-site archaeological excavations are often conducted during the summer. Outside, skilled Choctaw artisans fashion jewelry, weapons, and pottery. An annual August powwow is a highlight.

Dixon Gallery and Gardens (4339 Park Ave., Memphis, tel. 901/761–5250) blends art with nature, displaying French and post-Impressionist paintings and 18th-century Germanic porcelain in a museum surrounded by 17 acres of flowers.

Graceland (3717 Elvis Presley Blvd., Memphis, tel. 901/332–3322 or 800/238–2000), the city's most popular attraction, offers a glitzy and sometimes poignant look at Elvis Presley, who lived and is buried here and whose memory generates a sizable souvenir industry for a row of shops across the street.

Mud Island. The 53-acre Memphis park is accessible by walkway, boat, or monorail (boat terminal, 125 Front St., tel. 901/576–7241). Attractions include a 5,000-seat amphitheater, the 18-gallery *Mississippi River Museum*, and the exceptional *River Walk*, a scale model of the great river five blocks long, tracing every bend of the Mississippi on its journey from Minnesota to the Gulf of Mexico.

National Civil Rights Museum (406 Mulberry St., Memphis, tel. 901/521–9699). The civil rights struggle of the 1950s and '60s is documented in the former Lorraine Motel, where the Rev. Martin Luther King, Jr., was assassinated in 1968.

National Ornamental Metal Museum (374 W. California St., Memphis, tel. 901/774–6380). This one-of-a-kind place is devoted to preserving the art of metalworking, from gold to iron. Exhibits include a working blacksmith's forge.

Peabody Hotel (149 Union Ave., Memphis, tel. 901/529–4175 or 800/732–2639). This Memphis treasure was restored and reopened in 1981 after two decades of neglect. It's worth a trip just to see the resplendent lobby, where the hotel's famous ducks spend the day.

The Pyramid (on the Mississippi River at I–40, Memphis, tel. 901/521–1830). The 32-story stainless-steel structure has a 20,000-seat sports arena.

Shiloh National Military Park (off U.S. 64 on Rte. 22, tel. 901/689–5696). A beautiful country setting 100 miles east of Memphis is a grim reminder of the horrific Civil War battle and of the 4,000 soldiers buried here.

Sun Studio (706 Union Ave., Memphis, tel. 901/521–0664), a working recording studio by night, offers daytime tours on the hour through the famous spot where Elvis Presley, Carl Perkins, Johnny Cash, and Jerry Lee Lewis made their first records. The adjacent *Sun Studio Café* sells burgers and chili.

Restaurants

In Memphis, **Landry's Seafood House** (263 Wagner Pl., tel. 901/526–1966), on the riverfront, draws a loyal following for its seafood. In the Peabody Hotel (149 Union Ave.) **Chez Philippe** (tel. 901/529–4188) is worth the splurge, or for sandwiches and pastries made daily, try **Café Espresso** (tel. 901/529–4164). **Charlie Vergos' Rendezvous** (General Washburn Alley, tel. 901/523–2746), famous for its pork barbecue, is a real Memphis institution. **John Wills' Bar and Grill** (5101 Sanderlin Rd., tel. 901/761–5101) serves good barbecue, baked beans, and mustard-spiced coleslaw in an upscale atmosphere, while **Corky's Bar-B-Q** (5259 Poplar Ave., tel. 901/685–9744) is the place to do some down and dirty barbecue eating. **La Tourelle** (Overton Sq., 2146 Monroe Ave., tel. 901/726–5771), in an elegant turn-of-the-century bungalow, is one of the best French restaurants in the area. **Hemmings** (7615 W. Farmington Rd., Saddle Creek shopping center, Germantown, tel. 901/757–8323) is a departure from traditional Delta dining, serving excellent Southwest and California cuisine.

Tourist Information

Memphis Convention and Visitors Bureau (47 Union Ave., Memphis, TN 38103, tel. 901/543–5333). **Memphis Visitors Information Center** (340 Beale St., Memphis, TN 38103, tel. 901/543–5333). **Tennessee Department of Tourist Development** (Box 23170, Nashville, TN 37202, tel. 615/741–2158).

Reservation Services

Bed & Breakfast Memphis Reservation Service (Box 41621, Memphis, TN 38174, tel. 901/726–5920). **Tennessee Bed & Breakfast Innkeepers Association** (Box 120428, Nashville, TN 37212, tel. 615/321–5482 or 800/820–8144).

Magnolia Manor

Well off the beaten path in southwest Tennessee, Magnolia Manor creates an imposing presence along Main Street in tiny Bolivar, a historic burg that boasts the oldest courthouse in West Tennessee. It is one of two dozen or so antebellum homes in the neighborhood that were spared from Union torches during the Civil War; tours of the area can be arranged.

The two-story house is built in the Georgian Colonial style, its 1849 construction date noted on a bronze eagle mounted onto one corner. The walls, made of sun-dried, slave-laid red brick, are 13 inches thick. It was constructed as a symmetrical rectangle, with center halls upstairs and down separating the spacious rooms.

Elaine and Jim Cox, a reserved but polite couple, were inspired to open the inn in 1984 by the bed-and-breakfasts they'd stayed in on a long trip through Europe. Elaine is a former cosmetology instructor; Jim is a retired hospital administrator. Beyond travel, the Coxes' hobbies are interior decorating and cooking, both of which are evident at the manor. The house is ornately restored, and portraits of the four Union generals who occupied the house were commissioned by the couple and now hang in the entry hall. Downstairs, the inn's 14-foot ceilings provide space that mitigates the heavy furnishings

and a lingering, musty scent reminiscent of old houses in distant childhood memories. The downstairs suite, a double parlor, is furnished opulently with early Victorian, museum-quality pieces: a big rosewood headboard, a rosewood gentleman's chair, and others adorned with hand-carved roses. Upstairs are two double rooms and a spacious suite. One bed is graced with a massive walnut canopy; another is made of the same wood, its construction dated from plantation timbers. The suite has a walnut-and-rosewood Victorian bed and matching furniture, shipped upriver by steamboat years ago from New Orleans. All bedrooms have working fireplaces.

For history buffs in particular, Bolivar makes for a pleasant day trip from Memphis, 90 minutes away. An hour away is Shiloh National Military Park. Also of interest are the nearby Pinson Mounds, where there is a Native American museum. Historians believe Hernando de Soto passed through the area on his epic search for the Mississippi River, a journey noted by various markers.

Address: *418 N. Main St., Bolivar, TN 38008, tel. 901/658–6700.*
Accommodations: *2 double rooms share 1 bath, 2 suites.*
Amenities: *Air-conditioning, cable TV on sun porch, phone in hall.*
Rates: *$75–$85; full breakfast. No credit cards.*
Restrictions: *No smoking, no pets.*

Moss Rose Inn & Café

Formerly known as the Hurt House, this stunning Greek Revival home was built around 1857 and restored in 1993, transformed by owner Anne Stamps into Jackson's premier B&B. Anne is an experienced innkeeper whose ancestors include Dolley Madison. In fact, she has a side table supposedly owned by her famous relative, purchased at a White House auction decades ago and passed down.

A collection of antique Moss Rose china, owned before the Civil War by Anne's Virginia-born grandmother, is displayed throughout. Its dusty pinks and pale greens are echoed in the color scheme of the carefully restored mansion, which is decorated with family antiques. One bedroom has a queen-size sleigh bed covered with an antique quilt and romantic white wicker furniture circa 1910. Oriental rugs warm the hardwood floors in front of the fireplace. The other room is decorated in Colonial style and features a French desk and converted oil lamps. Its sitting area next to the fireplace is perfect for curling up with a good book. Coffee and a newspaper are delivered to your door each morning, and picnic lunches or a full-service dinner can be arranged for an additional cost.

Address: *586 E. Main St., Jackson, TN 38301, tel. 901/423-4777.*
Accommodations: *2 double rooms with baths.*
Amenities: *Air-conditioning, cable TV with VCR and phones in rooms.*
Rates: *$65; full breakfast. MC, V.*
Restrictions: *No smoking, no pets.*

The Peach Tree Inn

The Peach Tree Inn is on a West Tennessee back road an hour northeast of Memphis, not far from Interstate 40. Owner Mindy Campbell, who bought the inn in February 1994 and once handled catering at the Rose Bowl, handles hosting and kitchen duties with equal aplomb. The inn's location, on a 200-acre farm, is its biggest draw. The cypress building is a former lodge (built in 1978) that retains its original rustic charm, although Mindy has transformed its look into that of an English country farmhouse. She serves tea, coffee, and homemade biscuits in the afternoon, and fruit, cheeses, crackers, and wine on the big plank porch off the sun room in the evening. This vantage point offers a good view of the sunset on a small lake stocked with catfish (guests are welcome to drop in a line). Sports lovers will appreciate the adjacent field, a frequent volleyball and softball site, while spectators can watch the action from an old-fashioned swing on the wide front porch. The bedrooms are adequately furnished (one has a view of the lake) with beds that are a little soft.

Address: *1551 Skeet Rd., Brownsville, TN 38102, tel. 901/772-5680 or 901/377-7358.*
Accommodations: *4 double rooms with baths.*
Amenities: *Restaurant, air-conditioning, cable TV in parlor, Victorian gift shop; pool.*
Rates: *$47.50; Continental breakfast, afternoon and evening refreshments. MC, V.*
Restrictions: *No smoking, no pets.*

Directory 1:
Alphabetical

Directory 2:
Geographical

Alabama

Ashville
Roses and Lace *174*
Fairhope
Bay Breeze *187*
Church Street Inn *188*
The Guest House *188*
Florence
Wood Avenue Inn *173*
Greensboro
Blue Shadows *183*
Mentone
Mentone Inn *172*
Montgomery
The Lattice Inn *183*
Red Bluff Cottage *184*
Mount Meigs
The Colonel's Rest *178*
Prattville
The Plantation House
182
Selma
Grace Hall *179*
Talladega
Oakwood *180*
Orangevale Plantation
181

Georgia

Atlanta
Ansley Inn *139*
Brunswick
Brunswick Manor *158*
Rose Manor Guest
House *160*
Buena Vista
Morgan Towne House
Restaurant Bed &
Breakfast *165*
Chickamauga
The Gordon-Lee
Mansion *142*

Clarkesville
Glen-Ella Springs Inn &
Conference Center
140
Commerce
The Pittman House *143*
Concord
Inn Scarlett's Footsteps
150
Cumberland Island
Greyfield Inn *156*
Darien
Open Gates *157*
Fort Oglethorpe
Captain's Quarters Bed
& Breakfast Inn *142*
Macon
The 1842 Inn *148*
Mountain City
The York House *143*
Savannah
Ballastone Inn *158*
The Gastonian *155*
Magnolia Place Inn *159*
Olde Harbour Inn *159*
Pulaski Square Inn *160*
Senoia
The Veranda *149*
Statesboro
Statesboro Inn *150*
Tate
The Tate House *141*
Thomasville
Evans House Bed &
Breakfast *165*
Susina Plantation Inn
166

Louisiana

Abbeville
A la Bonne Veillée *255*
Cheneyville
Loyd Hall *265*
Covington
Riverside Hills Farm *240*

Destrehan
Ormond Plantation *250*
Folsom
Woods Hole Inn *241*
Lafayette
Bois des Chênes *258*
T' Frere's House *259*
Napoleonville
Madewood Plantation
248
Natchitoches
Cloutier Townhouse *264*
Fleur-de-Lis *266*
Jefferson House *266*
Starlight Plantation *267*
New Orleans
The Chimes *238*
Girod House *238*
Hotel Maison de Ville
and Audubon
Cottages *233*
Josephine Guest House
239
Lafitte Guest House *239*
Melrose Mansion *234*
St. Charles Guest House
240
Soniat House *236*
Sully Mansion *241*
Terrell House *237*
New Roads
Pointe Coupee Bed &
Breakfast *250*
St. Francisville
Butler Greenwood *246*
Cottage Plantation *247*
Green Springs
Plantation *249*
St. Martinville
Old Castillo Hotel/Place
d'Evangeline *258*
Slidell
Salmen-Fritchie House
235

Fodor's Travel Guides

Available at bookstores everywhere, or call 1–800–533–6478, 24 hours a day.

U.S. Guides

Alaska

Arizona

Boston

California

Cape Cod, Martha's Vineyard, Nantucket

The Carolinas & the Georgia Coast

Chicago

Colorado

Florida

Hawaii

Las Vegas, Reno, Tahoe

Los Angeles

Maine, Vermont, New Hampshire

Maui

Miami & the Keys

New England

New Orleans

New York City

Pacific North Coast

Philadelphia & the Pennsylvania Dutch Country

The Rockies

San Diego

San Francisco

Santa Fe, Taos, Albuquerque

Seattle & Vancouver

The South

The U.S. & British Virgin Islands

USA

The Upper Great Lakes Region

Virginia & Maryland

Waikiki

Walt Disney World and the Orlando Area

Washington, D.C.

Foreign Guides

Acapulco, Ixtapa, Zihuatanejo

Australia & New Zealand

Austria

The Bahamas

Baja & Mexico's Pacific Coast Resorts

Barbados

Berlin

Bermuda

Brittany & Normandy

Budapest

Canada

Cancún, Cozumel, Yucatán Peninsula

Caribbean

China

Costa Rica, Belize, Guatemala

The Czech Republic & Slovakia

Eastern Europe

Egypt

Euro Disney

Europe

Florence, Tuscany & Umbria

France

Germany

Great Britain

Greece

Hong Kong

India

Ireland

Israel

Italy

Japan

Kenya & Tanzania

Korea

London

Madrid & Barcelona

Mexico

Montréal & Québec City

Morocco

Moscow & St. Petersburg

The Netherlands, Belgium & Luxembourg

New Zealand

Norway

Nova Scotia, Prince Edward Island & New Brunswick

Paris

Portugal

Provence & the Riviera

Rome

Russia & the Baltic Countries

Scandinavia

Scotland

Singapore

South America

Southeast Asia

Spain

Sweden

Switzerland

Thailand

Tokyo

Toronto

Turkey

Vienna & the Danube Valley